SHULA

ALSO BY MARK RIBOWSKY

My Dad, Yogi: A Memoir of Family and Baseball
by Dale Berra with Mark Ribowsky

In the Name of the Father: Family, Football, and the Manning Dynasty

Hank: The Short Life and Long Country Road of Hank Williams

Sweet Dreams and Flying Machines: The Life and Music of James Taylor

*Dreams to Remember: Otis Redding, Stax Records,
and the Transformation of Southern Soul*

*Whiskey Bottles and Brand New Cars:
The Fast Life and Sudden Death of Lynyrd Skynyrd*

The Last Cowboy: A Life of Tom Landry

Howard Cosell: The Man, the Myth, and the Transformation of American Sports

He's a Rebel: Phil Spector—Rock and Roll's Legendary Producer

Slick: The Silver and Black Life of Al Davis

Don't Look Back: Satchel Paige in the Shadows of Baseball

The Power and the Darkness: The Life of Josh Gibson in the Shadows of the Game

A Complete History of the Negro Leagues, 1844 to 1955

The Complete History of the Home Run

Crazy and in Charge: The Autobiography of Abe Hirschfeld
by Abraham Hirschfeld with Mark Ribowsky

Eleven Days of Hell: My True Story of Kidnapping, Terror, Torture, and Historic FBI and KGB Rescue
by Yvonne Bernstein with Mark Ribowsky

The Supremes: A Saga of Motown Dreams, Success, and Betrayal

Signed, Sealed, and Delivered: The Soulful Journey of Stevie Wonder

Ain't Too Proud to Beg: The Troubled Lives and Enduring Soul of the Temptations

SHULA

The Coach of the NFL's Greatest Generation

MARK RIBOWSKY

LIVERIGHT PUBLISHING CORPORATION

A Division of W. W. Norton & Company

Independent Publishers Since 1923

New York | London

For information about permission to reproduce selections from this book,
write to Permissions, Liveright Publishing Corporation, a division of
W. W. Norton & Company, Inc., 500 Fifth Avenue, New York, NY 10110

For information about special discounts for bulk purchases, please contact
W. W. Norton Special Sales at specialsales@wwnorton.com or 800-233-4830

Manufacturing by LSC Communications Harrisonburg
Book design by Chris Welch
Production manager: Anna Oler

Library of Congress Cataloging-in-Publication Data

Names: Ribowsky, Mark, author.
Title: Shula : the coach of the NFL's greatest generation / Mark Ribowsky.
Description: First edition. | New York : Liveright Publishing Corporation, a division of
W. W. Norton & Company, [2019] | Includes bibliographical references and index.
Identifiers: LCCN 2019014727 | ISBN 9781631494604 (hardcover)
Subjects: LCSH: Shula, Don, 1930– | Football coaches—United States—Biography. |
Miami Dolphins (Football team)—History—20th century. | Baltimore Colts (Football team)—
History. | National Football League—History—20th century.
Classification: LCC GV939.S46 R53 2019 | DDC 796.332092 [B]—dc23
LC record available at https://lccn.loc.gov/2019014727

Liveright Publishing Corporation, 500 Fifth Avenue, New York, N.Y. 10110
www.wwnorton.com

W. W. Norton & Company Ltd., 15 Carlisle Street, London W1D 3BS

1 2 3 4 5 6 7 8 9 0

CONTENTS

Introduction: Shula Pride   ix

1   A SOVEREIGN MASCULINITY   1

2   CATECHISM   10

3   "WHO IS JOHN CARROLL?"   16

4   THE CLEVELAND CALIPH   25

5   ONE TOUGH SONOFABITCH   39

6   COACH SHULA   53

7   FLY ME TO THE MOON   63

8   NATIONAL FRUSTRATION LEAGUE   80

9   SWEET   96

10   SOUR   108

11   "THE BIGGEST THING SINCE BUBBLE GUM"   121

12   HIRED BY THE MAN WHO FIRED FLIPPER   138

13   BUTCH, SUNDANCE, AND A CUDDLY CYPRIOT   155

14   "STAY READY, EARL. STAY READY"   171

15   RAPTURE   187

16   "CAMELOT DISAPPEARED"   204

17   "IT'S ALMOST BIZARRE"   223

18   SUBPLOTS AND COUNTERPLOTS   235

19   "THIS IS STILL MY PRODUCT"   245

20   NEW KID IN TOWN   264

21   "SHULA IS GOD"   277

22   NO NEED TO RUSH   293

23   DON VOYAGE   309

24   A GRANITE-JAWED DEITY, STILL   338

Notes   351
Index   369

INTRODUCTION

Shula Pride

A long-ago interlude that today feels oracular was the brief moment in history when Donald Shula bisected with Donald Trump. It happened in 1983. That year, the boyish, bumptious Trump had bought into the last challenger to the NFL's hegemony, the United States Football League, as owner of the New Jersey Generals. He had Herschel Walker, arguably the best runner in football, and wanted unarguably the best coach in football. Shula, who knew little of Trump, listened. When he saw more of who Trump was, and the bull he slung, he stopped listening and bolted for the door. Trump naturally blamed Shula for the crime of . . . greed.

Trump's league went bust. His future bids to become an NFL owner were summarily dismissed. Shula—who is today nearing 90 and has never declared bankruptcy, and whose fortune of over $30 million is real[1]—remained in Miami, becoming football's first million-dollar-a-year coach[2] and a geographic landmark. Moral: Shula was a very winning coach, and a very rich one, because he could take the measure of men he respected, and quickly discard those he didn't.

Shula coached in some of the most memorable and important games in football history, and in keeping with the yin and yang of a long career, won some, but never enough. He seemed to suffer years of bedevilment, as if in a cosmic bargain for one single season of unprecedented success. That, his perfect 17–0 championship season of 1972, was itself seemingly earned by his ineffable defeat four years earlier to Joe Namath's New York Jets, when Shula's mighty Baltimore Colts came in as 18-point favorites and left as losers of the biggest upset in sports history. No mere career coach could have been on the sidelines for two such titanic events, which can fairly be discussed as markers of cultural history. The Jets loss carved out pro football's modern identity and threatened to leave Shula by the side of the road, in shame. For him, no win could ever expunge its sour taste.

But even after those two contrasting events were cemented in history, he had plenty left in the tank. Invested with a nail-hard, blue-collar Midwestern ethos and sensibility, he lengthened his shadow, always chasing the elusive return to glory. In that sense, he never changed. He took crap from nobody, ruled with a closed fist and deft, scientific methods gleaned from his mentor, Paul Brown. When he was unable to win, and had taken enough crap for it within his own league, he made a calculated decision to join the league he had, ironically, proved wasn't inferior by losing to it. He took over the Miami Dolphins when they were merged into the NFL in 1970 and immediately built them into a milieu, a fan base, and a corporate turnkey operation. Over the next quarter century, he would keep whittling his gnarled but handsome Teutonic face (actually Hungarian) into the football infrastructure, always defined by the perfect season and the repeat title a year later. He also led the Dolphins to two more Super Bowls, losing both, but for an unnaturally extended period of time, he seemed immune to the consequences of big-game defeat because he always won enough.

He was more than just a coach. Though, technically, he was born just a tad late to be a member of it, he was embraced as a pillar of the generation that journalist Tom Brokaw would retroactively celebrate in the 1990s as the Greatest Generation. From the glory of winning a world war and the passage of civil rights legislation, to the dishonor of undeclared wars of choice and the perpetuation of Jim Crow, Shula stood shoulder to shoulder with men both famous and infamous: on the one hand, a president who inspired a nation into space, and on the other, a demagogic senator shrieking about a red menace, a Southern governor who stood in the door of a university to stop black students from entering, and a president who lurched from landslide victor to unindicted co-conspirator. Shula has outlived them all, and has lived long enough to see the election of the very man he distrusted and foresaw as a destructive force in 1983.

In fact, men like Shula make it easier to cope with men like George Wallace, Richard Nixon, and Donald Trump. Not incidental to his strengths as a coach, he was a first-generation American, like Vince Lombardi the son of immigrants who, in their day, were reviled and scapegoated every bit as much as latter-day bigots have done to people of color. It was the qualities handed down to him by hardier men than most that took Shula into the fold of history occupied by Brown, George Halas, Lombardi, and Tom Landry, sturdy men who took pro football from a ragtag circus show into a respectable profession, and incidentally into a shiny but increasingly crass and soulless corporate megalith. He was never a Lombardi, and he knew it; indeed, like Tom Landry, his defeats at the hands of Lombardi determined the latter's legacy. Almost forgotten now is that, in the early and mid-'6os, any one of that holy trinity could have, by winning at the summit, claimed immortality.

They all hailed from middle-class, Depression-era slices of America: south Texas, the Italian ghettos of Brooklyn, a Hungarian migrant community in Ohio. All were ruthlessly ambitious. Viewed through the lens of history, Lombardi's hair-trigger emotions and tragically premature death seemed to render his lionization predestined. But Shula had his own mythology, and as it goes with contemporary giants, it was nuanced and subject to the heartache that humanized him. Shula's greatest success wasn't perfection; it was living with failure by cramming so much winning around it.

Spending time in Shula's company feels like an honor. In the fall of 1978, a commoner with a pen and notepad on assignment for a sports magazine visited him just before the season and found him untouched by the ravages of high-pressure football. It seemed almost irrelevant that Landry's Dallas Cowboys and Chuck Noll's Pittsburgh Steelers had passed the Dolphins by; or that three years before, another short-lived pro football league had ripped the spine from his offense, taking fullback Larry Csonka, halfback Jim Kiick, and receiver Paul Warfield from the Dolphins. Or that his All-Pro but rapidly declining quarterback Bob Griese was out injured.

"You never get used to injuries," he lamented, "but once they happen you forget about 'em. You just get off your can and figure out where to go from there."[3]

He spoke with his flat-voweled Midwestern dialect, rich in saliva, a slight lisp. His meat-hook hands clasped in front of him, his thick brown hair graying, he was stately—ruggedly handsome in the standard coach's Ban-Lon couture: white belt matching white shoes. His idiom was bromidic coach-speak, his answer to every problem seemingly to "roll up your sleeves" and get to work. But the takeaway was that he really seemed to believe he could, by the force of his will, impose winning. And by season's end, as if demonstrating the transferable quality that gave the article its title—SHULA PRIDE—he was in the playoffs.

Even then, at 48, he had been coach of the year four times—still a record—and compiled 166 wins, behind only George Halas, Curly Lambeau, and Brown. The only coach to win 100 games in his first decade, he had made four Super Bowl appearances and had won two world championships and a pre-merger NFL title. Tempered by some of the most torturous defeats of all time, he admitted, "I've never considered myself to be a coaching giant like a Halas or Lombardi." It hurt to his core to have lost big ones. But he had reason to bask in the limelight of his march toward the record for wins—which he took to 347, including playoffs, and which may stand forever.

Shula, whose reign spanned 10 presidents, seemed immune to attrition. As *Sports Illustrated*'s great football writer Paul Zimmerman noted in 1993, Shula "has thrived in a world of pressure so intense that it has burned out even those who have succeeded at the highest level."[4] He coached 490 games in the regular season, more than anyone but Halas, and 526 in total, more than anyone, period. This is remarkable given that the NFL played a 14-game season until 1978. His regular-season record was 328–156–6, for a winning percentage of .677—a hair behind Halas's .682 and Belichick's .680 (as of 2019). The result was seven conference titles and six Super Bowls, with Shula the first of just six coaches to lead two different teams into Super Sunday.

That he came away with a ring only twice is the rub. While his teams finished over .500 all but twice in the regular season, he won "only" 53 percent of his 36 playoff games, as opposed to Noll's 66.7 percent, Bill Walsh's 71.4, Lombardi's 90. He had to live with being the losing coach in the biggest upset in history, as well as the one whose team scored the fewest points in a Super Bowl (three). In retrospect, that seems like the bargain he made to also be the coach of the most dominant team in sports history, a pendulum swing only possible for a coach with nine lives. Not for nothing did Shula regularly have the highest, or close to it, salary among coaches, his half million a year by the late '70s, million by the late '80s, and two million in the '90s, also coaching milestones.

Consider, too, that when the Coach of the Decade was named for the 1970s, it wasn't Noll, who had won four rings in as many tries; it was the guy who won two in four tries, the guy with the perfect season. Even when Noll's team took apart Shula's, 34–14, in a '79 playoff game, a *Pittsburgh* writer correctly judged it a contest between "football's best team against football's best coach."[5]

Shula wasn't Lombardi, and to call the '72 perfect Dolphin team the "best ever" really means "best team of its era." But this is hardly a demerit. In his time, Shula was a unifying figure as he aged from youngest coach ever, to young elder, to elder statesman. If not immortal, he seemed indestructible. He could move men, keep teams with less talent at or near the top, avoid paying a high price for bad drafts and trades. In 1981, Nick Buoniconti, the undersized, overly ferocious middle linebacker of Shula's great Dolphin teams, said Shula had won his eminence by being "such a positive influence on the game," the proof that, "under the worst conditions, Shula will still be competitive."

Most impressive of all was that he reestablished himself after his personal Little Big Horn—and in the same Orange Bowl where he had been fed to the lions by the Jets. Yet he never shook that day. "If I would've lost the [1973] Super Bowl," he told me, "the 16 previous wins would've meant nothing. I would've been crucified as the loser." For this obsessively churchgoing Catholic, not even perfection was absolution enough for the original sin. Though sometimes it seemed easy for him to win, it never was. Someone was always ready with criticism. He even had to fend off his own allies, including two of the most headstrong, unstable owners in sports, Carroll Rosenbloom and Joe Robbie.

He was intensely insular. Running a tight ship, he hired top adjutants like Bill Arnsparger, Chuck Noll, and Howard Schnellenberger, but was loath to share power; he let his quarterbacks call the plays—as long as they did well; if not, then it was Shula to the rescue. As omniscient as he was, he felt his flaws were more magnified than those of Lombardi and Landry. Which is why Shula protected the honor of his perfect season like a pit bull refusing to let go of a bone. When Belichick's New England Patriots stood one win away from updated perfection—a 19–0 season—Shula's famous jaw tightened, and he called the coach who got caught spying on an opponent's coaches' signals during a 2007 game "Beli-Cheat."[6] No one was giddier when the Patriots lost the Super Bowl to the underdog New York Giants, making Belichick feel what Shula had in '69. To Shula, that was justice.

He learned from the best. As a young man, he was drafted by his own personal football Jesus, Paul Brown, absorbing Brown's methods and genius during a gritty decade as a defensive back in the '50s for the Cleveland Browns and Baltimore Colts. He retired to become a college assistant coach, and then got his break as head coach of the Colts. Over the decades since, he coached a holy trinity of quarterbacks—Johnny Unitas, Bob Griese, and Dan Marino, gearing his offense around each in different ways, according to the surrounding casts and best chances to score (though, with Marino, he let the seduction of the big pass turn his head, and his inattention to the running game derailed many of his teams). But in his salad days, when no facet was overlooked, his system was plug-in. Not even the loss of Unitas in '68 could stop him from going 13–1 with the journeyman Earl Morrall at quarterback; and when he lost Bob Griese in '72, he still went perfect with . . . Earl Morrall.

His mythological powers were nothing like Lombardi's, but just the thought of making a mistake in Shula's presence could induce cold fear among his players, many of whom went into the Hall of Fame. Even Csonka and Kiick, whose shared countercultural insolence tested Shula's tolerance, wound up toeing the line. They had a near-allergic reaction to losing. As safety Charlie Babb told me back in '78, "We're all poor losers around here. That's why we never seem to lose two games in a row." Shula craved being a dictator, but made the subtle distinction that "I want their respect, not their fear." Well, he got both.

It's remarkable how much he squeezed out of teams that only rarely made good draft selections. Shula told me, "I didn't concern myself with drafting because I didn't want to know about kids' college careers," and until late in his coaching tenure, he proved it didn't matter that his team's picks were, as Buoniconti once said, "pitiful, horrible." Of course, he had little choice but to settle for leftovers, since he rarely had high first-round picks and even primordial draft gurus like Bobby Beathard and George Young, who began Hall of Fame careers as NFL executives with Shula, couldn't dig up enough talent to make the task any easier. What Shula had, he won with.

Not all of his players loved, or even liked, him, but none blamed him for gut-tearing defeat. Words like *honest, real,* and *fair* trailed him around, testament to both his coaching and his character. That meant a lot to a man who wanted to be a model of moral probity and Christian values. He demanded of himself what he did of his players. Even into his 60s, he was running the same post-practice "gassers"—wind sprints that drained the will to live—that he put the team through. His teams were always the best conditioned in the league, and the most

verbally strafed. Shula didn't lose his temper without a tangible purpose, a means to add emotion to a dispassionate, machinelike system.
One of his buffet of All-Pros and Hall of Famers, center Jim Langer,
told me, "He does things in an adult way," albeit an adult who could
get so impatient that he once spit profanities at a player who had the
nerve to bend over and tie his shoelace.

Shula insisted, "I try to relate to my players, and try to be fair in
whatever I do and I think they know that. I can't appreciate a win-at-
any-price philosophy because I have to live with these guys all year
round. . . . They all have different egos and psyches." The key word
there was *try*. It didn't always work out that way. As Buoniconti noted,
Shula "would cut his mother, if it meant the team would be better."[7] He
was once said to have signed a picture of himself to his immigrant parents, "To Mom and Dad, best wishes, Don Shula"—which sounds like
a joke, but wasn't, since he had grown up in a family that emphasized
respect above affection. He did the same with his own sons, David and
Mike, who both became college and pro coaches. It was all he could do
to call them by their first names, rather than "Coach Shula."

Shula's parents had hopes for him becoming a priest, before football claimed him. But religion stayed a major facet of his life, even
if he eschewed smarmy, self-serving piety and facile applications of
Christianity to football, saying, "It's what I feel within for God that
makes me a Christian, not my emotions during a game." He still began
every day praying over his rosary beads, just as he did back when attendance was mandatory at the team's daily Mass, and Augustine priests
lined the field during the team's workouts. In his old age, he loved
to hear such testimonials as Bill Arnsparger dubiously saying that all
of the head coach's decisions were "based on his religion."[8] Even so,
he was part of the football-equals-religion-and-patriotism equation
that would, at its crude extremity, allow a feckless president to imagine ordering players who knelt, in silent protest of racism, during the
national anthem to stand or else risk *deportation*—a position Shula no
doubt agrees with, at least the standing part.

Still, he kept religion in the background when asked to provide his own epitaph, which, with mock seriousness, he once said was: "Didn't lie to anyone, didn't screw anybody, traveled first-class."[9] The version he shared with me even earlier was: "If I'm remembered for anything, I hope it's for playing by the rules. Winning by breaking the rules perverts the meaning of winning." However, this was also a coach who wanted to give jobs back to two linemen who had done time for dealing cocaine, a rising plague in Miami during his reign, saying they had "paid their debt to society"—or, more accurately, to Don Shula. Robbie vetoed the idea, but Shula maintained that he had not been a hypocrite and that his moral code did not have loopholes. Maybe not, but he was either remarkably naive or insentient when he also signed, for a brief time, Thomas "Hollywood" Henderson, who had once snorted cocaine on the sideline *during* a Super Bowl game before Tom Landry dumped him.

Shula played by his own codes, such as the gamesmanship that had him ordering pregame ceremonies at the Orange Bowl to stretch on seemingly forever, so that opponents baked in the burning sun before the kickoff. Shula also knew how to exploit his image, his baleful scowl on the sideline aimed at the cameras. The money quote about Shula is his own: he was, he said, as "subtle as a punch in the face." But the best-kept secret about Shula was that he had a weak side, that of an old softie. The porcine, garrulous Hall of Fame defensive tackle Art Donovan, who roomed with him in Baltimore when they were Colt teammates, once said Shula was "one tough sonofabitch" who "got everyone in Miami kissing his ass and running scared of him . . . But I'll tell you what, Shula doesn't like to see me coming, especially when his players are around, because I've got stories that knock that hard-guy image right on its keester."[10]

Shula indeed seemed to have a double standard at times, letting some players get away with conduct he fined or even released other players for. He let his emotions and fondness for players dictate how he treated them, cutting slack to those he thought needed it. For the others, who needed a dictator, he was, as his defensive back Lloyd Mumphord put it, "a man who can't compromise."[11] Shula played favorites, but expected loyalty from all. It hurt him that three men he regarded as sons—Csonka, Kiick, and Warfield, and especially Csonka—did not return to him when the WFL went under, but that didn't stop him from making room for Csonka when he wanted to play out his career back in Miami. Any feuds Shula had with players dissolved in the long light of their shared glories. After Eugene "Mercury" Morris served time for cocaine smuggling in the '80s, Shula recommended him for a radio job, and appeared as his first guest.

He held few grudges against players—not openly, at least—even when he knew that more than a few players couldn't stand him, most notably Unitas. He himself couldn't stand Rosenbloom and Robbie, nor they him. Rosenbloom was so irate when Shula broke his Colts contract to sign with the Dolphins that he savaged him as a "pig" and worse. Robbie got Shula so riled, he threatened, "I'll knock you on your ass."[12] But few fans around the league hated Shula. When he won his record-setting 325th game, they cheered him—even in *Philadelphia*, where they boo funerals and Santa Claus.

Shula was briny, and brainy. While playing at John Carroll University, the small Jesuit school near Cleveland, he majored in sociology and later endowed the Don Shula Chair in Philosophy. (His roots run deep at the school, where they play football in Don Shula Stadium, inside which is a Don Shula memorabilia room. In 2014, his grandson Chris put in a year as the team's defensive coordinator, en route to his current job as the Los Angeles Rams' linebackers coach.) He played psychological games, picking an argument as a means to test others' knowledge. Ed Pope, the late sports editor of the *Miami Herald*, told me on my trip to Miami that Shula was a "very complex fellow. The moment makes the mood with him. Sometimes, you can go tooth and nail with him for an hour, then he'll tell you how much he enjoyed the conversation. You walk out scratching your head."

He also habitually reads everything written about him, looking to humiliate those who had reasonable questions. Zimmerman found that out, writing, "Do not—repeat, do not—challenge Shula on a football matter unless you're on very firm ground. You don't remain so high, for so long, by being confused."[13] Few writers or broadcasters ever did rag him. During a *Monday Night Football* match in 1983, Shula raged at a referee after a call, screaming, "Bullshit!" and "Horseshit!" When this was picked up by a field-level microphone, broadcasters Frank Gifford, Don Meredith, and Howard Cosell slung some cloying BS of their own, saying that Shula "feels the emotions of the game" and that "the strength of the man is written on his face." So was self-pity. Another time, Shula bellowed to a ref, "You're ruining my life!"—during an exhibition game, no less. On yet another occasion, when a ref tried to calm him by saying, "Don, it's only five yards," Shula confessed, "Five yards is my life."[14] He may have even believed it.

Even so, there is at times a Zen-like calm about him. As Zimmerman observed, "Shula does not become haunted by the terrors of the night, and if he ever did, he would keep his feelings well hidden." He came onto the field serene, always believing he had a dynasty in Miami. When he retired—a euphemism for being forced out—in '95, Shula was 65, still the fighter, and his team was in the playoffs as if by rote. Only two years before, *Sports Illustrated* had named him Sportsman of the Year, mainly for the overall mileage and hardships he had weathered—the most egregious being the tragic death of his wife of 33 years in 1991 from cancer. He owes much to Dorothy Shula, who knew him like no other, but he rebounded when, two years later, he married a rich society divorcée 15 years his junior; their net worth was over $400 million, about one-ninth of it his, and if fans and old friends believed she had hooked him for ongoing status, he considered it a reward for a life very well lived.

He himself had a lot of life left, and a lot of punch to his brand, which remains profitable, as proven by his chain of eponymous steak and burger restaurants, a golf resort, and a conveyor belt of TV commercials, many with Marino as sidekick. He has bred a family dynasty. Two of his five children, David and Mike, though not born with great talent, made it to the NFL. The Shula surname was hardly a hindrance, then or thereafter, when they moved up through the coaching ranks, David getting his shot as a head coach with the Cincinnati Bengals when he was a year younger than the old man had been when he got his—though Dad didn't give him an inch, beating him twice. Mike Shula, Alabama's starting QB for two years, became an assistant coach for his father and he moved on as the Carolina Panthers' offensive coordinator and the hand behind Cam Newton's rise, and is now the New York Giants' offensive coordinator.

The patriarch, meanwhile, kept selling himself and the "Shula way," the "secrets" of which—among them, conviction, consistency, honesty—he laid out in two motivational books. When he went into the Hall of Fame in 1997, the football world beatified him. And why not? His victories on the field traced the growth of the game itself, from junkyard dogfights to a $20 billion-a-year corporate entity. He had shaped the nature and rules of the game as a member of the league's competition committee for 18 years, leading one rival owner to grumble that Shula "runs the league,"[15] about which Shula could have only thought: *If only.* He had also won the battles with himself over humiliating failure. Indeed, as the last hero standing, there was nothing left for him to prove, except perhaps for one thing: being able to expunge that goddamn Jets game.

SHULA

1

A SOVEREIGN MASCULINITY

In 2016, the Don Shula Chair in Philosophy at John Carroll University, Professor Bonnie Mann, gave a speech that, unwittingly but definitively, codified the essential nature of the man who had endowed that chair. The oration, which dealt with the war on terror, mass shootings, and the Trump campaign, was entitled "Sovereign Masculinity." Reporting on the speech, the school paper, the *Carroll News*, wrote:

> According to Mann, "Sovereign masculinity is composed of five key parts. It is the exceptional, the self-justifying, the rejection of human vulnerability, the shame and the redemption from shame. The redemption from shame is the moment most aspired to in order to become a masculine male." Sovereign masculinity describes the "need to prove one's masculinity, or manliness."

Mann posited that the third factor is the reason why sovereign masculinity is doomed to fail. "The rejection of human vulnerability means that the sovereign male must never be physically vulnerable to others," she said. "Because humans will always fail in one way or another, this key is the key to sovereign masculinity's downfall."[1]

Mann pulled no punches, illustrating her thesis with the examples of mass murderers and Donald Trump, the ultimate sovereign male, who proved that "sovereign masculinity involves a very particular relationship to shame." But she probably had no idea that the man who founded the very chair she sat in might well be the exception to that rule, on will alone, given that he wore his shame on his sleeve and, through vulnerability, found redemption, not self-destruction. That was partly a measure of the DNA of his forebears, who had to fight through life as immigrants in a strange land, in the days when it was possible to believe a man could tough his way through any obstacle, even if trying too hard could kill him. The rest was up to him to learn, on a very long journey.

The true grit was common law in Shula's breeding ground, the Steel Belt in northern Ohio. In the first half of the 20th century, Ohio played a central role in determining America's character and fiber, having bred seven presidents, second only to Virginia. The bustling ports that lay along the vast waterways of the Great Lakes and the nexus of highways snaking across the map were booming, opening commerce in small towns and drawing scores of immigrants looking for a good job and hoping to raise good American children.

The Shula footprint first touched American soil in 1901, when a 38-year-old Hungarian named Frank Sule set off from his small farming town of Mulenshook in Baranya County—today known widely for its wineries and quaint vineyards. He sailed for the New World, leaving behind his wife, Rosa, their 18-year-old son Paul, and a newborn son, Denes. Promising to send for them when he settled, Frank Sule made the long, seasickness-inducing journey across Europe and the Atlantic, sailing into New York Harbor. Rejecting the tenement life in New York in favor of the promise of a better, less-congested opportunity, he headed west on a rickety railroad toward the greener pastures of the American breadbasket.

He didn't get off the train until around 30 miles east of Cleveland, in Painesville Township, a narrow sector of Lake County where he understood there was a pocket of Hungarian immigrants living in a village called Grand River, a speck on the map not far from Lake Erie, built around the river. Only around 200 people lived here, in small but resolute two-story brick and stone homes. Frank found a room in one of them and began working in what seemed to some who labored in sootier jobs a less-than-masculine profession: in a hothouse nursery, planting seeds and collecting flowers. After six years, he sent for his wife and sons. Frank never did learn how to speak proper English, conversing almost always in his native tongue, Magyar. The baby boy, Denes, went off to school, learning the new language and even gaining a new identity. His teachers couldn't easily pronounce his name, so they called him Dennis—or, more often, Dan—Shula, anglicizing both names. It felt right to him; within a few years, when he reached 18, he legally changed his name.

He had matured quickly and dropped out of school in the sixth grade so that he could help his father at the nursery. When he was 18, he made it his business to become the first member of the family to become a naturalized citizen. He met a girl named Mary, who had also come to America with her Hungarian parents, Joe and Anna, who by way of assimilation had changed their surname to Miller. Two years younger than Dan, pretty and dark-haired, Mary Miller had dropped out of school, too, to work at menial jobs. Meanwhile, Dan had grown tired of the overcrowding at his folks' home and felt more comfortable at the Millers' home at 625 River Street, in the Richmond Village section, where the backyards of the homes on the east side of the street ran nearly to the banks of the Grand River. They lived in a multiple-family apartment building with a ground-floor store that Joe and Anna were renting and operating as a grocery. Dan spent most of his time with the Millers, causing a rift with his own parents, and it was assumed that he and Mary would wed.

With a little help from Frank, Dan was able to sink his own roots. He put down $500 for a mortgage on a house right next door to the Millers' at 615 River, where he and Mary would live after they married. As do many other homes of the era, the two adjacent structures still stand today. The old Miller grocery is now Sammy's Family Restaurant.

Heavily influenced by the town's immigrant history, its tables built by masons, it serves fat Greek omelets, Polish sausages slathered in gravy, Irish skillets, and deep-fried scallops—the sort of food they used to make at home back in Dan Shula's day, when families sat around the kitchen table, said grace for their daily bread, and meant it.

Though the most overused stereotype of Hungarian immigrants was of gypsies looking for a storefront, many brilliant minds came from that subset of the population. Three of the scientists who helped develop the atomic bomb—Leo Szilard, Eugene Wigner, and Edward Teller—were Hungarians. If these men had anything in common with Dan and Don Shula, it was that they had the ability to think logically and work as if their lives depended on it, such that they had little time for anything but work and Mass, which was basically the template for the Hungarian community in Grand River. They were tight-knit, deeply religious, mostly Catholic, and while they sang loudly from their prayer books, they were not overly demonstrative otherwise. The men didn't fancy holding hands with their wives or toting their kids on their shoulders in the playground. Indeed, many of the sons were out working in their early teens, no longer in childhood.

The women, some marrying in their middle teens, accepted subservience, but with their men working all hours, it fell to them to enforce discipline at home. Mary Miller Shula all but ran the family. As one future newspaper retrospective on the Shulas of Grand River told it, "Dan was the breadwinner, Mary the vocal leader. Family members and friends say Dan was a quiet man. Mary [was] 'a strict Hungarian mom. She laid down the law,' said Lou Gurbach, a pleasant woman and distant relative of the Shulas. Mary Shula also seems to have had the most telling effect on her son. She was disciplined, dedicated to detail and competitive."[2]

Dan converted to Catholicism, to the dismay of his parents, who were Christian Orthodox. Though they were becoming estranged, he was their pride and joy, after all, having grown into a swarthy, barrel-chested man with bushy eyebrows, a long nose, big ears, and a wry smile. A classic strong but silent type, he had socked away sufficient money to pay his father back and support a wife, and the inevitable wedding to Mary Miller happened on October 18, 1921, in St. Mary's Baptist Church in Painesville, whereupon she moved in with him at 615 River Street.

The neighborhood was, commonly for the times, segregated, and Dan was more fortunate than many native-born African Americans who had come to Ohio from the Deep South to work in the mines and factories Dan Shula had avoided. And for Dan, life went on productively, though not without tragedy. He and Mary's first child was a daughter, Josephine, born in 1922. Their first son, Joe, came a year later. Then, in 1927, five-year-old Josephine fell and sustained a broken skull. She was rushed to St. Mary's Hospital, where doctors operated on her, but after 10 agonizing hours, she was pronounced dead. Dan and Mary resolved to have more children. Another daughter, Irene, had been born in 1926, and they were nowhere near done.

The continued expansion of the brood would proceed without the anchors of the family, Frank and Rosa Sule. They had seen their brood grow in America, yet they had never completely given their souls to their adopted country and had longed for years to return to Hungary. In 1928, they did, bidding adieu to America and reversing the route they had followed two decades earlier—though they were the victim of terrible timing. Within a few years, Hungary would fall under the thumb of Hitler's Third Reich, at a grievous toll, with nearly half a million Hungarian Jews sent to the death camps, though the couple made it through. The Shulas, meanwhile, made the most of the American Dream. On the 1930 census, which mistakenly listed Dan and Mary's birthplace as Czechoslovakia, the census taker somehow filled in Dan's occupation as "laborer—tin factory" and estimated his income at $1,400 a month—which, if so, represented a hell of a lot of flowers. The property at 615 River Street was valued at $3,500, quite a step above the average home; their neighbor George Wilson's was valued at a mere $1,000. And their next child would be born into a degree of relative comfort not common to most kids in town.

Relative because the blue-collar, working-class ethos was the only one that Donald Francis Shula would ever know after he was born on January 4, 1930. That year, the most popular song in America was Irving Berlin's wistful fantasy "Puttin' on the Ritz," though for most people a more relevant wish would have been "Pennies from Heaven." Indeed, all that Dan Shula had worked for seemed to suddenly be in jeopardy, as his second son arrived almost exactly when the Great Depression did, the stock market having tanked just two months earlier on Black Tuesday, October 29. Spreading like wildfire, unemployment would hit 25 percent across the country, and in Ohio. There would be wildcat strikes and civil unrest in Cleveland, and violence that local authorities blamed on Communists—an alarming thought for Dan and Mary Shula, who had read letters sent by Frank and Rosa Sule about Hungary being carved by political factions. With less demand for his flowers, it was all Dan could do to keep his head above water, and those were the days that made the most enduring impression on his second son.

In his memoirs, the first sentence of the brief chapter about Shula's childhood began: "My father was a Hungarian immigrant [and although] my dad never mastered his adopted language and left school after the sixth grade, the people in the town thought enough of him to elect him to the town council."[3] He had no stories to tell about Dan, other than that he was usually absent, leaving Mary to run the household. Oddly, he never identified his parents by their names, just Dad and Mom. Of Mary, he wrote that she was "a proud woman" and that "even though money was scarce, I always remembered having clean clothes to wear. She made sure that if there were any rips or tears in our clothes that they were always sewn and that the buttons were always on."

Unlike the sentimental tales of matronly immigrant matriarchs that were later featured in radio programs and movies, the Shula household did not echo with laughter and sentimental expressions of love. The closest Shula came to describing his childhood home with warmth was "a great many of the ideas and thoughts that I have, as far as my relationships with God, stem from those early years and the lessons I learned around the house about being God-fearing and doing things the right way." That, of course, was not an option; God's word was law within the walls of the home. He wrote that his parents were "strong-willed, intensely moral people" and, per their dictum, "from second grade on, I went to a Catholic school, including college, and even today I try to attend Mass every day."[4]

When the streetlights went on, Dan's kids had to be home. His son, who started playing sports expressly so he could escape those four walls, told the story of trying to slip through a loophole when the power went out on the block. He stayed out late, though his excuse "didn't save me from a pretty good spanking." Strangely, the children were prohibited from stepping into the living room. "It was strictly taboo. The only time it was used was when there was company. Otherwise, it was nothing more than a show place with everything in its proper place all neat and clean. I could never understand it. We did all our living in the basement. It was fixed up and painted and we had a stove down there where my mother often cooked."

Shula got his high school diploma at Thomas Harvey High in Painesville. For decades, he would ride past these neighborhood landmarks when he returned to the old neighborhood for "weddings and funerals."[5] Out of habit, and the bargain he made with Jesus, he would find his way back to the St. Mary's pew, under the arching roof that still stands on North State Street. In time, he would take his marital vows there.

By 1936, the Depression had eased at least enough for Dan and Mary Shula to resume making babies, though they got more than they bargained for. Mary gave birth in Lake County Memorial Hospital to no less than *triplets*, daughters Jane and Jeanette and a son, James, an event that was written up in the *Cleveland Plain Dealer*. Three months later, the paper ran a photo of the trio in a bassinet, under the headline THEY'RE THE TALK OF LAKE COUNTY VILLAGE.[6] With all those mouths to feed, Dan decided to make a career move. There was more money to be made now in the major industries, and he began to moonlight as a commercial fisherman.

As Shula would recall, "There were some commercial fishhouses and fishing boats that would go out and lift the nets in Lake Erie and take the fish out and come back with two tons of fish in the bottom of the boat." Dan would get his boys Joe and Don to wade out into the lake with him, the better to pull in more fish, and would clear about 15 bucks a week. Shula detested every minute of it, and he could not approach his old man without being overwhelmed by the stench—high irony considering that, for years, Dan came home smelling like roses. "One of the early summer jobs I had," said his second son, "was going out with him on the boat and learning how to fillet fish and pack them and ship them out in ice and do all the things you had to do. I never got used to the rough seas. I'd get seasick a lot when I'd go out on Lake Erie." The memory never left him: "When I got to Miami, everybody wanted to take me deep sea fishing. I said, 'No thanks. I've had enough of seasickness.'"[7]

Down the road in Painesville, there was better pay for a fisherman, so it became a magnet for Dan. Bold as always, he had sold the house, quit the flower business, and bought a new place in Painesville. Each morning, he woke in the dark to head out in his pickup truck, driving the gaslit streets to drop his nets in the lake. He had bought himself a boat that could hold up to two tons of fish, and he and Joe, who was now fishing full time, loaded Erie blue pike into 25-pound cans. Taking the catch to market, they would earn around six cents a pound. Like the flowers, it added up, but there wasn't enough with so many children at home. And so he bent to reality and took on the kind of factory labor he hated, in exchange for a steady paycheck and some benefits. The job was in a nearby plant on Walford Avenue run by the Rayon Corporation, which produced 12 million pounds of synthetic silk a year. Dan's tasks there were monotonous, shredding and spinning liquid carbon disulfide into sheets of cellulose.

His daughter Jeannette Shula Moroz, one of the triplets, once said,

"Our father may not have been as outward with his emotions, but he had to be tough to go out to work every day, day after day, even when he was sick. He used to ride to work with another man. He could have asked that man to come pick him up when it was cold, but he never did. He always made the walk over there." He wanted nothing more than for his son to avoid such tedious work and make something of himself. The more Dan thought about it, the priesthood was the preferred path.

In his early teens, Don Shula was around five foot six and 150 hard pounds, fast on his feet, shifty, tough, quick-tempered. His brother Joe once called him "Sir Galahad," for his sense of fair play and sportsmanship. But one former chum recalled him a "pugnacious lad with an appetite for schoolyard scraps."[8] Shula never denied it, saying, "I don't think I ever started a fight. But I had a short fuse." The neighborhood remembered him as a tough and smart kid who would be the first to show up on a field across the street from his house where kids would choose up sides and play tackle football games without pads or helmets.

But he was not invulnerable. In 1941, when he was just 11, he was playing defensive back on his junior high team. He closed in to make a tackle on a receiver who, he recalled, had "a sharp object," a clamp of some sort, holding together his tattered uniform. Upon hard contact, the metal object "cut the side of my nose and ripped it open."[9] He was ready to line up for the next play, but the coach saw the blood and insisted that an ambulance take him to a hospital, where they wrapped a bandage around his face and sent him home. The nose would blow up like a balloon and seem to remold, becoming wider and flatter. Dan and Mary made much of it. Seeing the ugly gash, Mary screamed, "Dear God. What kind of game is this?" She laid down a rule: no more football. And she began to watch him like a hawk, seeing to it he wasn't sneaking into games. Their vigilance made it plain that they knew whatever he had to do to get around their interdiction, he would. Not even Jesus himself could stop him.

2

CATECHISM

on Shula was a few weeks shy of 12 when Pearl Harbor was attacked. For Dan Shula, who had been too young to fight in the last world war, and too old in this one, his work at the rayon factory took on an even more frenetic pace, the demand for textiles production keeping the plant humming nearly around the clock and producing greater income. Joe, now 18, enlisted in the army. His younger brother continued his schooling. Turning 14 in 1944, he entered Thomas Harvey High School, named for a 19th-century Ohio educator. It was the only public high school in Painesville, and because it was a magnet for teenage athletes, it would pose a fatal hurdle for his parents in trying to keep him from the ball fields.

From the start, he was smitten with the scholastic sports scene. The football team was coached by Howard Baughman, who also coached the basketball team, and both teams often had undefeated county championship seasons. As a sophomore, the young Shula, still under his parents' embargo on sports, could only watch Red Raiders games from the stands, despondent that he wasn't out there, kicking tail. When he turned 15, as a junior, he tried out for the football team, forging his parents' signatures on the permission slip. Baughman had left to coach at a Cleveland Heights high school and was replaced by

Clarence Mackey. Shula quickly made the team. However, he soon caught measles. When he recovered, he thought he had lost his place on the squad. An assistant coach, Don Martin, saw him in the stands and told him to put on a uniform.

That was when he had to fess up to his parents that he was again playing, and that he had a game the following Saturday. But, to his shock, his father didn't blow up at him for the forgery. His boy was now around the same age as Dan was when he had dropped out to work. He could see that his flesh and blood had the same mulish individualism, the rugged self-belief. And so Dan approved, and he and Mary even attended the game, the first they had ever seen. That day, they watched him return a punt for a 75-yard touchdown, and stood up and cheered for him like any other American parents.

Being allowed to play came with conditions. He still had to work and contribute to the family pot. And, even with scant spare time, he did various odd jobs for a dollar a day; at week's end, he would give his mother five dollars; she in turn would give him a dollar allowance. Dan and Mary could be proud of him. With everything else going on, he earned honor-roll marks. What's more, he had become a BMOC at Harvey, his striking face appearing on numerous pages of the school yearbook, *The Anvil*, on the football and basketball teams and in student activity groups. In his second year on the football team, Mackey made him tailback in his single-wing T formation, and he looked smugly confident in the team picture in his number 15 uniform. "There were other guys who were more talented, but Don was tough, fearless," remembered Tony Cimaglio, a teammate. "Don was always the aggressor."[1]

Don Martin, though, believed he was a too-angry kid who needed a few lessons in humility—and realized as much himself. Martin recalled:

> One day during a scrimmage, he and another boy exchanged a few heated words, and were told to drop it and stick to business. A few plays later, it happened again and Coach Mackey asked if they understood what he had said. When Don started to justify his actions, Coach Mackey, usually a very mild-mannered man,

slapped him. Don's face flushed with embarrassment and anger, but not another word was said. After practice, he hung around until the players had left and came into the office. I was fully prepared to hear him say he was quitting the team. Instead, he said, "I'm sorry coach, it was all my fault."[2]

That 1945 season came four months after President Franklin Roosevelt died, and only weeks after Hiroshima and Nagasaki were leveled by the awesome and awful new weaponry of mass destruction. Shula was the Red Raiders' big weapon. Along the way, Mackey began to use him at quarterback. Not that he owned the greatest arm, but Shula had an instinct for when and where to throw it, or keep it and go off on one of his headfirst rushes. In the season's fourth game, reported the yearbook, "the first touchdown was made from the [Willoughby] 45 yard line on a pass, Shula to [Charlie] Schupska." Against Fairport High, Shula learned how quickly success can go south. Though he scored the first touchdown, a bad interception led to Fairport taking it in late for a 12–6 win—sending Shula under the bleachers for a good cry. But he came back tougher. The climactic game was the big rivalry match against Ashtabula. It was, said the school paper, "the hardest fought game of the year," though it ended in a 14–9 loss. Their 8–2 record was good for second in the circuit, damned with faint praise by the paper as "a fairly successful football season."[3]

As for Shula, it went on, "Don did an outstanding bit of ball carrying this season. He has the knack of feinting a would-be tackler off balance so that he misses. He is also a defensive man. Being only a junior this [coming] year we will expect a lot from him next year"—an expectation that he would one day need to become very familiar with.

In some of those yearbook photos, he looked surly, eyes narrowed. His public persona was not far from the Marlon Brando–esque tintype that would define a whole new era of antiheroic manhood in the late '40s. How much of this was real and how much a pose was debatable. In other shots, the non-athletic ones, he was draped in sharp-creased slacks and preppy cardigans, looking as straight an arrow as any well-mannered college boy in postwar America. He was courtly to his teachers and other students, didn't cut class, didn't cuss. In a shot of the junior class officers, Shula seemed to grab the camera, leaning forward where the others sat back. One might have suspected he had something nagging inside him, something that drove him beyond the normal pursuits of his classmates. Time would tell.

In his senior year, he was a polished performer on the gridiron. The Red Raiders were 6–3 entering the finale against Ashtabula, who were 5–0 and had already clinched the county title. But Shula ran in a touchdown from the 2-yard line in the fourth quarter for the lead. Playing defensive back as well, he also made a game-saving tackle by cutting through a wall of blockers, leading the opposing coach to come into the locker room after the game and congratulate him for making the finest defensive play he had ever seen. That won Shula honorable mention on the All-Shore schoolboy team.

In his high school career, he won three letters in football, three as a shortstop and pitcher in baseball, three as a forward in basketball, two running track—11 in all. He lost the election for senior class president to Charlie Schupska, his big receiver and the captain of the football team. But he was a class officer, and basketball team captain. His picture in that capacity, in a dark, double-breasted jacket, half-grin on his face, read: "An athlete strong and competent." He also won for having the best build. No prude he, with each senior asked to compose a mock self-testament for *The Anvil*, he wrote that he was the author of "How to Be a High School Casanova."[4] Mocking or not, it was accurate.

When Shula looked back at his days at Harvey High, he had little to say of his athletic achievements. Rather, he spoke of an English teacher who had gotten through to him as no one else had:

All the other English teachers I had had would pat me on the back and give me a B because they liked me and wanted me to like them. Not Miss Symmes. The first essay I wrote for her she returned with an F and told me I was better than that. Since I was already a student leader, I thought I could get by with my gift for gab, but she insisted that I needed to learn to write, too. And she wouldn't back off. She pushed me and pushed me until, on the last paper I turned in to her, she was proud to give me an A. I was proud too. I'll never forget her.[5]

His swagger seemed to embody the words of the school's valedictory song—"Our Solemn Will"—which was played as he accepted his diploma, a teary Dan and Mary Shula in the audience. All of his considerable qualities, however, did little to impress the recruiters, whose eyes seemed to be trained elsewhere than on the only high school in Painesville. Two offers did come, one from no less than Ohio State— but for track, not football, and with very few expenses covered. Mackey had also gotten him a tuition-only scholarship from his alma mater, Emory and Henry College in Emory, Virginia. But neither of these bids seemed worth leaving his home turf, and so he prepared himself to become one more working stiff.

Then came a fateful encounter. Filling up his jalopy at a gas station in Painesville, as he waited at the pump, the nozzle stuck into his gas tank, he saw a familiar face. It was Howard Baughman, the coach who had first noticed him at Harvey High before leaving. They hadn't seen each other since. Recognizing him, Baughman strode over and struck up a conversation, saying he'd followed his high school varsity career in the papers and through the coaches' grapevine. He assumed Shula would have no problem getting into college, and asked which one he'd be playing for in the fall.

"I didn't get any worthwhile scholarship offers," Shula told him, "so I decided to go work instead."

"No, no, that'll be a mistake, Don," he said. "You should go to some college."

"But where?"

Baughman thought a moment. He knew Herb Eisele, the coach at John Carroll College, later John Carroll University, an all-male school run by the Jesuits, who took greater pride in turning young men into priests than into professional athletes. "I'll talk to Herb," he said, getting back into his car. "I'll get back to you in a couple of days."

"That would be great," Shula said, not at all convinced anything would really happen.[6]

But the coach shot straight, and as it happened, Shula's teammate Roy Kropac had also appealed to Baughman for help. He was able to package both kids to Eisele, who had them come into the Carroll admissions office for a joint interview. That netted each a one-year scholarship, at first for tuition alone. If they made the freshman team, they'd be given a full ride. It was a foot in the door to a school that Shula believed was perfect for his goals, the possibility of becoming a priest still in the back of his mind. To be sure, at Catholic schools like these, football *was* a religion. At Notre Dame, the library wall would one day be covered by a mural depicting the son of God, arms upraised as if resurrected as a referee signaling a touchdown—which they shamelessly called "Touchdown Jesus."

But Shula was already forming his rationale, separating Jesus from the touchdowns. He had an idea of which way the wind would blow. He had been in enough scrapes and sneaked enough beers and back-seat whoopee—and been to the confessional enough—to know he was not ideally suited to the Sacrament of the Holy Orders. The pop cultural themes of the day, heavy on Irish Catholic guilt and redemption, as seen in almost any Jimmy Cagney movie, caricatured life for many Catholic boys, but the cool guys in these morality plays usually weren't the priests; they were the straying best friends of the priests, their sometimes dark betrayals of the church soothed by a Father Flanagan. In Shula's purview, being Catholic was noble, and ever-binding; he had his own Father Flanagan, many of them. But in the hard life of the Steel Belt, tough guys went their own way, down the road to sovereign manhood, even if it meant chasing a football.

3

"WHO IS JOHN CARROLL?"

In the late summer of 1947, the stolid, intense, sometimes eruptive son of a rayon factory worker began commuting daily to University Heights on the eastern edge of Cleveland, to the school named after America's first archbishop, who ruled over the Baltimore diocese and founded Georgetown University in the early 1800s—though John Carroll's pseudo-sainted status took a hit two centuries later, when modern researchers revealed him to have been a slaveholder on his Maryland plantation.[1] The school was founded as St. Ignatius College in 1886, but it wasn't until 1923 that it had a sports program. It took as its nickname the Fighting Irish before quickly bowing to the hegemony of Notre Dame and adopting the less romantic Blue Streaks, its mascot a big, drooling St. Bernard dog.

Carroll's campus was, and is, a bucolic place to walk through, its stately Gothic architecture highlighted by the central landmark, the Grasselli Tower, which rises a hundred feet into the air over the practice field. But the school had a low-rent college football program. Playing mostly small schools around the Steel Belt, in 1932 the school joined the lower-level Ohio Athletic Conference, which, while the third-oldest conference in America, dating back to 1902, never saw its players get much national attention, nor All-American awards.

Carroll played most of its games on a weedy field at Shaw High School, though one game a year was played in Cleveland's crumbling, 22,500-seat League Park, where the Indians played baseball until 1946 before switching to the cavernous 78,000-seat Cleveland Municipal Stadium, and which was home to the NFL's Cleveland Rams before they split for Los Angeles that same year.

The school, strapped for players, had suspended football for the duration of the war. When the sport started up again in 1946, it was with 45 war veterans among the 51 players, two of them Purple Heart recipients. The coach, tall and bushy-haired Gene Oberst, had played for Knute Rockne at Notre Dame as one of the "Seven Mules" on the offensive line that sprang holes for the Four Horsemen backfield led by "The Gipper," George Gipp. He was also the first American ever to win an Olympic medal in the javelin, at the 1924 Games in Paris. He had coached the line for Carroll in the 1930s, and then, after a four-year hitch in the navy, returned to coach basketball and track, and finally, football. Oberst was no Rockne. The Blue Streaks went 1–7, after which he was kicked upstairs, as athletic director. The new coach, Herb Eisele, a bald, beak-nosed Ohioan, had been an All-American at Dayton as a receiver. His first year at Carroll, he turned their fortunes around, finishing 6–3, with Shula on the junior varsity, which was enough to earn the youngster a full ride and a varsity roster spot in '48.

That year, tired of playing the same small-time rivals, Oberst scheduled matches with bigger attractions including Youngstown, Xavier, Marshall, and Bowling Green, preceding Oberst's intention to pull Carroll out of the conference and play as an independent in 1949. Shula would mature along with the program, coming to a reckoning about his faith and football. That spring, as he prepared for his varsity debut, he attended a three-day retreat conducted by a popular Jesuit priest named Clark Cook, known for spending time praying with prisoners on death row. Shula remembered Cook as a "very intense person," and that "I was about ready to follow in his footsteps."[2] But then came the sights and sounds of pads colliding on autumn afternoons; in later years, in memoirs, he made a joke of his inevitable decision that he could not commit himself unconditionally to the divinity and still give his all on those afternoons, deflecting the serious considerations and implications of such a choice to say it was "my inability to carry a tune" that would make him a poor priest. More accurately, it was his ability to carry a football.

Shula chose sociology as his major, adding a minor in math—perfect for a guy with a thirst for broad thinking and a tightly empirical mind. His first roommate was one of those rough-and-tumble vets, Carl Taseff, who had gone to Cleveland East High School before shipping out with the marines to the South Pacific. Two years older than Shula, his own nose had been busted up a few times. Taseff was two inches shorter and no heavier than Shula, but his toughness led Eisele to play him at fullback and defensive back. Taseff liked Shula, but didn't know which version he would encounter from day to day. Sometimes, Shula seemed to obsess on the meaning of life; other times, he burrowed into the minutiae of a game. All Taseff really knew about the kid was that when he spoke, people had a tendency to listen, because he sounded like he knew what he was talking about.

To be sure, college life widened Don Shula's world view. Off the gridiron, he could be pulled from one academic or social activity to another, such as a debate club's discussion—as reported by the school paper the *Carroll News*—of the question, "How can civil liberties be guaranteed to all those living in the United States?" The paper was filled with editorials and reporting about issues contentious even then, one being "socialized medicine and increased social security." Not overlooking more primal activities, another article cheered that "practically every prewar tradition has been revived," and that "Hell week" would feature "beer parties and beanies."

There were, naturally, plenty of stories about the football team. Eisele certainly was a VIP. Like most Ohio-bred coaches, he was a Paul Brown devotee, copying the short-passing, ball-controlling methods some would much later call the "Ohio River Offense," which produced Brown's four straight titles in the All-American Football Conference.

The third, in '48, the same year Don Shula made his mark as a collegian, came at the end of pro football's second unbeaten, untied season. Eisele was so eager to learn from the master that he and his assistants would attend the Browns' practices and games, taking copious notes. Those notes, Shula would say long in the future, would form "the basis of my football training."

Shula was a keen observer of Eisele's play calling and would spend time with backfield coach Dan "Zip" Mormile, who had been captain and quarterback at Carroll in the mid-1930s and said of the still-unproven Shula, "I think he's going to rate with the best we've ever had."[3] That was saying something, since the roster was well stocked, mainly with tough-edged sons of immigrants with names like Harcsarik, Holowenko, Janiak, Kowalczyk, Kubancik, and Zupke. Shula would play each home game with his own immigrant parents in the grandstand. The Blue Streaks began the '48 season against their coach's alma mater, Dayton, in a sparsely attended Municipal Stadium, where Oberst booked three contests that season.

Shula played well, and also got in at halfback, spelling senior starters Jim Moran and Lenny Soeder, banging out 85 yards on 10 carries. Taseff ran for 109 yards on 14 carries, earning the sobriquet "King Carl" in the school paper. However, Dayton controlled the ball for most of the game and had a 75-yard touchdown run and a 100-yard kickoff return. That set the stage for Shula to make the game's biggest play. In the fourth quarter, he floated out of the backfield for a short pass. When it came to him, a Dayton defender seemed to get his hands on it for an interception, but Shula tore it out of his grip, righted himself, and ran it all the way for a touchdown, making the score 26–18, which is how the game ended. That got Shula's picture and a short bio in the paper, under MEET SHULA, which the world was just now doing.

Shula indeed began to make a name for himself. Against Youngstown, broadcast to a few well-heeled souls in Cleveland on the brand new medium of television, Shula replaced the injured Moran at halfback. As sportswriter Charles Heaton wrote in the Cleveland Plain Dealer, Shula "proceeded to take advantage with vengeance, scoring both of Carroll's touchdowns and blasting through the line for 179 yards from scrimmage," sewing up a 13–6 victory behind the team's season-high 396 rushing yards. That week, he was the talk of the campus, and again in the big-city paper, with another headline on October 14 that read: SHULA, CARROLL'S SOPHOMORE FIND, STARTS AGAINST B.-W. SATURDAY, followed by the subhead SPEEDSTER WILL SUB FOR MORAN. He actually was a speedster then, and the story contained a quite dashing photo of him from the team's program, his chiseled face and dark hair cropped into a crewcut, assuming what would become commonly known as the "Heisman pose," imitating the form of the trophy that had been launched in 1935. Moran's absence, reported Heaton, "is causing little consternation in University Heights. The reason for this unusual state of affairs is a 175-pound rookie halfback—Don Shula of Painseville Harvey High School [who] a week ago . . . was just another substitute on the Blue Streak squad [until] his brilliant performance against Youngstown College."

By the tail end of the season, injuries had shriveled the roster to only 30 healthy players. Shula, too, was hurt, with sore ribs. Carroll still routed Niagara 20–6. And while Shula missed the next two games—Eisele practically had to clamp his butt to the bench to keep him out—the Streaks clinched a postseason invitation to the Knights of Columbus Great Lakes Bowl, the first bowl appearance in the school's history. Though Heidelberg had won the conference at 5–0–0, the bowl was a reward and a high-water mark for the school. In the game, the 7–1–2 Streaks met 7–1 Canisius, the Jesuit college in Buffalo, on December 5 in what the *Carroll News* called the culmination of "the dreams of 25 years of grid warfare" at Carroll. The teams had a history that left bad blood—the last time they met, in 1925, Carroll trailed 12–0 with three minutes left, but then a near riot broke out and they walked off the field, forfeiting the game. Now, before 17,964 fans on a cold, gray afternoon at Municipal Stadium, they were down 13–7 entering the fourth quarter. Then they moved all the way down the field and Taseff took it over for a touchdown. The extra point made it 14–13, Carroll.

Shula and Taseff racked up some amazing numbers that season.

Shula finished far behind Taseff, with 414 rushing yards, but he gained 6.5 yards per rush to Taseff's 6.1—both among the best in the nation, if anyone cared to notice. And Oberst could now go ahead with his plans to play as an independent. For the '49 season, Carroll had lost key players, including Moran, and had only five returning seniors. They were huge underdogs on the road against Texas Western, though the *Plain Dealer*'s headline on September 21 was CARROLL UNAWED BY MENACING TEXANS. That day, in El Paso, they tore onto the field all hopped up—and were dismantled, 33–7. They did regroup to beat Toledo 28–14, but then fell to Youngstown and Xavier.

Thus, they were only 1–3 when they routed Marshall 26–7 and Bowling Green 38–24. In the latter, Heaton reported, "With the ball on the Carroll 30, third down and nine yards to go, Rudy [Schaffer] arched it to Shula, who pulled it down on the Falcons' 30 and traveled unmolested the remainder of the distance."[4] Shula also caught a 14-yard pass that set up the score that put it out of reach. The next week, the Blue Streaks beat Case Tech 27–0, then Canisius 26–12.

What concerned Eisele was that Shula was playing *too* hard, that he was always one carry from an injury of some sort; he had missed several games over two seasons with banged-up ribs. Accordingly, the coach put the load on Taseff, who was now the unquestioned star, his two touchdowns in a win over Baldwin-Wallace covered on the front page of the *Plain Dealer* sports section, right there with Ohio State's 7–7 tie with Michigan that same day. The Blue Streaks completed the season at 6–3, Shula having rushed for 409 yards. Though Carroll was still a speck on the football map, Shula's senior year loomed as a last chance to save himself from the factories and fisheries of Ohio, or the collar. Oberst played a key role here, booking a big-time opponent, the Syracuse Orangemen, for the next-to-last game, a November 10 match in Municipal Stadium, which was sure to draw the press and the pro scouts, if mainly to see the Syracuse players.

Shula did well enough during the 1950 season. In the opener against St. Bonaventure, in upstate New York, Taseff broke a 78-yard touchdown run and Shula picked up key first downs, though he also had a key fumble. With six minutes left, Carroll led 19–14, but the Bonnies ran off 14 points to win 28–19. It was the kind of loss that made Shula sick; afterward, he sat at his locker, back turned to the room, staring motionless at the wall for several long minutes. Everyone knew to leave him be, that even putting an arm around his shoulder might ignite a fuse. The next week, they again kept away, after the Streaks lost 24–19 to Xavier. But now came his big push. He went on a rampage against Kent State, gaining 113 yards on just 11 carries in a 41–0 laugher. The headline the next day was SHULA IS LEADER OF GROUND ATTACK.[5]

He had also caught 6 passes for 122 yards and a touchdown, Heaton praising his "combination of speed—he does the 100 in 10 seconds and was a member of the Carroll track team last spring—and agility make him hard to cover." And he played defensive back every game. Eisele could only rhapsodize, "I can't praise the boy enough. We pile the work on him but there's never any complaining."

The Streaks blasted Youngstown 27–0, Shula notching a 23-yard touchdown run, then Case Tech 51–14, Marshall 39–2, and Dayton 24–12 in a snowstorm. In that game, covered by the Associated Press, another breakthrough, the wire service reported that "the star for the winners was Don Shula, who accounted for 165 of the Streaks' 273 yards of gain. Shula scored the really decisive touchdown in the fourth quarter on a one-yard smash."[6] That cued the arrival of the team's biggest test, Syracuse, under the lights at Municipal Stadium on a Friday night. The Orangemen, a Division I school, came into the game with a 5–2 record, winners of four straight, and giving quotes to the newspaper asking, "Who is John Carroll?" Eisele pasted the clippings on the bulletin board for motivation. But Syracuse already regretted booking the game because, having anticipated a share of receipts from a good crowd in the big stadium, only 16,724 paid their way in.

That was a damn shame, considering that Shula and Taseff put on a show, one that Shula would be able to live off of, and cash in on, for years to come. He amassed 124 yards on 23 rushes, beating Taseff's 115 yards on 25 carries, a rare instance when he outshone his roomie, though it was "the bandy-legged senior fullback," wrote Heaton, who put it away, erasing a 16–7 halftime deficit by taking in two touchdowns in the fourth quarter. The second, a one-yard plunge, put Carroll ahead with a minute to go, after which the defense held off a furious Syracuse comeback attempt.

In his memoirs, this exhilarating victory was the only non-pro game Shula wrote anything about, calling it "the biggest highlight of my career at John Carroll" and "the biggest and best game John Carroll ever played."[7] Gilding that lily, he recalled that he had "tremendous anxiety" before the game, and was knocked so silly on one play that "I had to be dragged off the field." On the sideline, he was given smelling salts and came back in after missing just one play.

His performance bailed out Eisele, who at halftime raged at the players for so long that they were late returning to the field, incurring a penalty. But when the gun sounded, wrote Heaton, Eisele and "his happy warriors were carried to the dressing room on the arms of several thousand jubilant students." The *Plain Dealer* played the victory as a titanic event, splashing page one of the sports section with CARROLL'S LAST-MINUTE SCORE GAINS UPSET OVER SYRACUSE. Heaton gushed about "the courageous Streaks" having "crashed through with a major upset and one of the finest triumphs in the school's 30 years of football."

Carroll closed out by beating Baldwin-Wallace 33–25 to go 8–2, the best record in school history. Taseff was the nation's second-leading scorer, and he made the first-team all-Ohio team, while Shula earned honorable mention. And while it meant little within the national college scene—or even the local scene, given that Ohio State halfback Vic Janowicz won the Heisman Trophy—the good timing of the Syracuse game would pay dividends for both Shula and Taseff. That day, Paul Brown and his coaching staff decided to do some scouting of their own. They came to check out Syracuse, but left humming about Shula.

Knowing nothing of this, Shula completed his studies in the spring, earning his degree. On June 11, 1951, Dan and Mary Shula ventured to Cleveland Heights and found seats close to the stage when their son strode across the stage in his cap and gown for his diploma. He would leave Carroll grateful to the school for keeping him out of the factories. He also left behind any notion that he might join the clergy.

Proving how tenaciously competitive he was, that spring he also ran the anchor leg on Carroll's 880-yard relay team, which won one meet by setting a school record of 1:33.7. But he had faint hope that someone in the pros would give him a shot, not with so many high-quality guys at the bigger schools capturing the scouts' attention. Yet that game against Syracuse did more than he could have imagined. It put his fate in the hands of a higher authority, one only slightly less elevated than God.

4

THE CLEVELAND CALIPH

T hose hands belonged to Paul Eugene Brown, whose path through life seemed similar to that of Don Shula's. Born in Norwalk, Ohio, in 1908, Brown predated Shula as a product of the Steel Belt ethos. Growing up in Massillon, near Canton, the son of a railroad dispatcher, he was an undersized kid, but, with a yen for football that people thought strange, he worked his way up as a single-wing quarterback in high school, and then as a small-college All-American at Miami University in Oxford, Ohio. Like Shula, the uncertainties of pro football led him to pursue a fallback—pre-law— but when offered the job of coaching at a prep school in Maryland, he took it and won the state title. In 1931, he returned to Massillon High School as its coach, a job he held for nine years, winning the state crown six times.

Even at this low level, he formulated highly advanced theories and modes of behavior for players, turning high school into a Plato's forum of football study. It was here, developing his split-T, perpetual-motion offense and complex zone defense, that Brown wrote the first play-book, with any given play determined by what the sports geeks today call analytics—predictive models based on the chances of success for a play on a given down and distance. Nobody ever really understood it all except Brown, who used hand signals from the sidelines to call plays. He also utilized a tightly organized nexus of allied coaches and scouts to attract players from across the state, not caring a whit if they happened to be black.

Glowering and distant, he was a strict taskmaster, close to a martinet, always in a tie and gray suit with cleats, almost never smiling or indulging jokes. Few players, worked as they were like chattel, went as far as *liking* him, but they swore their souls to him. And by 1941, Brown was ready to take his arcane ways to big-time college football. Ohio State hired him at age 33; bringing some of his schoolboy players with him, he also signed purebred talent, such as the trucklike defensive lineman Bill Willis. In '42, with the country at war and many team rosters thinned, Brown's Buckeyes won the national championship. But then the Buckeyes were also at the mercy of the draft, and in '44, Brown's own number came, turning him into a lieutenant in the navy.

He was assigned to Naval Station Great Lakes, near Chicago, and did little else but coach the base team. Brown was far from unique in this respect. Early in the war, various arms of the service opened training programs at colleges, such as the navy at Purdue and Michigan. When the best football players arrived at their bases, commanding officers wanted them to keep playing. Among Brown's players were two future Pro Football Hall of Famers: Willis and another pachyderm, the 240-pound prototypical fullback Marion Motley. In an acrid irony of the times, both of these African Americans were the stars of their base team, yet could only have served in segregated units. Another player on the squad was a Miami of Ohio halfback, Ara Parseghian, who hurt his ankle and never played, but could observe Brown on the sideline—an education he called "priceless" as his coaching path carried him to a national title with Notre Dame two decades later. Brown's team became a national power, losing only to Notre Dame and his own Buckeyes. But then his path took another turn. As the war was winding down, in September of '44, a competitor to the NFL, the All-America Football Conference, was born, the brainstorm of Chicago newspaperman Arch Ward. It began play when the war ended as an eight-team circuit of mainly big cities, including Cleveland, where the team's owner, Arthur "Mickey" McBride, went after Brown with an immense offer: a $17,500 a year salary—more than any coach, college or pro, was earning—and a monthly stipend of $250 until the war's end. Brown was loath to quit Ohio State for good, but that kind of bread proved irresistible.

The NFL in those days was hardly a model of how to run a business, but few believed that even Paul Brown could make the fledgling AAFC a success. Still, when the league began play in the fall of 1946, its owners had ponied up enough cash to sign over 100 NFL players. They even brought the first pro team to Florida, called the Seahawks. Out in LA, a team called the Dons was owned by a group that included Louis B. Mayer, Bob Hope, and Bing Crosby. But Brown was the great equalizer, a one-man league. He came to Cleveland bearing talent loyal to him, including Motley and Willis, the only two black players on the roster. Coming shortly after the Rams had signed two black players, pro football had thus beaten major league baseball to integration; it would be seven months before Jackie Robinson arrived in Brooklyn.

The last thing Brown wanted was for the team to bear his name, but McBride forced it on him, and it fit. The rise of the team paralleled the postwar industrial boom and the explosive growth of a middle-class culture eager for new heroes. In this maw, the Browns became synonymous with the potential of pro football, a nearly unbeatable force mirroring the unlimited power of an America that held, for now, all the nuclear weapons. Future Hall of Famers abounded in Cleveland, the most celebrated being quarterback Otto Graham, who, when he was at Northwestern, had handed Brown his only loss in '41 and another in '43, proving one of Brown's adages: anyone good enough to beat him belonged on his team. He paid Graham top dollar, $7,500 a year, to keep leading the Browns to their titles without interruption. In 1951, the NFL merged with the AAFC, taking in two other teams, the San Francisco 49ers and the original Baltimore Colts, just to be able to get the Browns within its purview; the Los Angeles Dons also merged separately with the Rams. And that was when the nearly obscure Don Shula entered into the pro football culture, as an afterthought.

The NFL draft—which began in 1936 with the first player ever chosen, Jay Berwanger, saying thanks but no thanks to pro ball—occurred on January 18 and 19, 1951, at the Blackstone Hotel in Chicago, where cigarette and cigar smoke choked an airless room as general managers made their picks over 30 monotonous rounds. There were no scouting combines, no workouts with individual teams, no football gurus weighing in with projections, no real-time media coverage. Players were either notified by phone or telegram. When it commenced, Shula was busy winding up his studies and running track.

The likes of Kyle Rote and Y. A. Tittle went early, and few took note of the last pick of round nine, when Paul Brown selected Don Shula. The next day, with the last pick in round 22, he picked up Taseff. Or at least that's what the two roommates saw in the papers; no one from the team bothered to let them know. They were, of course, elated that the pro football caliph—who just weeks before had capped his first season under the NFL banner by defeating the team that once played in Cleveland, the LA Rams, on a last-minute field goal—had taken them; even better, two of their Carroll teammates were chosen, too, by other teams. But after two weeks, they still had not heard from the Browns. Shula, not one for sitting back and waiting, recalled, "I couldn't have been any happier. [But] I couldn't take the suspense any longer so I called them myself. They told me they were waiting until track season was over before contacting me. I felt greatly relieved, to say the least."[1]

Brown may have grinned at the kid's impudence. As it was, there was no guarantee he would make the team. Shula was prepared to fight like hell for a spot, but the realist in him told him to apply for a job with area high schools just in case, and he quickly had an offer to coach and teach math at Lincoln High School in Canton, where the NFL was born and where, in 1963, it became the home of the Pro Football Hall of Fame. The offer was for $3,750 a year, but Brown was willing to sign him to a contract, sight unseen, for $5,000. The roommates traveled together to the Browns' office, then went to a bar down the street and ordered martinis, which they'd never had before but believed was in order for men of their new status, and for Shula, his status as a 21-year-old able to legally imbibe—until he threw up all over the bar.

But now came a complication. Before they could report to the team's summer camp at Bowling Green University, they got their notices from the government to begin their impending military commitments. When the draft board learned that they were about to begin playing for Paul Brown, they were allowed an extraordinary concession: they would report to the national guard's 37th Infantry Division at Camp McCoy in Wisconsin, but for only a month, after which they would be able to return to the gridiron, the balance of their hitches with the Ohio National Guard to be fulfilled at a future time. Any delay was welcome. At the time, the shadow of the Korean War was lengthening, and the country was steeling itself for more years of war, not that many could understand why; unlike the last war, there were no attacks on America and the objective wasn't to free the world, but to contain the vague threat of "Red China" conquering a distant peninsula with two Koreas—one good, one not.

This was not easy for a man like Shula, who had clearly defined values and precepts of good and evil, to make sense of. Still, quite clear was that a football career seemed to be his means of avoiding picking up a rifle in anger. Taseff, who'd already seen combat, was made a sergeant at the base while Shula had to figuratively lick his boots, as a private. During this interim, a reporter from the *Plain Dealer*, Bill Cobbledick, caught up with the pair at the camp. Shula, his mind on football, told him, "Just say we hope to make the [Browns]." Taseff added that they were keeping in shape "running up and down these hills" and that, at his orders, "Don dug two foxholes today."[2]

Shula met Paul Brown for the first time when he got to the Browns' camp in mid-July, and it was all the kid could do to keep his knees from knocking. "I was," he recalled, "completely in awe of the man."[3] For years, he had scrounged up enough money to buy Browns tickets, watching and making mental notes about how Brown coached, sounded, *looked*. He even took to walking around with his arms crossed at chest level—the iconic pose imitated by coaches everywhere. He read instructional pamphlets written by Brown, and thought about how to play within his sytem both on offense and defense. Once on the inside, theory became law. The first day of camp, Brown asked, "Why do we have a playbook?" The players, even the 30-something veterans, would begin scribbling on paper like grade-school kids. He'd do the same with complicated concepts, expecting in-depth essays about things like trap blocking and strong-side zone coverage. It was, Shula recalled with epic understatement, "tedious work."

Brown explained his canons on the chalkboard and also had games— and even practices—filmed from different angles. At team meetings, he would run plays back and forth through a projector, with players called on, pop-quiz style, to answer impossibly technical questions. The meetings would stretch into the evening. The entire time, Shula said, Brown would "dictate and the players would write it down word for word." They would surprise themselves when, after endless repetitions, they actually understood more than a little of the subject matter and took it into games. From the start, Brown, with Motley at fullback and halfbacks Dub Jones and Rex Bumgardner, never considered Shula or Taseff as offensive players; they were put on the depth chart as scrub defensive backs, where they had split their time at Carroll. Impressed by Shula's quick reflexes and sure hands, Brown and his defensive backfield coach, Blanton Collier, penciled him in at safety. They were again impressed, and a tad amused, by the kid's chutzpah. During a scrimmage, Motley broke through the line and rumbled down field, right at Shula, whom he outweighed by at least 40 pounds. Shula described what happened:

> It was just the two of us in the open field. I came up to meet him, force against force. I lowered my head and put everything I had into the tackle. I wrapped my arms tightly around his legs and Motley went down. What a feeling of satisfaction I had. All of a sudden I heard Paul Brown's voice.

"Nice tackle, Taseff!"

I couldn't let that pass, not after the tackle I made. I looked back and yelled.

"It's not Taseff who made the tackle, it was Shula. S-H-U-L-A."[4]

Brown, he remembered, "broke into a laugh." The coach seemed to be getting used to having him around. Midway through camp, though, he and Taseff could hardly believe it when they received letters from the government informing them that, just weeks after their first hitch, their national guard unit was being called up and their notices to report would be sent in the near future. As a result, Brown began reducing their playing time, not wasting that of other players who would still be around. Shula, in rare form, decided to march down to the unit's armory in Cleveland. Confronting the commanding officer, he asked for an exemption, telling him, "Sir, my pro career is at stake." And damn if the top cat didn't see things his way, agreeing to wait until the end of the season to call Shula and Taseff to duty.

As crippling drills in the hot sun gradually turned into longer scrimmages, Shula's name began showing up regularly in the *Plain Dealer*'s team reports. He was also gradually taken into the cliques of the veterans, he and Taseff invited to go out carousing with grizzled bears like Lou "The Toe" Groza—the left tackle/kicker who had booted the winning field goal to beat the Rams in the '50 championship game—and Lou Rymkus, the right tackle. Ends Dante Lavelli and Mac Speedie worked one-on-one drills with him, on their own. Even the famously icy, glowering Otto Graham shot the breeze with them.[5]

A tougher task than fitting in was learning Brown's system. A reporter ventured that the players "more often look like scholars than bruising exponents of the 'play-for-pay' ranks."[6] As the season approached, Brown, with only 33 roster spots to fill, was apparently about to cut bait on Shula, perhaps relegate him to the "taxi squad," so named because McBride also owned a fleet of cabs and would give these players jobs driving while they sat around doing nothing. Only some urging by linebacker Tony Adamle, the defensive captain, kept Shula aboard long enough to prove he belonged. That happened in the final preseason game, against the Rams, when all he had to do was prevent future Hall of Fame receiver Tom Fears from catching passes from future Hall of Fame quarterbacks Bob Waterfield and Norm Van Brocklin.

Shula, wearing a rookie's number, 96, had no hesitation in getting into a scrap with Fears on the first pass thrown to him. Making a hard tackle, Shula rolled Fears over. Thinking Shula was twisting his ankle, Fears kicked at Shula's unprotected face, mashing his nose. Normally, this might have sent a Shula foot or fist back at him, but that would have gotten him run from the game and irked Brown. Instead, he coolly went back to his position—and proceeded to intercept two passes in a Browns win. Still, the *Plain Dealer* noted a week before the September 30 opener against the 49ers that among those expected to be cut were Shula and Taseff. The way Brown made his cuts, envelopes would be given to the victims. When Shula and Taseff got theirs, they were loath to open them; when they finally did, the letters inside told them they had cheated the hangman; they were the only rookies to make the team. "I was," Shula would recall, "the happiest guy on the face of the earth."

He and Taseff, who wasn't totally safe, being put on the taxi squad, shared an apartment at 1596 East 34th Street. He also gave his parents a hefty portion of his paycheck. That had been part of the bargain for rejecting the priesthood: his assurance that playing football for a living was honest work.

Brown's defensive system worked out of a 5–3–3 alignment: the five down linemen, including a middle guard—or nose tackle—and three mobile linebackers. His defensive backfield was held down by rangy, hard-hitting cornerbacks Warren Lahr and Tommy James. An opening did develop when safety Ken Gorgal, who had six interceptions as a rookie the season before, was called into the service for two years. Brown said that four guys might get that job—Shula, Stan Heath, Ace Loomis, and Ken Carpenter—but he went with a veteran, Cliff Lewis, who was also Otto Graham's backup. Shula, assigned to special teams, would have to wait for his shot. Taseff would come off the taxi squad and be used, rarely, as a kick returner and scrub fullback and defensive back. The season began with a rare poor effort, a 24–10 loss to the 49ers. The Browns then had an early critical match against the Rams in LA. After falling behind 10–0, they awoke and came away 38–23 winners. Typical of Brown's teams, they would not lose thereafter, and only two games were remotely close.

Shula had more to do with the team's performance than anyone would have thought. Before the third game, against the Washington Redskins, Tommy James was hurt in practice and Brown started the mouthy kid he had nearly cut. That week, Brown personally tutored him during practices, giving him a priceless education in four days. Brown's teams were so strong that the substitution hardly mattered. With Shula meshing perfectly with the veterans, they beat the 'Skins 45–0—typically, not good enough for Brown, who moaned that they had played "sloppy" but had gotten the breaks. Shula remained in the lineup when the Browns met the New York Giants, whose flinty coach, Steve Owen, was past his championship years but still employed a suffocating array of complex zone/man schemes of his own, dubbed the "umbrella defense," and whose offense was led by Chuckin' Charlie Conerly. Owen had beaten the Browns the year before in the regular season, but fallen in a playoff game. And the Browns had to scrape by, winning 14–13, the difference being a missed New York extra point. So intense was this affair that Motley, who had a bum knee and wasn't supposed to play, got off the bench and limped into the huddle, without Brown's permission, and pounded out key yardage.

This was a common dynamic for the Browns. Graham never missed a game in his career. When someone did miss a game, and the replacement did well, Brown kept the latter in the lineup. Thus did Shula make James a forgotten man for most of the season. He would play nine straight games, intercepting four passes—though in his memoir, he believed it was six. Against the Bears, on a day when Dub Jones scored a record-tying six touchdowns, the paper ran a stirring photo of the novice Shula, his outstretched fingers grabbing a pick. But Brown figured he needed to restore James for the final regular-season game, to prepare for the playoffs. Shula, gritting his teeth, was allowed the cold comfort of returning a kickoff, for six yards.

"Although I didn't agree with Brown's decision," he would confess, "I kept my mouth shut. But it hurt. Oh, how it hurt. I felt as if my world had collapsed."[7]

This was an early tell that when Shula later said that five yards was his life, he was dead serious. His life, his world, was football. To be sure, the season was a rush while it lasted for him; less so for Taseff, who rushed for 49 yards and scored two touchdowns, as well as catching a TD pass for 18. (The Plain Dealer, in a glorious typo, reported in October that he would be "filling in with the dickoff and punt return units.") Accordingly, while Shula would look back with reverence for Brown, his judgment of the coach would become nuanced, and in some ways negative. As a member of a changing culture in the game, Shula bridled at the caliph's antiquated rules that were, in reality, destructive— such as not allowing players to drink water during practices, however scorching-hot the day. Not only Brown, but, he would say, all coaches believed that water "was supposed to give you cramps or something, just like weightlifting supposedly made you muscle-bound." Another was Brown's favorite exercise, the duck waddle, which required players to walk through practice with their knees bent. That, Shula believed, "was absolutely the worst thing for your legs."

There was an even greater imposition, if only for those who actually obeyed it: mixing the sporting life with archaic Episcopalian folderol about self-denial. Most players laughed about Brown decreeing off-limits any sexual activity except for Sunday night and the Monday day off, as well as smoking or drinking in public. Said Shula: "The no-sex-after-Tuesday thing was just something to kid about. . . . Brown used to talk about it in the meetings, and everyone would laugh and tell jokes. I mean, how would they check?"[8]

He stopped short of saying whether he himself made any effort to comply, though as a young bachelor with a healthy store of aggression and testosterone, his modern concept of piousness had loopholes for such manly norms. To be sure, willing women were available for the taking, a reward for men who made a good living on athletic fields.

As it was, Shula could see tension between Brown and Graham, who admitted years later—at Brown's Hall of Fame induction ceremony, no less—that he had often "cussed out" the imperious coach.[9] That was something other players, especially green, precociously hot-headed, individualistic ones like Don Shula, might have wanted to do but didn't have the status, or the stones.[10] While Brown would endure in the game until the dawn of the next millennium, his best years would fit into one decade and dim with acrimony between him and his players and McBride. When, years later, Shula spoke of coaches needing to deal "with sensitive kids, getting them to feel confident, the *personal* angle—and never to assume they knew what they didn't,"[11] it was clear that he was, by long distance and implication, putting Paul Brown behind him.

Though the Browns finished at 11–1, the close call they had the year before against the Rams was a sign the rest of the sport was catching up to them. Brown faced the Rams again in the '51 title game in the Los Angeles Coliseum. They led 10–7 at the half, then wilted. Graham, who won the first of his three league MVP awards that season, and who played in the championship game every year of his career, coughed up a key fumble and threw three interceptions, while Motley and Jones ran for a combined 37 yards. The Rams went ahead, the Browns tied it late, and then Tom Fears snared a 73-yard pass from Norm Van Brocklin to win it, 24–17—Brown's first defeat in a title match. "We just lost one—period. We lost a football game, that's all," was Brown's stony postmortem. For Shula, however, no one deserved more blame than Brown—for benching him.

"I felt I deserved to start," he said years later, taking his token appearance late in the game as an insult.

When the final gun sounded that day, he and Taseff were immediately eligible for duty with the national guard, again with the 37th Infantry, now bivouacking at Camp Polk in Louisiana. Found there by a reporter, Taseff said, "This is taking us away from a good job, but it has to be done and we might as well do it with a smile."[12] In truth, the only thing the pair could smile about was that, as the stalemated Korean War raged on, they never got any closer to Pork Chop Hill than the bayou, mainly playing on the camp baseball team. During a road trip, they even jumped the team to catch the College All-Star game and bend their elbows in Chicago, a side trip Shula would later admit was technically AWOL, though he admitted the jaunt was "a gas." However, given the feral competition on the Browns, missing the team's summer drills and the first two months of the 1952 season would put them on borrowed time with the team. When they were honorably discharged in mid-November, Shula brashly called Paul Brown to ask if he had a job. As it happened, Brown needed to replace an injured Tommy James again. After asking whether Shula was in shape, Brown said, "Get here by tonight."

He and Taseff returned to Cleveland to be signed for another year at a $500 raise to $5,500. Starting the very next day against the Eagles, a typical face-first tackle left Shula with a busted, bloody lip and three loose teeth. He'd be stitched up and be ready for the next game, a plastic face mask—the kind being worn by some quarterbacks—nailed to his helmet, though this was a break with convention; as a *Plain Dealer* know-it-all believed, "Defensive backs cannot wear [them]. It ruins their chance to see enemy passes."[13] Shula played five games until James was healthy, intercepting no passes. He was then on the bench as the Browns finished their stroll to the '52 championship game, though with a less-than-preeminent 8–4 record and with a spate of injuries.

They were an aging, brittle team now—Dub Jones and Mac Speedie would miss the next championship game, and Motley was crumbling—less sturdy than the Rams and the newest NFL power, the Detroit Lions, who edged out the Rams to face the Browns in the title round. The Lions were a team on a hard rise under coach Buddy Parker, with a quarterback who would have given Brown the vapors: the boozy Bobby Layne. The onetime Texas All-American could barely stand erect or focus his eyeballs, prefiguring Joe Namath as he partied and flaunted dates with beautiful women; out of vanity, he would never consent to wearing a face mask. Layne was All-Pro in '52—even with a sub-.500 completion percentage and 20 interceptions to 19 touchdowns, hampered by favorite target, Doak Walker, being injured most of the season. In the title game, however, Layne threw an early touchdown, Walker ran another in from 67 yards, and the defense stymied Brown's offense to win 17–7.

Shula and Taseff, who never came off the taxi squad, felt like they were dead to Brown. It was a logical assumption considering that, when Brown divvied up the losing share of the playoff pool—a full share came to $1,712.49—Shula was given a half-share for his half-season, one of several Browns who were stiffed.[14] Shula had spent parts of the past two off-seasons working toward his master's degree in physical education at Western Reserve Academy, a small college and prep school in Hudson, Ohio, to bolster his credentials as a coach/teacher. That March, still waiting to hear from the Browns about '53, he picked up a paper, saw his picture, and read that he and Taseff had been part of a massive trade with the expansion Baltimore Colts. He was so livid that he had been dealt without as much as a call from Brown, or anyone else in the Browns' front office, that he slammed down his coffee cup.

There was relief for young men like him when the fruitless conflict in Korea finally ended, in a stalemate, just before that 1953 season, after over 36,000 American combat deaths. The world had dodged a nuclear bullet, but was trapped in a Cold War mentality; the specter of commies hiding under beds would sacrifice innocent reputations and lives in televised witch hunts by the likes of a besotted Wisconsin senator. Once again, sports would be a narcotic for those with disposable income in a decade unfolding with placid, self-satisfied calmness, under which a rumbling of *anti*-heroism could be detected in the rebellious, laconic stereotypes up on the movie screens, exemplified by Brando in a T-shirt or leather jacket. The men who gave birth to the Baby Boom generation had their subdivisions and strains, but pro football had made it through the stormy years, auguring a boom soon to come. But from where Don Shula sat, his cashiering by Paul Brown posed a dilemma. If this was how they treated people of his high moral and physical fiber in the NFL, maybe he had given enough of his time to a dream that seemed less plausible every day.

5

ONE TOUGH SONOFABITCH

I t couldn't have helped Shula's disposition that a previous iteration of the Baltimore Colts had already failed, in the AAFC and then for one awful season in the NFL, going 1–11 in 1950. That the name got another chance was the doing of NFL commissioner Bert Bell. The former owner of the Philadelphia Eagles, Bell had a fondness for the Baltimore–Philly corridor and the Colt fan base, which had supported the soon-defunct team with fan clubs, marching bands, and cheerleaders. When the Dallas Texans went under in 1952, Bell sought out clothing millionaire Carroll Rosenbloom, a former teammate at Penn, to take over that team and move it to Baltimore. He did, for a mere $15,000. Needing warm bodies, Rosenbloom made the mass trade with the Browns—the biggest ever in terms of the number of players moved (the famous 18-player deal in 1989 that sent Herschel Walker from Dallas to Minnesota involved mainly draft picks). Paul Brown leapt at the chance to unload *ten* players and get five good ones back, including tackle Mike McCormack, meaning that two future Hall of Famers were involved in the swap. McCormack, a former star at Kansas, would become a Hall of Fame lineman for Brown, and then turn to coaching. The other: Don Shula.

Brown said he was loath to part with Shula. As the *Columbus Dispatch* reported, he relented because he had drafted Ohio State's All-Big Ten defensive back Fred Bruney. "I sincerely believe Fred Bruney can make our team and be a help to us," he explained.[1] In the end, Bruney washed out after a few weeks before he, too, was traded, to the 49ers (later to become a longtime NFL assistant coach). Shula, was who nearing completion of his graduate degree, didn't want to make a decision about his future until he could speak with the Colts' general manager. He picked up the phone and called Don Kellett, who had been given the job by Rosenbloom even though his only experience in sports was as an infielder with the Boston Red Sox, after which he was a sportscaster. When Shula got through to him, he concluded that the affable, low-key Kellett was "quite impressive." Kellett gave Shula a $6,500 salary, a $1,000 raise.

When Shula arrived at the Colts' summer camp in Westminster, Maryland, he had gone from the top to the bottom. While Brown had paid his men $40 a week during the preseason—teams weren't obligated to pay players anything before the season began—all Kellett could manage was $15. Most Colts felt like mercenaries in a profession that, despite the highly professional methods of Brown, Halas, Parker, et al., was still often a freak show. One of Shula's most memorable teammates, defensive tackle Art Donovan, was a Bronx native and the son of a boxing referee of the same name. Portly and with voluminous appetites, he wore the nickname "Fatso," yet his proud gluttony did nothing to stem him from terrorizing offenses, an attribute that would get him into the Hall of Fame. Others with his dimensions usually had less ability, and waddled about, mostly looking for a fight.

That sort of chain-gang mentality was not frowned upon by most owners, or by Bell. The professorial Brown notwithstanding, the league was marketed similarly to pro wrestling—which was winning enormous ratings on early TV. The biggest names in football were often talented players like Donovan, but with near-homicidal instincts and appropriate nicknames. Hardy "Hatchet Man" Brown used his shoulder to clock guys in the head. Ed Sprinkle was called "The Claw." The Eagles' defensive line and linebackers were called the "Suicide Seven."

Shula, of course, was well aware of offensive players who were also headhunters. All that just came with the sport. Increasing sophistication was welcome, but sportsmanship was meaningless once the kickoff went into the air. Within this framework, pro football was the alter ego of baseball, which was historically resonant, well manicured, and undeniably the country's main leisure-time attraction, the New York Yankees drawing comparisons to IBM and General Motors for their machinelike perfection in a culture of courtly manners fending off loud, unruly new norms. This was an effective con, inasmuch as the beau ideal of impressionable Baby Boomer children, Mickey Mantle, lived off the field inside a whiskey bottle. Still, while the national pastime was rising to its apogee, the muddy-faced, bloody-nosed identity of pro football was more in line with the changing of the culture than most thought. And what Don Shula didn't know was that his ragtag team was going to be his ticket to places he couldn't have imagined in 1953.

The Colts' rookie coach, 47-year-old Keith Molesworth, had played quarterback for Papa Bear Halas's Chicago Bears in the same backfield as Red Grange and Bronko Nagurski. Seeing what he had now, he grimaced. He had no serviceable quarterback; the starter was the journeyman Fred Enke. Molesworth did have some solid pieces, like Donovan, Gino Marchetti, and Bill Pellington. The son of Italian immigrants, Marchetti had fought in the Battle of the Bulge and had been a star defensive end on the undefeated 1951 University of San Francisco team. Pellington, a willowy outside linebacker, was a tough Jersey boy, throwing his forearm around like a billy club and making horse-collar tackles that would eventually be banned. When Pellington tried out with the Browns in '52, Paul Brown was so aghast at his violence, he cut him the first week. Molesworth believed he needed such feral men to compete.

Shula fit the bill, and he gained attention early. The Colts' defensive secondary coach, Russ Murphy, wanted to play a Paul Brown–style defense but had no idea how, so Shula found himself tutoring his coach. In late August, the Associated Press ran a photo of Shula in a preseason game, reaching way up to deflect a pass, the caption reading, SHULA SPOILS IT.[2] On opening day, he was the starter at right cornerback against Halas's declining Bears, in the Colts' horseshoe-shaped Memorial Stadium. Erected a few years earlier on 33rd Street, near Johns Hopkins University, the stadium's capacity was in the process of being increased to 47,000, mainly in a bid to lure baseball's St. Louis Browns to Baltimore for the '54 season. (They would be renamed the Orioles.) But even the bottom-feeding Colts had no trouble filling ther still-under-construction stands. On September 27, they drew an impressive 23,715, who celebrated when the Colts won 13–9.

After they split the next four games, bringing in a full house of 34,031 against Washington, and seeing several inspired performances, people were starting to take notice. The secondary, anchored by Shula, had dubbed itself the "Radar Corps," for the way it closed in on passes. At 3–2, the team was a Western Conference contender, briefly. With a paltry offense, however, they lost their last seven games. As Shula recalled, "The Radar Corps cracked."[3] At 3–9, the Colts finished the year as a doormat, last in the league in both offense and defense. But they did lead the league with 56 fumble recoveries and interceptions, and Donovan, safety Tom Keane, and guard Dick Barwegen went to the Pro Bowl. Shula made strides of his own. He reeled in three interceptions, as did Carl Taseff. It was enough to convince Shula he needed to stick with it. And as his life came into focus, a woman came into the picture for the first time.

Back in Painesville for the off-season, he supplemented his income by selling cars at the Stanton Motors dealership, the kind of thing most professional athletes in that era had to do. He was at a bowling alley in his off time when he struck up a conversation with a swarthy, spunky 20-year-old woman on the next lane. Her name was Dorothy Bartish. For many years, he would say he met her for the first time that night. However, in 1987, he admitted they'd actually met in Catholic school. As he related it, "I was in the eighth grade at St. Mary's School, and she was in the fourth, and we boys did something we shouldn't [have]. This little gal squealed to the nuns."[4] He said this in a lighthearted manner, and never went any further about what it was he had done, and neither did Dorothy. Whatever it was, she was forgiving. That night at the bowling alley, they had a drink in the lounge, though she was under drinking age, and then began dating. The first date was at a dance club—her idea. "I was very reluctant to dance," he recalled. "But when she got me on the dance floor, she made things easy, made me feel comfortable. We hit it off."[5]

She had led a hardscrabble life similar to his. Her mother died giving birth to her, and her Hungarian father worked on the railroad and was rarely home, so she was entrusted to her maternal grandmother, a stern woman who watched her every move. When Dorothy introduced him to her grandmother, Shula said, "she was a bit cold toward me,"[6] because she regarded Hungarians as layabouts. This caused a clash between her and Dorothy, who vowed that if her granny didn't give permission to marry him, they should elope. Shula would never have done that, given that, for him, marriage was a sacred covenant, blessed by a priest and Dan and Mary Shula. For now, they carried on their careers, she as a music teacher at a Cleveland high school, and he spending the entire autumn away from her, but telling friends he had found the girl he would marry.

That winter, Molesworth was out as coach, kicked upstairs to be personnel director when Carroll Rosenbloom hired Paul Brown's 46-year-old defensive line coach, Wilbur "Weeb" Ewbank. A tiny man with a pug nose, Ewbank, who had also been Brown's assistant at Great Lakes, was the rare coach who could teach Brown's complex defense, which relied on reading "keys," the subtle moves or body language of offensive players that tipped off plays. He had also been Brown's personnel director, so integral to the team that when the Colt job came up, Brown warned him not to take it. He did let Ewbank go, but not before the draft, during which Ewbank stealthily passed notes to Baltimore sportswriter John Steadman to relay to Don Kellett about who the Colts should pick. When Ewbank finally got to Baltimore, he brought with him another Ohio native and student of the Paul Brown method, Joe Thomas, who'd been coaching at Indiana, as his defensive coach.

Most of the Colts could barely stand Ewbank. Like Brown, he was dour, repetitious, demanding of absolute perfection. He could scream himself red-faced at players who screwed up and was accused of playing favorites with the stars. He was also a bit ditzy. One early game in Baltimore, he insisted the team needed a field goal to tie—when the Colts actually led. Bill Pellington had to scream at him, "Weeb, for God's sake, we're fucking *winning* by three points!"[7] Still, if you mastered his tedious playbook, good things happened. And the Colts' draft picks that year, secretly made by Ewbank, were inspired. He chose Baylor quarterback Cotton Davidson first, who didn't do much that year, but down the list were some amazing stock futures: defensive end Ordell Braase, guard Alex Sandusky, and—at number 232, in the 20th round—SMU receiver Raymond Berry, whose glue-like hands and balletic feet would take him to the Hall of Fame and a long coaching career. Neither Berry nor Braase could play right away in the NFL because their college eligibility wasn't done. But Ewbank knew that Paul Brown was high on both, and he secured them to keep them out of Brown's clutches—Berry until 1955, Braase until 1957. They, and Sandusky, would play 38 years, every single one with the Baltimore Colts.

Ewbank also made a trade for Don Joyce, a behemoth defensive end who also was a pro wrestler. Art Donovan called him a "madman," one who solidified the line. But Fatso had less than good vibes about the new coach, saying years later, "Weeb was a screwball who held insane grudges. [He] thought he was smarter than God, and deep down inside was one mean sonofabitch . . . a tremendous coaching talent and a rat bastard." That first exhibition season, he said, Ewbank intentionally put an injured rookie lineman in a game just so he could say the kid wasn't playing hard and could cut him. Ewbank only encouraged the wild-man tendencies of his toughest guys, who blew off steam in endless excursions to the local bars, with no hedging for the curfew. Shula fell in with that hard-core group. In 1995, Paul Zimmerman wrote of that lesson in manly education:

[Shula] hung around with the rougher elements on the team—Gino Marchetti, Artie Donovan, Don Joyce, Bill Pellington—and choirboys didn't survive in that company. "We'd be drinking in Baltimore, and we'd have to drive back to camp, in Westminster, Maryland, to beat the curfew," Shula says. "One night I said, 'C'mon, I'll drive us back,' because I was the one who was sober. One guy grabbed the keys out of my hand and said, 'We ain't going anywhere.' And we weren't—until they were good and ready. When I finally got us back, we'd missed bed check by five minutes, and the whole bunch of us got fined.

"Some rough guys there, but you know, you could learn a lot from some of those old players. . . . Gino Marchetti revolutionized defensive-end play. Most of them were bull rushers in those days, but Gino was a grabber and thrower, a guy with moves who'd blow by the tackle so fast sometimes that he'd never touch him. There were guys who'd play against Gino and say, 'Joyce is much tougher. Look, my uniform isn't even dirty.' But Gino got a lot of quarterbacks and running backs dirty."[8]

Tough as they were, the '54 campaign was no more rewarding for the Colts than the year before. In the opener against the Rams, Shula learned on the very first play what it felt like to be publicly razzed by Ewbank. The Rams tried an old trick—the hideout play, which was soon to be banned. They huddled with 10 men while an 11th, receiver Skeets Quinlan, seemed to be jogging off the field. But he dallied and, at the snap, took off down the sideline. Ewbank, seeing Quinlan going and Van Brocklin loading up to throw to him, yelled to Shula, who was slow to see the fake-out. Quinlan caught the pass and ran 80 yards for a touchdown. Four decades later, Shula was still livid. "Damn right I remember it," he said. "I remember thinking, 'Where the hell is the Dutchman throwing the ball?'" But he believed it wasn't Quinlan who beat him. "It was Bobby Boyd who caught that pass. The track guy they used to bring in as third wideout. Not Quinlan." No matter that official league stats disagree, or that Boyd had four catches that day, the longest for 45 yards. Shula would never budge on what his memory told him. And neither would Ewbank let him off the hook for getting suckered, which built static between them.

Shula was always publicly kind to Ewbank; in his memoir, he wrote that Weeb was "a very meticulous person who put in a great deal of time in planning and actually was the coach that the Colts needed at the time."[9] Not that it seemed so clear at the time. They won the rematch with the Rams, 22–21, but finished 3–9 again. Shula turned in another fine year, intercepting five passes. But the confusion of trying to play the Paul Brown short-pass attack was a disaster, the team coming in last in offense.

Around the game, the sense was that the Colts were a dangerous-but-erratic, semi-psychotic bunch. Shula was leavening as a player of importance, never to make the Pro Bowl but gaining a reputation among hard-core fans as a hard hitter smart enough to be an adjunct coach, a lowercase analog of Tom Landry's role with the Giants in the defensive backfield. Shula was actually one up on Landry; as Zimmerman wrote in hindsight, Shula was "the only defensive halfback (they didn't call them cornerbacks then) in the league to call defensive signals." John Steadman, who began covering the Colts in 1952 and then witnessed every pro game in Baltimore until his death in 2001, moonlighted as the Colts' publicist for much of the '50s. He recalled Shula as "one of the finest tacklers in the game. If you wanted to run a clinic on how to tackle, you'd get Don Shula."[10] Donovan had his own coda. Shula, he said, "would throw an elbow into a receiver's eye as soon as look at him."[11]

In '55, when Shula was re-signed, with another $500 raise, the Colts had the first and third picks in the first round and drafted Oregon's All-American quarterback, George Shaw, and Wisconsin's Heisman Trophy winner, fullback Alan Ameche, the latter dubbed "The Horse." He would gallop for a league-high 961 yards and nine touchdowns, and make first-team All-Pro for the first of four straight seasons. The

Colts won their first three games, but Shaw never got the hang of the T formation in the pros. And Shula, who had five early interceptions, went down for the season on November 20 after breaking his iron jaw against the Rams. The Colts finished 5–6–1, improvement enough to be considered progress and for Shula to become quite comfortable within the gallery of talented goofballs on the team. Tales would be told at future banquets about how Shula, Taseff, and Pellington, on the street after a sudsy dinner in Green Bay, saw a taxi, its motor running, but no driver. Freezing in the cold, they decided to hijack the cab, Pellington putting on the driver's cap he found on the front seat. Shula's winking skew of the theft was that "we really didn't steal it. We just borrowed it," but he added, "In the early years, there wasn't anything we *didn't do*."[12] Soon, Shula, Donovan and Pellington rented a townhouse in the Campus Hill section; when Pellington honed his wrestling holds on the other two, it left expensive furniture in pieces all over the living room.

Even during those "Animal House" escapades, he was still *Shula*, the autocrat, the almost-priest, the blue-nosed scold with a semblance of propriety between shots of gin. Donovan told of a postgame party at San Francisco's St. Francis Hotel where Shula, who was nicknamed "Shoes" by the team for the alliteration and the spiffy spit shine on his loafers, came bounding in with a woman he had picked up and was "strutting around the room" with her. Then the woman lit up a cigar, causing Shula, a believer that women had clear, submissive roles—and that a man with a fiancée could step out on her if he chose—blew his top. As Donovan recalled, "Jesus, he kicked her right in the ass and threw her out of the hotel. I thought he was going to kill her."[13]

Watching him in those years in Baltimore was enough to convince Fatso that Shula would make a great general. If so, it was more like Patton than Eisenhower—sharp and mindful of rules, but not overly concerned if he bent them. And he wasn't the only young man on the rise with that MO. During the '53 season, a Brooklyn-born sharpie who had talked himself into coaching the cadets at Fort Belvoir, Virginia, did some scouting work for Ewbank and began to hang around the team, bragging on himself as a pigskin seer. That guy was Al Davis.

Shula immediately distrusted Davis, whose loyalties could shift on a dime, but he wasn't the only one Shula had his misgivings about. He never quite melded with Carroll Rosenbloom. "C.R.," as he was called, had the cauliflower ears and nose of a boxer and the daring of a riverboat gambler. When his father died, he took over the old man's clothing business in Baltimore and sold it to invest in more profitable businesses. After buying the Colts, he put together local TV and radio deals that would be the model for league-wide advances in coverage and sat on the owners' committee that made the rules. His teams never had a money-losing season, and, feeding on power, he was tight with Joe Kennedy, father of the senator who would soon become president. Yet he could be vindictive, and years later, a fellow owner described him as "an odd person," another as "one complex individual. Very smart, very tough, often very nasty. He always gave you the impression that, if you crossed him, he was capable of slitting your throat, then donating your blood to the Red Cross blood drive."[14]

Yet most of his players loved him. Many of them were set up in off-season jobs in his or friends' companies, and he kicked in bonuses for big plays; after the '54 season, he gave each player $500. He would also be instrumental in getting the league to accept a players' union. Indeed, parlaying his closeness with Commissioner Bell, C.R. moved up rapidly within the league power structure, even as he waded into deeper waters—an apt metaphor, as it would turn out—by falling in with gamblers.[15] Shula, who generally clashed with men who had over-sized egos—witness Paul Brown—at best tolerated Rosenbloom, and certainly didn't fawn over him, something C.R. craved. The owner, for his part, liked Shula's fearless instincts and leadership, but, like Brown, found him abrasive, distant, too calculating for his station. Mutual respect was about the best they could muster, for better or worse.

Adapting to the TV age, uniforms were becoming sleeker and players encouraged to look less like genital-scratching gorillas, so that they, too, could be seen in cigarette and shaving cream commercials. In '55, the leatherhead era gave way to the era of most players wearing fiberglass and plastic helmets. That year, Paul Brown hired the Riddell company to develop padded headgear specifically for the Browns, including one or two metal bars protecting players' faces. Within months, every team wore the masks, though a handful of rebels like Bobby Layne refused. Not that a helmet, with or without a mask, could keep a guy from getting his face smashed. In one Colts game, George Shaw's ankles were held by Ed Sprinkle while another guy caved in Shaw's mouth with his elbow, knocking out all of his teeth and leaving him bloodied. Shula, who gave as good as he got, was covering Tom Fears in a 1956 game when Fears barked at him, "Shoes, goddammit, keep your mitts off me!" The next time down, Donovan recalled, Fears "coldcocked" him "with an elbow that turned his lights out. Smashed [Shula's] jaw."[16]

That night in Campus Hill, Shula asked his roommates to cook him up something soft to eat, like eggs. But, said Donovan, "the choosy prick didn't like the way we cooked them. So Pellington said, 'Screw you, cook your own eggs,' and threw the whole plate at him. So much for being a nice guy."

However, owners needed to protect their investments, and Bert Bell moderated his appetite for savagery, handing down new regulations against such transgressions as fighting, punching, kicking, and gouging. Not that these rules were strictly enforced. Carl Taseff, in fact, nearly bled to death after John Henry Johnson broke his nose so badly, he began to hemorrhage. And the helmets themselves could be useful weapons—Don Joyce, after being kneed in the groin, ripped off his helmet and crashed it into his opponent's, cracking it open like one of Shula's eggs. This was still the essential nature of the game, and few shied away from it; even quarterbacks, the matinee idols like Graham and Van Brocklin, fearlessly ran with the ball, none of them sliding on their knees to avoid taking a hit. As middle linebackers became the stars of the defense, one could hear the soothing voice of Walter Cronkite narrate a classic CBS documentary about the Giants' star middle linebacker called *The Violent World of Sam Huff*.

Back there in the secondary, Shula—"a wild man," as Donovan affectionately defined him—played every down like a caged animal, wearing his scars like war ribbons. He played hurt throughout the 1956 season with a badly sprained ankle that necessitated injections of pain-killers before games. But he was breaking down. Again, the parallel with Landry is striking; the latter was also nearing the end of one foot-ball career and the start of another. Made the Giants' defensive player/coach in '54, he'd retired after the '55 season, at the age of just 31, to become the team's defensive coordinator. He and his offensive counter-part, Vince Lombardi, were regarded as the Giants' real coaches when they won the title that year. Still, Shula hung in there with the Colts, who were on the cusp of a breakthrough.

With rookie halfback Lenny Moore's speed and Ameche's bull-like rushes and pulverizing blocking, the Colts now had arguably the best backfield in the NFL. But, viewed through the looking glass of history, '56 was notable for another find—*the* find, and one that came in through the back door. Before the season, the bowlegged, buzz-cut Johnny Unitas was working as a pile driver in Pittsburgh. A throwaway ninth-round pick of the Steelers out of Louisville the prior year, he was cut in training camp by Buddy Parker. However, here again, Ewbank heard that Paul Brown was about to offer Unitas a tryout and signed him first. Ewbank noticed a quirk in Unitas's throwing motion: on his follow-through, his arm came so far down that it turned over, "like a pitcher throwing a screwball."[17] That quirk seemed to guide the ball on a pre-cise journey. At first, Unitas sat behind Shaw, but in the fourth game of the season, against the Bears, Shaw tore a ligament in his knee and the Unitas era began—unsteadily, his first pass picked off and run back for a touchdown. The Colts lost four of their last six to finish another disappointing season at 5–7. Yet Ewbank knew what he had in Unitas, which was no less than the catalyst of pro football's growth spurt.

Shula would see what Unitas could do when his tight spirals whizzed past his head in Colts practices and landed softly in Ray Berry's pre-hensile hands. To give Unitas as many weapons as possible, Ewbank junked the T formation's normal three-man backfield, taking one out for an extra receiver, and continued to broaden the role of the tight end as a pass catcher, using ex–Notre Dame star Jim Mutscheller to great advantage. Shula could see these revisions becoming football law. His only recourse as his skills diminished was to open his mouth, trying to unnerve receivers in practice. Nor did he spare the new QB, who took a fast disliking to the mouthy, fist-faced cornerback.

Shula and Unitas had similar backgrounds, the latter's surname also modified, from the Lithuanian Joanaitis when he was a child in Pittsburgh steel country. Like Shula, he had to constantly prove himself; rejected by Notre Dame coach Frank Leahy for being too skinny, he played at Louisville, though he was often injured. A good many coaches and scouts thought Unitas was too soft, and prissy. A highly insular man, he had no affection for the coterie of Colt carousers, rarely joining in their night crawling. He kept a distance from Shula, whose brashness he found irritating, to work for hours almost exclusively with the receivers on patterns, to the point where they read each other's minds. Ewbank gave him the slack to go his own way. The irony was that "Johnny U" had so little self-awareness that he couldn't see how irritating *he* was. And how little it took for him to get all over players who messed up, while never taking any blame.

Like all the Colts, Shula lauded Unitas to the sportswriters, and in later years delighted in recalling how Unitas would carve him up in practice. "John was just starting to time up with those [receivers], and I wasn't good enough when Unitas had the ball," he said. George Shaw, he noted, "was just a good athlete trying to play quarterback. John *was* a quarterback." Shula could play that public game. Unitas, by contrast, had almost nothing to say about Shula. They rarely spoke. Unitas, who seemed to resent even having a backup, no doubt disliked Shula even more when Ewbank, seeing how Unitas responded when he thought he had competition, dropped hints that he might even try Shula, who was listed as the third QB on the depth chart, at the position. It never happened, though it could have stuck in Unitas's craw that Shula might be after his job. Shula wanted to have a chummy relationship with Unitas, but wouldn't beg for it. And that rule held when history would unite them, with Shula the boss, at the highest level.

Shula's ego didn't get in the way of reality. Never did he think of himself as more than an "average player," as he put it later, and that was perhaps too kind in '56, when he intercepted a single pass and the Colts' defense sank to 11th in the 12-team league. His leverage sank, too, just as the league was coalescing. The Colts had a growing fan base, attendance at Memorial Stadium swelling at times to over 50,000. Shula would have liked a place amid this mounting swell. In mid-July 1957, the papers reported that he had signed a Colts contract for the upcoming season. But then, in an August exhibition game, he broke two ribs. On September 24, days before the season opened, he was given his release by Ewbank. This, he said, came as "a tremendous disappointment . . . I had contributed quite a bit to them."[18] His release, reported one story, "came as something of a surprise and disappointment to the Colts." His boy Taseff remained a Colt, something of a Ewbank pet, until 1961.

Not immediately picked up by another team, on opening day Shula sat forlorn in the stands in Memorial Stadium, watching the Colts beat the Lions. He took some comfort in the fact that, as he recalled, "The guy who replaced me—Henry Moore, I think—got beat for a touchdown." When he walked into the home locker room after the game, he was stunned when his old teammates presented him with the game ball. That, he said, "meant a great deal to me."[19] Then, four days later, he was signed by the Redskins, who anted up the highest salary of his playing career, $9,750—about the best he could do in a sport where even Otto Graham never made more than 30 grand. He had at least a little more time to stick his nose into tackles, but reality now meant he needed to start gearing himself up for what many thought was his real calling.

6

COACH SHULA

The third team on Shula's budding journey had begun in 1932 as the Boston Braves, then the Redskins, before owner George Preston Marshall moved them to D.C. in '37. They won two NFL championships, in '37 and '42, and played in six title games by '45, but had ebbed since the end of the war, though they usually contended under coach Joe Kuharich, who had played for Elmer Layden at Notre Dame and would later coach there. His team had several Pro Bowlers and a top quarterback in the sawed-off Eddie LeBaron, and Kuharich liked Shula's smart, scrappy style. Shula arrived for the second game, a 37–14 laugher in which Kuharich brought him off the bench. However, he went through an emotional three-week stretch in November when the team played the Browns twice, sandwiched around a game with the Colts.

The first was in his old digs, Municipal Stadium. Paul Brown had Jim Brown now, but the 'Skins led 10–7 at the half and hung in, though they lost 21–17. The Colts then came into the Erector set–like Griffith Stadium, and if Shula thought he'd be less vulnerable to Unitas and Berry than he had been in those practices, he learned otherwise. The first scores of the game were identical—Unitas to Berry, twice, the first for 67 yards, both times in Shula's area. In the Colts' 21–17 win, Berry set a team record with 13 receptions, and

Shula guessed years later that "nine or ten" were against him. Afterward, Unitas may have been tweaking him when he said, "It was asking too much for their wingbacks [cornerbacks] to cover deep passes and also come up to stop the running plays." In the rematch with the Browns, the 'Skins had a 10-point lead entering the last quarter, then had to salvage a 30–30 tie. It was satisfying, but at 2–5–1, they were out of contention. They would finish strong, winning three of the last four, and in the loss to the Eagles, Shula picked off Sonny Jurgensen and rambled for a 30-yard return. In the end, their 5–6–1 season was another waste for Shula, who had three picks but was also picked on. When Kuharich filled out his depth chart after the new year, he listed a rookie as the starter at right cornerback and ranked Shula third.

Shula saw that and knew the score. He received no offer from the 'Skins for 1958. He could have tried to sign on with another team, but he was 27 now—an old 27. And if he didn't want to lose Dorothy, it was time to shift his focus to more permanent pursuits. Apparently tired of waiting for him to finally propose, she applied for and was offered a teaching job in Hawaii. Recalled Shula: "She informed me of that, and I said, 'What?!' "[1] He tried to convince her she was making a mistake, but she was as stubborn as he and split. Knowing his halting career wasn't going to win her over, he began thinking of coaching, a more long-term plan for the future, and resolved to pop the question if she'd come back home. He explained all this in a flurry of love letters to her. And she began to weaken. She was able to get a job back home, and so she returned in the middle of the bitter-cold Painesville winter, expecting a ring to be put on her finger. He had one for her, and the pair agreed on a date after the next football season, provided he landed a job as a coach.

"You can't get along in my profession unless you have somebody at home," he wrote in his memoirs. Toward that end, he had been calling around, seeing who needed assistants. When he went to a coaches' convention in Philadelphia, he ran into Frank Lauterbur, an assistant coach at Army. The Cadets' defensive-line coach, Dick Voris, had just taken the head coaching job at Virginia, which had a rich history but whose football program was hurting. Voris, he said, was looking for assistants, but could not convince the better ones to come. Lauterbur told Shula he'd put in a good word for him, and when a job offer for $6,500 was proffered in mid-February, Shula accepted without even speaking with Voris first. On February 18, Voris announced his new assistant, who would "specialize in defensive play."

To be sure, it was a culture clash: the son of Hungarian immigrants in the land of the old Confederacy, making his coaching bones at the Charlottesville school founded in 1819 by Thomas Jefferson, awash in the antebellum aristocratic heritage. At the time, only a handful of black undergraduates had been admitted, none to be allowed on the football squad until 1970. Even a half century beyond that, Charlottesville was infamously chosen as a rally site for white supremacists. Football had its own heritage in the South within the folds of racist exclusion, dating back at the school to 1888 and the South's oldest rivalry, Virginia versus North Carolina. Through the years, the Cavaliers regularly ranked in the top 20. However, when Shula got there, school president Colgate Darden had all but gutted the program, blasting the influence of "big-time football" on academics, even refusing a Cotton Bowl bid. Playing in the Atlantic Coast Conference since '53, its teams had given almost no scholarships since then.

Still, it was a job. And even with the pay cut he took, Shula was now able to marry Dorothy, who always melted when he put aside his macho preening and spoke of things like love, family, and God. They wed at St. Mary's on July 19, 1958, leaving just enough time before training camp for a honeymoon at the New Jersey shore and for her to move into his cramped, off-campus apartment, the beginning of a life she would live in constant flux until they could become settled, and with a husband totally immersed in the minutiae of football.

Shula helped Voris erect a defense based on the Paul Brown model, putting the players through its highly repetitive paces. The Cavaliers had a quality running back, Sonny Randle, but little else. They finished 1–9, with an offense, ranked 102nd among 112 college teams, that scored just five touchdowns, all on passes to Randle—who praised Shula for taking time off from the defense to give him a few tips on running strategy. "Coach Shula," he said, "has really helped me on my movements this year. It takes a lot of extra work. You have different situations as the game progresses."[2] Shula's defense, meanwhile, came in 111th. Worse, the games were surrounded by none of the pomp and wild fan support that flavored Saturday afternoon football in the rest of the South. At Virginia's home grounds, Scott Stadium, there were more mosquitoes than fans. As Shula glumly remembered, "The college spirit wasn't anything like I thought it would be."[3] Seeing no reason for hope—wisely so, as Virginia was in the midst of losing 28 straight, the second-longest losing streak in NCAA history—he talked it over with Dorothy and submitted his resignation, then went about searching for a job not on the *Hindenburg*. Indeed, Dorothy was all for it. Sharing his ambition, she had gotten in Voris's face, arguing that her new hubby would never get to be a head coach if Voris kept sending him on the road to scout players. "I surprised myself," she once said of that incursion. "Don, of course, was mortified."[4] Still, having her so fiercely behind him would always steel his spine.

Not incidentally, his old team was lifting the pro game to a level not far below the colleges in terms of public attention. In '58, the Colts went 9–3, winning the NFL championship against the Giants in Yankee Stadium, a game forever to be known, fancifully, as the greatest ever played. In the first-ever sudden-death overtime, when Unitas led a long drive and Ameche ran through a gaping hole for the game-winning touchdown, the drama of continuously shifting tides kept building with each play, as did a national audience, establishing pro football as a sport for the TV age. Shula, watching at home in Painesville in his old apartment, where he and his new wife spent the off-season, figured he belonged in the coaching arc of the pro league, but he needed more on his coaching résumé to get there. He was prepared to pay some dues at the college level, where he seemed to be able find a job quickly.

He made a repeat trip to the Philadelphia coaching convention and came upon Blanton Collier, his old backfield coach with the Browns. At 53, Collier had been the head coach at Kentucky since he replaced Bear Bryant in 1954. Surprised to see Shula looking for a job, he gave him one, as the Wildcats' defensive backs coach. Offered $7,500 and a rent-free house on the campus for him and the now-pregnant Dorothy, Shula left the convention employed.

A couple months after the Shulas moved in, Dorothy gave birth to a son, David, in a Lexington hospital. As would become a fixed habit, Shula had scant time to be a dad before turning his attention to the job. The university, founded in 1865 just as the Confederacy expired, remained soldered to Jim Crow, going 84 years before admitting a black student in 1949, though none would be on the school's sports teams until the late '60s. Not that this was much of a concern to Shula, or to great numbers of white Americans conditioned to accept inbred racism. A coach, not a crusader, he entered a daily grind of skull sessions, again teaching the Paul Brown method. Collier's brain trust were all football academics; indeed, this may have been the greatest assemblage of coaches on one staff in football history, with Shula joining assistants John North, former Kentucky All-America tight end Howard Schnellenberger, Bill Arnsparger, Ermal Allen, and Bob Commings. The first three of those would become NFL head coaches, and Schnellenberger also a championship college coach; Allen would be an assistant coach for Tom Landry, Commings the head coach at Iowa. The Wildcats' backup quarterback, Leeman Bennett, would also become an NFL head coach, as did a later Collier assistant, Chuck Knox.

Schnellenberger, an engagingly windy man three years Shula's junior who would assist five Hall of Fame coaches before becoming a head coach himself, sized up Shula this way:

> I liked him and he liked me. But he was a pain in the ass. We used to play tennis after practice. We'd fight over each point, because he cheated. He would always yell, "It's in!" on every ball that hit near the line. It could be ten feet away. We'd fight the whole time.

I could do that when I was on his level. Later, when I was his assistant, we still played. But when he'd say, "It's in," all I could do was say, "Yeah, it was." That's what he did as a coach. He didn't cheat, but he fought over every point.[5]

The problem for Collier, an avuncular fellow with thick glasses, wasn't his coaches, but his players—or, rather, lack thereof. He was unable to recruit quality players to a school a cut below Southeastern Conference giants like Alabama, Georgia, LSU, Ole Miss, and Auburn. The football team was also a sideshow next to Adolph Rupp's glorified roundball team coming off its fourth national title in '58. As in Charlottesville, fan support for football in Lexington had waned. At historic Stoll Field—where the first college game in the South was played in 1880, and the first SEC game in 1933—attendance at some games didn't reach the 30,000 capacity. With thin talent—not a single Wildcat would make All-SEC that season—they lost five of their first six and were thrice shut out.

The defense was solid, the 24th best in the nation, giving up 10.7 points a game. But, as with Virginia, the offense scored exactly zero rushing touchdowns all season, and only five overall. They ended at 4-6, and Shula put the blame for the mediocre season on the state of Kentucky itself, something he never would have dared to do in Ohio. There were, he said, only around a hundred quality players in the entire state of Kentucky, leaving scraps after the big programs took the best. The upside for Shula and the other assistants was that their work was recognized around the football meridians.

There was also a bigger employment pool for incipient pro coaches in 1960, with the American Football League starting up. Al Davis, for one, took his first pro job in the AFL, on Sid Gillman's staff with the original Los Angeles Chargers. And Shula, having had two years to make his case to pro coaches like Gillman, reckoned that was enough to get out of the South. After the season, calls came from the Detroit Lions and Chicago Cardinals' coaches, George Wilson and Pop Ivy. It was clear to the Wildcat staff that he already had a foot out the door. Said Schnellenberger, "Blanton wanted Don to stay. But you can't stand in the way of a guy getting a better job." A laugh. "Shit, we all wanted out. There was nothing to do in Lexington. It was a graveyard."

Shula was interviewed by Wilson and Ivy on a single weekend in January, and he was offered the position of defensive backfield coach by both. The Lions intrigued him more. They had, of course, been an elite power in the '50s. Wilson, a Papa Bear Halas protégé, had been on their staff since '49, becoming head coach in '57, when they routed the Browns in the title game. They had tanked since, though, perhaps hastened by Wilson trading Bobby Layne to the Steelers in exchange for another quarterback, Earl Morrall, a lumbering but talented former standout at Michigan.

Wilson, a respected coach, was relatively easy on his players. With top veteran talent, he glided along, letting his assistants do the grunt work. He already had a defensive-backs coach, Bob Nussbaumer, and wanted Shula to be more of a coordinator. Signed by general manager Edwin Anderson, his salary was $11,000 a year for two years—a pretty penny then, especially for a new father who had another child on the way; his daughter Donna was born on April 28, 1961. The Lions' owner, automobile heir William Clay Ford, personally welcomed him aboard, and Shula made tracks out of the graveyard. "All he said to us," said Schnellenberger, "was 'adios.'"[6]

For Collier, it was just the beginning of the exodus of his staff. Within a year, Schnellenberger, too, would be gone, hired as his old coach Bear Bryant's offensive coordinator at Alabama, where he recruited the teenage Joe Namath. Collier himself would fail upward; fired after that '62 season, he leaped to the NFL—as the successor to Paul Brown, no less. In the small world of football coaching, Don Shula was already just a few degrees of separation from a good many coaches who would go on to mold the game.

Shula rented a house in suburban Allen Park for his growing family, though he spent most of his time in the Lions' training headquarters in Bloomfield Hills, surveying the talent he'd have. He could almost hear a faint bluesy trumpet in the movements of Dick "Night Train" Lane, a four-time Pro Bowler, who came in a trade with the St. Louis Cardinals that year. At 31, he still wore the name of the 1952 blues song well, retaining much of the speed, stealth, and catlike reflexes that had enabled him to set the interception record—as a rookie—with 14. He'd become available because of gambling losses, but Wilson took a gamble on him—and won.

Shula also had a great safety, Yale Lary, and a real buster at middle linebacker, Joe Schmidt, who Art Donovan once said "had a neck like a killer turtle and was about as subtle as a heart attack."[7] Schmidt would win 10 first-team All-Pro selections and later coach the team, but there were also future All-Pros in cornerback Dick LeBeau and linebackers Wayne Walker and Carl Brettschneider. The draft brought another star, massive defensive tackle Roger Brown, a future six-time All-Pro who solidified the latest incarnation of the Fearsome Foursome front line with Alex Karras, Bill Glass, and Darris McCord. On the sideline, the Lions' other assistant coaches included former Packer coach Scooter McLean, whose 1–9 record two years before got him fired and replaced in '59 by a guy named Lombardi. The defensive line coach, Les Bingaman, a former Lions All-Pro, had once been arrested for domestic abuse. He also owned a downtown bar. One night, after he served Bobby Layne seven scotches, the quarterback was arrested for drunk driving. He got off easy when Bingaman admitted that he saved money by putting only a small amount of booze in his bar's drinks.[8]

Spending the first half of games in the press box, getting a feel for the flow of things, Shula would then make changes at halftime and spend the second half on the sideline, barking out signals. His key was Schmidt, who got less publicity than Sam Huff or Bill George, the other elite middle linebackers, but was clearly better than either, and ranked ahead of Shula's old Colt teammate Bill Pellington. Schmidt was even more sneering and snarling, taunting opponents by calling them "honey" and blowing them kisses, which he could get away with because he almost always nailed the ball carrier. No defense was as scary as the Lions', but on the other side of the ball, it was a mess. During the 1960 season, the quarterback, Jim Ninowski, would throw two touchdowns and *18* interceptions. But Shula was helping to rig up suffocating zone defenses, and after the team stumbled early, losing the first three, the repeat champion Colts came into Briggs Stadium. As Ewbank feared, Shula knew them like the back of his hand and could decipher any shifting the Colt offense did to hide its tendencies. The score was 19-all in the fourth quarter, but the Lions kicked two field goals. Then Night Train Lane picked Unitas and ran 80 yards for the touchdown to ice the game. Six weeks later, they did it again, whipping the Colts in Baltimore, 20–15, intercepting Johnny U three times.

They also beat the Green Bay Packers in the annual "black and blue" Thanksgiving game, 23–10—the game entered team lore as the "Thanksgiving Day Massacre," in which the Fearsome Foursome swarmed Bart Starr like a pack of rottweilers, sacking him 10 times (sacks were charted, but were not yet an official league stat), once for a safety. The home crowd was so eager for more hits that they booed when the offense took the field. Still, there were not enough of these moments. The Lions wound up 7–5, behind the Packers, who went to the NFL championship game. There, Lombardi lost his only postseason game as a coach, to the Philadelphia Eagles. The Lions' consolation prize was to play in the inaugural Bert Bell Benefit Bowl, a really bad idea that would be dubbed by players and the press as the Runner-Up Bowl or Loser Bowl. Held a week before the annual Pro Bowl all-star contest, it pitted the divisions' second-place teams against each other, honoring Bell, who had died in 1959, and benefiting the players' pension fund. Both postseason games were more like expense-paid vacations. But *Sports Illustrated* has retrospectively called the Bell event "the worst kind of garbage time,"[9] staged in the Orange Bowl, under the hot Miami sun, with players preparing mainly by lying around and drinking margaritas. Though no records were recognized, and the games were classified as exhibitions, Shula could take some pride in winning the first one 17–16 over the Browns; moreover, the Lions would win the first three Bert Bell Bowls. Garbage time or not, it went on the résumé and earned the winners up to 600 bucks in mad money.

Don Shula had definitely solidified his job. The Lions' defense had forced and recovered 15 fumbles and, after giving up 275 points the year before, yielded only 212, third-best in the league. Night Train, freed by Shula to use his favorite weapon—grabbing opponents' face masks, twisting their heads like a bottle cap—was so terrifying that the league thereafter banned the move. In the '61 season, the Lions ticked up a notch, but again finished behind the Packers at 8–5–1, sending them back to the Loser Bowl, to beat the Eagles.

More and more, little by little, Shula was making gains and being noticed for his work. Back in Cleveland, the *Plain Dealer* seemed eager to pimp him. One puff piece by Gordon Cobbledick read: "Much of the credit for the uniformly fine performance of the [Lion] defense is given by the Detroit staff to Don Shula. . . . 'Definitely head coaching material,' is the way admiring Detroiters now describe the ex-Blue Streak."[10] To be certain, Shula was not content to remain a highly respected adjutant. As it was, Wilson trusted his judgment enough to send him on spring scouting missions, watching college scrimmages prior to the '62 draft. On his recommendation, the Lions' first pick was Kansas quarterback John Hadl. But Hadl was kept away from the team by Sid Gillman's top lieutenant with the relocated San Diego Chargers, Al Davis, who in the parlance of the day "babysat" Hadl, keeping him under his watch until he eventually signed with the Chargers. Hadl would be a four-time AFL All-Star and then lead the unified NFL in passing yards and touchdowns in 1971, and failing to get him for the Lions left a burr under Shula's saddle. Shula and Davis were interlocked in history, and if Shula lacked Davis's boastful grandiosity, they both shared a desire for world domination. As yearlings, the two of them were already in a race upward, their ambitions burning so brightly that neither of them had to wait long before they could snipe at each other from the very top of the football sanctum.

7

FLY ME TO THE MOON

The '62 season began while a very nervous America tried to somehow carry on as the Cuban Missile Crisis intensified, raising the nightmare scenario of Russian nukes being launched 90 miles away from Florida. As schoolkids were taught how to duck and cover under their desks, that's what many NFL teams were doing that fall against the Lions. Shula's defensive backfield was stifling, second-best in the NFL, garnering 24 interceptions. The day President John F. Kennedy declared the crisis over, Sunday, October 28, the Lions choked the Bears 11–3. That sparked a seven-game winning streak, including a 26–14 win over the Packers (to whom they lost the first warlike meeting, 9–7) on Thanksgiving, and finished at 11–3.

The offense was smoothly led by quarterback Milt Plum, acquired from the Browns, with a strong running game and All-Pro receiver Gail Cogdill. But the win over Green Bay was Lombardi's only defeat that season. With playoff rounds still years away, the Pack's 13–1 record put them back in the title game, while the Lions went back to Miami to win their third straight Runner-Up Bowl, over the Steelers. For Wilson and Shula, this foxtrot had become too familiar. And, ominously, the defense was spent. While Night Train Lane made All-Pro again at 34, he was breaking down. He was also about to divorce his first wife and marry jazz singer Dinah Washington. Late in 1963, he would find her dead from a drug overdose in their home.

Shula could see diminishing returns. He admired Wilson, but could not see himself in that mold as a laissez-faire coach, though he said he took from Wilson the desire to be "a man-to-man type coach," able to relate to players on a human level. As he put it, "My own personality had to emerge." He always would borrow from Paul Brown's methods, but would be open to "sitting down and rationalizing, talking and joking a little."[1] Very little, to that point. As Howard Schnellenberger recalled, "You couldn't really joke around with him." Indeed, as the clock was running out in one of those Runner-Up Bowls, a Lion player, thinking of the bread, told a teammate, "It's a hundred bucks a minute." Overhearing that, Shula blinked hard and got in his face. "Cut that out!" he barked. "That's a heckuva thing to say."[2] Joe Schmidt said life with Shula was no day at the beach, but no one could claim he wasn't head coaching material.

Shula had begun to put feelers out before the end of the season, not bothered by the fact that no NFL head coach had ever been as young as he was at 33. He set his sights on his old team, the Colts, well aware that Weeb Ewbank's job was in trouble. Ewbank's lack of feeling for players he railed at did not wear well in defeat; the Colts were rumored to be in open revolt over him. Shula, not minding a bit that he was aiming a knife between Weeb's shoulder blades, made it his business to call up Carroll Rosenbloom in his hotel room when the Colts came to Detroit in late October and tell the man who had traded him he wanted to coach his old team. It was a hell of a ballsy request—one that, if it became public knowledge, could have gotten Rosenbloom in dutch for tampering. Shula didn't leave it there, either; he asked his old confreres Gino Marchetti and Bill Pellington to pimp him to C.R., coyly recalling in his memoirs that the owner "had a great deal of respect for their recommendations."[3] Especially that of Marchetti, to whom Rosenbloom had loaned a hundred grand years before so he could buy a chain of burger joints with Alan Ameche that now was earning $8 million a year. Shula would say years later, "Gino was the one who got me the job" by advising the owner, "There's only one guy [for the job]. Shula."

Ewbank, who was still youngish at 55, had two years left on his contract. If he was fired, he would have to be paid $60,000 for those remaining years. When the season ended, he said, "As far as I'm concerned, I'm all right."[4] But he wasn't. He had been embroiled in feuds with Rosenbloom and Johnny Unitas, who steamed when he constantly pricked him for deviating from the conservative game plan. When the battered Ameche quit in 1960 after just six seasons, the running game sputtered, leaving Unitas to have to pass more, amassing lots of yardage but also lots of interceptions. Although he made All-Pro by rote, in '62 he threw 23 touchdowns and 23 interceptions—a microcosm of the Colts' 7–7 season, which included a 53–0 shellacking by the Bears. Shula had experienced great schadenfreude by kicking the Colts' tails twice in '62, deepening Ewbank's slide.

Shula met with C.R. during the Runner-Up Bowl in Miami's Golden Strand Hotel. The owner asked him if he thought he was ready to be a head coach. Shula replied, with his usual smugness, that the only way to tell would be to hire him. On January 8, John Steadman reported that Shula was "far out front" as the choice. Only hours later, Rosenbloom fired Ewbank, saying it was "the most difficult task I've ever faced," and that he had signed Shula to a two-year deal, $15,000 a year. Ewbank was offered a paper job with the team, but refused, instead signing a three-year, $100,000 deal to coach the AFL's New York Titans. That team's new ownership, a syndicate headed by showbiz agent Sonny Werblin, had bailed the bankrupt team out of a million-dollar debt and in March 1963 changed their name to the Jets, a year ahead of their move to Shea Stadium, adjacent to LaGuardia Airport.

Weeb still had loyalists on the team; even Marchetti ventured that Ewbank got the gate because he was, in fact, "too nice"—far from a unanimous opinion. Ewbank, who would be paid by teams in both leagues for two years, was in an enviable position, and could be believed when he said coaching "is in my blood."[5] But so, too, was it in Shula's, and he and his old coach would have a future rendezvous with destiny.

Shula's task was not easy, but there were still nine players left from his Colts days, and they still had a quality roster. Defensive tackle Billy Ray Smith had been acquired in a trade to replace the retired Art Donovan. Also coming in a trade was a new target for Unitas: the small, light-footed Jimmy Orr, a onetime rookie of the year with Pittsburgh. Five Colts made All-Pro in '62, including left guard Jim Parker and center Dick Szymanski. Still, they needed a coach to make them whole again. Rosenbloom clearly had doubts that Shula would be that coach, but whatever Gino wanted, Gino got. George Wilson, meanwhile, could be big-hearted about Shula climbing higher, wishing him the best and taking pride in grooming him, but, like Ewbank, confrontation with Shula waited down the road.

Shula came back to his old team with a swagger, and with no intention of kissing C.R.'s posterior. He began with a modest declaration of optimism: "I'm real happy to have the opportunity and for the faith Baltimore is showing in me"—perhaps pointedly substituting the town for the owner.[6]

Across the football divide, meanwhile, Al Davis had demanded and bluffed his way into being hired by the AFL's Oakland Raiders as their coach and general manager, given three years at $20,000 per year and unlimited power over all on-field decisions, including recasting the team colors to the sinister-looking black and silver. Rosenbloom made no such offer to Shula. But Shula had his footing, rooted not in a league built on flash and dreams, but on history and economic stability. Still, in retrospect, 1963 was the nexus when he, Lombardi, Landry, and Davis were all in place—and Paul Brown was old news, fired by the Browns' owner, Art Modell, who had finally determined, "This is a game of emotions. I am convinced Paul Brown is incapable or unwilling to become emotional."[7] Once, that had seemed a plus. But football was proving that America was a different place, its still-youthful members of the Greatest Generation given the levers of power. The future was theirs.

Having lived like a gypsy for a decade, Shula resettled his family, hopefully for the long haul. Dorothy was pregnant again, and they found a large townhouse near where he had bunked with his old Colt comrades. The first thing he did was to hire assistants. He flirted with Blanton Collier before he took the coveted Browns job. But Shula needed look no farther than Ewbank's staff: defensive line coach John Sandusky, an old teammate on the Browns, and offensive coordinator Don McCafferty, who had played for Paul Brown at Ohio State. Only line coach Herman Ball was let go.

Shula's deference to veteran Colt players raised questions about his ability to pull rank. A UPI story, headed NEW COLTS' COACH MAY FACE FRICTION, asked, "How will these veterans accept taking orders from a former teammate, one who was cut in fact while many of them remained with the club?" That was when Shula realized there was a price for pushing out a championship coach with allies in the press. Writers referred to him, with condescension, as "youthful Don Shula," "a former student of Ewbank," and noted that three Colts were older than their coach. Marchetti defended Shula, saying, "No one will walk over him." And Rosenbloom defended his choice, saying, "If it were just a case moving up to second place, I would not have made the change," he said. "I think we will win the title; that is why I hired Shula."

Introduced to the press by Don Kellett, Shula entered in a spiffy dark suit, smiling, engaging in easy banter, leading one of the scribes to write, "I liked the way he answered questions. Not once did he say, 'I have to look at the movies before commenting on that.'"[8] Still, to some, he would need further introduction. The AP ran a photo identifying the new coach as "John Shula."

At early spring camp at McDaniel College in Westminster, he eyeballed the squad. The NFL, trying to get the jump on the AFL, had moved its draft up to early December, and Kellett chose wisely, taking in the first round the massive Ohio State offensive tackle Bob

Vogel; in the second, Syracuse tight end John Mackey; and in later rounds, defensive back Jerry Logan, linebacker Lee Roy Caffey, and receiver Willie Richardson. Among the holdovers were quality role players like the feathery Jimmy Orr, who was heir to the aging Berry. Shula asked Artie Donovan to come out of retirement, but Fatso was not about to start over with a coach he used to rag as a teammate and who would now want him to lose weight and subject him to sterner rules.

Of course, Shula had what no one else did: the owl-faced, bowlegged Unitas, whose immense stature matched his ego. He hadn't particularly liked or spoken much with Shula during their sole overlapping year with the Colts, but knew enough about him to recognize that the new boss was not a passing kind of coach but a pound-it-out type. Unitas had had enough tension with Ewbank, and Shula was hardly laid-back. Early on, Unitas reacted with impatience as Shula re-created Paul Brown's grueling classroom dissertations, calling on players for answers and growling at them when they didn't know the answers. Shula could only hope winning would be the salve that might melt things between them.

He barely took time off when Dorothy gave birth in June to their second daughter, Sharon. By then, he was in his regular routine, flitting from church to his office, implementing his "scientific approach," as the military newspaper *Stars and Stripes* called it. Shula was fortunate, as Ewbank had been, to have as his conduit to Unitas the likable McCafferty, an old softie the other players called "Easy Rider." He may have been the only coach Unitas had any use for. Perhaps as a slap at Shula, he once said of McCafferty, "He doesn't shout and scream. He's able to look at football objectively without getting carried away emotionally." Not that Shula cared, as long as Unitas followed orders. Like Ewbank, he would need to bend to Unitas's will, but never let him forget who the boss was.

Rosenbloom, meanwhile, had other matters to worry about. Over the summer of '63, Commissioner Pete Rozelle suspended two top-line NFL players, Paul Hornung and Alex Karras, for a year after it was revealed they had bet on NFL games, though not involving their own teams. The investigation turned up evidence that C.R. was an even worse gambler, even betting against his team at times, and that he had won $1 million when the Colts beat the five-point spread in the '58 title game—when the Colts spurned a sure field goal in OT for the six-point touchdown.[9] That day, Unitas jokingly said he bypassed the field goal because he'd "placed a bet," for which Bert Bell called and, as Unitas said, "I got my ass handed to me."[10] But Bell apparently did not do the same with his old college roommate, even after a gambler came out and said he had given the Colts $25,000 to split after that game.[11]

Rozelle, though, made Rosenbloom twist in the wind, finally clearing him when one of his accusers recanted, grandly claiming "the Irish Mafia"—meaning the Kennedy family—was after him. Although C.R. dodged a cannonball, he was required to admit he had bet "substantial sums on activities other than professional football," but had stopped. Though it could have been much worse, he felt humiliated, but at least he could get back to work with his new coach. Observing Shula's no-nonsense ways, he predicted, "He's going to do all right."[12]

Shula added some Landry-style movement on offense, sending players in motion and changing backfield alignments from play to play. He returned 30-year-old Lenny Moore, who had been used by Ewbank as a pass catcher, back to halfback. With the hole left by Ameche still unfilled, Shula mused about using rookie tight end John Mackey at fullback—he was not sold on him as a receiver, and nor was Unitas, who said Mackey's hands were stiff as "a toilet seat." But a quality blocker/receiver at tight end was now a must, and Shula left him alone. In camp, most of the Colts sucked up to Shula. Backup running back Alex Hawkins gushed, "Everybody likes Shula. This is the best training camp I've been to. . . . All the old animosity is gone." The flattery worked. By opening day, Shula was so impressed with Hawkins's breakneck play on special teams that he made him special teams captain; for years, the Colts would have the league's best special teams, and Hawkins enjoyed the role of being a captain, even if he was otherwise generally anonymous, giving himself the nickname "Captain Who."

Trying to get his new role of benevolent despot right, Shula picked spots to joke around and make small talk. He hoped that doing so would earn him the goodwill to get away with blaming players for mistakes and not overlooking even the slightest breach. He lowered the hammer for the first time when a low-level rookie fullback, Roy Walker, walked out of camp; when he crawled back, he found he had been cut, his locker already emptied. The fines began in camp, and continued whenever anyone was late for a meeting or missed a curfew, even by a minute. Once locked into a room, or so it seemed, they would be bombarded with game film.

Shula was merciless. He had even veteran players stand and dissect why they had misread a play. Unlike Ewbank's meetings, nobody dared catnap in the darkened film room, too great the fear of sending him into a sputtering rage. When the Colts streaked to a 26–0 halftime lead against the Eagles in the first preseason game, then hung on and won 28–21, Shula was livid. He then faced Collier in Cleveland, a match that drew 83,000 fans to Municipal Stadium, and, preseason or not, he wasn't relieved and sweat-free until he walked off and shook Collier's hand, a 21–7 winner. He won four out of five of those meaningless games, but Unitas came away from the last with a sore arm. Then, two days before the opener, Lenny Moore had an emergency appendectomy, putting him on the shelf for a month.

Shula had to go with a pair of kids in the backfield. One, the first-round pick in '61, Tom Matte, had played quarterback at Ohio State, but in Woody Hayes's prehistoric system he mostly blocked and ran, using his talent for scrounging yardage from nothing. The other, freckle-faced Jerry Hill, carried the ball once as a rookie the year before and had little speed, but he could smell out holes to run through. They were both Shula's kind of guys, overachievers with abundant smarts and toughness. Matte especially seemed to fit the coach's mold. He could get so wound up for games that he had already developed ulcers. Still, both were unproven, as was Shula when he made his official debut as a head coach at Memorial Stadium on September 15 in front of the first of three home crowds of over 60,000 that season. The opponent was the Giants, whose aging team made the Colts seem like *Romper Room*. That year would be the Giants' last among the elite, as Y. A. Tittle, who was 37 going on a hundred, threw a then-record 36 touchdown passes. Against Shula's tough but unsure defense, Tittle diddled for a while as Marchetti, whom Shula had made a player/ quasi-coach along with Pellington, returned a fumble for a touchdown. Meanwhile, Unitas threw TD passes to Orr and Mackey for a 21–10 lead. Then Tittle toyed with them, hitting on three scoring passes in the second quarter and running in another in the third for a 30–28 lead. It ended 37–28—a "terrific letdown," said Shula, who bemoaned "mental mistakes," though he did say he was "really proud of these guys."

To be sure, the game wasn't a total loss. The offense showed its stuff, and while a still-sore Johnny U—whose left index finger was dislocated in the game—was picked off twice, he could put up points in bunches. The next week, in San Francisco, the Colts came from behind in the last quarter on a Unitas pass to Orr, beating the 49ers 20–14 for Shula's first win as a head coach. But here the schedule slapped him down. The Colts had three straight road games—the next of them in Green Bay, where Lombardi's Packers trampled them 31–20. Then he had to go to Chicago and suck up a 10–3 loss to the Bears, grimacing as Unitas was picked off twice and Moore was lost with an injury. However, Shula's work ethic had convinced the team he had the right answers. In Moore's absence, Matte teamed with Hill to keep the ground game alive, aiding Unitas, who began to lean on the amazing Mackey, a rolling cannonball on mid-depth pass routes, splitting zone defenses to reel in perfect passes. He would catch a modest 35 balls that year, but average over 20 yards a catch, unheard of for a tight end in those days, with a team-high seven touchdowns. With defenses needing to cover Mackey, six other Colts caught at least 20 passes and had at least one touchdown. And being freed to throw more, Unitas was, if not happy, at least not brooding.

Shula won two in a row for the first time in October. With Moore back, he won two more in November, putting him at 5–5. Then, late in the morning of Friday, November 22, the team was midway through its charter flight to LA to play the Rams. Some players were asleep. Marchetti and Unitas were playing poker in the back of the plane. Shula, who had recorded his weekly radio show in the morning, was up front with the coaches, going over scouting reports. It seemed routine when the pilot began to make an announcement, but this was no weather or turbulence update. He said that President Kennedy had been shot in Dallas. As guard Dan Sullivan recalled, "I wondered, is this an isolated incident or an attack on the U.S. We didn't know what kind of a world we were coming back to, until we landed."[13]

Marchetti, who had campaigned for Kennedy, felt the wind go out of him. "I'd just won a big pot and was bragging about it when the announcement came on," he said. "I was really shaken." Shula, a Catholic and the son of a blue-collar union man, admired Kennedy and led the team in prayer. When they got off the plane, they scrambled to get in front of TV sets in the airport lounge, where they learned that the president had died. A distraught Rosenbloom, a Kennedy family intimate, asked the league office to cancel Sunday's games. The AFL did so immediately, as did the National Basketball Association. The NCAA called off its Saturday football and basketball games. Players across the NFL said they had no desire to play, but what mattered to most owners were gate and TV/radio revenues. When Rozelle buckled to them, it only worsened his rift with Rosenbloom. The compromise was that there would be no TV coverage during the funeral and burial in D.C., and there would be no bands and no player introductions. Years later, Rozelle called it the worst decision he ever made.

The Colts would awake that Sunday to more shock and bloodshed. Said Sullivan, "I was in my hotel room watching TV when I saw Ruby shoot Oswald. I just about fell off of the bed. You tried to get the thoughts of all that had transpired out of your mind by game time, but it was difficult to do that." Like zombies, they were bused to the LA

Memorial Coliseum and they were silent as they changed into their uniforms. Shula, still in a daze, gave no pep talk before sending them out. To the surprise of many around the league, crowds showed up in large numbers, and after a two-minute standing silence and the playing of taps by a single trumpeter, the crowd of around 49,000 watched in near silence. The game proceeded in an atmosphere that was called "surreal," but once the players warmed to the contest, it actually turned into the most exciting of the season, a seesaw affair won by the Rams, 17–16, clinched only when the Colts' kicker missed a desperate 62-yard field goal attempt at the gun.

With the Bears losing only one game that year, the Colts were already out of the money—as were the Packers, who only lost two— but Shula had salvaged the season. Despite the loss of the hard-luck Moore again—with a head injury—and Orr being hobbled by knee trouble, the Colts routed the Redskins and Minnesota Vikings, and got even with the Rams, nipping them 19–16 in the finale. That let Shula go out at 8–6, just one win better than Ewbank the year before, but with the team on the rise. Unitas had 237 completions, then a league record, amassing 3,481 yards with just 12 picks. For Shula, who often gave in to Unitas's passing rather than fighting it, the late surge corrected an early flaw—the inability to cash in within the opponents' 20, which caused an anomaly in the stats: though the Colts had the most air yardage, they only rang up 20 passing touchdowns, eighth-best in the league.

Shula never did become more than a martinet to many of the Colts, but Dorothy Shula did her best to change that. Hearing him sound stiff and distant on the half-hour radio show he was given on WMAR on Friday nights, she worked to humanize him. Interviewed by the *Sun*, she said her husband "has a wonderful outlook on life and a good sense of humor . . . he'll come home and tell me something wild with a completely straight face. And I won't know whether to believe him or not." She spoke of relaxing afternoons at Art Donovan's home and around his pool.[14] And in time, when he also began hosting a pregame TV show in 1966, which moved to Saturday afternoons in 1967, he did become looser, and more of a players' coach—albeit not enough to suit Unitas and others, whose ears hurt from his wallpaper-peeling harangues.

The press soon began to junk the trope of the young coach and carve an image of the "square-jawed" Shula as a man of iron will, but also a mensch. "I don't like to lose," he said in one story, "but I don't go out and commit suicide when I do. Instead, I try to diagnose why we were beaten to be sure it doesn't happen the same way again."[15] Unspoken was: it had better not happen the same way again.

As many of the Colts of the 1950s neared their last hurrah, the '60s Colts were forming their own identity under Shula—not as rollicking ballbusters but smart, clawing overachievers. Outside of Unitas, Berry, Moore, and Mackey, no skill-position player seemed destined for stardom. Shula, despite his own growing status, wore the hunted look of a man with something to prove—as did Tom Landry in Dallas, who had to deal with coaching in an unapologetically segregated city. Shula had it easier on that count, but only by degree. Baltimore was technically a Southern city, and racial tensions quietly simmered, stirred by a white working class that stewed about black workers taking their factory jobs. Suburban flight was already underway in the city, where the population would decline by 200,000 between 1960 and 1990.

Shula could recognize this trend all through the industrial belt, and could look for confirmation to Painesville, where Dan Shula and his other sons were working harder but earning less than they had been. Working his way up the coaching ladder, and thinking of how much he could keep of his income, the romance of labor unions had given way in Shula's view to more narrow interests as his affluence grew along with his family—with Dorothy giving birth to yet another daughter, Anne, on May 7, 1964, and another son, Mike, on June 3, 1965. But Shula was a good Christian, a good son, one who was still sending money back to his parents, and he could not possibly pander to racial resentments that arose when blue-collar white men lost jobs to black men. He was colorblind about his team, with no hedging about drafting two African

Americans with his first picks in '64: defensive back Marv Woodson and running back Tony Lorick (though Woodson would quickly be traded to the Steelers).

Beyond race, Shula could also see inklings that in 1964, with the Beatles' invasion and rumblings about the war in the Vietnamese jungles being escalated, society and culture were turning a new page, the nation less innocent and predictable after the murder of a president. Given his own, now-fading antiheroic youth, he could sense the angst in younger players, who were mostly less willing to believe what they were told—even by their coaches. And he was young enough to stitch himself into both his own and the younger generation, as the face of a blue-collar team framed by Baltimore's row houses and smoke-belching factories.[16]

To those who went back with Shula, it was as if he could see himself in the good, but problematic, foot soldiers on the team, but he also saw himself in the mulish Unitas, whose respect he craved. Johnny U was making almost as much as Shula, and he retained the authority to call the plays, but not to ignore Shula's when he sent one in. Still, more than a few times, he went as far as to reject a Shula call, announcing in the huddle, "We're not running that play," then imperiously brushing off the coach when he came to the sideline. Unitas seemed to revel in those moments, and Shula wouldn't begrudge him; Unitas, like all great quarterbacks, could see the game two, even three plays ahead. Fortunate to have such a leader, Shula tolerated a lot of intransigence from him, snapping only when Unitas waved the field goal team off the field in a 1964 game, an act of defiance in plain view of the whole stadium. Shula waited until after the game, then summoned Unitas to his office and laid down the law, as calmly as he could.

"Look, John," he said, "if you're going to show me up like that, I can't be the coach of this team."

Marchetti, who was in the coach's office at the time, punctuated the directive: "He's right, John."

Unitas went into his petulant shtick. "If that's what you want," he said with a condescending shrug, "that's what you'll get."

He kept his word, but with a snide comment for Shula whenever he could get one in. When questioned about a specific failed play, he would tell reporters, "Don't ask me. Ask Shula. It's his team." Never would he admit what Otto Graham, now coaching at the Coast Guard Academy, ventured after watching the Colts during the '64 season, that Unitas "seems to be calling a better game under the direction of Shula."[17]

That 1964 season was almost too easy for Shula, even though the opener made Colts fans nervous. On the road, they lost 34–24 to the Vikings, but any worries evaporated the next week, when they went to Lambeau Field and ravaged Bart Starr, intercepting him three times to win 21–20, the winning score a 40-yard Unitas-to-Mackey pass. The next week, in the home opener, the champion Bears strutted in—and limped out, losing 52–0, Papa Bear's worst defeat ever. Shula was feeling so invincible that day that he sat Unitas in the fourth quarter, seemingly so as not to run up the score—but backup Gary Cuozzo then threw a touchdown, which might have been intentional and not beyond Shula's selective notions of sportsmanship, and which no doubt prickled Halas.

It would be December 6 before the Colts lost again, breaking an 11-game winning streak, two shy of Halas's single-season record, during which they swept the Pack. All season, opposing players and coaches vouched for the Shula effect on the team, which he defined after one typical rout when he giddily told the press, "Did you notice how the gang was hitting out there?" Which he said was "hard and quick." Shula had taken Paul Brown's methodology to a higher level. He had hired his staffmate at Kentucky, Bill Arnsparger, as his defensive line coach, and both Arnsparger and McCafferty would be up in the press box, as Shula had been with the Lions, peering through binoculars and relaying information by phone for Shula and his sideline coaches to assimilate. In time, they were able to review plays on a rudimentary videotape machine, which the TV people were using to show replays during the broadcasts.[18]

Shula captured his first title as a head coach, taking the Western Conference at 12–2, leaving Lombardi out in the cold again. The Colts scored the most points—including 40 or more in four games—and gave up the fewest. With Shula using him in and out of the backfield, Moore had over 1,000 yards of total offense, 16 rushing touchdowns— three receiving—and was named the league's comeback player of the year and a first-team All-Pro selection. Unitas, who was ahead so often and by so much that he barely needed to throw, racked up fewer than 3,000 yards, his lowest total since '58, yet won his second MVP—proof that Shula knew what he was doing. In fact, Unitas would only throw for more yardage once over the rest of his career.

The last roadblock to the NFL title was the Browns, whom the Colts faced on December 27 in the well of a packed Municipal Stadium, the wind whipping like a hawk's claw off Lake Erie. Had Shula had to stand opposite Paul Brown that day, his knees might have knocked. As it was, Blanton Collier posed similar qualms, but Shula believed the Browns were easy meat. The two teams hadn't met during the season, in which the Browns went 10–3–1, but Collier's defense had given up the most points in the league. The Colts were a seven-point favorite.

But the Browns—in their last hurrah, and that of Cleveland sports teams in general for 52 years—played the underdog role to perfection. When Shula remarked that Browns quarterback Frank Ryan, a PhD candidate in quantum physics, was the "best protected" QB in the league, Collier took this not as a compliment to his offensive line, but as a jab at Ryan. Collier also saw something intriguing in the film: when Unitas set himself to throw, he unconsciously shuffled his feet in the direction he would throw, a tell that had somehow escaped even Shula's sights. Collier also saw that teams usually played deep against the Colt receivers, conceding a lot of yardage. Instead, he put his deep backs up close to the line, right in their faces. Moreover, Collier had seven All-Pros, led by Jim Brown, in his penultimate season. And Ryan had big targets like Gary Collins and an antelope of a rookie from Ohio State, Paul Warfield, who had caught nine touchdown passes and made All-Pro.

Collier naturally wanted to keep Unitas off the field. Johnny U seemed primed, and not the least bit intimidated by the gaping dimensions of the stadium he had seen many times; younger Colts, who hadn't been to Cleveland, were awed by it, only to have Unitas bark, "Hey, haven't any of you seen a football field before?"[19] But he was harried that day, only able to throw 20 passes, many of them cut down by the wind, completing 12 for 95 yards with two interceptions. The first half ended scoreless, a perceived win for the underdogs. The Browns then made the killer plays, and Brown was on his way to rushing for 114 yards. In the third quarter, up by a field goal, Ryan fired two touchdowns to the acrobatic Collins for a 17–0 lead. Yet another, for 51 yards, made the final 27–0, a mortifying loss for Shula, and not for the last time.

While remaining classy in the face of national humiliation, profusely congratulating his old boss, Shula seethed. Decades later, he looked back in anger at that torturous day, saying "we messed up on our defense" and that he was "disgusted" by the offense, bemoaning "a fine season down the drain."[20] He also intimated that Collier had run up the score with that late TD pass—exactly what Shula seemed to do so easily to George Halas—and criticized Unitas, saying that he had "killed our own drives" because of fumbles and interceptions. On the flight home, he was stone-faced in his front-row seat. Unitas sat in the back, also steaming. The mood was foul. When they landed, someone called out, "Touchdown." From the back came the retort, "First one we made today."

Shula's mood improved when he coached the Western Conference team in the Pro Bowl—another symbolic step up—and beat Collier's Eastern team, 34–14. In fact, when Marchetti joined in on a gang sack of Frank Ryan, knocking him out of the game with a broken shoulder, some wondered if it had been ordered up by Shula in retribution. There was also satisfaction in winning his first Coach of the Year award, beating out Collier. Rosenbloom didn't sour on him for losing the big one. The free-spending owner re-signed him for five years starting at $40,000, close to Landry's salary on his 10-year mega-deal in Dallas.

Lombardi had them both beat, also owning stock in the Packers, and his income and éclat were soon to skyrocket further.

Having come so close to winning it all, Shula mainly stood pat with his roster. He had a successful formula, respect, awards; defeat didn't cause him to second-guess himself. But losing the big game had taught him that he didn't have all the answers. And while patience wasn't his strong suit, he would need to develop a whole lot of it.

8

NATIONAL FRUSTRATION LEAGUE

Only Don Shula had a real chance to keep Vince Lombardi from his throne. Because the Colts had been a headache for the Packers during the regular season—albeit losing to Shula by a total of four points over two meetings—their season-within-the-season in '65 loomed as a personal grudge match, with a shot at the title at stake for the winner. In the draft—held ridiculously early, on November 28, 1964—Shula and Don Kellett could make another down payment on the future. With the 14th and last pick in the first round, Baltimore took Duke fullback Mike Curtis. Shula, who hadn't kept his eye on the college game much, knew Curtis was an absolute mad dog—nicknamed "The Animal"—but he already had one of those in the backfield in Matte. Instead, he wanted to try Curtis at outside linebacker, utilizing his speed and ferocity. He liked what he saw in camp and made the switch, though Curtis would pay his dues, mainly sitting as a rookie.

Clearly, Shula needed youth on the roster. Before the season, Marchetti and Pellington called it quits. Gino broke the news to Shula when the two, along with Unitas, accepted an invitation from the air force to conduct a football clinic at the base in Weisbaden, West Germany. Without depth up front, Shula had to improvise, using the 30-year-old placekicker Lou Michaels, whom he had obtained in '64, back at his aboriginal position on the defensive line, putting faith in a guy who had tested his discipline, drawing numerous fines for beer-drenched curfew violations. Shula, foreseeing Pellington's exit, had made a key trade the year before, ridding himself of a problem child, halfback Joe Don Looney, who lived up to his name with some truly loony and violent behavior and general insubordination. Looney, who would die at 45 in a motorcycle accident, was traded for the Lions' Dennis Gaubatz, who eased in between the outside linebackers, Steve Stonebreaker and Don Shinnick.

But Shula must have been temporarily insane when he traded his second-round pick, Oklahoma offensive tackle Ralph Neely, to the Cowboys for punter Billy Lothridge, who was promptly sent off to the Rams in August. Neely would play 13 years for Landry and make the '60s All-Decade team. On the other hand, Shula drafted a future gem, Jackson State defensive end Roy Hilton, a steal with his 15th-round pick.

On balance, he had a strong if aging team. Marchetti's absence would mean teams could better contain the holdover defensive line-men, Fred Miller, Billy Ray Smith, and Ordell Braase. But they had a strong offensive line and secondary. And they had Unitas, Orr, and Moore, the game's best offensive triangle, with Mackey always a potent threat, and Shula hired a new assistant, former Colt Dick Bielski, as his receivers coach. However, disaster hit just as things looked rosy.

The Colts won the opener, a blowout of the Vikings, then pulled into Green Bay for the first critical Packer game. On a balmy 47-degree day, they pushed the Pack around, outgaining them 309 yards to 184. But turnovers—the biggest being a Unitas pick that was returned 44 yards by Herb Adderley for a touchdown—kept it close. In the fourth quarter, Unitas capped a drive with a five-yard touchdown pass to Berry for a 17–13 lead. The Pack were hurting. Both Paul Hornung and Jim Taylor had left the game, as had Bart Starr with a leg injury. But his sub, 34-year-old Zeke Bratkowski, lofted a lazy spiral for Max McGee. Lenny Lyles, the corner, missed bumping him and McGee beat safety

Wendell Harris for a 37-yard score. Down 20–17, the Colts had a last shot, but Matte caught, then fumbled a pass, gift-wrapping a win for Lombardi in what *Sports Illustrated* called "a thriller."

Lombardi, with a sigh of relief, hailed "two superb defensive teams." Shula, though, was upset. "We just gave them the game," he lamented. "This is tough to swallow."[1] Rosenbloom was less politic. "We blew it," he said. As the season wore on, Unitas battled injuries, coming out of one game with a bad back and missing another. Still, the Colts won eight straight, followed by a tie with the Lions, to lead the division. In week 12, against the Bears, Unitas was mauled—he completed just three of nine for 24 yards. With four minutes left in the half, he took a hit and fell to the turf, grabbing at his right knee. Unable to rise, he was helped, limping, off the field. After the Colts' 13–0 loss, he was diagnosed with torn ligaments and was in the operating room a day later, finished for the season.

Dauntingly, the next game was the rematch with the Packers, who loomed half a game back. Unitas's backup, Gary Cuozzo, a former Phi Beta Kappa student at Virginia, confidently proclaimed, "That's what I'm here for." He kept the Colts in it for a half, but the defense cracked, allowing Hornung and Taylor to go on a stampede and letting Starr, who hit on three touchdown passes, control the ball. But then Cuozzo went down, too, separating his shoulder seriously and undergoing surgery the next day. Matte, the nominal third-string QB, was probably more shocked than anyone when he was told to go in and take snaps, with Shula sending in the plays. He threw three passes, completing none, and had one intercepted in the 42–27 loss.

Suddenly, Shula was behind in the race, by half a game, and had no quarterback as he neared the finale, a Saturday game against the Rams in LA. During the week, he called Woody Hayes, Matte's old coach, for assurances about him. The garrulous Hayes said Matte could do the job. There was just one flaw in his game, said Woody: Matte was bad at taking the snap from center. As Shula recalled years later with a dollop of sarcasm, "That's all I needed to hear."[2]

Helpfully, the Steelers' owner, Art Rooney, offered Shula his team's third-string QB, 37-year-old Ed Brown. Shula said okay, but it took three days for him to clear waivers. Brown arrived in LA the day before the only game he would be eligible to play in, which would also be the last of his career. Shula had Brown come right to his hotel room, where he, his offensive coaches, and Unitas—on crutches—gave Brown a crash course in the Colts playbook. During pregame warmups, Shula recalled, the team looked "horrible. . . . Everyone appeared flat," and Matte and Brown "couldn't complete a pass." Fortunately, the 4–9 Rams were an easy touch, and if the Colts beat them, the Packers would need to beat the 49ers up the coast on Sunday to clinch the division; with a loss, they would have to face the Colts in a playoff.

Shula figured he could get by with defense and the running game. Matte started, a condensed Colts playbook written in code on his wristband so he could call a play if he had to. Shula, though, gave Matte and Brown strict orders not to pass unless told to. Despite Shula's exhortations, the Colts indeed came out flat. Matte had awakened that morning with a fever, and Shula alternated him with Brown, who looked lost. Over the entire game, Brown threw five passes, Matte two. The running game did its job: Matte, Moore, and Hill ran for 210 yards. But the Colts trailed 17–10 in the fourth quarter. Then, given one of Unitas's favorite plays, Brown hit Mackey over the middle on a stunning 68-yard touchdown to tie it up, his third and final completion of the game. With four minutes left, Michaels, who had made a 50-yard field goal earlier but blown three others, booted one from 23 yards. The defense preserved the lead when Roman Gabriel dropped back to throw with a minute and a half to go. The ball was tipped by Billy Ray Smith and grabbed by Bobby Boyd, icing the exhilarating 20–17 win.

The Colts hung around LA that night. Some of the players were invited to a party in Hollywood that Matte recalled was "full of young starlets." He and Unitas had a few beers, "chatting up the girls," when defensive back Jim Welch "came out of one of the bedrooms, whispering, 'They're snorting cocaine in there.' I turned to John and he was already gone. With a cast on one leg, he hopped down three flights of steps faster than you could believe."[3] On a more natural high, the team flew home, the Ram win treated in the press as some kind of bold statement. The next day, Bob Maisel opined in the *Sun*, "The Colts may not win the World Championship this year, they probably won't even get a chance to play for it. But, yesterday in Los Angeles, they played what might have been the most satisfying football game in their history." Cameron Snyder's take was that "a miracle [was] performed" and "the Colts looked like dirty-faced urchins caught in the act of stealing an apple after their astounding victory." All agreed with Matte's appraisal of the coach, which produced the headline HUMBLE MATTE GIVES COACH SHULA CREDIT.

The following afternoon, the Colts got the shock of their lives when the Packers could not close the deal, the game in San Francisco ending in a 24–24 tie. With Shula and Lombardi both 10–3–1, the league hurriedly set the playoff game—the 10th in league history—for the following Sunday, the day after Christmas, which normally would have been on a bye week leading up to the title game a week later. Lombardi got the home field by dint of the Packers' two wins over the Colts, and this was no small advantage over any team that had to come to Green Bay in late December and somehow function in finger- and toe-numbing arctic conditions.

With Brown's one-game contribution over, Shula had no choice but to put the task of beating Lombardi into the raw hands of Matte, who would once again wear the wristband containing the plays. As in the Ram game, he would be instructed to run on first, second, and, if possible, third downs. If Matte didn't hand off, he would roll out like an option quarterback and look for a hole—or else, if he saw a receiver close enough, shovel a short pass to him. All else was in the hands of the defense.

It was cold, of course, at Lambeau Field—22 degrees with a wind chill of 12—steam rising over the open grandstand from rabid fans' heavy breathing. But Shula's defense made the first big break. On the Packers' first play, Bart Starr threw a short one over the middle to Bill Anderson, who caught it, but fumbled on the Packer 25. Don Shinnick scooped it and ran it in for the touchdown. Worse for the Pack, Starr, trying to tackle Shinnick, took a spill and injured his ribs. So now Lombardi had a quarterback problem too. And the Colts were sky high after making a goal-line stand, blunting Hornung and then Taylor to take over on downs. Packers guard Jerry Kramer recalled that Shula used a surprise five-lineman, one-linebacker set, and on the Taylor run, it "fouled up our blocking, and [Dennis] Gaubatz had a clean shot at Taylor."[4]

All game, Colt pass rushers would harass Starr's sub, Zeke Bratkowski. At the half, Baltimore led 10–0. No one thought Lombardi would go down quietly, though. While Taylor gained only 60 yards on the day, he carried 23 times, battering the Baltimore front line. The Pack loaded up against the Colts run, daring Matte to throw, which he did 12 times for 40 yards. But Matte did his job, running 17 times for 57 yards, the same as Hill, though Moore was held in check. The game plan was indeed simple. As Matte recalled, "Every time I came off the field, I ran straight to John [Unitas]," who would tell him what to do.

Finally, the Pack began to move. A 33-yard Bratkowski pass to Carroll Dale set up Hornung to run it in from the one in the third quarter, cutting the lead to three. But the defense was tenacious. Bratkowski was intercepted by Logan, then by Boyd. As the clock ticked down on an astounding upset—the greatest ever, as Shula envisioned it—Bratkowski got one last drive going, aided by a dubious face-mask penalty on Billy Ray Smith that moved the ball to the Colts' 15. With 1:58 left, kicker Don Chandler came in to try for a 22-yard field goal for a tie and perhaps to force the game into overtime. Striding into the kick, Chandler sent up a wobbler that the wind ushered to the right. Chandler jerked his head in disgust. But when the ball crossed over the 10-foot-high upright, it seemed impossible to call. The ref, Jim Tunney, stationed under the crossbar, needed to make a decision immediately. He thrust his arms into the air, signaling that the kick was good. On the sideline, in a topcoat and fedora, Shula let out a scream, wildly gesturing "no good." Colt players cursed and kicked the turf, some sinking to their knees in disbelief. After the clock ran out, they had to regroup for the second overtime in NFL history.

As with the '58 Colts–Giants game, the league was picking up new fans by the minute, and the teams extended the contest deep into the extra period. The Colts had a shot when Michaels tried for a 47-yard field goal, but Bobby Boyd, the holder, botched a high snap from center Buzz Nutter and the kick dribbled short. That left it for the Pack to move it to the Colt 18, where Chandler kicked an undeniably good field goal after 13 minutes, 39 seconds of overtime, ending what was the longest NFL game to that point—a far more savage, and better, game than the alleged "greatest game ever played." Well after it was over, Chandler's hands were still shaking from the tension. Hornung had bruised ribs and could barely breathe. Packers Hall of Fame tackle Forrest Gregg called it "one of the toughest games I ever played. You got to give them a lot of credit for the way they played with what they had to play with. I'm glad it's over."[5]

Shula, who congratulated Lombardi at midfield, sending him on his way to decimate the Browns 65–12 in the title game, had come so close to changing the course of history that, inconsolable, he kept the locker room door closed to the media for 20 long minutes so that he and the players could blow off their anger. Shula then calmly engaged in coach-speak about how proud he was of his team, and that the ref didn't beat them, that they had their chances but let them slip. The only sour note came when a reporter bizarrely asked him, "What program are you planning for the Playoff Bowl?"—referring to the joke of a consolation game that would take place the following week. Glaring, Shula stared at the guy.

"I was thinking about that all afternoon," he said, oozing sarcasm.[6]

All he would say about the tainted field goal was that he thought it was wide, but he would never let go of the belief that he had been jobbed. A few days later, when NFL Films came out with its celluloid record of the game, the critical kick was shown in slow motion and stop-action, from behind the end zone—and, clearly, a few feet wide. Indeed, Chandler would tell John Steadman 30 years later,

"When I looked up, the ball was definitely outside the post."[7] Old Colt fans still curse Tunney and the NFL for what they swear was a conspiracy against Shula and for Lombardi, never mind the Colts' overtime foibles. The league, too, seemed to admit that the call was wrong when it made significant changes, lengthening the uprights to give the refs a better perspective on field goals, and putting a second official on the goal line under the bar. Whenever Shula ran into Tunney through the years, even a half century later, he would want to argue the call. Exasperated, the ref would tell him, "Christ, can't you let it go?"

C.R. was more vocal. "We didn't deserve to lose," he fumed in the locker room. "There was no justice out there." Under those circumstances, he added, "I was never more proud of any team I've ever had,"[8] which certainly appeased Shula. Indeed, the unexpectedly close contest only helped cement his reputation. Bob Maisel wrote that Shula "never did a better coaching job."[9] The Monday headline in the *Sun* accentuated the positive—"WE GAVE IT OUR BEST SHOT," SAYS COLTS' DON SHULA. A common theme emerged around town that the Colts were something like uncrowned champs. Nobody argued with Matte, who sank to his knees as the winning kick was made, and who later said, "We have nothing to be ashamed of." Least of all him. Matte came away a folk hero in Baltimore, his wristband itself a folk legend, to be enshrined under glass at the Hall of Fame. In the Runner-Up Bowl, Shula unwound, letting Matte throw all he wanted. He strafed the Cowboys 35–3 before the biggest crowd ever to see one of those vacuous games—over 65,000. Afterward, Tom Landry praised Matte for being able to dissect his famed Flex Defense, not that the Cowboys took the game seriously. Shula giggled at Landry's over-generous compliment. Matte, he said, "didn't have the faintest fucking idea what the Flex Defense was."[10]

As the '66 season began, months of secret negotiations had transpired between the most powerful executives in the NFL and AFL to end their costly war, one that had sent salaries soaring, and merge into a unified

NFL. In doing so, the AFL owners betrayed their own commissioner—none other than Al Davis, who had been given the job, ostensibly, to bring the NFL to its knees, begging to merge on the AFL's terms, with Davis as NFL commissioner. But in reality, Davis had been given the title to keep him from gumming up the negotiations between Cowboys president Tex Schramm and Kansas City Chiefs owner Lamar Hunt, who signed the deal on the tarmac of Dallas's Love Field. Davis was so infuriated at being shunted aside that he upbraided his league for capitulating too soon, quit as commissioner before he could be fired, and went back to the Raiders, gaining additional leverage as co-owner.

The merger was scheduled to commence with the 1970 season. In the meantime, the identity of each league was kept intact, and a world championship game between the two leagues' titlists would be played at a neutral site. Most NFL people thought the AFL's teams—all of them—were too inferior to play in such a game. Indeed, the NFL title was regarded by most as the real championship, while the newly made NFL-AFL Championship Game was viewed as merely a bow on top of the season. As such, it seemed unthinkable that Lombardi wouldn't be certified king or saint or god after that '66 season. And he was, but only after Shula made it close. Too close.

The Colts were an enigmatic team coming into the season. At 33, Unitas would need to have his knee drained periodically, further limiting his mobility, and Lenny Moore was clearly on the way down. Jim Parker had to move from guard to tackle because of a retirement. But Unitas was still Unitas. *Sports Illustrated*, in its preseason forecast, said the Colt roster was "not as deep as it could be, but should give the Packers a grim enough fight for the conference title."[11] The league had scheduled the first Colt–Packer game of the season for opening day, in Green Bay, and Lombardi took Shula down, 24–3. Unitas had two passes intercepted and run back for touchdowns in the second quarter. The Colts mustered just over 200 yards of total offense. That stung, but Shula got them back on track, winning seven of the next eight, even with Unitas hampered by injuries. Johnny U would have more interceptions than touchdowns over the season, 24 to 22, but again make All-Pro by rote.

When the Colts met the Pack again, on December 10, the Colts were 8–4, having just disposed of George Allen's Rams as a divisional challenger, and two games behind Lombardi with two weeks left. Memorial Stadium was full and loud on a mild Saturday afternoon on which a steady rain left the field a muddy bog. It was a physical test, with players dropping all over. Starr, after having back spasms, couldn't go back in. After a head-to-head collision with Matte, cornerback Bob Jeter needed smelling salts. Chandler missed three field goals, and the Colts controlled the ball. But Unitas, his shoulder aching, had one of the worst games of his career, throwing three picks. Shula yanked him briefly for Gary Cuozzo, who threw one pass—an interception. A seeming Unitas-to-Mackey TD was ruled incomplete.

Staying close at 10–7 in the fourth quarter, Bratkowski took the Pack on an 80-yard drive and found Max McGee for the go-ahead touchdown. Unitas took his men down the field, hitting Berry at the Packer 15. Then, flushed from the pocket, he ran for five yards, was clubbed by linebacker Willie Davis, and the ball popped loose. It skidded in the mud, and the other outside linebacker, Dave Robinson, fell on it, protecting the 14–10 victory. "I just said, 'Come to papa,'" Robinson said later, "and there it was."[12] *Sports Illustrated* called it a "million-dollar fumble."

When the latest grim frustration was over, Shula was numb. According to one report, he "sat on a training table smoking a cigarette and staring into space, as was Carroll Rosenbloom nearby. Finally Shula turned to a clutch of reporters and said, 'Anybody want to get it started?' There was a question and before it could be completed Shula said, 'They threw mud in Unitas' eye,'" swearing that some Packers had done that literally, to keep Unitas from seeing the loose ball on the ground.[13] He also slagged the official who had called the pass interference that wiped out a Colt touchdown. "You were there," he said, "you saw it." After losing four straight times to Lombardi, no greater an analysis was needed. Whatever it took for the Packers to win, it seemed

Lombardi got it. It held true the next week, when the Pack went to Dallas for the NFL title game against Tom Landry's Cowboys. With time running out, the Cowboys were near the goal line with a chance to tie, but a fouled-up pass by Don Meredith was intercepted, sending Lombardi to the first NFL-AFL Championship Game—unofficially, the Super Bowl, a term not adopted until the third game, in 1969—an event he dominated in blowing away the Kansas City Chiefs, and one he left in coronation.

Shula knew he would need to break that glorified narrative if he had any chance of supplanting Lombardi in their division. As it was, he ended the '66 season at 9–5, a step back, earning only one more trip to the Playoff Bowl, where the Colts beat the Eagles 20–14. He had assets, and, of course, Unitas, but whatever else the next season would bring, he was now almost obsessed with Lombardi. Everything Vince said provoked a reaction in Shula, who became even more fixated on beating him. And he would have no dearth of chances to do it.

That off-season, he and Dorothy moved their brood out to the suburbs, in Lutherville-Timonium, buying a newly built five-bedroom, four-and-a-half-bath split level on an acre of land at 2222 Pot Spring Road. This upward move was befitting his increased status and authority. When Don Kellett retired the year before, the new GM was former Colts linebacker Joe Campanella, who, after his playing career, had partnered with Alan Ameche and Gino Marchetti in their chain of restaurants, then ran his own eatery, the Rustler Steak House, which he sold off for a fortune. At C.R.'s urging, Campanella took the job, but was well aware that Shula, his old teammate, was the de facto GM. That deference was common within the front office, and Campanella easily complied; he and Shula worked well on drafting and personnel moves. Often, they made such moves after playing handball. However, in February 1967, during another handball game at the Downtown Athletic Club, Campanella felt faint before collapsing to the court. Shula rushed over, but Joe died in his arms as they awaited an ambulance. Killed by a heart attack at just 36.

Devastated—he would be haunted for years by that memory—Shula delivered the eulogy at his funeral, calling Campanella "a wonderful human being" and "one of my closest friends." He and Marchetti were overcome with grief at the service, as was Rosenbloom, who had to name a new GM. He promoted Colts PR man and former navy combat veteran Harry Hulmes, who also deferred to the coach on all decisions, though they relied heavily on the advice of another new hire, personnel director Upton Bell, son of the late commissioner and actress Frances Upton, who began as a Colts training camp ball boy. Their first order of business was the draft, held in mid-March, the first common draft under the merger agreement. The Colts, who had enough excess talent to trade up, decided that getting a high pick was worth parting with the only insurance they had to back up Unitas. With the expansion New Orleans Saints holding the top pick, they dangled Gary Cuozzo—a no-brainer, since Cuozzo had asked to be traded. For Tom Fears, the Saints' first coach, the prospect of gaining a reputable quarterback was seductive; he even threw in his third-round pick and the veteran ex-Packer center Bill Curry.

Now, with the top pick, Shula had options. The scuttlebutt had it that the Colts would use it to land Florida's Heisman Trophy–winning quarterback, Steve Spurrier, and groom him to one day replace Unitas. Instead, they tapped Michigan State's mammoth All-American defensive end Bubba Smith, a six-foot, seven-inch, 265-pound terror who had led the Spartans to a shared No. 1 ranking with Ara Parseghian's Notre Dame Fighting Irish. In all, four of Duffy Daugherty's players were chosen in that first round, eight in all.

Shula then used his existing first-round pick on Michigan running back Jim Detwiler, and in round two, another Wolverine All-American, safety Rick Volk. He did go for a QB in round six: Baylor's Terry Southall, who, like Detwiler, would wash out. That meant Shula would go into another season with no competent backup for Unitas; by default, the job went to the 14th-round pick from a year before, Jim Ward, who would throw 16 passes in six mop-up appearances. Fortunately, Unitas remained in one piece, which seemed all that was required to win his final MVP award. He passed for 3,438 yards, completing a career-high 58.5 percent, with 20 touchdowns and a manageable 16 interceptions.

While this was more passing than Shula was comfortable with, he had to compensate for the deteriorating ground game now that Lenny Moore, who was to retire after the season, was on his last legs. It also birthed a new receiving corps, transitioning away from the aging Berry and Orr, with Willie Richardson, who caught eight TD passes, buttressing Mackey. Unitas, Richardson, and Mackey were all first-team All-Pros. The offense was a monster, but the defense matched it. Shula had hired a new assistant, Chuck Noll, to oversee the secondary, into which Volk—a virtual Shula clone, a wily and tough nut who had also played fullback in college—fit right in at free safety. As he recalled:

> Sure, Shula was a dictator, but he could relate to you. Sometimes he'd get too wound up, drone on for half an hour, and Danny Sullivan would fart just at the right time and we'd all break up. Don, too, 'cause he knew we needed a break. People said the Colts were all business, a machine, but we had a good time. We knew we had the best team and the best coach. Yeah, better than Lombardi.[14]

Volk was a Pro Bowl selection as a rookie with six picks that year, setting a team record when he ran one back 94 yards for a touchdown against the Bears. The secondary, benefiting from the ravaging Smith up front, rang up a ridiculous 32 interceptions. The Colts gave up the second-fewest points in the league, helping Noll climb toward the Steelers' head coaching job two years later. And yet, because of the structural changes in the league as it moved toward the merger, Shula was faced with a crazy anomaly. That season, the NFL expanded to 16 teams with the addition of the Saints, and the Eastern and Western conferences were each split into two divisions of four teams (the Colts were in the Coastal), the winners of each division advancing to a playoff round to determine the title-game contestants.

After 13 weeks, the Colts were undefeated, at 11-0-2, the two ties on successive Sundays in October against the Rams and Vikings.

Shula could breathe easier, knowing that he had put distance between himself and Lombardi, whose team played in the Central Division, and the Colts handed them a bitter defeat in their one confrontation that season, 13–10, on a pair of late TD passes. Still, Lombardi faced little resistance en route to winning his division with a 12–2 record. While the win over the Pack was one Shula could savor, the Colts had a tougher fight in their division with the Rams, whom George Allen had turned into a terror, breeding All-Pros in Roman Gabriel, halfback Les Josephson, receivers Jack Snow and Bernie Casey, and three of their Fearsome Foursome defensive line, Deacon Jones, Merlin Olsen, and Shula's old charge in Detroit, Roger Brown. Allen had been able to tie the Colts in Baltimore and to keep pace with Shula all season. The season finale, on December 17, brought the rematch into the LA Coliseum, with Shula on the verge of the NFL's only undefeated season since Halas's two—13–0 in '34 and 11–0 in '42 (like the Colts, two other undefeated NFL teams were not perfect, the '22 Canton Bulldogs going 10–0–2, the '29 Packers 12–0–2)—while the Rams were 10–1–2. If Allen won, the Rams would tie the Colts, but would make the playoffs by sweeping the season series. Shula, with a single defeat, would be on the outside looking in.

That would be a nightmare scenario for Shula, and with more than 77,000 people in the Coliseum, he couldn't shake his men awake from it. They got off well when Unitas found Richardson for an early touchdown. But Gabriel hit Snow with an 80-yard bomb in the second quarter and the Colt defense, which had given up 30 points just once during the season, crumbled into dust. They allowed two more TD passes by Gabriel, who went 18-for-22 and whose passer rating (a geeky stat the NFL didn't adopt officially until 1973, but which has been applied retroactively to every past season) was 154.9 out of a perfect 158.3. Unitas, sacked just 18 times all season, ate turf seven times, Gabriel not once. Unitas was also picked off twice, once deep in Ram territory when Deacon Jones, a man who proudly made his name synonymous with sacks and dirty hits, slammed his forearm into him. Another pick, by linebacker Jack Pardee, was run back 29 yards. Unitas's passer rating was a puny 64.7, and no Colt runner gained even 40 yards. Two fourth-down gambles failed. The final tally was 34–10, at the end of which, wrote one scribe, "Baltimore's sun sank slowly in the West."[15]

Shula was loath to admit personal failing. Assessing the pass to Snow, he blamed Jerry Logan, saying that Gabriel "caught us with our strong side safetyman playing up."[16] According to one account:

> Shula went over to a training table and put his head in his hands for several seconds, then stared long at the ceiling. He had to be thinking, one loss—one loss—and we blow it all. "I feel really sorry for my team," he said finally. "We've held our heads high all season and now we've got to live with this through a whole winter. The Rams deserved to win, I'm not denying that, but what a way to go . . ."[17]

For Shula, who also lost the Coach of the Year award to Allen because of that season's one defeat, the worst of it was that history was robbed of what would have been a pivotal crossroads: an unde-feated Colts team against a seemingly mortal Packer squad, the winner to get the next crack at an overmatched AFL team and walk off with Lombardi's vestments. Instead, Lombardi, after brushing by the Rams in the first playoff round, broke Tom Landry's heart again, this time in a subarctic Green Bay, Bart Starr's quarterback sneak with seconds left codifying the "Ice Bowl" and entitling St. Vince to the highest level of idol worship—and another coronation in the warmth of the Orange Bowl, taking apart Al Davis's Oakland Raiders. In truth, the difference between the proud, aging Pack and both Shula and Landry's teams was small, but in the metaphysical sense, it was enormous. Both Shula and Landry marveled at the depth of character Lombardi could sink into his players' hearts and minds; neither of them could inspire that kind of loyalty. No athletes would ever really willingly die for a coach, but when Packers spoke of the spell Lombardi had on them, it didn't seem so far-fetched.

Shula didn't crave that kind of idolatry, nor accept it. What he wanted was Lombardi's apostolic manner of elevating players to a seeming state of calm when opponents were losing their equilibrium under duress. This was the one element no Paul Brown playbook could provide; it had to come from within Shula. That Shula didn't have it, at least not yet, had begun to make him sound like Hamlet, wondering how he could redirect fate, which his bible always told him was immutably ruled from above him. He had proven he belonged on the same consecrated fields as St. Vince, and though it wouldn't become clear for a while, he was better positioned than Lombardi. No one knew that better than Vince, who that winter suddenly abdicated as Packers coach, spending the next year as the club's general manager, then walked away from the sundered team a year after that to coach the Redskins, in a mercenary turn that shocked many who had bought the saintly jive. Shula could also see the shifting of the league's landscape, and that the field was wide open for him, if he could survive the fall he had taken.

He would enter the '68 season having already left his mark on history; as Bob Maisel pointed out in the *Sun*, "Never before in the history of the National Football League has a team gone undefeated all the way through until the last game of the season and then been eliminated from the chase in that final start."[18]

Okay, so it wasn't exactly the work of a saint or an apostle. And the fact that Shula *had* lost that last game made for a nagging suspicion that he was somehow predisposed to heartache. It would take only one more season to make that seem like an epitaph.

9

SWEET

Running parallel to Don Shula's upward thrust was that of Richard Nixon, whose own tunnel-vision ambition seemed to have been thwarted numerous times until he got off the canvas in 1968, when the political and cultural terrain was more fertile for his malignant pretensions. Shula and Nixon were two opposite sides of the Greatest Generation coin, Shula not built for deceit or exploitation of fear. But both were melding into a culture of post-'50s turmoil and confusion that threatened to consume the country more and more with each passing day. Shula began his training camp in Westminster just days after Bobby Kennedy was gunned down in a Los Angeles hotel kitchen, weeks after Martin Luther King was murdered on a motel landing in Memphis. What's more, the Baltimore streets that had stayed calm in the past detonated, as urban centers nationwide erupted in protest after the King slaying, followed by looting and violence in the D.C.–Baltimore corridor and 5,500 arrests. Governor Spiro Agnew called in the national guard and spouted off that black leaders were "circuit riding, Hanoi visiting, caterwauling, riot inciting, burn American down type of leaders"[1]—the kind of run-on bile that elevated Agnew to the vice-presidency in Nixon's administration, at least until 1973, when evidence that he took bribes as governor did him in, presaging Nixon's own fall.

In Baltimore, the migration of white residents to the suburbs was about to begin, leaving the city blacker and poorer. The mood across the country was volatile. As training camp stretched through the summer, cops in Chicago rioted at the Democratic Convention, beating and stomping protesters. Meanwhile, the war in the jungle was grinding on with no end in sight. But the football world remained shielded, a sanctuary of militaristic pretensions. "It's funny," said Rick Volk, "the year before, at Michigan, they had the worst rioting they ever saw in Detroit, and I never even thought about it, because in Ann Arbor we were so shielded. Then I came to Baltimore and it was the same. Even in Baltimore, we could've been a thousand miles away."[2]

Shula, to be certain, had moved away from his days as a Kennedy Democrat, the working-class, union-man roots of Dan Shula supplanted by greater wealth, more conservative beliefs, and reflexive dismissal of antiwar protests. His Colts had, not coincidentally, kept up with Lombardi's Packers as the bedrock of the old-guard NFL, the polar opposite of the looser, swingier tintypes of the AFL epitomized by the image of Joe Namath. Shula had some rebels, too, though to see the Baltimore Colts on the road, in an airport or a hotel, in their suits and ties and crewcuts, they might as well have been playing for the Chamber of Commerce. Shula clearly had his favorites—like Tom Matte and Mike Curtis, men much like him—and while race never meant a thing to his player transactions, some of the black men under his rule did not feel the same bond with him that white players did. John Mackey, for example, revered him as a coach, but like Lenny Moore before him, could feel a separation—not out of enmity or even anything specific to Shula, but because the coaching brethren seemingly lacked the sensibility to understand why African-Americans had rioted in the streets, or why Muhammad Ali had refused to join the military the year before, or why John Carlos and Tommie Smith raised black-gloved fists at the Olympics that October.

In Shula's eyes, culturally, the world still turned as it had in 1960. He was as contemptuous of the AFL as Lombardi had been, and that attitude carried over to many old-line football writers. During summer camp, syndicated sports columnist Louis Chestnut noted that Johnny Unitas and Joe Namath were expected to be the MVPs of their respective leagues, writing, "Unitas, maybe. I ain't too sure about Namath. I have this strange, weird feeling that old Shaggy Hair might fall on his mod fat face this year."[3] Weeb Ewbank had had to lose his old-world bent as the price to pay for tolerating Namath's excesses. And Shula knew he would need to make similar exceptions; though, if he had to coach Namath, Lord knows how he would deal with it. For now, there was no such dilemma, and he was just fine with the Colts' drab, machinelike regimentation that kept them winning.

And why not? They were loaded in '68. When Ray Berry retired and Ray Perkins blew out a knee, Shula could plug in Jimmy Orr, who himself was getting over a shoulder separation, to ease the load on Mackey and Willie Richardson. He also now plugged in Curtis at outside linebacker, where he would ravage offenses and earn first-team All-Pro honors. However, Shula would have to make a critical move to avoid being derailed before the season even began. Johnny Unitas, a time bomb at 35, immediately had problems with his right elbow. Shula planned to go with his backup, Jim Ward, for the exhibition games, but Ward hurt his leg in the second one. With Matte the only fallback, Shula started scouring rosters around the league for a quarterback. One stood out: Earl Morrall. Now 34 and all but stationary, he had become expendable in Detroit after injuring his shoulder in '65. Cleaning house, the Lions sent him to the New York Giants, where he fractured his wrist during a 1–12–1 season. The next year, with Fran Tarkenton's arrival, he was a mop-up man.

But Morrall had value to people who kept tabs on serviceable players, and Shula had hired one of them that year: George Young, an extremely bright man with degrees from Johns Hopkins and Loyola College. Scouting the league for Shula, Young signed off on Morrall, and Shula offered the Giants a fourth-round draft pick to get him. The Giants countered by also asking for backup tight end Butch Wilson. Shula thought about it, then made the deal, one that a thousand years later he would be able to call "the best trade I've ever made."[4] Morrall came to his fifth team with the purpose of spelling Unitas in preseason, then taking a seat. And then, in the penultimate preseason game, Unitas came off the field with his arm hanging limp. "I think I've torn something," he told center Bill Curry.[5] It turned out to be worse. Two tendons in his elbow that soldered bones in the joint were, he said later, "torn off at the bone." However, team doctors either misdiagnosed it or went along with the team's—perhaps Shula's—wishes to downplay the injury; the reporters obediently parroted the doctor and Shula's descriptions as no more than "tennis elbow" or "black-and-blue elbow." Shula even insisted that it was "the same old sore elbow. It's a chronic condition that John lives with and we can just hope it doesn't act up too much."

Unitas, though, knew this was no tennis elbow. Not playing along, he said he couldn't raise or straighten his arm, that the elbow was "real sore, puffed up, black and blue."[6] During drills the week before the opener, at home against the 49ers, he walked off the field, unable to do much of anything. Even this didn't seem to faze Shula. As Cameron Snyder wrote in the *Sun*, "Optimistic concern is the best way to explain coach Don Shula's attitude" toward his meal ticket.[7] Shula went only as far as to have Unitas sit out the game, naming Morrall as the starter. Fortunately, the defense did the heavy lifting, and with Morrall throwing two TDs, the Colts eased in, 27–10.

Unitas's arm was still limp for the next game, against the Atlanta Falcons, and Morrall threw three interceptions, but also three touchdowns and racked up 279 yards. As snaillike as he was, he could anticipate a rush and step out of the pocket, then thread a needle with a pass. Shula trusted him to change plays at the line of scrimmage, and he seemed to mesh perfectly with the powerhouse machine all around him that broke games open with brute efficiency, rolling up massive yardage and choking the life out of enemy offenses. The Colts won their first five, four of them by blowout. By then, Unitas was able to move his arm more freely and was begging to get in. Down 14–7 at the half against the Browns in week six, Shula started him to begin the second half. "I thought it would give us a lift," he said. But Unitas only lifted Cleveland. He went one for 11, was intercepted thrice, and heard boos in Memorial Stadium for what was arguably his worst game ever, a 30–20 loss. The Colts righted the ship the next week, beating the Rams 27–10, Morrall throwing two touchdowns, though also three interceptions. They would not lose again.

Over the next five games, they turned in three shutouts, surrendering only 19 points in total. Morrall became the story of the season, a scrub at the helm of a team people were already calling the best ever. Games were over early, with only two victories by fewer than 17 points. Entering the next-to-last game of the regular season with an 11–1 record, the division clinched, they had the distinct pleasure of storming into Lambeau Field on a 19-degree day, knowing the worm had turned. As Lombardi had reckoned when he stepped aside, the Pack could not compete with the Colts any longer. Worse, Bart Starr was out.

Shula relished every minute of a game that was essentially over when Morrall hit Willie Richardson with an early 26-yard touchdown pass. The defense limited the Packers to 163 total yards, and three field goals put it away, 16–3. However, a complication had now arisen, one that seemed an embarrassment of riches, but was in reality a monkey wrench thrown into the subtle mechanics of winning.

All through the season, Unitas had been a good soldier, helping Morrall get the hang of the system. But at times, he seemed a broken man, slumped on the bench, a Colts parka draped over him like a shroud. For years, he had taken a profound beating, without complaint. In his younger days, when a hit broke his nose, blood spurting, he jammed a wad of mud into his nostrils and went about his business. No quarterback ever stood in the pocket longer, waiting for a receiver to get open, seemingly daring linemen to bury him. But now he could do nothing but watch the Colts have their best season ever. The perennial All-Pro was a spare wheel. For Shula, the situation called for a delicate balancing act, between managing Unitas's massive ego and allowing a near-perfect season to congeal. He regularly soothed Unitas by saying he hoped for his return. But the Browns disaster chastened him into keeping Unitas benched until the playoffs were in the bag. Not until the 12th game, against the Falcons, did he give the iconic QB any playing time—and even then, only to mop up.

Unitas may have held it against Shula that he had been turned into a backup. When reporters would ask him why he wasn't playing, he would respond, snarkily, "Why don't you ask The Man?" Shula later described such comments as "cold," and to be sure, that season marked the nadir of their relationship. In practice, when Unitas could throw, he'd come off the field staring at Shula, who would stare right back. "Boy, I could feel the electricity between them," said the third quarterback, Jim Ward.[8] Still, while Shula personally liked Morrall better, he would subject him to the same bullying that he did the rest of the team. When Morrall deviated from a play Shula sent in, improvising a pass to Perkins that resulted in a touchdown, he was glad-handed by teammates. But when he got to Shula, the coach ragged him for throwing to the wrong guy, screaming, "Read the fucking defense!"

Shula would have been insane not to want Unitas back. And as the season wound down, the veteran showed flashes of Johnny U in a few mop-up appearances, throwing a touchdown to Mackey in one game. By the last two games, having made an amazing recovery, he was throwing easily in practice and was game-ready. He was also his old ornery self. In one game, he came off the field glaring at Shula after the coach called a play based on what he thought was a stolen signal for a blitz that never happened. "Unless you're sure of what you're doing, don't interrupt my play calling," Unitas snapped, the kind of insolence only he could get away with.[9] In the finale, their division clinched, the Colts played George Allen's Rams—who, in a delightful irony, had won 10 games but were frozen out of the postseason. When Morrall played badly, in came Unitas to throw a fourth-quarter touchdown and lead a drive that scored another, sealing a 28–24 win. That left the Colts at 13–1, tying Halas for the most victories in a season in NFL history. It also left the greatest quarterback in history believing he had made his case, and that with the playoffs about to determine whether all that goodness during the season prefaced a championship, or was just a giant tease, Johnny U had to be where he belonged, running the Colts offense.

Earl Morrall, the unassuming Walter Mitty who helped Shula step into the void left by Lombardi, won the MVP award by racking up Unitas-like numbers, compiling league highs with 26 touchdowns, 9.2 yards per pass attempt, and 16 yards per completion. Along the way, the fans seemed to transfer their allegiance from the old general to the slightly less old guy with a crewcut. During Unitas's disastrous midseason game against the Browns, they began booing him. The thorny Unitas merely said, "I could care less." Amazingly, Shula also took some booing for it. As one scribe wrote, "Fans [had] Shula on the pan . . . for going so quickly to Johnny Unitas," quoting a cab driver who said, "Shula blew that one."[10]

Unitas had continued to play the role of good company man, saying Morrall deserved to start in the playoffs. And indeed, there was a certain egalitarian aspect to the team. Tom Matte, whose nickname was "Garbage Can" for his less-than-artistic running form, piled up 662 rushing yards and nine touchdowns, making All-Pro. A rookie fullback, Terry Cole, added over 400 yards. In all, 13 players scored at least one touchdown, and the Colts scored the second-most points in the NFL. Mackey even lined up in the backfield to run the ball 10 times, for 103 yards. The defense gave up a meager 144 points, equaling George Halas's 1963 Bears. Bobby Boyd pulled down eight interceptions and went first-team All-Pro. Shula, without objection, won his second AP Coach of the Year award. It seemed they were all living in a dream state.

Morrall did get the nod to start in the playoffs. Against the Vikings, he tossed touchdowns of three yards to tight end Tom Mitchell and 49 to Mackey to take a 14–0 lead in the third quarter. Curtis then recovered a fumble and ran 60 yards to make it 21–0. It ended 24–14. But the next round would be harder, and the stakes higher. Cameron Snyder averred that the Colts were "no longer playing for wages," but rather immortality.[11] It almost seemed too much of a contrived fable that Shula would now face the Browns in Cleveland, he and his veteran Colts still scarred by the 27–0 carnage in the '64 title game and the October loss that prompted all the booing in the only game between them since. They now would need to win in Municipal Stadium, stuffed with 80,000 fans.

On Saturday, a nervous Shula held a practice there and complained that the turf was in poor condition, soft and patchy, unfriendly to the Colts' running attack. As it turned out, the next day would be much colder, the wind chill around 12 degrees, the field iced up. This was actually a help to him, given that Jim Brown's successor at fullback, Leroy Kelly, the league's top rusher, was a mudder, but less stable on a slick surface. Another help was that Shula had noticed from the game film that the way tight end Milt Morin got into his three-point stance tipped off when the Browns would run. And so it was that Kelly, skating on turf he normally pounded, was dogged and gang-tackled. He would carry 13 times for only 28 yards. By contrast, Shula confused Blanton Collier by using a formation he called "wing left opposite," with Richardson and Orr lined up on one side, Mackey on the other. As Bob Matheson, the Browns outside linebacker, recalled, "We hadn't seen anything like that since high school. It's all we talked about at halftime, but we didn't see it the rest of the game. And while we were looking for it, they ran all over us."[12]

Matte, who was built for primitive conditions, ate up turf, dragging Browns with him, scoring three times. He ran 17 times for 88 yards, Jerry Hill adding 60 on 11 carries. They rolled up 184 yards rushing, 353 overall, holding the Browns to 173. With Kelly nullified, quarterback Bill Nelsen had to throw, ineffectively—two of his hurried passes were grabbed by Colts. Bubba Smith blocked a field goal and recovered a fumble. On the sideline, dressed to kill in a sartorially splendid two-tone, fur-collared brown topcoat and matching fedora with a feathered snap-brim, Shula seemed over-caffeinated, leaping up and down, exhorting his men to "come on!" and letting out whoops of pleasure on each score.

He had to calm himself down when, the 34–0 win in the bank, he

met with Collier at midfield for the handshake he had been await-
ing for four years, the one that marked an NFL title. For Collier, it
could not have been a more bitter end, against the former assistant
who had quit on him and whose team, Collier later said, "gave us a
good sound whipping" in one of the most one-sided title games in
NFL history. Lenny Lyles's postmortem was simple: "We hit, we hurt,
we won." Tex Maule's take in *Sports Illustrated* was that, "seldom in
the long history of NFL championship games has one team so thor-
oughly dominated the other. . . . It was a prodigious display of almost
flawless football [achieved by] executing Don Shula's stratagems with
precision and flair."[13] Not to mention maniacal intensity. In the fourth
quarter, the game long over, Matte was still plugging away. On his final
carry, he was kneed in the back. He went down as if nearly broken in
half, and had to be helped off the field. Examined by the team doctor, E. J. McDonnell, he kept repeating, "When am I going back in?"
Afterward, he felt faint, telling the writers, "Back up, I'm starting to
get weak." He was rushed to a hospital; his kidney was punctured.

Shula, relief all over his face in the afterglow of victory, sat in his
office, draining a champagne bottle, uttering words a coach can only
dream about. "We ran well and were almost perfect with our pass
defense," he said. "I can't think of anything we didn't do."[14] That may
have been a first for him: not a complaint anywhere. He needed to convince no one that the win was "specially sweet," but hardly surprising.
"The things we accomplished this year," he said, "there was no way we
could be denied this."

He went on sipping, hogging the only bottle of the stuff that the
Colts had brought with them for the occasion. Someone wanted to
know about the field he had worried about.

"It was perfect," he said.[15]

Having lifted the Browns monkey off his back, Shula was convinced
that he had turned the corner for good, that he had coached, as the
title of *Sports Illustrated*'s game story put it, THE GAME THAT GOT RID
OF THE FRUSTRATION. Further underlining the trope of the Colts as

blue-collar leviathans, the story called them "The Irresistible Ones," a quality few had seen in Don Shula. Which might explain why he was practically giddy during the two-week interval before the NFL-AFL Championship Game, which many still preferred to call it rather than the seemingly nonprofound Super Bowl. By any name, it was sure to be the cherry on top of a season already defined and crowned. When the team arrived back in Baltimore, 10,000 fans were waiting on the tarmac at Friendship Airport, where some broke down fences to get close to them. No one in the crowd, or on the plane, gave much thought to the assumed formality of the next game and the team they would meet.

That, of course, was Weeb Ewbank's New York Jets—who, despite "Broadway" Joe Namath's gifted arm and the sybaritic theatrics that endeared him to his generation and Madison Avenue mad men, were regarded more lightly than the AFL's first two sacrificial lambs, the Kansas City Chiefs and Oakland Raiders. As Rick Volk remembered, with the contest in Miami, the Colts all but substituted this game for the usual Runner-Up Bowl, a semi-official vacation in the sun. Aside from maniacs like Curtis and Matte—the latter of whom, asked if he would play in the game, said he would play even with a broken leg— Volk said, "It felt like an exhibition game with a $15,000 paycheck [for each winning player]. Shula tried to tell us not to let up, that the NFL was depending on us, and he worked us hard. But he couldn't really sell it. Shit, I can recall that week the biggest issue for some of those guys was where to go to dinner and get some drinks. The mental preparation wasn't there," despite Shula's usual hectoring.

The point spread opened at 18 and pretty much stayed there. Word was that NFL elders now regretted the merger plan, and that it might be better to do some tinkering, maybe sprinkle AFL teams into the unified league rather than maintaining the identity of the junior league as the American Football Conference. That way, two old-guard NFL teams could still play for the title—which seemed a good possibility in any case, since, to balance the new league, the NFL would soon pay Carroll Rosenbloom $3 million to place the Colts in the AFC's

East Division, while the Browns and Steelers were to move into the AFC Central.

All this overlooked, or ignored, that, aside from Shula, there were arguably better coaches in the AFL, with the likes of Ewbank, Sid Gillman, Lou Saban, Hank Stram—and Paul Brown, who, as a way back into the game, paid $10 million for the AFL's expansion Cincinnati Bengals. Then, too, Namath was no simple party boy, but a wily, ferocious competitor who had endured a broken jaw the previous season and not missed a game of that or the Jets' 11–3 season of '68. With a more conservative game plan instituted by Ewbank, he threw 100 fewer passes than in '67, when he had over 4,000 passing yards but 28 interceptions. Gutsy indeed was how Namath led his team from behind in a savage AFL title game, firing a 65-yard bomb to old dog Don Maynard, then a short bullet to Maynard in the end zone to beat Al Davis's Raiders 27–23. The Jets also had a smallish but smart defense that gave up the fewest yards in the league.

Shula respected Ewbank, but the press now billed this game as a grudge match that would surely end badly for Weeb. Shula would say no such thing, but if that was to be the theme, so be it. Yet he had no real context for fully evaluating the Jets. Playing in Namath's glittery shadow, fullback Matt Snell and halfback Emerson Boozer could be overlooked, though their roles were vital. Similarly, it was impossible to gauge how strong the offensive and defensive lines were by their success against other AFL teams. The Jets had 11 AFL Pro Bowlers, but beyond Namath, few NFL fans knew much about defensive ends Gerry Philbin and Verlon Biggs, defensive tackle John Elliott, or offensive tackle Winston Hill and guard Dave Herman.

Said Volk: "They had talent, we could see that. But when you've put in a tremendous amount of work, you've just run the Cleveland Browns out of their own stadium, and you're reading that you're the greatest team of all the time, how seriously are you going to be working that hard against a team from a league the Packers treated like amateurs?"

In their hubris, the Colts told themselves that watching the films was counterproductive, because it made them too confident—the exact same thing the Jets were telling themselves about watching the Colt films. To them, Shula's men were the perfect avatars of the old, sclerotic league, led by a quarterback even less mobile than Namath and who was never pressured. Ewbank told his boys the majesty of the NFL was bullshit, a Potemkin village propped up by the ghostly pillars of Vince Lombardi. He wanted the Jets to keep that to themselves, to let the Colts believe they were too good to care about the game. But one player wasn't willing to keep his lip zipped.

10

SOUR

When the teams got to Miami a week before Super Bowl III, the Colts came off the plane in Shula-mandated ties and sports jackets, the Jets off theirs in groovy, '60s-chic leisure attire, Joe Namath in his customary bell-bottom slacks, white belt and white Gucci loafers. While Shula banned any unplanned contact with the media, the shambling, ample-nosed Namath—an odd sort of sex symbol (it must have been the blue eyes)—was soon inviting writers and photographers to join him one hot afternoon as he draped himself, clad in a bathing suit, on a lounge chair by the Galt Ocean Mile Hotel pool, shades over his eyes, glass of something not ginger ale in his hand, reminding Tex Maule of Dean Martin "in his relaxed confidence and the droop of his heavy-lidded eyes."[1]

He was openly hostile to what he called "NFL reporters," repelling questions with his own soliloquies. He spoke of Johnny Unitas as his childhood hero as if he were talking about a dinosaur, citing Unitas's "crew-cut" and "high-top shoes," contrasted by Namath's longish locks and famous low-cut white shoes. He said Earl Morrall would be the "third-string quarterback on the Jets," and that "there are maybe five or six better quarterbacks than Morrall in the AFL." The topper: "We're a better team than Baltimore." A couple days later, Namath was in a Fort

Lauderdale restaurant, Jimmy Fazio's. Lou Michaels—whose younger brother Walt was the Jets' defensive backfield coach—and Dan Sullivan came in. Seeing the burly kicker, Namath began a woofing match, shouting, "We're gonna kick the shit out of you, and I'm gonna do it." Michaels's comeback was, "I wish I had one minute with you outside."[2]

The spat escalated, with each arguing about who was the better Catholic, and who took better care of his mother—an argument Shula could have joined in if he'd been there.[3]

Three days before the game, honored by the Miami Touchdown Club at the Playhouse, a downtown banquet hall, Namath made his famous, Ali-like intonation, "Were gonna win the game. I guarantee it," which was provoked when Michaels, in the back of the room, heckled him with his own guarantee of victory. Namath's bold bravado got scant notice at first. Shula, like most sportswriters—in a poll of 55 writers covering the game, 49 picked the Colts—snickered. "Joe's the 837th guy Louis has threatened," he said, "and if he'd punched him, he'd have been the 30th guy he'd decked."[4]

Shula had more on his mind, needing to keep up his team's intensity with all the disruptive headlines and questions about being such a prohibitive favorite. He held closed-door workouts all week away from the circus, up in Boca Raton, and enforced an 11 p.m. curfew at the Hilton hotel. He avoided giving the Jets any bulletin-board fodder, even saying the Jets had a defense on par with the Lombardi Packers and had the edge at quarterback, Namath being "the best pure passer in the game" and "a tremendous competitor."[5] The only Colt to break rank, Bill Curry, said his team had played "ten or twelve teams" as good as the Jets, which hardly seemed a boast as much as a simple fact. Yet Namath's takeover of the pregame publicity unnerved the Colts. Morrall was offended at being openly insulted by an opposing quarterback, especially after what he had just accomplished. So was Shula.

"I don't see how Namath can rap Earl," he said, holding his temper. "How can he rap a guy who did all the things Earl did for us?"[6]

It was easy enough for the Colts to pity Namath for the destruction they were sure to wreak on him. Said Volk: "How could you take him seriously? That whole Broadway Joe thing, the wearing pantyhose. [Actually, Namath did that commercial in 1974.] We didn't wanna kill him, but we really wanted to beat him."[7] But, in a broader view, Namath did what no one else could have for his league: he broadened the scope and context of the game beyond the field, to an arena the Colts were not equipped to compete in. Paul Zimmerman would later recall "the circus atmosphere surrounding Weeb Ewbank's Jets versus Shula's buttoned-up and businesslike Colts," but it went farther than that. To old-guard types, Namath was subversive, a label worn by many simply for expressing different opinions than most.

The *Washington Post*'s longtime columnist Shirley Povich wrote, tellingly, that Shula "can't escape the Jets-Joe Namath syndrome." He noted that Shula stammered when asked how he would handle Namath if he coached him, saying only that he met him once and that he seemed "a nice guy." Of course, Shula never would have put up with what Weeb did, and was privately critical of Ewbank's permissiveness—some real irony, given Ewbank's Colt reign—whose manner of discipline, wrote Povich, "bordered on a musical appeal of 'Oh, promise me. . . .'"[8]

Adding context to these cultural shadings was that all of this was happening eight days before Richard Nixon would be sworn in and begin compiling an enemies list of imagined subversives, perhaps Namath among them. Though some Colts bridled at the notion they were too square to be hip, Shula only made that image resonate further. The onetime FDR and JFK-worshiping union man turned well-heeled Nixon supporter believed his generation did more than talk; they won, while spoiled Baby Boomers only complained. It had to tickle him that he could shut up the loudest one. Maybe it tickled him a bit too much.

Not that he prepared with any less meticulousness, and with a warning to his team that the Jets weren't exactly a semi-pro team and needed to be taken very seriously. Mostly, he feared the Namath-Maynard connection. The latter, a prickly former NFL reject who had played for the AFL's New York franchise since it was the Titans in 1960, had speed and cunning. But he had not caught as many passes in '68 as the other

Jet wideout, George Sauer Jr., the anti-establishment son of a former NFL player who was then the GM of the Boston Patriots. Cerebral and reliable, he was a clone of Ray Berry in running precise patterns and holding on to passes, earning first-team All-Pro in the AFL two straight years. Shula figured his zone defense would blanket Sauer, but Maynard's speed could beat them. And he was skeptical that Maynard, as the injury report said, had injured a hamstring in the Raider win, believing Ewbank was trying to play with his head.

Ewbank feared little about the Colts. He prepped his defense to ignore the run, swarm Morrall, and clamp down on Richardson, Orr, and Mackey. The Jet defensive backs were an opportunistic lot, intercepting 28 passes. Within the NFL bubble, though, arrogance ruled. Maule, who had worked as a publicist for two NFL teams, typed his verdict of the game in advance, writing, "The pro football championship of the world was rather definitely decided on a mushy field in Cleveland on Dec. 29."[9] Of Namath, Maule sneered that he had signed with the AFL because he was too "scared" to "excel against the best." His prediction: Colts 43, Jets 0. And the patron saint of the NFL? Vince Lombardi had no doubt. The Jets' chances were, he said, "infinitesimal."[10]

Shula worried what that kind of talk would do to his men. But not too much. One writer found him "in a merry mood" that week. Seeing a magazine with a picture of him clad so nattily in Cleveland, he passed the magazine around and said, "I bet I get some offers for modeling. You'll have to do something with that nose . . . not imposing enough."[11] Even so, he was every reporter's worst interview—even those who knew him well. Bob Maisel, comparing Shula's press conferences to Ewbank's garrulous ones, wrote: "He injects humor . . . but his answers are much more to the point and businesslike. There is no reminiscing, no bringing up names from the past. . . . Ask a question and he hits you right between the eyes with his answer. It's concise, orderly, logical."[12] Just like his team.

Carroll Rosenbloom had been praising Shula for the job he'd done that season without his star quarterback, ready to conclude right now that hiring him was an act of genius. Shula, he said, wasn't just the best current coach, but maybe the best ever. Anticipating such, he had given Shula the title of vice-president, though without stock in the team. As Shula recalled:

> He said he hoped that as long as he lived and that as long as he owned the Baltimore Colts, he would never have to look for another coach. There was a lot of warmth in his voice and there wasn't any reason why I should doubt his sincerity. It was a tremendous moment and I was touched by [it]. At that moment I couldn't possibly envision the day we wouldn't be together.[13]

Hours before the game, he and Rosenbloom strode around the field in the empty Orange Bowl. Ewbank was doing the same thing, and when their paths crossed, Rosenbloom grandly invited him to the Colts' postgame victory party. Whether this was an intentional dig, or just a too-little-thought-out attempt at collegiality, Weeb, hardly believing what he heard, walked away without a word. Still steaming, Ewbank would send his team out for the game with the exhortation "Let's have our own victory party!" At that same moment in the other locker room, Shula—this time wearing a blue windbreaker, as if the game was no more important than a scrimmage—had no rousing words.

"He wasn't a rah-rah guy; he didn't want us so high we'd forget what we had to," said Volk. "It was basically, you know, 'Let's go get 'em.' It was supposed to be that easy."

It was overcast in Miami, a cool, humid 66 degrees. The pro wrestling–style theatrics of the week swelled ticket sales to 75,389, about the same as the year before, when the game was also played in the Orange Bowl. More importantly, TV viewership would also hold, garnering over 41 million viewers and a 36 Nielsen rating, a 30-second ad selling for $55,000. (The 2017 game was seen by 72 million, and the same ads sold for $5 million.) The formalities done, the Colts took the ball first and moved easily to the Jet 19, but Michaels—still unnerved?—shanked a field goal. A few plays later, Namath heaved one long for Maynard, who beat the deep zone. He overthrew him by a few inches, but, according to Namath, it spooked the Colt defense into covering Maynard even more tightly, leaving room for Sauer.

Ewbank and Namath believed they could easily exploit the under-side of the Colts' strong-side rotating zone going to the possession guy, Sauer, which became more doable when Volk, on the second play of the game, collided head on with Snell, nearly knocking Volk cold. He would be given smelling salts and was cleared by the team doctor to return to the game after a few series. Namath and Sauer took note of his wooziness. But none of this would have mattered had the Colts not bumbled early, when they had the Jets on the run. After a scoreless opening quarter, Morrall got them to the Jet four. He aimed one over the middle for Tom Mitchell. The ball caromed high off his shoulder pad, and cornerback Randy Beverly dove and grabbed it at the back of the end zone. That preceded an 80-yard Jet drive that ended when, from the four, Snell rumbled around left end and sliced past Dennis Gaubatz into the end zone. After both teams missed field goals, Matte broke a 58-yard run to get deep into Jet territory. Morrall then aimed one for Richardson on the foot of the end zone, but aging cornerback Johnny Sample—who had been cut by the Colts after their two cham-pionship years and blamed Shula and the NFL for allegedly blackball-ing him—crept in to pick it off at the two.

A pattern was forming. Snell was pounding yardage behind savage blocking by Boozer, ultimately running 30 times, most of his carries against the right side of the Colt defense, where Braase and Miller were decimated. And with the protection of the offensive line, as well as his uncanny recognition of nearly every Colt blitz and stunt, Namath could take a quick drop and throw a daggerlike pass to Sauer—who would snare eight, only one of which, for 39 yards, went deep. He also hit Snell four times out of the backfield for 40 yards, halfback Bill Mathis thrice for 20.

Namath's command of his own offense, and the Colts' defense, was such that he called no plays in the huddle; rather, he'd get to the line, see the lay of the land, and call it then. It was surgical, classic old-style football—"one of the most masterful play-calling jobs I've ever seen," wrote Paul Zimmerman years later. It also kept the defense fresh. As the game wore on, Morrall could barely see blue Colt jerseys downfield—not even one that was left so free that he could have walked the ball to it. On the Jet 41, with 25 seconds left in the half, Shula got funky, calling a flea-flicker, with Matte taking the handoff, running a few steps, then tossing it back to Morrall. During the season, this play worked perfectly against the Falcons, with Orr making an easy catch at the goal line. And now, too, the Jet secondary bit on the fake, leaving Orr ridiculously open, frantically waving his arms for Morrall to throw him the ball in the end zone. Calling the game for NBC, Curt Gowdy shouted, "All alone is Jimmy Orr!" However, Morrall inexplicably sailed a pass down the middle for Jerry Hill, but strong safety Jim Hudson cut in front of him and intercepted.

Recalled Volk: "Earl didn't want to make an excuse, but a marching band was right behind where Jimmy was, getting ready for the halftime show. Earl lost Jimmy in the crowd of blue band uniforms and went for Jerry. Something like that doesn't happen on a good day."

Shula, whose grim, tight-jawed slow burns became a constant on the broadcast, knew he was in a dogfight of his own making. At halftime, he upbraided his men for losing their cool and deviating from the game plan. He could have inserted Unitas to give the team a shot of adrenaline, but figured that would be panicking, and insulting to Morrall. Unitas, for his part, believed Morrall didn't have it and that only he could save the season. On the sideline, he looked highly agitated when Matte fumbled on the first drive of the second half and the Jets kept on churning out long drives. With three minutes left in the third, they held a 13–0 lead. As the poet and longtime Colt fan Ogden Nash penned sadly, the Colts, "like the Florida snow that melts, seemed to have trickled somewhere else."[14]

At that point, Morrall was 6-for-17 for 71 yards, with 3 picks. *Now*

Shula motioned to Unitas to warm up, the sight of which titillated the crowd and the press. In he came, wobbling on his gimpy legs. It was a sight that Namath said scared him to death. But, with twilight casting a gloom over the field, Unitas's first two passes fell incomplete. After a punt, the Jets notched another field goal, making it 16–0 early in the fourth quarter. Unitas next got the Colts to the Jet 25, but a pass for Orr was picked off again by Beverly in the end zone. His weak arm and the Jet defense held him to 11-for-24 for 110 yards. Still, with three and a half minutes left, he led a long drive that was capped by a short Hill TD run to make it 16–7. The Colts recovered the onside kick, but the Jets held and ran out the clock, whereupon many in the crowd, not sure if they were dreaming, just stared as the Jets jumped on each other, though Ewbank begged off being carried on some of his men's shoulders.

A grim-faced Shula met Ewbank at midfield and put an arm around his old boss, who in his suit and Jets baseball cap came up to his shoulder, but stood tall on this day, the second coach after Paul Brown to win titles in different leagues. Namath, still the center of attention, was briefly congratulated by a gracious Unitas, then jogged off the field, index finger raised in the air. He was the game's MVP, despite Snell's then–Super Bowl record 121 yards rushing and Sauer's 133 yards receiving. His stats—17-for-28 for 206 yards, no interceptions—seemed secondary to the guarantee he had backed up. Inside the locker room, with the Jets bitching that the NFL had not put any champagne in the room for them to celebrate with, Namath felt he had to clarify his criticism of Morrall, not for Morrall's sake, but for that of the coach he had taken pains not to malign.

"I'm sorry that Don Shula took what I said about Morrall as a rap," he said. "I only meant it as a statement of fact."

In the other locker room, the mood was funereal. The Colts sat with their heads bowed, many just staring. Shula, who felt like the blood had been drained from him, mouthed the exact opposite of what he'd said in Cleveland two weeks earlier: "I don't think we did anything right."

Of Namath, he said, tersely, "He beat us. He beat our blitz three or four times and we beat him only once." Then, pulling out and dusting off the civil code of his generation, he stared straight ahead and said, "It's just a shame for us to face the winter after all of the good things that happened to us before today, but we've just got to be men."[15] As for holding back on Unitas, he said he felt he "owed it to Earl" to stick with him as long as he did. Of Morrall not seeing Orr? Pause, then, "Bad judgment." He finished saying what he never imagined he would have to.

"We realized what was at stake. We didn't represent our league or ourselves."

The veterans echoed him. Braase said, "We let down the entire National Football League. . . . My pride was bent. They just walked out there and beat us. They didn't beat us physically. They just beat us." Billy Ray Smith said, "When you're No. 1, you're the best, but when you're No. 2, you're nothing." Not seeing the irony, he seethed, "We played like an AFL team." Unitas, outwardly, was stoic. "You always hate to lose," he said. "But a football player can't feel sorry for himself," though he couldn't help but note that "I moved 'em . . . but time ran out on us." Morrall was pouring all the blame on himself. Someone congratulated him for a great season. "Thanks," he said, "but I'm sorry I can't agree with you."[16] Alex Hawkins, having played his last game for Shula, wept as he sat on his stool.

The aftermath of the game was every bit as much Namath's as the prelude had been. There were 1,290 press credentials issued for the game, a sample size large enough to influence public opinion by shamelessly serenading Namath in the next day's papers, many splattering headlines of the "stupendous upset" on front pages in type bigger than news such as HANOI REJECTS NEW U.S. BID. Turning on a dime, Maule called the Jets quarterback the "folk hero of the new generation [and] insouciant youth in the Jet Age," and that "the era of John Unitas ended and the day of Broadway Joe and the mod quarterback began." The *New York Times*'s Robert Lipsyte, elevating him to the level of the heavyweight champ still in exile for refusing to fight in that jungle war, reminded readers that the then Cassius Clay had beaten

Sonny Liston only a few miles away.[17] Namath was far less significant than Ali, but profound in the arc of team sports. St. Vince knew how lucky he was to escape Shula's pitfall. It felt unmistakable that something new had officially arrived. Tom Wicker, the astute *New York Times* political columnist, wrote that the Jets upset gave comfort to all challengers to the status quo, "their tattered faith [in change] preserved [and saved] from imminent extinction."[18]

Namath's rebel status, and relevance, would last only until the Jets went south and he quit in '77, his body ravaged. By then, he was jejune within his own generation, and many rungs below Don Shula on the distinction ladder. But even decades later, in his 70s, he was still riffing, "If we had played 10 times the Colts might've won one."[19] But Shula, too, would be forever synonymous with January 12, 1969, as the foil. No one seemed to know this more than he as he exited the Orange Bowl, wearing a hunted look and probably hoping never to see that house of horrors again.

Shula's longest day held more horrors in store. He had just gotten back to the Hilton when he heard a woman screaming in panic in the corridor outside his room. He opened the door and saw Rick Volk's wife, Charlene, calling for help. Shula ran into the room, saw Volk lying in the bathtub, his body wracked by seizures, and summoned Dr. McDonnell. Volk had been knocked out of the game late in the fourth quarter, barely conscious and dragged off the field by teammates. He had made it back to the hotel, but soon fell ill. With Shula holding him down, the doctor reached into Volk's mouth, keeping him from swallowing his tongue. An ambulance was called, and when Volk was taken to a hospital emergency room, Shula rode with him. Volk was taken to the intensive care unit, and when word got back to the team, they milled around the lobby, waiting for some good news from the hospital, where Shula would stay with Charlene through the night. It was determined that Volk had actually suffered two concussions during the game, and blood was seeping into his brain. "For a while," Shula said, "it was touch and go."[20]

The next morning, Volk was still in the ICU when a shaken Shula returned to the hotel for a final press conference, saying he was thinking more of his cornerback than the game, which he would later write made him feel "sick" and was "the darkest day of my coaching career." Happily, Volk, who received flowers from Namath, was soon released, though he would not fully recover for six weeks. But for Shula, the malaise about letting down the NFL never eased. And in the short term, the most important immediate consequence was that he had an entirely different relationship with Carroll Rosenbloom.

The owner, in a snit about becoming the first NFL owner to lose to the AFL, sounded an apocalyptic tone days after the game. "It's still like a bad dream to me," he mourned. "I can't sleep. If we don't get together and get our vindication we don't deserve to have a club. I am 60 years old. When will I ever get close enough for a Super Bowl again? We just must start right now to be better, in every aspect."[21] Only days after swearing allegiance to Shula, he said that he was not "big on coaches," who he insisted had less effect on teams than the players. His obligatory, throw-in paean that Shula "is as fine a coach as there is in football" seemed canceled out by his whine that "something happens every year, so we must be doing something wrong."

With this tension suddenly between them, they spent a fleeting few minutes at Rosenbloom's forlorn "victory" party consoling each other. But after reading the owner's turgid comments in the paper, Shula rang him up to ascertain whether he still supported him, and was stunned that the flighty owner was angered at being put on the spot. As he recalled: "He snapped at me that he had a right to say or think whatever he wanted to and was bitterly disappointed by the loss. . . . It was obvious to me that our relationship was beginning to deteriorate."[22]

Though no one other than Dorothy knew it, Shula had begun preparing himself to break free if the right opportunity came along. For now, he kept his feelings hidden, but they were percolating. Looking back 40 years later, long after C.R. was gone and Shula was out of football, he said:

I loved Baltimore—the people, the fans and everything that Colts football stood for. But Rosenbloom's New York buddies never let him forget [the loss], and he never let me forget it. If we had won that game, and continued to win, I certainly wouldn't have gone. I'd still be in Baltimore, eating crab cakes.[23]

That was a case of Shula "going there," to areas most football people avoided out of respect to Rosenbloom. His sly phrase "New York buddies" was fraught with dark meaning, a veiled reference to Rosenbloom's gambling cronies who had bet heavily on the Colts to cover the engorged spread. Art Donovan helped fill in the blanks when he once breezily ventured that Ordell Braase told him that the Super Bowl game was the day when "the Sicilian frogmen finally got to Rosey." If so, it meant "Rosey" had violated the pledge he'd given Rozelle, by doing the exact same thing that had gotten him into trouble back in '58. And perhaps this had something to do with Rosenbloom holding his full fire against Shula, knowing the coach was hip to it all and could create big trouble for him.

In truth, Shula's moral code, which made allowances for the conduct of an owner like this—and, over time, that of some of his players— would have precluded him from ratting out Rosenbloom, as he did for decades. But the implied threat otherwise might have served him well, at least in the short run. To be certain, winning the NFL title as the Colts did was no small matter, and firing "the best coach in football" for one clinker, as enormous as it was, would have been exceedingly petty. Thus, Shula was insulated for the time being from the avalanche of off-season criticism, during which one Maryland state senator grumbled, "I'm disgusted . . . The Colts let me down so hard." Another pontificating pol, a House delegate, added, "Shula has the best winning record in football—and the worst record in big games." A sign in a downtown office building read, "Due to unforeseen circumstances, the start of the Colt dynasty has been delayed." On an ad on a bus that featured Morrall saying, "How to be number one—you've got to hang in there," someone crossed out "in there." Callers to sports talk radio shows yammered about the game being fixed by New York mob types. Some Colts chose to lay low in Miami for a while rather than coming home.[24]

The most peeved, though, was Unitas, who beneath his stoic posing was sure he would have avoided Morrall's blunders and pulled it out had he been sent in earlier. He was livid that his brief cameo had made him look not heroic, but pitiful. For that, he held Shula in contempt. The coach was never far from his mind. Late in his life, Unitas let out the epitaph of Shula he had long chosen to use in private.

"I wouldn't walk across the street," he said, "to piss down Don Shula's throat if he was on fire."[25]

11

"THE BIGGEST THING SINCE BUBBLE GUM"

Many around Baltimore, and the NFL, wondered how Shula could possibly recover from the stain of the biggest upset any sport had ever experienced. Dorothy took the heat even more personally than he. When an expletive-laced "fan" letter criticizing him came to their mailbox, she couldn't sit idly by. Somehow tracing the sender's phone number, she called him, posing as a law enforcement agent and putting a good scare into the guy, threatening to come and arrest him.[1] All Shula could do was press on, cloaked in shame and with Unitas's once-golden arm rusting. Because the tendons in his right elbow would further weaken, after his career he would need to use his left hand to write. Yet he would be Shula's starting quarterback again in '69. The would-be hero of the previous season, Earl Morrall, the reigning MVP, went back to his accustomed spot on the bench. Not that this made Unitas any less irritable.

Shula had lived a charmed existence, held unaccountable for all the postseason failure. Even now, the goodwill he had built up shielded him. While there was predictable second-guessing about him keeping Unitas on the bench too long, among other grievances, no writers or fans were calling for his head. One letter to the *Sun* read, "Mr. Shula worked hard to make a team that is a real team [that] I'm sure will be right next year."[2] Still, the sorrow and pity seemed to cling to him, and was intensified by a sort of guilt by association when the similarly favored Orioles lost to the "Amazing" New York Mets in the '69 World Series; such titanic failure seemed somehow endemic to the descent of Baltimore itself. The Orioles' manager, Earl Weaver, a sort of blustery mini-Shula, would at least be able to say he broke this paranormal grip the very next season. But for Shula, there was a subtle difference in the way his men would see and play for him. Invincibility didn't drip off him; vulnerability did. In fact, Shula would confide to Howard Schnellenberger that he spent hours in church praying to get past the Jet infamia. "He was confused about why it happened, why God put him through that," Schnellenberger said.[3]

Just getting past that winter was a task. Shula and Dorothy got away, taking a vacation in Mexico, but the wounds were raw. Blaming the Baltimore writer who reported C.R.'s caustic remarks about him, Shula gave few of the local beat men his time; instead, he gave an interview to his old Cleveland bobo Chuck Heaton during the league's March winter meetings in Palm Springs, California. "It was tough for a while," he said of the post–Super Bowl malaise. "People [won't] let me forget it." Heaton's story was helpfully titled SHULA'S STAR STILL RISING.[4] But the past would always be present, keeping his insecurities close to the surface. During the winter meetings, he was at the pool at the El Mirador Hotel when a page came over a speaker: "Call for Don Shuler."

Looking for a phone, he half-laughed, half-grunted.

"If that was Vince Lombardi," he said, jaw clenched, "they wouldn't have mispronounced his name."

As it happened, Lombardi had returned to coaching that '69 season, as the new czar of the Washington Redskins. No one doubted that he would reclaim his imprimatur. Shula, meanwhile, approached the season searching for redemption, acknowledging, "We have to start all over again." Not kidding himself that his "all-time great" defense could stand pat, he used a second-round draft pick to take Miami's mayhem-making, two-time All-American linebacker Ted Hendricks, who at six foot seven and 220 pounds had been anthropomorphically nicknamed "The Mad Stork," or "Kick 'Em in the Head Ted." The second pick in that round brought a replacement for Bobby Boyd, who had retired at only 31, ranking third all-time in interceptions: Texas A&M corner Tommy Maxwell; both would start on an otherwise veteran squad. Shula and Arnsparger, a milquetoast-looking guy often mistaken for a schoolteacher, brainstormed a new zone scheme. "We called it a double zone, which they call two-deep now," said Rick Volk. "The safeties covered half the deep zone and everyone else was in shifting middle zones. It worked because Hendricks was so tall and fast, but it was really Curtis at middle linebacker that made it work. He could go from one zone to another on the same play, and even cover deep. To use a middle linebacker deep, I'd never seen that, but I sure as hell saw it after that, all over the league."[5]

As the last pre-merger season neared, Rosenbloom stopped kvetching. Shula's contract, which was structured to renew every five years, still had four years to run, and for all his diffidence about coaches, C.R. still needed him. The problem for Shula, who himself was still under 40, was that he had a geriatric team not unlike the Packers, who had come apart all at once. He also lost Chuck Noll to the Steelers, leaving Shula feeling much the way he had left Blanton Collier, saying how much he hated losing a "fine young man" to a better job, but in the lurch because of it. Shula moved in Bobby Boyd as defensive backfield coach. Braase and Szymanski had also retired, but still 11 Colts were 30 or over, and Unitas was 36, while Morrall was 35. Morrall contemplated retiring as well, but Shula talked him out of it. While many of the holdovers were in their prime, a free-spirited newbie like Hendricks could feel like he was walking into a corporate boardroom. As he would later say, the Colts were "an old team, very set in their ways." Shula had not drafted or traded for a young quarterback, putting his full bet on winning now.

The Colts were favorites to win it all. But Shula was being henpecked by doubters. Al Davis, still fighting the expired war between the leagues, popped off in late August that the Colts were "not that great a team," and that "their defense is suspect." Shula shot back that Davis was trying to "copy Joe Namath's psychology."[6] Yet slings and arrows followed the Colts into the season, with Shula feeling very much alone and on the spot, cold-shouldered by NFL executives. And it would only get worse.

Though Unitas was back, he took a hit in preseason that left his knee throbbing. Mackey, too, hurt a knee while Shula experimented with him at fullback. Multiple other injuries hit the team as Shula was refitting his defense, with two new starters at linebacker, Hendricks and second-year man Bob Grant, and two more in the secondary, Maxwell and third-year pro Charlie Stukes. A strange hybrid of tried and true and untested, the Colts swept all six preseason games and opened the season at home against the Rams. Leading 17–10, with Unitas throwing touchdowns to Mitchell and Orr, they crumbled. Unitas was intercepted three times, Roman Gabriel threw three touchdowns, and George Allen walked off with a 27–20 win.

Shula could brush that off as a wake-up call. But the next week, in Minnesota, he had no explanation for what he saw before his eyes. "Indian Joe" Kapp, who threw the feeblest-looking passes known to man, cranked up and administered the worst beating a Shula defense would ever endure. He threw for seven touchdowns and 449 yards. It was 31–7 at the half, 52–14 at the end. Unitas, after going 8-for-22, gave way to Morrall, who threw a touchdown and two more picks. The Colts were outgained 538–195. Shula looked like a ton of bricks had landed on him.

"This is the first defeat since I came here that I'm ashamed of myself and the football team," he said. "Hate to be connected with any of it." Accepting blame, he went on, "It's my job to get them up for the game [and] they weren't ready to play." Then, "I'm going to have to take a long, hard look at every phase," even using the word *quit*, and that he would evaluate everyone. "Something has to be done and it has to be done now."

Confirming fans' fears, the team still seemed hungover from the

Super Bowl, trapped in a crisis of confidence. Had Rosenbloom been in a mood, Shula might not have made it to the third game. But that was when he did some of the best coaching of his life. Against the Falcons, the Colts led early, only to fall behind 14–7. Then rookie Jim Duncan ran a kickoff back 92 yards to tie it, and in the fourth quarter, Unitas, who completed 18 of 24 passes, led a drive that ended with a six-yard touchdown toss to Mackey, winning it 21–14. Against the Eagles a week later, they never led until, again in the last quarter, a long drive and a short TD run by Matte gave them a 24–20 win, Unitas passing for 250 yards but also throwing two more picks. They beat the Saints 30–10, lost to the mediocre 49ers, blew away Lombardi's Redskins 41–17, and topped the Packers 14–6, even with three more Unitas picks.

The Colts were 5–3, but shaky, Unitas throwing so poorly that Shula yanked him in the 49er game for Morrall, who went down with an injury. Having refused to draft a quarterback, Shula had no third man, and Unitas came back and threw a touchdown to Perkins for a late lead, but John Brodie pulled it out with a TD pass to Jimmy Thomas. That was pretty much how the season went, the Colts on their heels. In November, Shula seemed ready to concede. "It looks like we are out of it," he said.

To Cameron Snyder, Shula seemed "strangely unemotional." Indeed, in his mind, Shula may have had a foot out the door. As Volk said, "We were taking a lot of heat, and I'm not sure Shula thought he'd be around to fix it, or wanted to be, because he knew Carroll wouldn't have any patience." Snyder defended Shula as the "whipping boy" for ills left unaddressed by management. Yet by midseason, Snyder wrote in a mock memo to Colt fan Spiro Agnew, "If you don't want your name associated with a loser, please stop following your favorite team, the Baltimore Colts."[7]

Bobby Boyd said years later that Shula was a dead man walking that season, never able to shake off the Jet loss. Before the Ram finale, Snyder reported "rumors of [Shula] leaving," which may have been fed by Shula himself in confidence. Openly, though, he dismissed them, saying, "I am perfectly satisfied here." Only partly giving him the benefit of the doubt, Snyder opined:

> Shula isn't a devious man [but h]e would be silly, which he isn't, not to want a deal like Vince Lombardi got at Washington, which included a piece of the action. But the first to know . . . would be Carroll Rosenbloom, because Shula would tell him immediately.[8]

Shula may well have made such a demand to stick around, perhaps as a poison pill that Rosenbloom would surely reject, thus giving Shula a basis for leaving. If so, it was all kept on the downlow as the season played out. And the Colts didn't quit on him. "We really were ready to pack it in a few times," Volk said. "He wouldn't let us." While Unitas was never healthy, and put up stats he would have sneered at in the past—2,343 yards, 13 touchdowns, 20 interceptions, 64.0 passer rating—they lost only twice over the last eight games, gaining the fourth-most yards in the league. Even when a loss to Landry in Dallas in the penultimate game finished them, their record 7–5–1, Shula leaned on them to rough up the playoff-bound Rams in the finale on the coast, winning 13–10, holding Allen's team to 153 total yards.

An 8–5–1 season wasn't exactly a disaster, and wouldn't seem to have been fatal to Shula. In fact, Rosenbloom could still smell a championship if things broke right the next season. Shula, too, looked ahead with enthusiasm. "This is the team you'll see next year," he said, adding the Rams win "justified all our beliefs." Bill Curry was so taken with that game, he gushed, "Right now I feel like we've just won the world championship," which only seemed to signify how far the team had fallen. But Shula seemed overly sensitive to criticism. He had been writing an innocuous weekly column for the *Sun* at the same time that Bert Bell Jr., son of the late commissioner, who had quit a job in the Colt front office in '66, wrote a sports column. Shula believed Bell was taking shots at him.

"Bert," he told him, "I'll pay you $35 not to write the column."

When Bell refused, Shula gave the editors an ultimatum: him or me. They sided with Bell. In spite, Shula gave up the gig.[9] Other small things peeved him, and he was clearly seeking a way out of Baltimore. If the right offer came along, he was prepared to listen, even though he was under contract and risked opening himself to allegations of tampering. He was too smart not to know this, but in matters as profound as maintaining his lofty status and self-respect, morality was not a factor. At least not until he could get to the confessional.

Rosenbloom apparently had his own agenda: keeping Shula while having the license to embarrass him. Right after the turn of the decade, Shula and his assistants went to Mobile, Alabama, to coach the South team in the Senior Bowl. During practices that week, word broke that Rosenbloom had upgraded the role of the Colts' general manager, hiring Don Klosterman from the Houston Oilers.

The 40-year-old Klosterman, who had once backed up Otto Graham with the Browns and Bob Waterfield with the Rams before being partially paralyzed in a skiing accident, was a big mover and shaker among the AFL elite. Previously, as GM of the Kansas City Chiefs, he'd set them on the path to two Super Bowls—the second of which would come just a week after the Senior Bowl, when they demolished the Vikings. For Rosenbloom, Klosterman would ease the transition to the AFC. Shula, though, was either not quite ready to elevate the Colts' new conference to parity, or else just not keen on ceding any of his authority. When the owner felt him out about making the move, Shula said he didn't think Klosterman could be pried away from Houston. Rosenbloom swore he could do it, and made it official on January 7, three days before the Senior Bowl. By then, his work done, C.R. prepared to set sail on a cruise to the Far East with his wife, former lounge performer Georgia Frontiere. He left it to his son, Steve, whom Carroll had made president of the Colts, to introduce Klosterman at a press conference.

Asked how Shula and Klosterman would work together, Steve said each had his duties. Then, throwing in some ill-executed but telling humor, he added, "Of course we all know that the only reason

Shula was made a vice-president is that we needed one more person around to sign checks."[10] Shula was said to be "highly disturbed" by the comment.

The next day, after Carroll Rosenbloom and Klosterman flew to Mobile to observe the Senior Bowl game, a prickly Shula told C.R. what he thought of the remark. The owner insisted his son meant it as a joke, but said he understood why it bothered Shula. Even so, seeing the two poobahs together, Shula would later write in his memoir that he could see "major changes" ahead, and that "they knew what was going on," but he didn't. Shula's one-off as a college head coach was a wild affair, his quarterback, Louisiana Tech's Terry Bradshaw, and the West's Dennis Shaw conducting a shootout that ended in a 37–37 tie.

Shula then returned to Baltimore, still preferring to believe he had control of the football operation. He and Klosterman put their heads together for the late-January draft, in which, with their first-round pick, they agreed on TCU's bowling ball–shaped fullback Norm Bulaich, passing on the Heisman Trophy winner, Oklahoma fullback Steve Owens.

But if the coach expected comity, he was more optimistic than Harry Hulmes, who had been demoted to assistant general manager and then, only days after smiling for photos with Klosterman, quit to take the GM job with the Saints (later to spend 25 years in the Giants organization). Shula, too, felt demoted. After having represented the Colts at the league's annual winter meetings every year since becoming their coach, he was informed by Steve Rosenbloom that his presence at this year's meetings in Honolulu was not needed; Klosterman would go instead. Growing more wary of his own allies, Shula demanded that Steve phone his father so that he could hear from the horse's mouth just what his responsibilities were. As Shula recounted, the elder Rosenbloom again became incensed, telling him he was ungrateful despite "everything he had done for me." Shula called the one-sided conversation "one big continual tongue-lashing." As a sop, Rosenbloom said he would pay for him and Dorothy to stay a few days at the own-er's oceanfront club in Miami Beach. He ended the discussion seeming to dare Shula to quit, saying that if Shula had "decisions" to make, meaning leaving, to go ahead and make them. He did not say anything about giving him permission to do so, but to Shula, that seemed no reason to keep from doing it.

By early February, rumors were flying that Shula was on the way out. One had it that he would become the Packers' head coach, though how he could do that, or make any jump without Rosenbloom's permission, and perhaps compensation for the Colts, wasn't explained. A reporter sought out Dominic Olejniczak, the Packers' chairman of the board, at the winter meetings. He said, tongue in cheek, "Yeah, we got him."

More seriously, a strong clue came when Bill Arnsparger suddenly resigned for what were called "personal reasons," to accept a "business opportunity," which left open the possibility he could rejoin Shula with a different team. However, it was already getting a bit late for such a move. The draft had already taken place, and Shula later said he had received only one call from another team about his availability, identifying it only as "one of the stronger franchises."[11] If it was an AFL-cum-AFC team, he may have concluded by now that the parity between the former leagues, which was only proven when an anvil fell on Shula at the Orange Bowl, was indeed complete. Indeed, jumping to a native AFL team seemed like a smart move. After several conversations, however, he said the mystery team had decided to stay with its coach.

The truth was, he was desperate to get out, feeling "ignored and left behind." He might even have quit, walking away from the contract that suddenly felt like paid servitude, until he could plot his return. But something else had happened, seemingly out of the clear blue, when in mid-January, Bill Braucher, a sportswriter for the *Miami Herald* and a former teammate of Shula at John Carroll, called him with a most unusual query: Would he be interested in becoming coach of the Miami Dolphins? That one was really out of left field. All Shula knew about the Dolphins was that his old boss George Wilson, after being fired in Detroit, had taken the head coaching job there when the AFL expansion club began play in '66. Wilson had gone 15–39 in three years, and both he and the team went nearly unnoticed. Startled, Shula asked his old friend if he was somehow making him an offer.

"I have the authority to speak about it," Braucher replied, a clearly unethical role for a journalist who covered the team, and possibly in contravention of the league's tampering rules.[12]

As Braucher explained years later, he and Edwin Pope, the *Herald's* sports editor who also wrote a popular column, had been called into Dolphins owner Joe Robbie's office the day before. Robbie, unsatisfied with Wilson, was thinking big. He had already offered the head coaching job to Bear Bryant, who considered it but begged off. That made it possible for Shula to be the next to get the offer. Robbie, a highly personable man of Irish-Lebanese descent, had fronted an eight-man cartel of Lebanese-Americans, including the actor Danny Thomas and entrepreneur George Hamid, that bought the fledgling Dolphins in 1965 for an $8 million franchise fee to the AFL. He was a savvy business guy and pitchman, much like Rosenbloom, and was also a player in Democratic Party politics, having once made an unsuccessful run for governor of his native Minnesota and a confidant of Hubert Humphrey. Although he had seemingly waited too long to make a coaching change for 1970, he asked the two scribes who they thought would be a good coach to hire.

Pope's first suggestion: Don Shula. All three men knew he was bound contractually to the Colts, so Robbie asked Braucher to act as his beard. Desperate as he was, Shula listened.

"So Robbie is aware of it?" he asked Braucher.

"That's right."

"Tell him I'll call him in the morning."[13]

He did—technically a breach of league rules specifying that any initial contact by a team with an interest in another team's coach must be from management to management. Shula waded in deeper, asking about being given part ownership in the Dolphins, which Robbie said would be possible. Robbie asked how many more years he was signed for. Shula said three. "That wouldn't be a problem," Robbie replied. All this was treading on dangerous ground, and Shula's conscience kicked in—though not so much about Wilson being sacrificed. He told Robbie he had to talk first with Steve Rosenbloom and request permission to talk turkey with Robbie.

"What about Carroll?" Robbie asked.

Shula told him he was on his cruise, and "unavailable." But was this true? Was C.R. unavailable even by ship-to-shore radio, or telegram? Was a business mogul like him ever out of the loop? Or was it simply more fortuitous for Steve to be put on the spot and have to make the momentous decision to grant his coach permission to skip out, bare months before spring camp?

Whatever the case, the next day, Shula called Steve, whose snap decision was that he wouldn't stand in the way of his advancement. Shula then notified Robbie, and said he could contact Steve for confirmation. It's plausible that Steve acted this graciously because he did not believe the Dolphins, who operated on a shoestring playing in the sparsely attended Orange Bowl, could afford Shula, or that Shula would be eager to coach a team so unfulfilling. But Steve underestimated Robbie. A lawyer and lobbyist for the tobacco industry, he seemed to be able to raise other people's money—he had only ponied up $100,000 of his own for the partnership that bought the team, and then, as Al Davis did a few years later in becoming the Raiders' managing general partner, consolidated his power by systematically buying out the original partners. He had long-range plans to build a new stadium, so he could stop paying the city rent to use the Orange Bowl, and he was starting to recruit well-heeled donors for the project. And he was prepared to make Shula a very rich man.

Over the next few days, Robbie flew to Washington, D.C., to meet with Shula and his lawyer, David Gordon, at the Marriott. The pair then traveled to Miami to hunker down with Robbie at the chic Jockey Club. When Shula looked up from his table, he saw none other than Vince Lombardi at the bar, along with the New York restaurant owner Mike Manuche. He bade Vince to join him and Lombardi—who, unknown to most people, was dying of cancer—asked what Shula was doing in town. Shula lied that he was on vacation.

A deal in principle was reached the next day, and Shula flew back to inform the Colts. For that, however, Steve wouldn't do. He needed to give the word to Carroll Rosenbloom, who suddenly was available, after all. Shula recalled the owner acting "kind and understanding," echoing Steve's original judgment that he couldn't stand in the way of Shula moving on. Rosenbloom said he would talk to Robbie to give his official assent and to discuss proper compensation. That conversation only occurred on Wednesday, February 18, with Shula having been prematurely signed and about to be introduced by Robbie as his new head coach, regardless of when the Colts would assent. And Rosenbloom didn't make things any easier. He told Robbie that the latter would have to notify Pete Rozelle that he was giving permission for Shula to terminate his Colts contract, and had attached a new condition that precluded Shula from speaking with his Colt assistant coaches until a new head coach was named, so that they wouldn't flee to Miami. A joint statement was hurriedly released by the teams that day, but the issue of compensation was still to be worked out.

That afternoon, Shula, Dorothy, and Gordon, their plane fare to Miami picked up by Steve Rosenbloom, came to the Dolphins office to sign his contract, hours after Robbie fired Wilson, offering him a lesser role in the organization. Then, at the hastily arranged press conference in a side room at the Jockey Club, the beak-nosed, bespectacled Robbie read the statement that rocked the sport. "With mixed emotions," he began, "I announce that Don Shula is the new coach of the Dolphins after four highly satisfactory years of work by George Wilson."

The details were still under wraps, but they were impressive. The "handsome young" Shula, as the AP called him in its report, would be paid $70,000 a year for five years, $10,000 more than he'd been making with the Colts. He would also be a team vice-president and own a three percent stake in the team, which at the time was valued at $15 million, making his stock worth $450,000. The deal finally gave him the perks that put him on the same plane as Lombardi, if not quite the same level (when St. Vince sadly died soon after, on September 3, 1970, his salary was $110,000 a year and his Redskins shares worth half a million dollars). Still, Robbie acknowledged the obvious: he had conceded quite a bit to land his man, who he said would own "a sizable chunk of the club." Aware that his defection was thorny, Shula said that it had come about only because of "immediate and substantial interest" from Robbie, insisting, "The last two weeks have been murder. I weighed this deal from every angle." And: "I have regrets in leaving Baltimore and a fine owner in Carroll Rosenbloom and I regret leaving that fine ball club of young men."[14] In the end, it was business, not personal—"Being active in ownership while still coaching is something I've always wanted," even if he felt he needed to say "money certainly wasn't the decisive factor."

Because people were already blithely saying Shula had broken his contract, he made sure to point out that both Rosenblooms had given him permission to negotiate with Robbie. Putting a positive spin on it, he enthused that a new rivalry had been birthed, given that the two teams would play in the same division, as would the Jets, to meet twice each season starting that fall. "I expect the Baltimore-Miami rivalry will get pretty hot because of my move," he added. Playing down the hard feelings sure to come out of Baltimore, he sounded quite believably sad to be "leaving a great organization" that "treated me very well," as well as his friends and "a fine bunch of football players [who] I'm sure would enjoy beating me when we meet." He concluded that Miami "wants a winner," and that they would have one. "I don't have any magic formula. I'm not a finesse man. I've always been straightforward with my ball players and we'll depend on hard work." Watching his new coach slickly handle the delicate matter of his mercenary exercise, Robbie swore to the fan base he hoped to ignite, "This is a red-letter day for the Miami Dolphins." He repeated it more than once.

With beneficial timing, Shula was spared scrutiny and opprobrium in the Baltimore papers, as both the *Sun* and the *News American* had gone on strike on January 2, not to publish again for 74 days. In Miami, meanwhile, the papers were crackling. In the *Herald*, the headline DOLPHINS NAME SHULA COACH, GIVE HIM PART OWNERSHIP dwarfed lesser news such as NIXON REVEALS STRATEGY FOR PEACE IN '70S, 5 OF "CHICAGO SEVEN" GUILTY ON RIOT CHARGE, and UNIFORM INTEGRATION APPROVED BY SENATE. Finally free to reveal the details of the process that lured Shula to Florida, Ed Pope wrote in his column that an "acquaintance" of Robbie had recommended Shula—that man being himself. He made sure to say, not quite accurately, that the acquaintance "fulfill[ed] both legalities and protocol."[15] The other player in that plot, Bill Braucher, passed up self-congratulation to hail the new man with a column titled DON SHULA—DETERMINATION-PLUS.

But Pope's *Herald* writers were also reporting that the Dolphins players were hardly thrilled at the change. Luther Evans wrote that they were shocked that Wilson had been sacrificed after four years of slow progress. Quarterback Bob Griese said, "I hate to see George go." Middle linebacker Nick Buoniconti said it was like "losing a father."[16] Sensing this undercurrent, Shula insisted that replacing Wilson was "one of my biggest regrets" about taking the job. "The man I'm relieving is a personal friend." Wilson, for his part, gritted his teeth and said he wasn't blaming anyone for the loss of his job. And, in a moment of goodwill, Steve Rosenbloom said, "We're sorry to see Don go," but "it's our policy that, if anyone has a chance to better himself, never to stand in his way."

Still, the notion that he was a contract breaker rankled Shula to no end. Some in the press did provide cover for him, one writer wondering if Klosterman had been somehow responsible for his defection. When the *Sun* published again, Bob Maisel would boil it down to "Don simply got too fantastic an offer to turn down. . . . You can't blame him for accepting it. He was hemmed in here. He'll be missed." And, "If Don Shula isn't an honest man, then I'm a poor judge of character. [And] I feel sure Shula thought he was acting in accordance with the rules." Maisel also absolved Steve Rosenbloom for giving Shula permission, since Shula was going to sign that very day. "What could Rosenbloom say then except 'yes'. . . . If he said 'no,' he had a disgruntled coach on his hands."[17]

But now, some Colt players felt liberated to snipe at him. Don Shinnick said he felt betrayed that Shula hadn't put him back into the lineup after he missed four games with an injury. The most savage was John Mackey, who believed he had been jerked around by Shula during the backfield experiment. Mackey—who had just been named the first president of the NFL Players' Association and would sue the league over its restrictive free-agent policy known as the "Rozelle Rule," which subjected player movement to prohibitive compensation—let loose a jeremiad, calling Shula a "dictator" and "two-faced," and claiming that Shula had made Unitas a "puppet" and had "panicked" during the Super Bowl loss.

"I'm not a bit sorry he's gone," he said. "He thought he was the biggest thing since bubble gum."[18]

As wounded as Shula was by epithets, he turned the other cheek, praising Mackey and his family, and wrote in his memoirs, "You never really know what a player thinks of you until after you have gone."[19] Shula had tried to head off snipe hunts like that by meeting with Klosterman before he left. Said Klosterman at the time, "Don said he realized the timing couldn't be worse . . . leaving right after I came. He was concerned how that would look, and I appreciate his concern. I always liked Don." Giving him the benefit of the doubt, Klosterman said he believed Shula "wouldn't even have considered leaving except for the chance to become a part-owner."[20]

But the elder Rosenbloom, who wouldn't match Robbie's offer, wasn't so magnanimous. When he bumped into Shula, now representing the Dolphins at the winter league meetings, Shula stuck his hand out, but C.R. "completely ignored me and turned his back on me."[21] Yet, when the owners took a vote in late May to approve Shula's stock windfall in Miami, it was a unanimous aye.[22] That was good enough for Shula to believe he could move on in peace, granting that "a lot of unpleasant things happened," but that only one thing mattered: doing what was right for No. 1. Especially when it came with stock.

In Baltimore, though, there was no healing. Not so long as compensation was still to be determined. Despite his sanguine parting with Shula, Klosterman, no doubt at the behest of Carroll Rosenbloom, began tossing out words like "tampering," "subversive," and "unfair." This was a slender thread indeed, given that both Rosenblooms had approved Shula's defection. The senior Rosenbloom, once he had a chance to reflect on the irony that his underling had escaped to a place where he himself owned a home in Miami Shores, along with a beach club and several condos, and would have loved to own the team there, piped up, "Everybody in the country knows that fellow Robbie was tampering when he took Shula away from us. They waited until I got out of the country to continue their little talks." Shula, he went on, "has very few fans among the players and I certainly am not one, either." Not since Weeb Ewbank, C.R. said, did his coach have a rapport with the players, and Shula "left me with a legacy . . . the first NFL owner to lose the Super Bowl." In the end, he claimed, Shula's exit had actually saved him from having to fire him.[23]

Irrational as he sounded, Rosenbloom did have one real grievance—the tampering issue—and he took it to Pete Rozelle. In April, Rozelle saw it his way. Conceivably, he could have sent Shula back to Baltimore because of it; instead, he ruled that the Dolphins had palpably tampered because they had made Shula an offer before being permitted to, and because Shula had not told the Colts he was signing with Miami until after he already had. Rozelle rewarded the Colts with Miami's first-round draft pick in '71, which would rob Shula of a vital building block.[24] That ruling hurt Shula the most, implying that, for him, the ends justified the means.

Defending himself, Shula called the decision "unfair," claiming that other teams had done worse and gone unpunished. Though he conceded in his memoir that, under a "strict interpretation" of the rules, "I guess [my actions] could be wrong," he argued that "there weren't any undercover dealings." That being so, he concluded, "I believe the Dolphins were victimized," perhaps inferring that the old league was exacting retribution for losing to the AFL.[25] That would also explain why he grumbled that Rozelle kept quiet about fining Rosenbloom $5,000 for his vicious personal insults.

Back in Baltimore, there was chaos, and even scuttlebutt that

Unitas might be named head coach, a hell of a way to show up Shula. But Unitas wanted to keep playing and would sign a new contract. Rosenbloom would keep the team in familiar hands by promoting Don McCafferty and rehiring Shula's assistants before the latter could get at them. This meant that both teams would bear the stamp of a coach who had not yet won the big game, but had caused more fuss than any other coach in football. It also meant that Shula had scant time to justify earning his salary and stock. Around the new NFL, though, the smartest people sensed the timing was perfect for Shula and his team. Perhaps partly in envy, Al Davis declared that the Dolphins had "bought themselves into contention."[26]

12

HIRED BY THE MAN WHO FIRED FLIPPER

In Miami, as in Baltimore, Shula would not have the luxury of a silent owner. Joe Robbie never quietly receded into the simple life of rubbing—and bending—elbows in a VIP suite with other swells, leaving the team to the football people. Like Carroll Rosenbloom, he was an unapologetic fop and meddler, a man with an opinion about everything and eager to make it everyone else's opinion. He loved to tell the story of how he had morphed from a lawyer in South Dakota to Hubert Humphrey's trusted money raiser to the mover of the Lebanese cartel behind the Dolphins. Robbie, as *Sports Illustrated*'s Mark Kram wrote in 1969, "just isn't right, especially not for Miami, the capital of the smooth façade. He looks like the business agent for a labor union, wears electric-green anklets, and his grip on a cocktail glass is that of a longshoreman holding a schooner of beer."[1]

Maybe, but Robbie was no interloper. Like "despotic emperors of commerce," Kram went on, "he certainly has their tunnel vision, their touch at the wheel and deal and their insensitivity to intimidation . . . even his detractors . . . suggest that he may be without peer in the cobweb corner of sports finance. He is, they say, a shrewd manipulator of men and money, tough as a wharf rat and as charming as a rent collector." Indeed, when the city stopped paying for the celebrity TV dolphin

Flipper to swim in a tank at the Orange Bowl, Robbie wouldn't pick up the tab. Thus was Kram's piece titled THIS MAN FIRED FLIPPER. Despite the criticisms that accrued as the Dolphins failed to swim, Robbie gave himself high marks. "I brought pro football here when nobody else would get near the place," he said. "I protected football in this community."

Robbie put Don Shula into his own fishbowl, but Shula quickly became the clenched-jawed face of the team. He had a half-hour weekly TV show, co-hosted by Dolphin radio announcer Joe Croghan, on Channel 10, directly preceding the brand-new *Monday Night Football*, which in time would regularly feature his team. But he would never hold all the power of a Lombardi, who could dominate his small market in Green Bay, and he would constantly need to please Robbie. He also had to share power with one of the regime's holdovers, Joe Thomas, who had been Robbie's first hire in 1965 as director of player personnel. Thomas, who started out as Weeb Ewbank's scouting maven in Baltimore, was a shrewd team builder, having put the Minnesota Vikings into the elite. So, while Shula was the titular general manager, Thomas was the de facto GM. Shula would share power without complaint, at least for a while.

Any complications that may have lay ahead were not on Shula's mind as he began packing up for his new home in Miami—Dorothy and the five kids were moving with great regret, having sunk roots deeply into the Baltimore community. They sold their house on Pot Spring Road—with apt symmetry—to Gene Shue, coach of the NBA Baltimore Bullets, then found a sumptuous home on the 16th green of a golf course at 16220 West Prestwick Place in Miami Lakes, a six-square-mile grid on the southeastern tip of the state. The location offered the Shulas what they wanted, a slice of suburbia just miles from downtown. But he had no time to settle in. Needing to hire a staff yesterday, the first—surprise, surprise—was Bill Arnsparger, who'd had a change of heart about his "business opportunities" when Shula got a new job. He was hired as defensive coordinator and line coach. Shut out from his Colt aides, Shula next reached back for old cronies, plucking Howard Schnellenberger away from George Allen to be offensive coordinator.

As Schnellenberger recalled, "The team hadn't won, but Shula always had the smell of a winner. He said, 'I didn't come to Miami to change the players. I came to change the attitude in the locker room.' I said, 'You talked me into it.'"[2]

Shula hired as offensive line coach Monte Clark, whose work containing Gino Marchetti in the '64 title game still made Shula shudder. Clark was about to retire, but Shula played by the book and got permission from Blanton Collier to sign him. Next to arrive was Mike Scarry, an NFL lifer, one of the old Paul Brown gang, who had played center and linebacker in the dinosaur days and in his 60s was scouting for the Redskins. It was an offbeat selection, but Shula saw his staff as a mix of football minds and personal chums. That was obvious enough when he hired Carl Taseff, who had replaced his old running buddy as defensive back coach with the Lions, but had been out of the game since '66. Sentimentality overruled need, since Shula had already retained Wilson's defensive back coach, Tom Keane, whom he had also played with in Baltimore. Shula assigned Taseff to the offensive backfield, but his real role was to spread the gospel of Shula as a peerless potentate. Carl did just that, ensuring his employment virtually in perpetuity.

As for the players, the talent was there, which Wilson freely took credit for. Indeed, Robbie's "highly satisfactory" judgment of the previous years was not lost on Wilson. The Dolphins' 12 wins over their first three seasons, he said, "equaled or bettered the record of any expansion team in history," and in the fourth, "we were taken out by injuries." Feeling slighted, he refused to stay in the organization; instead, he left the game, muttering about Shula. Two years later, he was still saying he had turned over "a ready-made team" to Shula, and "Joe Doakes could have coached that team" to great success. Painting Shula as an ingrate, he recalled that he'd doubled Shula's Lions salary and helped get him the Colts job—"I practically wrote his contract for him"—claiming he himself turned down the job.[3]

Wilson overstated his success and understated the enormous differ-ence Shula would make. Right from the get-go, Shula's hiring sparked thousands of new season-ticket sales. But he was right that—as with Shula's first pro team—the Dolphins were not doormats. Mercury Morris, the team's hip-swiveling halfback drafted in '69, agreed that "the nucleus for a championship team [was] already in place."[4] Wilson handed Shula an offense led by a young and proven quarterback, Bob Griese; a deep backfield with battering-ram fullback Larry Csonka and halfbacks Jim Kiick and Morris; and a defense anchored by middle linebacker Nick Buoniconti and right defensive end Bill Stanfill. Griese and Csonka came as first-round picks in '67 and '68, Stanfill as the first-round pick in '69.

Buoniconti, a former team captain at Notre Dame, came in a trade in '69 after seven seasons with the Boston Patriots, five as an All-Pro. Judged an "old" 28, at five-eleven and 220, he was undersized for his position, but was the only linebacker with a law degree, and he could think as fast as he could cover a play. In Miami, he made first-team All-Pro; Griese had gone to the AFL Pro Bowl twice; Kiick, Stanfill, and center Tom Goode once. The biggest need was on the offensive line, which resulted in Griese being sacked an AFL-high 33 times in '69 despite missing five games. He also threw more interceptions than touchdowns. When Shula first met with him, in spring camp at St. Thomas University in Miami Gardens, he told Griese to quit scram-bling; he wanted him to stay in the pocket.

"Make me a pocket and I'll stay in it," the quarterback replied.[5]

Shula also saw problems in the secondary, his area of expertise. He and Arnsparger would install the same double zone scheme that had failed with the Colts, and he figured he had two keepers: right corner Lloyd Mumphord, who as a rookie in '69 grabbed five inter-ceptions, and third-year strong safety Dick Anderson. Unhappy with the other holdovers, he would start two rookies, Curtis Johnson at left corner and Jake Scott at free safety—a gamble, but one he thought he could win, based on a week-long interval over the sum-mer when a wildcat players' strike called by John Mackey left only rookies in camp, their ears blistered by Shula's verbal fusillades, prompting a headline reading "HIT, HIT, HIT," CHANTS SHULA TO DOLPHIN ROOKIES.[6]

Shula had more high cards than he knew. When he arrived, he had been given a splendid gift from Blanton Collier, who, saving on payroll, made arguably the worst trade ever, sending the balletic receiver Paul Warfield, an All-Pro for the third time in '69, for a third-round draft pick. Shula had been a fan of his since Warfield played for Harding High in Warren, Ohio. The son of a preacher, he was in his prime at 28, with remarkable athletic ability. He would look almost lazy loping down the field, then make a subtle pivot, shift gears, and get open, the product of hours of repetitive practice and film study. A highly sensitive man, Warfield believed the trade was racially motivated, and he nearly quit rather than accept the trade to a city he wanted no part of. And he was just one of many African Americans on the team who felt the same way, something that threatened to wreck Shula's efforts before he ever coached a game.

They weren't wrong. Dade County, wrote a local reporter in 2016, "has [a] long and hideous history of discrimination—particularly in Miami Beach, where wealthy elites could enforce their biased whims."[7] At one time, incredible now, signs in hotels read, "Always a view, never a Jew." By the '50s, African Americans were the ones denied those views. There had been small gains by the time Shula got to town—in 1971, a black woman would be named Miss Miami Beach—but the first black Dolphins players felt Jim Crow lived in their own locker room.

Of the various cliques on the team, one had been a beer-chugging pack of good ol' boys led by the South Carolina–born Georgia graduate Jake Scott, who proudly called themselves the Redneck Club. Mercury Morris, in a bylined article in the *Miami News* in 1969, wrote of "a sticky situation here at the Dolphins' camp. . . . There's a de facto segregation being practiced here and it's as much my black brothers' fault as anyone else,"[8] for putting up with it. Years later, Morris wrote a memoir in which he claimed Buoniconti had "whacked" the black runners in practice while going easy on Csonka and Kiick, and that he and the linebacker almost came to blows over it.[9]

Other recently arrived black players had also had to think hard about coming to Miami. One was free-agent Packer tight end Marv Fleming, who had spent seven years in Lombardi's liberal regime. Guard Larry Little, who had grown up in south Florida and been signed by San Diego out of all-black Bethune-Cookman, was traded to the Dolphins in '69. Looking back, he admitted, "I didn't particularly like the trade."[10] He liked it less when Shula greeted him not with hello but "How much do you weigh?" When he answered 286, the coach ordered, "I want you at 265." (He'd made a similar demand of Csonka in their first encounter.) Little made the target, and as Shula expected, he became quicker, paving the way for him to be named the AFC's outstanding lineman three years in a row. Left unspoken in public was the companion negative opinion black players around the league had of Shula, which was stoked by several black Colts players. Not only Mackey, but now Bubba Smith went on the record, saying:

> When things went wrong, it seemed to me [Shula] picked mostly on the black guys. I can't function right when someone is always hollering in my ear. If the team was having trouble, he'd come over to me or John Mackey or some other black player and ask us to try harder. No one has to tell me or Mackey to put out more in a game. Hell, that's insulting.[11]

To most players, Shula was an equal opportunity scold, save for the slack he had shown Unitas, and white players who had been ripped by him had little sympathy for black men who felt the same sting. It's revealing that no one ever labeled Shula as racist, unlike some of Tom Landry's players in Dallas, where the racial divide was starker and the assumption was easier to make, given Landry's deep Texas roots. The truth was, Landry, caught in a cultural clash, simply didn't know how to deal with racial clefts on his team, and for years just left them hanging with passive indifference. By contrast, Shula, the son of immigrants, had a clear sense of cultural differences. Another of his early signings was a bald, pint-sized, left-footed soccer-style place-kicker born in Cyprus, Garo Yepremian.

Yepremian, who made ties as a supplemental craft, looked like a Muppet and had been ridiculed by Alex Karras when he'd played for the Lions, as the guy who would allegedly say, in a thick accent, "I keeck a touchdown." Actually, he had once "keeked" six field goals in a game, but sidewinding soccer-style kickers with funny-sounding names and accents were not yet fully accepted. For Shula, it was enough that Yepremian had become a citizen and enlisted in the army for him to be convinced the little man had the right stuff to play for him. Yepremian was grateful. After losing his job in Detroit, he said, "I wrote letters to 21 pro teams but Don Shula was the only one interested in giving me a chance."[12]

Diverse characters seemed to find refuge on the Dolphins. Wilson had also left Shula with defensive tackle Manny Fernandez, a descendant of Spaniards who sailed to Hawaii. The front office wanted him to do some publicity for the team, speaking what they assumed was his native tongue in Miami's Little Havana section. "Sorry," he said, "I don't speak Spanish at all. Not a word."[13] Fernandez arrived at camp on his Harley, shortly after he had broken his jaw and nose and lost seven teeth when he crashed it going 120 miles an hour.

Shula's Dolphin rosters would include men of disparate backgrounds, some eccentric, some left-wingers, some right-wingers, black men and white crackers, some atheists, some holy rollers, some suck-ups, head cases . . . all of whom were united by a common gene: a willingness to do anything to play.

Still, Shula had to address the racial tensions. Already, he was working on a historical trend, with the Dolphins' highest-paid players being Warfield and Fleming, the former under a four-year, $280,000 contract. Knowing he had to make important symbolic gestures, in the first full team meeting of spring camp, he watched the whites congregate on one side, blacks on the other. Shula ordered everyone to group by position. Whereas many teams, including Wilson's Dolphins, had blacks room with blacks, whites with whites, during training camp, Shula put Warfield in with Griese, with whom he would have to develop an innate connection on the field, and Fleming with backup quarterback John Stofa; similar interracial pairings were made in this manner.

Detail-oriented as Shula was, he even placed pick combs and Afro Sheen in the locker room, though he seemed not to understand what they were for. Once, he asked Csonka, "How did the Afro Sheen go over?" Replied the hirsute fullback, "What the heck are you asking me for? I'm Hungarian like you are."[14] Shula's attempts at being a brother from another mother may have been, as Morris said, "a bit awkward," but the effort counted.

His mission was to apply his system, a conservative, low-risk attack built around the running game, mainly passing when the defense was softened up. Csonka was a six-foot, three-inch, 240-pound slab who ran in short, pigeon-toed steps with no outside speed, but a keen sense of where the hole would open. He would blast through it, head down, not falling until gang-tackled. Once, when he was knocked out cold, they called for a stretcher. Csonka, coming to, refused it. "I'm not gonna be carried off in front of all these people," he said, and half-crawled to the sideline.[15] Kiick, smaller and not much faster, had the same fanatical drive and was a jarring blocker and dependable pass catcher.

They had come to the pros at the same time, Csonka, indeed a Mid-western Hungarian like Shula, having starred at Syracuse and then been the Dolphins' No. 1 pick in '68. Kiick, a Jersey-born son of a World War II army lieutenant who also played briefly as a running back for the Steelers, went all the way to Wyoming to play college ball, then was drafted in the fifth round. They quickly complemented each other, both married, both carousers—as Csonka would often say, "Me and Kiick and Jack Daniels had a big night together."[16] But they were also men of intellect, wit, and sarcasm. As if out of a comedy sketch, they had names no one could spell right and a *Cuckoo's Nest/Easy Rider* sensibility. To Mercury Morris, they were "a clique unto themselves."[17]

They fit in quite well under Wilson, in an atmosphere more like a men's smoker—or, as Schnellenberger called it, "a floating cock-tail party." Griese recalled Wilson and his assistants drinking their lunches at Johnny Raffa's restaurant near the Orange Bowl, then "returning for the afternoon practice breathing alcohol into the hud-dle."[18] Csonka, with no pushback from Wilson, lauded him as a "great guy"—a description few players ever offered for Shula. Wilson, he said, "wasn't too concerned with the room check. . . . He told everybody, 'If you've got something good going somewhere and you're going to miss the curfew, give me a phone call.' That's the kind of coach that most football players appreciate, that they want to win for. Just to keep him around." When Shula arrived, Csonka's world changed. "For football knowledge," he said, "George wasn't as meticulous as Shula is. And he wasn't as good a sideline coach."

Schnellenberger, characteristically, was blunter. As a coach, he said, Wilson was "horseshit. Everyone knew he was horseshit." Shula's coaching style was a change. His low-key pep talks, to Csonka, were "rational, not rah-rah. He's smart enough to know he can't bullshit bullshitters. . . . That's what Shula keeps saying. 'Be yourself.' " The problem was, Shula knew all too well who and what he and Kiick were, because he used to *be* them.

> He didn't trust either of us. He knows a hell-raiser when he sees one, because he was one himself. When he [played,] his team-mates used to go get him the night before a game and put him in a car to get back for curfew. He's up every morning for mass and communion. He'd like everybody to believe he's always been this way, but he knows that me and Jim know better. We've heard the stories from guys he played with.[19]

Shula had less success trying to understand other players, who reflected a different side of the Baby Boomer crowd. Mercury Morris, for example, was a human paradox few could grasp. He had come to the team as a third-round pick in '69 out of West Texas State, where he set NCAA rushing records quickly broken by O. J. Simpson. At six feet and a sinewy 200 pounds, he had blinding speed—he had been given his nickname, after the wing-footed god, in college—and Wilson played him mostly as a kick returner. He led the AFL in return yardage that rookie season.[20] He surely had a mercurial mouth—when Wilson said he'd be happy with a 7–7 season, Morris clucked that he wanted to go 14–0—and some of the best moves were off the field; he would leave games and practices with two women, one on each arm.

Unsure that Morris had the proper attitude to be a pro, Shula would also relegate him to kick returns, making him the first of many Dolphins to grouse about playing time. Before long, all three runners would be in a cat-and-mouse game of tweaking Shula, whom they feared, but never saw as sacrosanct in the Lombardi sense. This was likely the better way to go about coaching men in the '70s. And Shula could always get his point across, no matter who was balky. Csonka learned that on day one of Shula's first spring camp, when he called in sick with the flu. When he did make it in, Shula was all over him, blistering him as too fat, and had him run a 40-yard dash. Somehow, Csonka ran it in 4.7 seconds, his best time. As Kiick learned about the new guy, "Shula's not the kind of coach you want to win for as much as you want to win for yourself. Because . . . winning keeps him off your ass."[21]

Knowing what he had in Csonka, Shula leaned on him hard. As a rookie, he had sustained two concussions, a broken eardrum, and a busted nose, his 10th since high school. But he was indomitable, incurring a penalty once for knocking a would-be tackler cold with a forearm shiver. According to Buoniconti, Shula "literally had to teach Csonka how to run with the football. He used to run straight up and down and Shula [got] him to lead with his forearm rather than his head." Shula and Taseff, he said, all but "reengineered" Csonka to be a top performer.[22]

Shula himself needed refining. He was still young, still blue-collar, still old-guard, but the unyielding shell around him loosened a bit. As he had done with Tom Matte, he bonded with analogs of himself, often Ohio-bred fire-breathers. Csonka sort of qualified, and if he was easily the most scabrous, Shula gave him the most slack to prick him. But when he spoke, grown men jumped. As part of an overall professionalizing of an operation that sorely needed it, players were ordered into the gym daily to lift weights, run endless laps, sweat through four-a-day practices, and jog those dreaded gassers at the end of the day. When the player strike called by Mackey ended in early August, he had the veterans do a 12-minute run before breakfast their first day back. Some, like Csonka and Little, used to piling it high at the buffet table, were put on strict diets.

Shula mandated wearing sports coats and ties on the road, while forbidding long hair or "excessive" beards, which no one really knew the meaning of but didn't test. The 11 p.m., lights-out curfew in training camp, barely an hour after all the team meetings were done, was inviolate; no time was allowed for visits with wives or girlfriends. Csonka called it "a system designed for children, not adults," and described Shula's camps as "prisons." Shula was the warden, Monte Clark the enforcer, taking names, lurking in dorm and hotel corridors, handing down fines. Since Shula knew all the ways to beat a curfew, those avenues were shut down. He would hand a football to the hotel elevator operators, instructing them to ask any player who broke curfew to autograph it, so that he knew who to fine. Ego-driven players always fell for it.

On the field, Griese was his generalissimo. He looked like a farm boy, missing only a stalk of hay in his mouth, but had proved at Purdue that he had a killer instinct. He also had a refreshing lack of ego, accepting the role of "game manager" rather than long bomber, which AFL quarterbacks had seemed to believe they had to be. Never would the mild-mannered Griese sass Shula or, Lord knows, refuse to run a play he sent in. He was a natural defense reader, a masterful play faker, and never pretended he had a great arm, though he could deliver one deep when needed. Even Schnellenberger, his own position coach, said Griese "couldn't beat you with the pass." But he could with his brain. The apotheosis of Shula football: low-risk, high-percentage, pounding all the time. At last unfettered by the polar opposite of Unitas, Shula had the ideal mechanic to run a game the way he had always wanted to.

Cracking the whip during the preseason games to show he meant business, Shula beat Chuck Noll's Steelers 16–10, Paul Brown's Bengals 20–10—Shula's first game at the Orange Bowl, where, at his urging, artificial turf had been installed—and Dick Nolan's 49ers 17–7. Then the Colts came to Miami for a game meaningless to everyone except Shula, the Colts, and over 76,000 fans who jammed their way into the Orange Bowl on a humid Sunday night, the most that had been there since Shula's longest day. Despite all the negative quotes from the Colts—Bubba Smith now vowing he would "make Shula sorry he left"[23]—Shula shied from any inflammatory comments, though Schnellenberger recalled him as being "wound tight as a drum." The secondary picked Unitas twice, Kiick ran for 78 yards, Griese threw a touchdown, and the Dolphins won 20–13. It left Shula grinning, crowing that his new team was "finding out how much fun it is to win," but it also gave the Colts incentive to bring him back to earth in their two regular-season matches.

The south Florida papers, already kissing up to him, ran splashy headlines about Shula's "Debut Success" and "Winning Start." Another was: THE INCREDIBLE MIAMI DOLPHINS DO IT AGAIN, above a story swooning that Shula "could run for mayor. Maybe even governor."[24]

They remained primed, though they lost the last two preseason exercises, one to an emotional Packers team only three days after Lombardi died on September 3, the other to the Falcons on a field goal with four seconds left. Yet Shula wasn't entirely sold on his own team. Though key positions were held by good, smart, tough pieces, the offense had little speed save for Morris, who would see little time in the backfield. Shula flirted with signing the Olympic sprinter Jim Hines, but would go into the season with Warfield as his only game breaker; the other wideouts, Howard Twilley and Karl Noonan, were dependable but not exactly scary. Shula did deal for his old Colt receiver Willie Richardson, who would catch only seven passes all season and so detested Miami that he went right back to Baltimore in 1971.

It would be Shula's defense that took him up or down. It was strong, mobile, with the peripatetic Buoniconti flanked by linebackers Doug Swift and another rookie, Mike Kolen. Up front, the incumbents on the line—ends Stanfill and Jim Riley, tackles Fernandez and John Richardson—could stack up well against opponents' running backs but were less adept at swarming quarterbacks. The deep backs, especially the two rookies, were gambles, though Anderson and Scott were gems. There were holes to plug on both lines, tweaks needed. But Shula came into the season with his usual swagger, knowing that Lombardi's death had made him the champagne of coaches. One newspaper story quoted an oddsmaker as saying that Shula was the only coach who could influence a point spread the way Lombardi had. But then, Shula knew all about point spreads, and the thought made him shudder.

The Dolphins began the Shula era against the Boston Patriots (they weren't the New England Patriots until a year later) on September 20 in Harvard Stadium, one of the worst fields to play on. The Pats were one of few teams who would be underdogs to the Dolphins. But while they would suffer a disastrous season, their coach fired midyear, they ruined Shula's debut. It looked good after Scott intercepted a pass and Kiick ran in a five-yard touchdown in the second quarter to put Miami up 14–3. But they never scored again. Griese, forced to throw, was held to 13 completions in 32 attempts and was intercepted twice, leading Shula to yank him for backup John Stofa. He and Griese—who called it the worst game of his career—were sacked eight times. The final was 27–14, Shula's men outgained 301 yards to 214.

A loser one week into the merger, Shula was in no mood to spare the players. "I gave the team a tongue lashing," he said, grousing that "we were giving away offensive gifts."[25] He had to stay on the road for the second game, against the Houston Oilers, another lesser team. And now a more controlled Griese completed 10 of 17, one a short touchdown to Twilley, and handed off 41 times to Csonka and Kiick, who in tandem gained 136 yards. The defense made a goal-line stand

and forced three fumbles. It ended at 20–10, Miami. "I thought we had a good football team," a relieved Shula said, "but we wanted to prove it."[26]

The team now began to roll. In the home opener, against Al Davis's Raiders, the Orange Bowl nearly erupted when Griese hit Warfield in full stride with a 49-yard TD in the second quarter, Warfield eluding three defenders with a 360-degree pivot. The 20–13 victory was the first Dolphin win ever over the Raiders, with the defense intercepting Daryle Lamonica four times. Griese only had to throw 16 times, completing eight for a stunning 180 yards, Warfield with 120 yards on just three balls. Csonka and Kiick rushed a combined 30 times for over 100 yards. The template was formed.

The next week, savoring every minute, Shula stomped Weeb Ewbank's Jets in the wind tunnel of Shea Stadium, 20–13, the Dolphins' first-ever win there. Shula handled Namath the way he expected to in the Super Bowl. With the Dolphins taking the lead early, a far less confident Namath threw into the teeth of the double zone 40 times, and completed 17 for 240 yards but was picked thrice. Hounded all day, his passer rating was 31.2; Griese's hit 100, as he went 14-for-24 for 240 yards, throwing touchdowns to Warfield and Twilley. Braucher happily wrote that the Dolphins had "shocked" and "humbled" the Jets with "the best defensive effort of its 5-year history."

Shula called it "our most important victory, wonderful, just wonderful."[27] But this reverie was premature. After beating the Buffalo Bills 33–14, Shula had to play the two games that gave him palpitations. First, Blanton Collier's Browns came into the Orange Bowl and left with a 28–0 win, outgaining Miami 339–165. Griese would hear boos late in the game, leaving some writers to ask if the Dolphins wilted in the 83-degree heat, supposedly their home advantage.

After Shula insisted, "We're a better football team than we showed today," Braucher wrote, "They'd better be,"[28] since the next game was in Baltimore, with the Colts still stinging from the preseason loss. Under McCafferty, they were riding high at 5–1. The media Shula once owned was in a taunting mood, Cameron Snyder cheekily writing of the "return of the prodigal coach," calling the first-round pick gained as compensation a "dowry" for the Colts.[29]

McCafferty kept a lid on any snark from his players, while Shula heaped praise on the city and team he ditched. Gracious fans gave him an ovation before the kickoff. But that was it for the niceties. McCafferty's team, favored by seven points, piled it on, scoring on an 80-yard punt return and a 99-yard kickoff return. A series of flubbed punts by Larry Seiple and two more Griese picks made it easy for Unitas, who threw a touchdown to Eddie Hinton. Then Morrall, mopping up, ran up the score with a TD pass to Tom Mitchell. Final toll: 35–0.

When Shula, who now had lost consecutive shutouts, giving up 63 points, congratulated McCafferty, he was given a mock ovation as he jogged off. Asked if he appreciated that, he glared, "I found absolutely nothing nice about today," adding that "things can't look any bleaker for us than they did today."[30] The Colts were smug, speaking of Shula as if he were yesterday's news. Tellingly, they gave the game ball to Carroll Rosenbloom.

Shula was now 4–3 with half the season left. If there was any good to being drop-kicked by the teams that haunted him, one significant development was that Mercury Morris, finally given a shot, glittered. He carried eight times for 89 yards against the Colts and caught three passes for 68 yards, displaying speed the team badly needed. Morris still wasn't content with the action he saw, and Kiick wasn't happy with his carries being reduced, but the running game was a three-headed hydra, all three backs with their own strengths. It didn't do much good in the third week of hell, against the Philadelphia Eagles, when they again fell behind, 24–0—having yielded an astonishing 89 straight points—and lost 24–17. Surveying the wreckage, a caustic Shula said the team had excelled only in "ineptness," though he didn't help matters when, down 24–0, he sent in Yepremian to kick a field goal.

To Braucher, the Dolphins were "floundering," the defense "porous."[31] The season seemed beyond redemption. And that's when they found their backbone. Because of Shula's drill-sergeant methods, they were in shape to win the last six games, tuning up for the rematch with the Colts with a 21–10 win in New Orleans. The schadenfreude after the first game disappeared in the broiling heat of the Orange Bowl turf. The Dolphins toyed with the Colts. Scott returned a punt for a 77-yard touchdown, Griese ran in one score and hit Warfield for another. The linebackers blitzed Unitas silly, forcing him into two picks. The final was 34–17. There was no game ball for Rosenbloom this time—now it went to Shula.

Saying he was "totally pleased" with the triumph, Shula was now in the hunt and his team thumped the Falcons, Patriots, and a Namath-less Jets. The Dolphins closed by decimating the Bills 45–7—bringing their record to 10–4, not far off the Colts' 11–2–1—and taking the sole wild-card slot, a major success for Shula, who nonetheless was snubbed in the Coach of the Year voting, won by Dick Nolan. Still no sweet-heart, he had certifiably become more human to writers who used to dread talking to him, but now were warming to him as an underdog.[32]

Shula's gamble on the secondary paid off. All four starters excelled, picking off 31 passes, Anderson leading with eight. Still, the defense, though second against the run, came in 22nd against the pass. The run-based offense was solid, leading the AFC with 148.7 yards a game, Csonka the leader with 874, winning him a Pro Bowl slot. Griese and Warfield also were honored, though it was glaring that Griese had 12 touchdowns and 17 interceptions. But success seemed to only accentu-ate the bitching. While Morris's carries were a breakthrough for him, his and Kiick's gripes would become a recurring, tedious theme. No one complained about winning, though it hardly seemed a reward that the Dolphins' first-ever playoff game was on the road against the Raiders' motley cast of outcasts and chain-gang refugees.

Two days before the December 27 game, Robbie picked up the tab for a team dinner at a local restaurant on Christmas. But Al Davis wasn't big on Christmas spirit. It rained all week in Oakland, and on the morning of the game, the field at the turbid, foreboding Oakland-Alameda County Stadium was like quicksand. This was the kind of thing Raider opponents had come to expect, including groundskeepers drenching the field with hoses if need be. It paid off, too. The Dolphins, slipping in the mud, gained 118 rushing yards, but Csonka would carry only 10 times, Kiick 14, Morris eight. With Shula believing it would be more formidable to throw, Griese went 13-for-27 against the Raiders' infamous bump-and-run coverage and had two touchdowns, the first a 16-yard dart to Warfield to put the Dolphins up 7–0. It was 7–7 at the half, a real battle. But in the third quarter, the great veteran cornerback Willie Brown cut in front of a sideline pass, snared it, and flew 50 yards for a touchdown. Then, in the fourth quarter, Lamonica sailed one that Rod Sherman reeled in and took all the way, 82 yards. It ended 21–14; for Shula, the same story, different team.

He seemed itchy to indict Davis, but held back. In the locker room, wrote Ed Pope, Shula looked like "he had spent the afternoon making mud-pies" and brooded about the "treacherous" conditions. "But I don't want to say too much about that," he said, biting his lip. "After all, both teams had to play on it. . . . The fact is, our season just came to a screeching halt." He was asked if the Dolphins were a Super Bowl–level team. Flashing the Shula glare, he said, "How can I answer that at a time like this? All I know is that I'm not happy with things right this minute."[33]

13

BUTCH, SUNDANCE, AND A CUDDLY CYPRIOT

Despite its painful end, Shula's maiden season in Miami was a marked success. He came in second to the old guru Paul Brown in the Coach of the Year voting, though Brown's Bengals were just 8–6, and he certainly had justified his hiring, getting somewhere fast with a team that had had no idea how to win and soon developed a hip, collective persona. In his game story after the December 13 win over the Jets, Bill Braucher wrote of the apostates in the backfield with a brief reference to the hip Newman-Redford Old West buddy flick just out:

> Larry Csonka and Jim Kiick—the Dolphin version of Butch Cassidy and the Sundance Kid—sat in a triumphant glow in their customary corner. "What's the matter?" Csonka jibed a later-arriving interviewer. "Don't you even bother to talk to me unless I gain over 100 yards?"[1]

Braucher wrote up some byplay between Csonka and Kiick regarding an option pass Kiick threw, which was caught by Karl Noonan for a big gain. "Hey, ask Kiick about that pass," Csonka said. "Ask him why he didn't throw it to me. I was open." Kiick said something about it being his first pass in three years and how he wouldn't waste it on a fullback. Delivered with their dry cynicism, the dialogue indeed seemed Butch and Sundance-like, aided by Csonka's Wyatt Earp mustache, Kiick with his Fu Manchu and frizzy mop top—though, somehow, in the transition, Csonka came out as Sundance and Kiick Butch, reversing the logical roles for each. Taking it onto the field, Kiick in one game was buried under a pile of bodies. Gazing up at Csonka, he asked, "Who are these guys?"—a catchphrase from the movie.[2]

Even more of a freethinker was linebacker Doug Swift, who ambled around wearing earphones, grooving to psychedelic music. He was also the team's player-union representative, which pitted him against Howard Twilley, a throwback right-winger. The two of them would argue for hours, always with Twilley threatening not to pay his union dues. Watching the story lines grow, Joe Robbie was pleased that Shula could run herd over what seemed a freak show at times.

In Baltimore, meanwhile, Carroll Rosenbloom was pleased that the Shula melodrama was over. Of course, Shula had made it possible for the Colts to go 11–2–1 that year, and for Unitas to be bailed out often by Shula's holdover double zone defense. The Colts tamed the Raiders in the playoffs and got back to the Super Bowl, winning on a last-second field goal against Tom Landry's hard-luck Cowboys in the Orange Bowl—pitting two old NFL franchises, just as the NFL brotherhood had hoped. A good many Colts, including McCafferty and now even Rosenbloom, could be magnanimous about the guy who had walked away, who watched from the stands with mixed emotions as his "other" team won the ring that had eluded him.

C.R. clearly enjoyed not sharing any of the spotlight with his coach, few people knowing who McCafferty even was. And now, after 15 straight winning seasons, Rosenbloom talked of retiring. He made Steve president, retaining for himself the title of chairman of the board. But he had a bigger conquest in mind: going Hollywood. When Rams owner Dan Reeves died in April 1971, C.R. typically came up with a novel idea. Having increased the value of the Colts to $20 million, without legally ever paying a dime in tax,[3] he would face a

$4 million tax bill if he sold the club outright. The solution: *trading* the franchise for the Rams. It would take a while, but, as it would play out, Shula's growing authority in Miami would play an indirect role in the making of that history as well.

Shula got his first crack at drafting his own Dolphin players at the '71 draft, though without a first-round pick—the Colts, given the 22nd selection for the tampering business, took running back Don McCauley. Shula's first selection, in round two, was Iowa State receiver Otto Stowe. Often forgotten is that, in the fourth round, he picked Joe Theismann as an insurance quarterback. He might have given Griese a stiff challenge, but the latter caught a break when the flashy Notre Dame star's salary demands were rejected by Robbie and he went to the Canadian Football League for three years—his rights subsequently traded to the Redskins.

The real gem came in round nine: six-foot, six-inch defensive end Vern Den Herder out of minute Central College in Pella, Iowa, where, despite garnering little attention from the scouts, he had set records that put him in the College Football Hall of Fame. Den Herder would mainly sit during his rookie season, as Shula's lineup was mostly set. The only changes were second-year pro Tim Foley platooning at left corner with Curtis Johnson, and second-year tight end Jim Mandich with Fleming.

Shula worked furiously to refine the team. In '71, everything was just a bit tighter, quicker, smarter. The zones meshed more fluidly. The missteps were fewer. As crafted by Bill Arnsparger, the defense began to utilize the in-vogue 3–4 alignment. The wrinkle he introduced was to use the fourth linebacker in passing situations, either rushing the passer or dropping into coverage. The man for the job was Bob Matheson, whom Shula had acquired from the Browns the year before. At six foot four and 240 pounds, tall and mobile, his range on the weak side provided cover for the other linebackers to blitz. As Arnsparger explained in footballese, "We were able to rush five guys and cover with six. That's what you need to run a zone blitz. We could usually drop a linebacker into that slot zone, and that gave people a lot of problems."[4] In the Dolphins' schemata, the alignment was dubbed "53," for no reason more complicated than that it was Matheson's number, and when it got enough attention, the "53 defense" would become not only terminology, but the stuff of mythology.

The crux would again be the running game. But when training camp came around, Csonka and Kiick weren't. Their contracts had run out— each had been making around $30,000 a year—and rather than take what Robbie offered, they chose to hold out in tandem. Paul Warfield had recommended his agent, Ed Keating, from Mark McCormack's Cleveland-based IMG agency. A brass-knuckle type, that same year Keating made Ole Miss quarterback Archie Manning the highest-paid football rookie ever, after he was drafted by the New Orleans Saints. For Butch and Sundance, he demanded that Robbie deal with them as a unit, not separately, and that they would split a three-year, $300,000 package. Robbie refused, and, reminiscent of the famous dual hold-out of Sandy Koufax and Don Drysdale with baseball's Los Angeles Dodgers, they remained out into August, the negotiations with Robbie called "acrimonious" by Csonka.

He and Kiick were "training" by living in Keating's penthouse hotel suite. When Joe Thomas, who had recently undergone bypass surgery, threatened that if they didn't sign, they'd get no raise, Kiick, in his best Butch mimicry, said, "That really chaps me."[5] Thomas repeated the threat, supported by a less than sympathetic Shula.

Butch and Sundance did some posturing of their own. Hanging out one night at Joe Namath's short-lived Fort Lauderdale bar, Bachelors III, they told the manager, Bobby Van, to tell Namath they wanted to be traded to the Jets. Van did, and Weeb Ewbank made an inquiry. But it was an empty threat, one that Csonka had made before, telling Shula that life would be a lot easier for him under Ewbank. Shula always shut down that argument with a quick comeback.

"You wouldn't win," he would say. And Sundance knew he was right.

Butch and Sundance didn't think it wise to cross Shula for any longer than necessary. They came to camp unsigned, and Keating didn't stick with the united front, though in the end, the backs would sign for what they held out for: identical three-year deals splitting $100,000 per, minus a combined $6,000 in fines.

Shula never did fully understand Csonka and Kiick or their generation. Nor they his. While most of the players were, according to Csonka, "totally afraid of Shula," a hard core didn't sacrifice their individualism. John Stofa, whom Csonka called "a fellow Hungarian, truly crazy, a real gypsy," decided during camp to have a party in the dorm. He brought in "an all-time corner-bar sexpot," who bumped and grinded in a G-string as Dolphins danced around in jockstraps. He said Shula "sat there not moving, not too sure what to expect. All of a sudden, she flipped off her G-string." At which point, reported Kiick, "Shula's eyes about popped out of his head. He didn't smile"—though he apparently lingered for a better look.[6] Coincidence or not, Stofa was cut before the season; the new backup would be 49er and Eagle retread George Mira, a former star at Miami University.

For a time, Griese, too, was a holdout, among 14 Dolphins still unsigned when camp began. Dealing with Shula and Robbie on his own, he came to terms. And he would improve the most. In '71, his throws were zippier, the scrambles more contained. Most of the team's peaks and valleys of the year before were smoothed into a steady mainline. After another stumbling start, with a 10–10 tie in Denver and a loss to the Jets in week three, the season was smooth sailing. They ran off eight in a row, then had a letdown that nearly cost them big. At 9–1–1, they tanked against the lowly Patriots, 34–13. Next came the Colts, whom they had beaten three weeks before in a fierce battle in Miami on a late field goal.

Shula's old team was a half-game behind in the division, looking for retribution—and they got it. Tom Matte capped two drives in the first half with touchdown runs. The Colt defense was suffocating, picking Griese twice and holding the Dolphins to a field goal in the 14–3 win. Both teams were on safe ground, having already clinched playoff berths, but for Shula there was undeniable pride in winning the division. And the Dolphins, a half-game behind, took it as a character-defining moment that they whipped the Packers in the finale at the Orange Bowl, 27–6, while the Colts were upset in New England, 21–17. That gave Shula his first division title in Miami; awarded another game ball, he turned it over to Csonka, who had played on a bad leg.

At 10–3–1, his team had racked up impressive numbers. They came in fifth in offense—first again in rushing, with 2,429 yards—and fifth in defense. Griese, ever closer to perfection, had 19 touchdowns with just 9 picks, and a career-high 90.9 passer rating. Csonka cracked 1,000 yards, while Kiick gained 738 and Morris 315. Griese, Csonka, and Warfield (11 touchdowns, 23.2 yards per-catch) all made the Pro Bowl and first-team All-Pro, as did lineman Little. Yepremian, who led the league in points, also made the first team. Jake Scott was a second-team All-Pro.

Shula had prepped them perfectly, the intensity of those last two weeks a launching pad for the playoffs. They would need that intensity, the playoffs taking them on Christmas Day for a war against the Chiefs in Kansas City.

Hank Stram's boys had also finished 10–3–1, winning the AFC West. They were a finely tuned bunch. Stram's endless sets and innovative "moving pocket" gave old pro Len Dawson time to throw—most effectively to Otis Taylor, who was as smooth and deadly as Warfield. Their offensive and defensive lines were massive, and they had the best line-backing corps in the game with Bobby Bell and Jim Lynch flanking Willie Lanier, and maybe the best secondary, right cornerback Emmitt Thomas having made eight interceptions. Eleven Chiefs went to the Pro Bowl, including the kicker and the punter. The game was held in ancient Municipal Stadium—the last one there before the team moved to Arrowhead Stadium. On an unseasonably warm, wet, 60-degree day, a war of attrition took hold, an endless sequence of parry and thrust that lasted all day and into the night.

The Chiefs went ahead 10–0 in the first quarter. The Dolphins broke back in the second to tie. The Chiefs regained the lead in the third and in the fourth, the Dolphins tying the score each time. Both teams racked up enormous yardage—the Chiefs 213 rushing yards, 100 by Ed Podolak, who accounted for 350 total yards by himself, including punt and kick returns. But the mistakes were big, too; each team had four turnovers. Griese, needing to pass more, went 20-for-35 for 263 yards, seven to Warfield. His five-yard touchdown to Fleming with 1:25 left made it 24-all. Podolak ran back the ensuing kickoff 78 yards, kept from a game-winning TD by, of all people, the elfin Yepremian, who got in his way and made him run out of bounds. It still looked like the end was near when, four plays later, Jan Stenerud, the AFC's second-team All-Pro kicker, came in for a 32-yard field goal. Both teams had their own priest on the sideline—Shula two of them: Father John McDonnell and no less than the Archbishop of Miami, Coleman F. Carroll. Only divine intervention seemed responsible for Stenerud sailing his kick just wide.

All through the game, the toll was heavy. "Guys were exhausted on the sideline," said Buoniconti, who had a hellacious game with 20 tackles. "Everyone was getting cramps in his legs." Center Bob DeMarco had cramps in both hands, making every snap torture. And now came overtime, in the gathering darkness. Both kickers missed game-winning field goals, Stenerud again when Buoniconti got a hand up to block his kick. Then, deep into the second overtime—the first time in history a game had gone that far—players seemed to be carrying safes on their backs, as if trying to run up a hill. Something had to give, and it did when Griese called an against-the-grain cutback run by Csonka, who rumbled like a runaway milk wagon for 29 yards, deep into Chief territory. At the 12:21 mark—after a record 82 minutes, 40 seconds—Yepremian booted a 37-yard field goal for a 27–24 sudden-death victory.

Shula grabbed and hugged a couple of his coaches by the shoulder, ran to midfield to console Stram, and ran off the field, lineup chart still in hand, stepping so lightly his feet seemed not to touch the ground. In the locker room, a call came from Florida governor Reubin Askew. Trying in vain to hold a serious tone while celebrating what he called his "greatest victory," when a reporter asked who made the big block to spring Csonka, Shula shrugged.

"Let's not get technical, the hell with that! This is too joyous a moment to start going into football science and tactics"—a remarkable deviation from the norm.[7]

The most joyous of the players was Yepremian, who had come a long way since the season opener, when he blew four field goals in Denver. Though he missed that first OT field goal, he was the hero. Across page one of the *Herald* the next day was the headline IN THE LONG RUN, DOLPHINS WIN BY A TOE. The cover of *Sports Illustrated* had him following through on the kick, the game story titled UP, UP, UP AND AWAY! The last time a kick meant so much was when Shula's Colts were screwed on Don Chandler's tainted field goal; the *SI* story noted the ironic twist that "the longest game in the history of American professional football [was] decided by the smallest player on the field. . . . A Cypriot, with an accent. . . . And cuddly."[8] Stenerud, by contrast, suffered enduring emotional scars. He would play another 14 seasons and become the first kicker inducted into the Hall of Fame. But he would never get over having blown three of four field goals in that game, and decades later, when asked to recall the game, he replied in earnest, "Do you want to talk about my mother's funeral, too?"[9] As was shown that day, the difference between heaven and hell was a few inches.

As it was, Shula's stomach had already come through more than a few of these gut-churning affairs, usually on the short end. But when the high wore off, he had to train his sights again on the Colts. They had swept away the Browns 20–3 in the same round, meaning that the AFC title would be determined the following Sunday, January 2.

In Miami, where it was said that thousands of people had turned off their ovens while cooking Christmas dinner as the Chief game went on and on, 25,000 fans were at the airport when the Dolphins arrived home. When Shula and his son David, whom he had taken to Kansas City, got in their car in the parking lot, it wouldn't start. The other Dolphins had cleared out, it was Christmas Eve, cabs weren't around, and Shula said they'd have to hitch a ride.

"You're kidding, Dad," David said.

The first car to stop had two couples inside. They all recognized him, flabbergasted that Don Shula was asking for a lift to Miami Lakes. The Shula men squeezed into the back seat, gabbing with the others all the way home. When they got there, Shula invited the four in for drinks. Shula loved telling this tale as his Christmas story, a parable of the town's newfound adoration for the team, and for him.[10]

The Orange Bowl was quickly sold out for the Colts, the theme of the game set by Cameron Snyder in the *Sun*: "For Shula, playing the Colts is always like looking into a mirror," an assessment Shula confirmed by noting, "Our styles are so similar" that "the team that executes best will win."[11] Of course, they really weren't so alike. At 38, Johnny Unitas was crumbling, again beset with arm and shoulder woes. He had started just five games, mopped up in others for Earl Morrall, while throwing three touchdowns and nine interceptions. Morrall, at 37, started the rest and won seven, but his touchdown-to-interception ratio was also unsightly, seven to 12. Unitas's passer rating of 52.3 was the lowest of his career until then, save for his injury-ravaged '68, and Morrall was only marginally better at 58.2. But McCafferty's rushing game was the league's fifth-best, Norm Bulaich was a Pro Bowler, and the defense gave up the fewest yards and second-fewest points.

Shula, who the day before the game was named Coach of the Year, 16 votes to five over McCafferty, stood again on the high road. He said he thought Unitas was throwing better now than he had all year, though he was only so-so in the Colts' 20–3 playoff win over the Browns. Unitas was equally solicitous of the Dolphins, calling Griese "the best young quarterback in the game." McCafferty only gently tweaked Shula, citing the latter's expanding waistline, which he said was due to "all that good living down there."

In truth, though, the game loomed as a walkover for Shula, given that the Colts would be without their starting backfield of Bulaich and Matte, both injured. But, coming down from the Kansas City slog, Shula described his team as "tired and beat," a good number of them unable to practice until midweek. He also fretted about the condition of the cement-hard, jagged Poly-Turf surface of his home field, which would be more ragged with the college Orange Bowl played the night before. And while the Dolphins were favorites, it was hard to bet against Johnny U in what could be his last big-game roundup.

The Dolphins, on the other hand, were a fairly unknown commodity, save for the backfield. Part of this was because Shula kept his team in rigorous balance, no one ever seeming to do something more than necessary or spectacular. Csonka and Kiick rarely carried 20 times in a game, Griese rarely threw 30 passes, Warfield rarely caught more than five balls. The shifting zones and strategic substitutions made for a different hero every week. Shula had seen and heard the team called "the no-Name Dolphins," its defense "the No-Name Defense," despite All-Pros on both sides of the ball. He himself would repeat those terms to stoke a communal sense of being overlooked and underestimated. Days before the game, a reporter, noting that the Colts had scored 14 points in both games of the season series, jokingly asked if the Dolphins defense would "concede" 14 points. As it was reported, "Shula's expression hardened briefly into what he calls his 'dull sideline look.' 'I don't think,' he said quietly, 'that this defense would concede two touchdowns to anybody.'"[12]

Late in the afternoon of January 2, it was cloudy and drizzly, at 73 degrees a relief from the usual tropical Miami heat and humidity. The Orange Bowl was stuffed with a record 78,629 humans. Shula's game plan was to make the replacement Colt backfield of Don Nottingham and Don McCauley feel the hurt. The zones would allow shallow screen passes to the backs, then defenders would hit like jackhammers. Shula would call it his "rubber-band defense." If the Colts had a wrinkle, it might have been to rattle *Shula*. As the game wore on, Mike Curtis and Fred Miller, on plays near the sideline, would woof at him, and Shula went right back at them.

"Don't ask me what was said," he said later, "it's unprintable."[13]

Beyond that, the Colts had little to say. On the Dolphins' second drive, from the Miami 25, Griese play-faked and, Rick Volk recalled, "I bit, I admit it. I froze."[14] Cornerback Rex Kern also froze as Warfield flew

down the sideline. Kern tried to bump him, but missed. Warfield reeled
in the pass over a leap by Kern and pranced into the end zone—a 75-yard
lightning bolt. It was still only 7–0 at the half, after McCafferty went
for it on fourth-and-inches on the Dolphin nine, whereupon Buoniconti
nailed Nottingham, spinning him around in midair for a loss.

The hitting on both sides was savage. Griese would take borderline-
legal shots from Bubba Smith that left him with blurred vision and his
left shoulder throbbing. Seeing double, he kept the ball on the ground,
throwing a mere eight passes, completing four, but for 154 yards. Because
the defense bottled up the Colts' running and short-passing game, the
Dolphins didn't need to blitz. Playing straight up, they indeed bent,
giving up more yardage than they gained, but clamped down in the red
zone. The Colts missed two field goals and Miami blocked another.
Unitas kept chucking, going 20-for-36 for 224 yards, but was sacked
thrice and also intercepted three times—the killer being when Curtis
Johnson got a hand on the ball and it deflected to Anderson, who ran it
back for a 62-yard touchdown. Griese then hit Warfield with a 50-yard
strike and Csonka blasted it in to put away the 21–0 victory.

They were going to Super Bowl VI on the back of the first shutout
of the Colts in 97 games, dating back to Shula's third season as coach.
This point was not lost on Shula, who relished telling the press, "They
talked about the Colt defense before but now they'll be talking about
ours." The players spoke mainly of the relief of surviving two pressure-
packed games. But Csonka was typically grouchy. Sitting on his stool,
wincing and sucking on cigarettes as a trainer pulled off his socks for
him, he moaned, "God help us if they don't do something about that
damned Poly-Turf. I don't know how much more of that stuff I can
stand. The buzzing in my head [from landing head-first on the turf]
was so noisy I couldn't hear Griese's calls." Griese, his head hurting as
well and his vision still cloudy, sat mummified by bandages, seemingly
not knowing where he was. Shula would need to have them all healthy
and amped after two weeks of hell, but at least the Colt albatross was
off his neck.

To many, Shula really *was* the team, those All-Pro no-names just chess pieces. In the *Sports Illustrated* game story, the first words were: "Who are these guys?"—the favorite inside-joke line of the Dolphins. One newspaper game story called them "the incredible Dolphins," their playoff march an "impossible dream." Shula's explanation was simpler: "The Dolphins," he said, "weren't pushovers anymore." Before he could leave the stadium, though, a reporter rubbed up an old blister, asking if his epochal failure the last time he got to the Super Bowl had left any "lasting wounds."

"Not except when someone like you brings it up," he said, in full glare.

Earlier that afternoon, Tom Landry, seeking redemption for the Dallas Cowboys' loss to the Colts the year before, made it back to the summit by beating the 49ers 14–3 in the NFC title match. This meant that the Super Bowl would match the two most erudite—and, to some, overbearing—coaches in the game. Not that everyone was willing to consecrate Shula. It was now that George Wilson chose to make his derogatory remarks about Shula being an opportunist and ingrate who had won with Wilson's team. To Shula, Wilson was a footnote, and he brushed him off, saying, "I'm not going to lose any sleep over it."[15]

Landry had, of course, also paid the piper in pain and humiliation. He had lost two excruciating NFL title games to Lombardi, his agonized sideline reactions both times enduring as rare displays of emotion by the famously stone-faced World War II fighter pilot. A brilliant tactician, Landry had prefigured the future not only with the flex defense in the '50s but by using computers in formulating game plans. But, like Shula, he also had to put up with disgruntled players, centrally his star halfback, Duane Thomas, who had run for 11 touchdowns in 11 games, averaging 4.5 yards a carry, making it easier for Roger Staubach to shine at quarterback. Employing a Griese-style attack—conservative passing set up by punishing running—the ex-Navy midshipman went to the Pro Bowl. He, too, was able to uncork a bomb to receivers like the molten ex-Olympic sprinter Bob Hayes and Lance "Bambi" Alworth, the doe-eyed, graceful former AFL star now in his final season. Staubach threw 15 touchdowns and only four interceptions, and—with Landry hating it as much as Shula did with Griese—scrambled for over 300 yards.

The Cowboys had led the league in offense and were third in defense. They had eight Pro Bowlers, including the bedrock of their "Doomsday Defense," the massive, terrifying right tackle Bob Lilly. The offensive line was anchored by right tackle Rayfield Wright, and Landry had gotten important contributions from the old, but still ironclad Mike Ditka at tight end and the ex-Packer fixture Herb Adderley at left cornerback. Shula, who knew the pitfalls of being a prohibitive favorite, came in now as a six-point underdog. Even he seemed lowercase beside Landry, whose knowing, Lincoln-like rectitude and mythology starkly clashed with Shula's red-faced, sputtering temper. As one reporter framed the game, it was SHULA'S FIRE VERSUS LANDRY'S PATIENCE.

After he arrived in New Orleans 10 days before the contest at rickety Tulane Stadium, a reporter at Shula's first press conference actually called him Tom. Having lived with a Lombardi inferiority complex, Shula could only laugh.[16] The old-guard NFL bias in the media was still extant; John Underwood, jabbing his *Sports Illustrated* stablemate Tex Maule, the magazine's lead football writer, ventured that if Dallas won, "the Cowboys' enduring advocate will finally be vindicated" and should get the game ball.

But Landry had to pay a price for getting to that precipice: putting up with Thomas, who got most of the ink that week, as one story said, "confounding even his teammates with sullen silence augmented by a missed practice." Landry even had to promise that Thomas would show up for the game, and, with fullback Calvin Hill's right knee aching, carry the load. Shula could certainly promise every one of his men would be there. What's more, he didn't lock them up. On the Friday night of their arrival, he gathered them in the lobby of the Fontainebleau Hotel and told them they could cruise the French Quarter. Buoniconti said it was a chance to "turn loose, raise a little hell, and get our minds off football."[17] Shula's reasoning, from experience, was familiar, that "the kind of guys you need to keep under surveillance for all but 20 minutes a day would find something to do in those 20 minutes."[18]

However, gauging the Dolphins' practices, Shula would write in his memoir, "Our momentum seemed to be going the wrong way."[19] Fortunately, he had a brilliant football strategist on his side. That week, Richard Nixon made his famous phone call to Shula, suggesting a can't-miss play: down and in to Warfield. Shula had little choice but to be gracious, noting that Nixon had sent him a comforting letter after the Jets' loss "when no one was calling or writing me." In that letter, the impending president wrote that losing is the predicate for winning. He had no idea how relevant the reverse of that equation would be, over time, for both of them.

Super Bowl VI, witnessed by 81,023 people, the largest crowd for the game up to then, was played in perfect football weather: 35 degrees with a cool wind. At least it was perfect for one team. Shula had said the game would be won on "physical merit, the hitting will decide it." It was evident in the opening moments that the Dolphins hadn't gotten their minds around the demands of the third such game in succession. In the first quarter, Csonka, who had not fumbled all season, lost the ball, setting up a field goal for a 3–0 Dallas lead. Moments later, in what would be the lingering highlight, or lowlight, Griese was flushed from the pocket. He started retreating on a crazy backward scramble, reversing field three times as he went back . . . and back . . . until Bob Lilly caught up and dropped him for a highly embarrassing 29-yard sack—still the longest loss of yardage in Super Bowl history.

On the other side, Thomas kept slicing through gaping holes to gain 95 yards on 19 runs. Landry's scheme was to misdirect Buoniconti by having the backs take a step or two one way, then cut back to the middle as he was sealed off by two guards—Landry called it a "slip-wedge." Running behind it, rugged halfback Walt Garrison added 74 more yards, Hill 25. Nor did it help that, after one loud helmet-to-helmet hit, Buoniconti blacked out for several moments. He came to and played the rest of the game—today, according to the NFL's concussion protocols, a player would need to sit out until receiving clearance from the team doctor—though he would be unable to remember even playing in it years later, when numerous such head shots took a grievous toll on his health. Meanwhile, muzzled by a swarming Dallas front seven, Kiick, playing on a bum knee, led the team with just 40 yards on 10 carries, Csonka the same on nine carries. Morris never got a single carry, only returning four kickoffs.

Staubach, the game's MVP, passed only 19 times, completing 12, with short touchdown passes to Alworth in the second quarter and to Ditka in the fourth, sandwiched around a one-yard TD run by Thomas in the third. Dominant all the way, Dallas led in first downs 23–10, yardage 352–119, plays 67–43, and rushing—gulp—252–80 in setting a Super Bowl record.

Playing from behind, Griese was red meat for the defense. He went 12-for-23 for 134 yards, and was picked by linebacker Chuck Howley, who played a monster game. Warfield caught four passes, but for only 39 yards, also muffing one at the Dallas two. Only a goal-line fumble by Hill kept the score from being worse than 24–3.

The "Cowboys stampeded," Maule happily wrote of a contest made the most memorable by the halftime tribute to the recently deceased Louis Armstrong, featuring Ella Fitzgerald and Al Hirt. Losing the big one, naturally, was familiar territory for Shula. Having been the first NFL coach to lose to the AFL, he now was—and still was until Super Bowl LIII—the only one whose team failed to score a touchdown in a Super Bowl. Things got so bad that, after he ragged the officials, one of them warned him, "Shula, if you open your mouth one more time, it'll cost you." Minutes later, he shouted, "Hey, dummy, move over." An official threw a flag, though Shula insisted he was saying it to one of his players. He asked the zebra what the penalty was. "Coaching from the sidelines," he was told.[20]

For the Cowboys, it was hard not to gloat. Even when they tried to compliment the Dolphins, they could hardly keep from sounding condescending. They pointed out that when Csonka ran, Warfield cheated a few steps to the inside to block for him, a sure tip-off that got by Shula and his coaches. The usually fawning Florida papers weren't sympathetic. IT'S DOOMSDAY FOR DOLPHINS was the *Herald*'s banner headline. Ed Pope quoted Shula as saying, "The only way we can ever be completely happy now is to win the Super Bowl. We can't just drop our heads and cry. We have to walk away feeling as though we have gained something." He concluded, "That 'something,' though, was hard to define after this kind of trampling."[21] Bill Braucher, who had started the Butch and Sundance thing, wrote that the outlaws "came to the end of the glory trail." Kiick added that the movie characters had it better—at least they went out with guns blazing. "They were dead and didn't know it. We're alive, and we'll feel it for six months."

Csonka, admitting that his fumble was a killer, insisted the Chiefs and Colts were actually better than the Cowboys. But Shula's own postgame words in a *Herald* headline were the epitaph: "WE NEVER CHALLENGED." Still, he wasn't as deflated as he might have been. For him, that enigmatic "something" was the valuable experience of a Super Bowl baptism for a young and growing team. The first thing he did was tell them, "We have to dedicate ourselves to getting back [here] next season and winning it."

Csonka could see how badly Shula needed to do that. The coach, he said, had a "monkey on his back," and it would be holy hell on them as long as it stayed there.

LEFT: The ravages of the game, and of time, seemed kinder to Shula than to many of his players. One of the perfect-season Dolphins, defensive end Bill Stanfill, glad-handed here by Larry Csonka when Stanfill was inducted into the team's Ring of Honor in 2010, underwent multiple hip and spine surgeries and was diagnosed with dementia before he died in 2016. *(AP Photo / Al Messerschmidt)*

BELOW: A moment of comedy—and, for Shula, agony—came during Super Bowl VII, when Dolphin kicker Garo Yepremian's field-goal attempt was blocked. The ball caromed back to him and, trying to pass, he batted it into the air, to be grabbed by the Redskins' Mike Bass, who ran for a touchdown. But nothing could keep Shula from destiny. The Dolphins won the game to cap his perfect season. *(AP Photo / NFL Photos)*

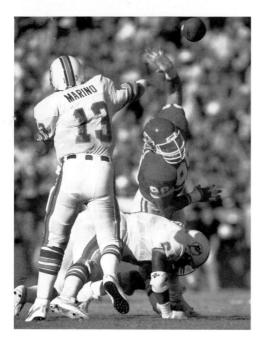

Dan Marino, displaying the perfect mechanics that defenses dreaded, uncorks a typical quick-release pass in a 1985 game against the Kansas City Chiefs. Marino's arm and leadership led Shula to revamp his conservative game plans and usher in the era of exploding pass yardage. Marino took the team to a Super Bowl in his second season, which would prove to be Shula's final appearance in the title game. (AP Photo / Al Messerschmidt)

RIGHT: Never mellow, Shula flashes his storied temper during a 1979 game in Oakland, unleashing a stream of well-chosen adjectives on a helpless referee. Being named the coach of that decade didn't ease his fanatical desire to win, explaining why the Dolphins were almost always in contention, right up until he was forced out as coach in 1995. (AP Photo / Al Messerschmidt)

LEFT: While Shula never got over his mortifying loss in Super Bowl III, he could look back with good humor when Joe Namath attended the 2018 Reid & Fiorentino Call of the Game Dinner in Miami to receive the Don Shula Sports Legend Award. At 88, Shula was confin to a wheelchair but was still spunky ar handsome, a fixture in South Florida a the last of football's greatest generatio (Sipa USA via AP / Alberto E. Tamargo)

Reflecting the social culture, the Dolphins' backfield tandem of fullback Larry Csonka, left, and Jim Kiick were tagged "Butch and Sundance." Here, in groovy shirts, they pose before Super Bowl VIII with toy guns. Often at odds with Shula, they betrayed him by defecting to the World Football League in 1975, though Csonka would end his Hall of Fame career as a Dolphin. (AP Photo)

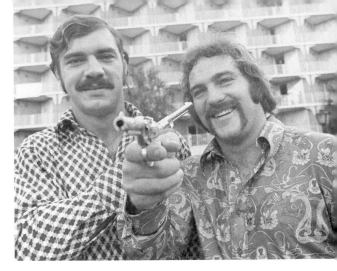

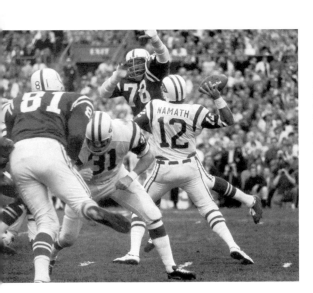

LEFT: A sight that has given Shula nightmares for 50 years: Joe Namath fires a pass, oblivious to the massive Bubba Smith, during Shula's longest day—the New York Jets' 16–7 victory over Shula's 18-point-favorite Baltimore Colts in Super Bowl III on January 12, 1969. Shula would reboot his record-setting coaching career in Miami, on the same Orange Bowl field where he suffered his greatest humiliation. (AP Photo)

RIGHT: Shula always assembled top-notch teams of assistants. Seen here in 1964, his second season with the Baltimore Colts, his staff comprised: in the front row, left to right, Don McCafferty, John Sandusky, and Dick Bielsky; flanking Shula are Charley Winner and Bill Arnsparger. The latter two would also join Shula in Miami—Sandusky for 19 years, Arnsparger for 12, mainly as his much-heralded defensive coordinator. (AP Photo / WAS)

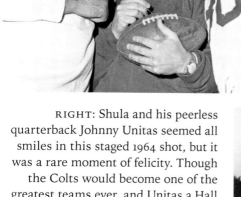

When Shula took over the coaching reins of the Colts, some wondered whether he could exercise authority over his old running buddies on the team. But he could share a good laug with two of his hoariest former croni Gino Marchetti (left) and Bill Pelling ton, as he signed a football after the team went 12–2 in '64, winning their conference and earning him the first his four Coach of the Year awards. (A Photo / WAS)

RIGHT: Shula and his peerless quarterback Johnny Unitas seemed all smiles in this staged 1964 shot, but it was a rare moment of felicity. Though the Colts would become one of the greatest teams ever, and Unitas a Hall of Famer, they regularly feuded, Unitas at times even disobeying Shula's play calls. While Shula cut him greater slack than any player he ever coached, Unitas nursed the grudge to his grave. (AP Photo / NFL Photos)

Shula's apprenticeship included a stop as an assistant at the University of Kentucky in 1959, under coach Blanton Collier (right). One of his fellow assistants, Howard Schnellenberger (left), began a long personal and professional relationship with Shula there. He was on Shula original Dolphins coaching staff, as offe sive coordinator, and also won a nation title coaching Miami University in 1983. (AP Photo)

As a player, Shula wasn't the biggest or most talented, but nobody was smarter, tougher, or more pugnacious. Here, at defensive back for the Baltimore Colts in 1957, he returns an interception against the Green Bay Packers in a 37–14 win. He would be traded the next year, missing out on the Colts' first championship season, but would return five years later in a far more important capacity. *(AP Photos / NFL Photos / Vernon Biever)*

February 18, 1970: Shula is introduced as the new coach of the Miami Dolphins, hired by team owner Joe Robbie (wearing glasses). Though Shula would win two titles and more games than any other coach in history, and become the highest-paid coach in the league, he and Robbie would clash for two decades, Shula once threatening to knock Robbie on his posterior. *(AP Photo / Jim Bourdier)*

Shula's early march to a championship in the '60s was stymied by Vince Lombardi, whose Green Bay Packers edged Shula's Colts in several nail-biting playoff games. Shula had to get used to leaving the field, as he did here after a 20–17 loss to the Pack in September 1965, with Vince seeming smug and Shula in agony. *(AP Photo)*

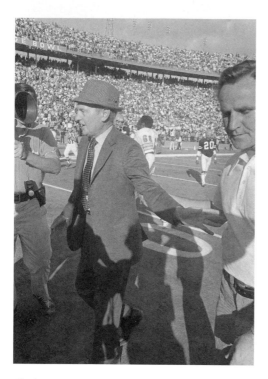

Shula's mentor was Paul Brown, who drafted him to play for the Cleveland Browns in 1950. He absorbed Brown's brilliant, cerebral coaching methods, but disliked Brown's cold indifference to players. When the Dolphins trounced Brown's Cincinnati Bengals 34–16 in a 1973 AFC playoff game, the iciness between them was obvious when they met up after the game. (AP Photo)

In this 1973 photo, a relaxed Shula s beside his wife, Dorothy, surround by their children: Anne (foregroun Michael (leaning on Shula's leg), a behind them, Donna, Sharon, and Dav Shula's family wasn't only his sanctua but a budding NFL dynasty, both sc becoming pro coaches. So popular w Dorothy that all of football grieved wh she died in 1991 after a courageous bat with breast cancer. (AP Photo / MT

A freeze-frame of Shula and the Dolphins during their glory days: Shula on the sideline, hands on knees, jaw clenched, intensity etched on his face, watching his defense like a hawk as quarterbacks Bob Griese (12) and Earl Morrall (15) plot strategy, speedy receiver Nat Moore (89) close by. Shula's teams were called dull and businesslike, but in Miami, they were mor exciting than early-bird dinners. (AP Photo / David Durochik)

Shula groomed his son Dave to follow in his giant steps. As a teenager, he charted plays for the Dolphins; then, after a brief career [a] pro, he was hired as an assistant coach. Here, watching warm-ups [w]ith his old man in 1985, they look [e]erily alike, with many of the same [m]annerisms. Dave became coach of [t]he Cincinnati Bengals in the '90s, [los]ing twice to his father. *(AP Photo / Al Messerschmidt)*

[Bel]ow: In 1993, Shula married [wea]lthy divorcée Mary Anne Ste[ve]ns (second left), the two becom[ing] South Florida's ultimate power [cou]ple. Raised as a New Deal Demo[cra]t, he retained a blue-collar sensi[bili]ty, endorsing candidates for office [sele]ctively, such as when he and [Ma]ry Anne hosted a 2003 fundraiser [for] Democrat Bob Graham when [the] Florida senator and ex-governor [ann]ounced a presidential run. *(AP [Pho]to / Wilfredo Lee)*

TOP: Denied a White House invitation in 1973 because Richard Nixon was preoccupied with Watergate, Shula and the veterans of his perfect team finally got there 40 years later, hosted by President Barack Obama on August 20, 2013. With smiles all around, Shula and Bob Griese presented the president with a Dolphins jersey signed by the team and inscribed "Undefeated." *(AP Photo / Jacquelyn Martin)*

BELOW: In retirement, Shula and his meal ticket for the final 12 seasons of his coaching career, Dan Marino, remained close, doing joint appearances and commercials for everything from weight-loss products to car dealerships. Both also stayed close to their old team, as informal consultants. Here, they share a ride in a cozy golf cart before a Dolphin home game in December 2017. *(AP Photo / Wilfredo Lee)*

14

"STAY READY, EARL. STAY READY"

Both Don Shula and Tom Landry would have to continually keep their teams' thirst for winning intense in the '70s—Landry, as he had hinted, rid himself of Duane Thomas after he was busted for marijuana possession in February, a prelude to a bigger plague that would most destructively affect the Cowboys and Dolphins, who played in the country's busiest drug ports.[1] Landry would not get back to the Super Bowl for another six years. And Shula still had to get his first ring. For now, his men had a $7,500 loser's share, on top of the $8,500 winner's cut from the AFC title game. But after all of Shula's henpecking about getting back to the summit and leaving as winners, it felt like money for nothing.

Shula could be pleased that the run-up to the '72 season left him with the power he lusted after. He had gotten Joe Robbie to approve a budget for his assistant coaches to scout college kids and file reports to Shula and Joe Thomas. The latter seemed to accept the arrangement, but may have felt that, as vice-president, Shula had the upper hand. What's more, Robbie may have sought to keep Thomas content; in February, he offered him a promotion to vice-president. However, he would be making only around $40,000 by 1974; indeed, the Dolphins were one of the most underpaid teams in the NFL, half the players making less than $20,000 a year, forcing most of them to take off-season jobs to make ends meet.

Whatever excess funds Robbie had—and he would rake in more by adding 5,000 seats to the Orange Bowl bleachers that season—he applied to the bottom line, and to Shula. Thomas, it was said, "chafe[d] over Robbie's red pencil striking the nickel-and-dime stuff on my expense accounts."[2] Meanwhile, Robbie exalted Shula. As a result, Ed Pope wrote, Thomas's "rapport [with Robbie] was [not] always complete."[3] And so he refused Robbie's offer and quit. But Shula, too, was beginning to have reservations about the owner's increasingly unstable behavior. Since the tragic death of his 22-year-old daughter Kathleen while on vacation in Mexico in September 1971, Robbie had been hitting the bottle harder.[4] Shula would now have to deal directly with him as Robbie descended deeper into alcoholism and personal grief. Four years later, his son, Dr. David Robbie, twice arrested for drunk driving, leaped to his death from the Golden Gate Bridge.

Thomas, meanwhile, turned to another volatile owner. When Carroll Rosenbloom went ahead with his plan to "swap" the Colts for the Rams and needed someone to buy the Rams, then flip them to him, Thomas enlisted Chicago heating contractor Robert Irsay, a winter neighbor of his in Miami. The bizarre plan was consummated in July, when Rosenbloom, described in one account as "acne-scarred and Gucci-tailored,"[5] began living in posh Bel Air with his wife, Georgia, keeping the Colts' Vince Lombardi Trophy for himself. Thomas, with two owners in dutch to him, signed with Irsay as the Colts' general manager, with total power. Soon, he would blow up the whole team, making Shula's exodus from Baltimore seem brilliant.

The last draft Shula and Thomas collaborated on, only weeks before Thomas fled, was a bust. The only picks to stick were linebacker Larry Ball and safety Charlie Babb. With Thomas gone, Shula had Robbie hire Bobby Beathard as the player personnel director. The 35-year-old Beathard, an Ohio native and the older brother of former USC and AFL quarterback Pete Beathard, looked like a windswept surfer boy, but his scouting had been crucial to the Chiefs' title team before he took his computer punch cards to the Atlanta Falcons for four seasons. Still, all decisions would run through Shula, who began to feel the prickly effects of running a winning team with no dearth of players who had grievances.

Mercury Morris was the loudest of them. Minutes after watching the Super Bowl from the bench, he had broken Shula's 11th commandment, telling reporters, "Hell, no, I wouldn't mind going somewhere else. I want to play." Shula waited until the media were gone and then confronted him. As Morris recalled, "He came out of the shower with that wet-head look of his and found me. We were among the few left in the locker room. It was like a scene from *Gunfight at the O.K. Corral*."[6] Shula ordered Morris to come to his hotel room the next morning. He did, and apologized for speaking out. Pacified, Shula then told him he would be starting the next season: "This is your shot."

But it was hardly the end of Morris' griping. During the off-season, Morris boasted, "The only runner who can run the sweep is me. The only one who can get outside is me. But except for the national anthem and kickoffs, I don't get off the bench." Shula again cut him slack, having decided he needed that outside speed. He committed to use Morris and Kiick in a semi-platoon—one of several he employed, such as Fleming and Jim Mandich at tight end—not only soothing egos, but creating a competition in which the players would fight hard for their jobs. If it meant maximizing talent, Shula would try just about anything. And if it kept guys' mouths shut, even better. But it rarely did.

When George Mira signed with the Canadian league in August, Shula's only backup quarterback was Jim Del Gaizo, an undrafted free agent in '71 who did not play at all that season. And so, once more, Shula sought Earl Morrall, who was assumed to be through when Thomas released him from the Colts over the winter. But it took only a $100 waiver fee for a team to claim him, and Shula did. Morrall then got on the next plane to Miami, likely to be a well-paid scrub. Shula kept telling him the same thing: "Stay ready, Earl. Stay ready."

Jim Kiick, however, didn't appreciate hearing the same thing when Shula began giving Morris an expanded role. He and Csonka's heads had swelled, making them even more self-absorbed. The August 7 issue of *Sports Illustrated* ran a cover story on them, calling them "The Blood and Thunder Boys," the blood referring to Csonka's nose gushing so often. John Underwood wrote that " 2,000 posters of them in Western costume" had been sold and that a TV movie was made, "featuring them on horseback, riding into the sunset at the close of another tough day on the trail (actually hotel row on Miami Beach)." Shula pitched in by calling Csonka "the image of manhood." On the cover, they posed under a goalpost, smirking, Csonka seated cross-legged on his helmet, slyly slipping his middle finger against his shin.

More than Shula, they were the faces of the Dolphins. Women gathered outside the locker room, begging the team's equipment manager, Dan Dowe, to fetch them a jockstrap signed by Csonka. A Kiick impostor made the scene in Miami, renting a luxury home and picking up women. And the fandango with Shula went on. Almost every practice, before almost every game, there would be some kind of episode, some argument about his rules. Shula always won, but each episode was fodder for the book they were writing, which came out late in the season, a sort of dual autobiography mostly given to cataloging the dust-ups with Shula. For Csonka, the most satisfying sentence may have been, "I say shitty things to him all the time and I get away with most of it." For Kiick, Morris was the coach's payback. "Shula," he said, "stuck it to me."[7] By the opener, Shula gave the starting halfback role to Morris. Not that Kiick would be glued to the bench; Shula would use either according to down and distance, and would still rely on Kiick's blocking. Years later, Kiick would recall how perilous even that role was:

I had many, many discussions with Coach Shula, arguing, "I don't understand why a guy at 215 is blocking for a guy at 240." He gave me a dirty look and said, "Just get back in there." I got dizzy, got dinged a few times. You'd come to the sidelines and they'd ask, "How many fingers have I got up?" And you'd say four or three or whatever, and they'd say, "Close enough." We were playing because we enjoyed the game. We were too naive to realize that, in the future years, this could affect us, our life, the brains."[8]

Shula landed another ten-strike before the season, reeling in Marlin Briscoe. In 1968, he had been the first black quarterback to start in the NFL in 15 years, then the Denver Broncos traded him to Buffalo, where he was switched to receiver—a sore issue for black players who, like Briscoe, believed racism was involved. He was rotting in Buffalo, but Shula was willing to part with a first-round pick for him, and all he would do that year was ring up the most touchdown catches on the team. Briscoe was impressed with the mind-set on the Dolphins on game day, if not always before and after, when they bitched. Then, he said, "The players only cared about winning, the only team I found it to be like that."[9] Csonka already knew that. He said of Shula on the eve of that season, "As soon as we reported to training camp, he mentioned the Super Bowl thing. . . . Every few days he mentioned the Super Bowl. . . . It got to be the underlying spirit of the team."[10]

Shula wanted more versatility and depth of strategy. The 53 defense was his sina qua non, he and Arnsparger adding such wrinkles as two blitzing linebackers, and even having Manny Fernandez drop off the line and into coverage. Buoniconti figured there were now "seven or eight variations" to the 53. While such refinement meant Shula would work his team to exhaustion, his practices were briefer so that they could spend more time in the classroom.

The '72 season seemed to justify a greater intensity. Three of the first four games on the schedule were on the road, all against recent Super Bowl teams. The first was in Kansas City, in the new Arrowhead Stadium. Again, the priests were there, but Shula needed no divine help this time. Morris collected 67 yards on 14 carries, supplementing Csonka's 118 on 21 carries. Griese went 8-for-15 for 111 yards and a 31-yard touchdown to Briscoe. Baffled by the 53 defense, Len Dawson threw for 237 yards and a TD, but was picked twice. Miami won 20–10.

Said Shula, "I'm proud. Mighty proud."[11] The second week, the home opener, was an expected stroll over the Houston Oilers, 34–13. Then came the formidable Vikings in Minnesota. For nearly the entire game, the Vikings had them stymied and brutalized. On a pass to Csonka, linebacker Roy Winston jackknifed into his lower back, seeming almost to tear him in half, a moment that would be replayed over and over. As Csonka lumbered to the sideline, he crumpled, facedown, right near Shula, who had little sympathy.

"You can't get hurt," he yelled down at him. "You've got to go."

"I don't want to hear your shit," Csonka yelled back. "I think my goddamn back is broken. Screw the game."

Shula backed off, saying, "Take it easy. Take it easy."[12]

Minutes later, Csonka got up and returned to an escalating defensive battle that swallowed up both Griese and Fran Tarkenton, who were intercepted a combined five times. Trailing 14–9 in the fourth quarter, Griese took the Dolphins down the field and threw a three-yard touchdown to Mandich, pulling the game out, 16–14. Gritty as it was, the poise of that final drive looked so familiar that the *Herald* summarized the game as "just another day's work." So was the third road trial, against the Jets. Falling behind early, the Dolphins erupted in the second half, piling up nearly 400 total yards, Griese outpassing Namath 220 yards to 156, Csonka gaining 102. The final score was 27–17. Now at 4–0, they were in a groove.

The following Sunday, against the Chargers, a new record of 80,010 spectators crammed into the Orange Bowl. Midway through the first quarter, Griese rolled left. With the still-fearsome Deacon Jones, who'd been traded to the Chargers that year, and tackle Ron East closing in on him, he set and heaved one over the middle for Kiick. As he released the incomplete pass, Jones and East slammed into him. They got up. Griese didn't. His right fibula was fractured and his right ankle dislocated. It was a sickening sight, his mangled leg bent in different directions as he was placed on a stretcher and rushed to Mercy Hospital. Driving home after the game, guard Norm Evans, who had missed his block on Jones, stopped his car and began weeping, telling his wife, "I just cost us the season."[13] Jones, who coined the term *sack*, deflected any blame for the hit, saying he'd hit Griese high. "I don't like to see nobody hurt," he said. "Nobody, man."[14]

Like Evans, the Dolphins believed the ride was over when Griese was taken off the field. But Shula, who said he "wanted to throw up," at least had the smart old goat who'd bailed him out before. Getting his mind back into the game, he told Morrall to check Schnellenberger's flowchart of down-and-distance play options. "I said [to Morrall,] 'Look for this, look for that,' and he stopped me and said, 'Coach, I know.'" The big crowd, still stunned by the apparent sudden death of the Dolphin season, barely made a sound as he trotted in. Some players made an attempt at levity to break the gloom. "Old man," Bill Stanfill told him, "get those cataracts in motion and turn up your hearing aid, and let's go!"[15]

He was slower than ever, his gray-flecked crew cut as much a relic as the man, yet he began to seamlessly carry out the job. In Dolphin style, he mainly handed off. But after Anderson had picked up a Mike Garrett fumble and run it for a 35-yard touchdown to make it 10–3, he found Howard Twilley for an 18-yard TD, effectively putting the game away by halftime, 17–3. With the defense strangling the Chargers, picking off John Hadl twice, Morrall added some icing on top with another scoring pass, 19 yards to Warfield. The 24–10 final, leaving Miami 5–0, showed, according to Shula, "how a good team plays under adversity."

Morrall, who went 8-for-10 for 86 yards, was named Offensive Player of the Week. Chargers coach Harland Svare called him "the best there is at rescuing a team." Shula must have felt he was living in a *Groundhog Day* scenario, facing the same gargantuan task of '68, with only the uniforms different.

With the only backup for Morrall the green Jim Del Gaizo, everything rested on Morrall. The next game was a cautionary tale. They played the 2–3 Bills in Buffalo. But while the Dolphins contained O. J. Simpson and gave up a mere 188 total yards while racking up over 300, Morrall threw an interception returned for a touchdown. At halftime, the Bills led 13–7. It stayed close, the Dolphins' lethal ground game negated by three fumbles, but when Morris swept in from 15 yards for his second TD run, it gave them an eight-point lead and they survived, 24–23.

Now came the Colts. Shula's old team was going through hell, losing five of its first six games. Then, when Don McCafferty refused Joe Thomas's orders to bench the now-feeble Johnny Unitas in favor of Marty Domres, he was fired and replaced with John Sandusky as interim coach. Coming into their coach's old home ground, Memorial Stadium, Shula's men walked all over them, 23–0, Csonka plowing in two touchdowns, Morris another. As they churned on, they would tally 20 points in every game until the finale, and only one was close— a 28–24 edge in the second Jets match.

Always, it seemed, Shula had an answer when he needed one. Even when he strayed from his boilerplate system and played hunches, it worked. That was the only way he could manage the Kiick–Morris competition, sometimes choosing which one would start on a whim. Kiick got the nod in New York, because his family would be there, and Morris in Pittsburgh for the same reason. Other decisions he had less control over. More than a few Dolphins, like their peers nationwide, smoked weed in their spare time. More ominously, however, there were regular decisions made in the locker room to have players take injections of a concoction of liquefied Xylocaine and cortisone—or, as this mix of the anesthetic and anti-inflammatory steroid was called in the clubhouse, a "Xylocaine cocktail." Griese recalled that the most regular injections went into the arm of Bill Stanfill, but he was far from the only one.[16]

This sort of thing was hardly exclusive to the Dolphins. Cortisone injections and speed concoctions had been common for years, and been routinely prescribed by team doctors for pain relief. As ex-Cowboy Pete Gent's savagely satirical 1973 roman à clef North Dallas Forty described, players eased the pain freely, shot up by team trainers on game day, with little regard to the perilous toll being taken on their organs and immune systems, presaging the era of harder, more lethal drugs and steroids. Shula apparently had no objection to "cocktail" hour in his locker room, having taken a few shots for pain back in the day. It was legal, and normal to do so. But he had no clue, said Schnellenberger, about the rise of recreational drugs—a possible cause and effect in the case of Morris, some Dolphins ascribing his erratic behavior to dabbling in pot and coke. Shula, whose only frame of reference for illegal drugs was his old Colt teammate "Big Daddy" Lipscomb dying of a heroin overdose while with the Steelers, would get wind of such things and ask a player if he was "on anything." They would say no. And that was that.

Morris revealed in a 1988 memoir, written after he served three years in prison for cocaine trafficking, that he did the hard stuff freely, but not as much as the opioid painkiller Demerol, which he said he took before every game in '72; by game time, he said, "I was banging. And then I wondered why I would stay awake until 3 a.m. and chew my gum for fifteen hours."

Sometimes, inexplicably, the team doctor, orthopedic surgeon Herbert Virgin—or Virgin's son Charles, who was the assistant team doctor until 1984, when his father retired—prescribed him the barbiturate Seconal, a drug Morris said was "sold on street corners for junkies to go into a nod," the night before a game, when Shula allowed players beer. "Barbiturates and alcohol," said Morris. "That can be automatic death." Telling the trainer he was groggy after waking up one Sunday, he said one of the Virgins pulled out two vials and gave him two green pills and one brown pill.

"Take these," the doctor said.

"What are they?" Morris asked.

"Mood pills."

"What do they do?"

"They get you in the mood."

Morris added, "I wasn't the only one 'under the influence' on the field. There were jars of these pills over every players' lockers. Did the coaching staff know? In my opinion, they must have."[17]

Feeling no pain, the Dolphins clinched the dreadful AFC East in midseason. As the argosy of their undefeated season became a running headline of the season, only two games loomed as hurdles. The first was when, at 12–0, they played the New York Giants in Yankee Stadium. The Giants were out of the playoffs, but at 7–5 were good enough to believe they could derail Shula's runaway train. Intense as they usually were, the Dolphins were loose geese before the game. The week before, in practice, Csonka saw a strip of rubber under the goal post. He picked it up and tossed it toward Shula.

> [H]e went, "Yow." . . . I thought he had a heart attack. But it scared him so bad, he didn't get pissed off. He didn't know what to do. He chuckled. Then he walked around looking like he was going to get pissed off. Then he chuckled again. By then he looked lost and everybody was laughing at him. He can't stand that. But he really didn't get mad. I don't know why.

The obvious reason was that he was too happy with what he was seeing week after week. The Dolphins trampled the Giants with 204 rushing yards. Morris had 98 on 19 carries and another touchdown, while Warfield racked up 132 receiving yards and a TD. The defense intercepted Norm Snead twice and recovered four fumbles. The win tied Shula with Papa Bear Halas, whose 1934 Bears went 13–0. (Paul Brown's 14–0 season of 1948 in the AAFC technically didn't count.) And so, what normally would have been a meaningless finale at home was now one for the ages, against, of all people, the ravaged Colts. They were 5–8, and Unitas would be wearing the Colt uniform for the last time, riding the bench.

As it turned out, the game was over early, and the only real drama of the 16–0 win was Morris's pursuit of 1,000 rushing yards—if he got there, he and Csonka would become the first tandem of 1,000-yard rushers in history—and the return of Griese, who no one thought could make it back this season, but came in to make a couple of nice throws. The Dolphins also set a new record for team rushing on the season, with 2,960 yards. The fans cheered themselves hoarse, saving some love for Unitas, who walked off to an ovation, waving to the crowd.

However, players and reporters were out of sorts about Morris, who gained 86 yards on 16 carries, but had to leave the game late because of an ankle sprain, nine yards shy of 1,000.

Csonka blasted the dreaded Poly-Turf for the injury, and for making Morris slip all game. Shula had to take heat for playing Morris so long just for the record. On a day when the headline was 14 AND 0, THREE TO GO, Ed Pope griped, "For all its sentimental aspects, the venture was foolishly prolonged, [risking] serious injury to Morris." The happy ending to that minor squall was that Morris did get his 1,000 yards—after the Dolphins petitioned the league to review a play on which he fumbled a lateral, losing nine yards, but which they claimed was actually an incomplete pass. In a highly unusual and illogical move, since the series of downs couldn't be replayed, the league agreed, restoring the nine lost yards, thus enabling him to hit 1,000 on the nose. People around the league gritted their teeth; was there anything Shula couldn't get to go his way this season?

From any perspective, Shula had done the impossible. The offense and defense were ranked No. 1, the defense pulling down 26 picks. The Dolphins' 2,960 rushing yards, the third-best ever, worked out to over 210 per game. Csonka finished fourth with 1,117 yards, Kiick over 500 as the third wheel. The hitch was that the passing ranked 16th, though this was a product of the system. Morris went to the Pro Bowl with a league-leading 12 rushing touchdowns, though he did fumble eight times, a recurring problem for a guy who once fumbled four times in a game. Nine other Dolphins made All-Pro—Morrall, as in '68, on the first team, as were Anderson and Stanfill.

And yet, for a team with a perfect record, the Dolphins were a tough sell as the greatest of all time. Shula would be duly honored as the NFL's Coach of the Year, for the fourth time. But the players would be shut out in the individual awards. Some contended that the Dolphins' schedule was too soft, the ordeal of the opening month aside. Another postseason failure would expose them, especially Shula, to unending scorn. Which is why he had declined the game ball the team bestowed after the finale; the only game ball he wanted was for a Super Bowl win.

Again, Shula had to decide on his playoff quarterback. Griese, a class act, ventured that Morrall was healthier and "there should be no doubt who should start." Morrall, though, even with a 91.0 passer rating, received no assurances from the coach. "Nobody's told me who'll start," he said, sounding disappointed. "I haven't asked Don Shula. I don't know." Morrall was surely the sentimental favorite. But while he was undefeated—as was Griese, of course—he wasn't quite an MVP this time. Then, too, unlike Unitas in '68, Griese had no problem with his arm.

Shula seemed to dither back and forth, willing to commit to neither. In the end, he went with Morrall in the first playoff game, against the Browns on Christmas Eve day. They were now coached by Nick Skorich, who took over when Blanton Collier quit in 1970. He had a thin roster; with quarterback Mike Phipps throwing 13 touchdowns and 16 interceptions, the rapidly aging halfback Leroy Kelly was basically the Browns' whole offense. But on this day, he could gain only 11 yards. Phipps, meanwhile, was picked five times, including twice each by Anderson and Doug Swift. Charlie Babb picked up a blocked punt and scored for a 7–0 lead. Morris, his leg just fine, led the rushers with 71 yards. And yet, Morrall was a bit off, throwing just 13 times, completing six for 88 yards. The offense stalled. And when Anderson fumbled one of his interceptions, Phipps's touchdown pass to Fair Hooker midway through the fourth quarter had the Browns up 14–13.

With an inconceivable upset looming, the Dolphins went on an 80-yard drive kept alive by two crucial slants to Warfield and an interference call. Kiick then ran it in for the lead. Needing a touchdown to win, Phipps heaved one toward tight end Milt Morin. Swift dropped back with him, and his second pick saved the 20–14 win.

Afterward, the lingering, and still familiar question was why Shula had stuck with a "floundering" Morrall and "committed himself to an overly dangerous degree."[18] Another question was whether the Dolphins were repeating the previous year's malaise against the Cowboys.

Not wanting to show any panic, Shula stuck with Morrall for the AFC title game against Chuck Noll's Steelers, who had also gone down to the wire in their playoff opener and had come away on a high after beating the Raiders on the flukiest play in memory—Franco Harris's "Immaculate Reception." That came when Terry Bradshaw threw a desperation pass to Frenchy Fuqua that ricocheted when the halfback collided with the Raiders' Jack Tatum. Harris picked it off his shoe top and took it in for the winner. Shula could only pray that when it came to such fortune, "the Lord spreads it around a little bit."[19]

Despite the Dolphins' unblemished record versus the Steelers' 11–3, under the NFL's yearly rotation, the New Year's Eve afternoon game would be played in Three Rivers Stadium, a snake pit with fanatics waving "terrible towels" and bearing bed sheet signs pledging allegiance to favorite players. (The league didn't start awarding home-field advantage to the team with the better record until '75.) Noll had not lost there all season, during which his men had surrendered the second-fewest points in the league. Noll and his defensive coordinator, Bud Carson, had built a "Steel Curtain," led by the fire-breathing left tackle "Mean" Joe Greene and right end Dwight White, Pro Bowlers both, as was versatile outside linebacker Andy Russell. But they were young, still ascending, the considerable talents of Jack Ham, L. C. Greenwood, and Mel Blount still solidifying. In his first two seasons, Bradshaw had thrown 19 touchdowns and 46 interceptions; even in year three, he was just 12–12, aided greatly by Harris gaining over 1,000 yards on the ground.

During the week, Bradshaw was hospitalized with a bad flu, and Shula figured if he could force him to throw, it might turn the game, while controlling the ball would keep Greene and the Steel Curtain pacified. It wouldn't be easy. If the Dolphins' precocious cast and storybook quest were endearing, the Steelers were a highly sentimental favorite, vying for the first NFL title in their 40-year history of misery, their owner, the hearty, stogie-smoking Irishman Art Rooney, beloved in league circles. Warming to the battle, someone from "Franco's

Italian Army"—which included, so he said, Frank Sinatra—arranged to drop 2,000 leaflets on the Dolphins' base, the William Penn Hotel, urging them to "surrender." But a stiff wind blew the leaflets blocks away. Both teams fancied themselves as "no names," were spectacularly coached, and gave ground grudgingly. Evenly matched as they were, it would be another nail-biter.

Shula wasn't about to play it safe. While most teams double-teamed Greene, Larry Little—who said he was in a "deep concentration bag"—would have a savage head-on battle with him. Morrall, heavily pressured early, was picked by safety Glen Edwards, who ran it back 28 yards. Bradshaw tried to carry it in himself, but was hit by Scott and fumbled, and even though tackle Gerry Mullins recovered for the touchdown, Bradshaw came up limping and was replaced by Terry Hanratty.

Shula couldn't take control, though he tied it on a nervy call. Seeing a flaw on the Steelers' outside punt coverage, he had Larry Seiple fake a punt, and he rambled for 37 yards. Morrall then hit Csonka with a nine-yard TD pass. In the third quarter, a Steeler field goal put them ahead. Now, with the game hanging in the balance, Shula decided to bring in Griese. His first pass clicked for 52 yards to Warfield, giving the offense a jolt. The Dolphins would get several enormous breaks: one when Griese was intercepted by middle linebacker Ham, but it was wiped out by an offside penalty; another when Harris muffed a pass; still another when they blocked a Steeler field goal. With the Dophins' ball-control game in gear—they would rush for 193 yards, led by Morris's 76 yards on 16 carries—an 80-yard drive ended with Kiick taking it in from the two; in the fourth quarter, he did the same from the three. So it was 21–10, enough to absorb Bradshaw returning and throwing bombs, one of them a touchdown on a crazy one-handed snare by receiver Al Young. He had two more shots to win, amid pandemonium in the stands. But he was intercepted both times, by Buoniconti and Mike Kolen.

Game over, 21–17. Shula, as daring as he ever would be, had tested the odds by going for it on fourth down three times, converting each time, leading to the three touchdowns—"Fourth-Down Shula," Braucher called him the next day. Explained the coach, "You have to go for the short ones if you want to be champ."[20]

Super Bowl VII—played, like the first two title matches, in the smog of the Los Angeles Coliseum—had the same lingering feel of settling old NFL–AFL arguments, more so because Shula still bore the legacy of the league he was again trying to slay. Having lost the argument to Landry so convincingly, he might have included in his daily prayers a thank-the-Lord that the Cowboys had lost the NFC title to George Allen's Washington Redskins.

Allen was definitely a handful—or mouthful, the exact opposite of Landry, and he provoked strong opinions, good and bad. After being fired by the Rams in '71, he had signed with the Redskins as coach and GM, receiving the fattest coaching contract yet seen: seven years at $125,000 per, with a five percent stock option. He took with him seven of the Rams' best players, and gave them such high salaries that owner Edward Bennett Williams lamented that he had given Allen an unlimited spending account, "and he has already exceeded it."[21]

He also got himself into trouble. Back in the summer, he was fined $5,000 by Pete Rozelle for trying to trade draft choices he had already dealt. To Schnellenberger, who had coached for him in LA, Allen was "a promoter" and "a strange guy" who would "chew his food exactly 15 times, then spit it out."[22] Among his other obsessive-compulsive habits was to constantly lick his thumbs on the sideline, where he wore a manic, jack-o'-lantern grin. In the locker room, he conducted tribal dances to choruses of "Hail to the Redskins."

Allen had molded the team as the "Over the Hill Gang"; his middle linebacker, Jack Pardee, was 36, as was his quarterback, the paunchy Billy Kilmer, whom Allen saved from the NFL trash heap. Belly hanging over his belt, socks drooping to his ankles, Kilmer was crudely effective, tossing 19 touchdowns against 11 picks. He also had the benefit of Larry Brown, who ran for 1,216 yards and caught 32 passes—winning him the MVP nod—and had a glittering pair of receivers in Charley Taylor and Roy Jefferson. Allen's defense was the fourth-stingiest in the NFL, though if its age was a major problem, it was worst in the defensive secondary.

To better exploit it, Shula decided to start Griese. Schnellenberger wasn't so sure it was the right choice. "Earl had a better working relationship with the team," he said. "Griese was always a little standoffish. It would have been nice for Earl to make up for the [Jets] Super Bowl. But Shula said, 'Griese's gonna be the guy.' When he gave an order, the conversation was over."

15

RAPTURE

Despite Shula's pedigree, the old-guard sportswriters assumed that the resumption of the old league's primacy in the Super Bowl (the Colts' win as an AFC team included) was the natural order of things. George Allen, who had never coached his way to a Super Bowl, was pimped as a stabilizing force. Tex Maule, always loyal to the old NFL, believed the Redskins were "The Top-of-the-Hill Gang," who "appeared to grow stronger as the season progressed," while Griese "cannot be expected to be in top form." Allen's geezers, he concluded, "should win . . . by at least 10 points and perhaps by as many as 21."[1] Another eminent scribe, Jim Murray, wrote in the *Los Angeles Times*, "The Redskins are sure to hand the Dolphins their shoes and ask that they bring them back by morning shined and leave them outside their door." This consensus altered the point spread; at first favored by a point, by kickoff the undefeated Dolphins were a three-point underdog.

Shula was not without tinsel of his own. Weeks before, he had stepped into Lombardi territory when an illustration of his bulldog features was on the cover of *Time*, though casting him somewhat tepidly as MIAMI'S UNMIRACULOUS MIRACLE WORKER, who had turned a "lotus land" of sun and mah-jongg into a cauldron where "hoarse cries of 'Dee-fense! Dee-fense!' [emanate] from a bathing-suit sales-man dressed in a robin's-egg blue sports jacket."[2]

For Shula, more distracting than the puffery about Allen's team was Allen himself, who even the anal Shula granted was methodical to the point of being annoying. Although the two men were close and often spoke on the phone, Allen clearly wanted to get under Shula's saddle. He called the Dolphins "a fundamentally precise team," but added, "I haven't seen Csonka—what's his name? Larry?"[3] He also said that the Dolphins executed so well that "they're not that impressive. They're like a baseball team with six guys batting .300, not home runs but singles and doubles." Shula also was slightly paranoid about longtime rumors that Allen—a prototypical Bill Belichick—spied on his opponents. He sent Dolphin equipment boys to check the trees outside the practice field for guys with binoculars; when they shook a few, so the story went, a hobo fell out of one, but no spies.[4]

Although Shula obligingly praised Allen's team—Larry Brown, he gushed, was "great"—he believed he could lose only if his team screwed up.[5] Trying to harness their concentration, tightening the slack he cut them a year before, he put his players into a hotel in Long Beach, the Edgewater Hyatt, though Csonka and Kiick easily found their way to Newport Beach and Marina del Rey on free days to hang out in whatever bars they came across. Shula by now had stopped even trying to control them.

And, truth be told, in general he seemed almost mellow. Tex Maule believed he was "relaxed and amiable throughout, and almost elfin" in interview sessions. He allowed the players to wear informal attire like jeans and sneakers, and some black players looked very un-Dolphin-like in *Soul Train*-style leather vests and caps. Ed Pope saw those pregame days as "Don Shula's loosey-goosey week," compared with a "jittery and testy" Allen—who was more so after Rozelle fined him again, $2,000, for concealing a player injury during the playoffs.[6] But Kiick, for one, didn't quite buy Shula's outward calm. "Shula kept telling us that he was more relaxed than the year before," he said, "but I think he was fighting it. I think he was trying to make himself believe it."[7]

Shula was no amateur at mind games; while he acknowledged that Jake Scott had hurt his shoulder in the Steeler game, he never let on whether it was separated or just bruised, leaving Scott's status as questionable, which affected the betting line and Allen's plans. But what curdled him the most that week was Carroll Rosenbloom. Livid that the man who ditched him would be playing for the title on his home grounds, Rosenbloom lamented that both teams had coaches who "broke all the rules in football." Getting uglier, even for him, he called Shula a "pig" and "a loser of the big ones," and predicted he would lose because "Allen is a winner" and "I've seen [Shula] freeze up too many times in the big ones."[8]

Shula hit back, saying his old boss "has done nothing for three years but downgrade me not only as a coach but as a human being." The worst part, he added, was that his family had to read the hurtful remarks. His son David, he said, told him, "Dad, I thought you were honest," breaking his heart.[9] But he wouldn't take the bait, refusing to "get in a verbal battle with a man of this nature because I'm no match for him." Rather, he called Rozelle, hoping for some kind of action against Rosenbloom. Rozelle said he'd get back to him about it. He never did.

The game plan was again simple. "We wanted to take away their short, inside passing and we wanted to whip them up front, which takes away the run," he said. He also knew that Kilmer's weak arm couldn't beat him with sideline throws, and thus the Dolphins would overplay the slant-ins to the middle. The X factor would be the intensity that drained from the team in the last Super Bowl. But he was helped out in this respect by no less than Richard Nixon, who this time stuck his nose into the game's hype by picking the Redskins, Allen being a loud courtier of his. "I wouldn't want to be Griese," said the man whom no one in America would have wanted to be within two years. Csonka, who despised Nixon, not to mention all dilettante politicians, who he said turned football into "an apple pie thing," responded by making it a battle cry. "If he's rooting for the Redskins," he said, "I don't see how we can lose."[10]

The Dolphins were also loose on game day. Leaving the hotel, Scott, whose status was still in question, was late. Shula, impatient, growled at him, provoking Scott to say, "S'matter, coach, you thinkin' about going down as the coach with the most losses in the Super Bowl?" Staring straight ahead, Shula said, "Just be ready to play."[11] He had, of course, told Earl Morrall that months ago. But now Morrall was the forgotten savior, about to see another Super Bowl he had led his team to end with him on the bench. On the other hand, Kiick, who had started only four games so far, got the nod, sending Morris onto the field with a scowl.

That late afternoon of January 14, 1973, was a typical warm, smoggy winter day in LA, the crowd in the ancient tureen 90,102. A TV audience of around 75 million tuned in. The field—covered with smooth grass, now Shula's favorite surface—was like a soft green bed as he led his team out of the tunnel. Clad in a white polo shirt, matching belt, and gray slacks, he had been typically terse in the locker room. "We've waited in line," he told his men. "We've worked too hard to lose this one." Once on the field, he seemed almost serene compared with the manic, overwound Allen, who in his maroon slacks and white shirt immediately descended into a mass of tics and thumb licking. Early on, the defenses ruled. Then Griese, who would pass only 11 times, completing eight for 88 yards, found Warfield on the sideline for 18 yards on a first down. Three plays later, from the 'Skins 28, an unhurried Griese saw Warfield doubled. His second option, Howard Twilley, who had suffered a broken jaw and elbow during the season, faked a down-and-in on diminutive cornerback Pat Fischer and cut outside as Griese sent the pass skyward. Twilley caught it at the five and, with the five-foot, nine-inch Fischer clawing at him, tumbled in for a 7–0 lead. Elated, Twilley handed the ball to the back judge, Tom Kelleher, and patted him on the behind. "Don't do that again," Kelleher warned him.

Meanwhile, Kilmer was in the Dolphins' crosshairs all day. Arnsparger's wrinkle was to have Fernandez line up in an unbalanced front, as a nose guard, head to head with veteran center Lenny Hauss, who needed help from the guards to contain him, which freed up Buoniconti to pour in. Redskin guard John Wilbur, victimized often by Fernandez, said later of the Dolphin defense, "They're like swarming bees. You think you've blocked them well, and you only get two, three, four yards before they're all over you."[12] Coming in, Kilmer had planned to exploit cornerback Lloyd Mumphord, who replaced injured Tim Foley. But he never counted on the Dolphin linebackers and safeties sniffing out his passes. On the opening drive of the second quarter, he sent one for Charley Taylor, but it sailed over his head. Matheson, playing deep for a linebacker, tipped it, and Scott, lying on his belly, snared it one-handed.

However, the Dolphins hurt themselves, with a penalty nullifying a 47-yard TD pass to Warfield, so Kilmer was down just 7–0 when he took the 'Skins across the 50 for the first time. With a third-and-three on the Miami 48, as soon as he dropped back, a blitzing Doug Swift zeroed in. Kilmer forced one down the middle to tight end Jerry Smith. Buoniconti, in his mid-zone, barely had to move to pick it off. His 30-yard runback set up a short drive, during which Griese, on a third-and-four, threw to Jim Mandich, who made a diving catch at the two. Kiick then scored on a one-yard plunge, making it 14–0 at the half.

Shula's blueprint was flawless. Griese had gone 6-for-6. Misdirection runs and trap blocking plays would propel Csonka 112 yards on just 15 carries, and Kiick and Morris 72 more. Larry Brown, meanwhile, was being targeted as soon as he lined up, combinations of linemen and linebackers erecting a wall he couldn't get through. On the bench, he was wincing in pain. And things got worse for Allen in the second half. His kicker missed a 32-yard field goal. A Kilmer pass to an open Smith in the end zone hit the crossbar. On the next play, another end-zone pass went to Taylor. Scott, the game's MVP, again intercepted it and took it back 55 yards.

But finally Allen got a break, if an incredibly strange one. After giving up a 49-yard run by Csonka, his defense made a big play, intercepting Griese in the end zone near the end of the third quarter. And then, with 2:38 left in the game, Yepremian attempted an insurance field goal from the 42. The snap to Morrall, the holder, was low and to the outside, and when the left-footed Yepremian sent it up, the 'Skins Bill Brundige got a hand on it, sending the ball skipping backward near the sideline. Yepremian got to it first. In such a situation, Shula had told him, he was to fall on the ball. Period. But the wee tie maker thought he could *pass*—though to whom, no one knew. Trying to get a grip with his tiny hand—his *right* hand—his arm went forward as the ball squirted straight up. As if playing volleyball, when it came down, he batted it into the air with both hands. It came down in the hands of cornerback Mike Bass, who tripped lightly down the sideline to score a ridiculous 49-yard touchdown, officially a fumble return.

The NFL Films clips would show spare Dolphin linebacker Al Jenkins on the sideline, unbelieving, shouting, "Damn!" While almost everyone else watching guffawed about the *Gong Show* play that seemed to prove Alex Karras right about "keeckers." Shula, who'd seen some wild kicking plays in his day, could have had a coronary. But he had a game to win. All he said to Yepremian was, "Next time, fall on it!" He later said he felt "terrible" for Yepremian, pity not shared by all. When Yepremian came to the bench, the scabrous Bob Kuechenberg told him he'd made a "chickenshit play." Buoniconti double-teamed him: "I'm gonna kill you, you little cocksucker. I'll hang you with one of your ties."[13]

With the game suddenly in doubt with two minutes remaining, Shula kept cool as he sent in his kickoff return team, yelling after them to watch for an onside kick. Allen, though, inexplicably kicked deep, and the Dolphin offense went in. Griese kept the clock moving with a gutty sideline pass to Warfield for a first down. With a minute left, they punted and the defense came in, the ball at the 'Skins 30. Two Kilmer passes fell incomplete. On third down, he tossed an ill-conceived screen pass to Brown, whom Stanfill dragged down inbounds for a four-yard loss, the clock ticking under 40 seconds. The last gasp ended, aptly, when Kilmer dropped back and Stanfill and Vern Den Herder made him into a ham sandwich, dropping him for a nine-yard loss as his helmet flew off, his face in agony.

A victory 42 years in the making for Don Shula was finally won. On the sideline, the Dolphins had begun moving toward him to carry him off on their shoulders, the now-customary ritual of ultimate coaching success. It was, after all, his win more than anyone's, paid for by years of his own agony. With security lax, people were gathering around him, some of them strangers, shaking his hand, patting him on the back. As time ran out, he and Arnsparger embraced, Shula's arm clutching his coach's neck. He then was lifted on top of a scrum of players, his fist shot into the air, and he shouted as they lifted him. Symbolically, he was on top of the world, looking down at the rest of the NFL, his past failures seemingly momentarily irrelevant. He felt something tugging at his wrist, looked, and saw his gold watch gone. Clambering down, he saw the guy who took it, screamed "Hey!" and ran after him, yanking the watch out of his hand and glaring at him, deciding whether to lay him out. He decided he shouldn't. Not now. Not on this perfect day.

Up in the stands, Dorothy, clutching a crucifix, had done a slow boil all game as boozy Redskin fans around her recognized and taunted her. As she began to shed joyful tears, one sore-loser fan mocked, "Aw, look, isn't that touching? The poor thing's gonna cry." Upon which, it was reported, she didn't let it go. Instead, doing what her husband always *wanted* to do at such moments, she "spun around and unloaded" with a punch to the guy's nose.[14]

In the locker room, Shula stood beside the weeping Robbie as they took the Lombardi Trophy from Rozelle, Shula calling it the "ultimate" moment in his life, his men "the greatest team I've ever been associated with." He joked that he didn't know what he would tell them the next year, having used up his supply of motivational fodder, though he would surely find more.

He was, of course, the story, his redemption complete, though in a locker room full of men so conditioned by him, even in a victory of this magnitude, they seemed somber. Reporters sought out Yepremian, the man who almost marred perfection. Most who saw it had to laugh at the volleyball "pass," but it wasn't at all humorous to him. He sat at his locker, head buried in his hands, near tears, saying, "I almost caused a disaster." Then, like a line from a Shakespearean tragedy, "That championship ring will hang heavy on my hand." That night, at the team's victory party at the hotel, he felt a sharp pain in his side, apparently from stress, and was helped to his room, where he sat in a tub of ice water until it eased.

But that was the only blight on the day when the axis of the NFL changed forever. Quoting Shula, the page-wide headline in the *Herald* read, FOR MIAMI, "THIS IS THE ULTIMATE," a photo of Shula being hoisted running above a story about peace talks in Vietnam. *Sports Illustrated's* story was simply called "17-0-0," the cover photo showing Griese poised to throw. Maule, every word like a molar being pulled, granted, "It was not always easy, and far less dramatic than it might have been, but the Miami Dolphins finally demonstrated rather conclusively that they are the biggest fish in the pro football pond."[15] Ed Pope, whose suggestion to hire Shula had paid its biggest dividend in what he wrote was "a cake walk," reported that President Nixon had called Shula, which Maule suggested might send Allen "into a catatonic state."[16]

Schnellenberger saw Shula at that moment as a man who had found the holy grail. "He wasn't relieved, he was cocky. I could see it on his face. He thought he had discovered the formula, the elixir. That he would win again and again. That there was nothing anyone could do to beat him. We all did. And you know what, he should have. Ask him today, and that's the first thing he'll tell you."[17]

A year earlier, Pope had questioned the team's courage and fiber. That was now replaced by giddiness all around south Florida. Another airport mob scene awaited the return of the team. In Miami, where the game kept almost everyone off the streets and beaches, the game's highlights were shown over and over, and car horns blared for days. When that 40-minute movie of the game from NFL Films came out, it redefined the AFC as the new face of the once-unrestrained AFL, with Shula's pug-like countenance the new bedrock of the league. The sublime basso of John Facenda's narration identified the contrast between "the enthusiastic Washington Redskins" and "the somber Miami Dolphins." The Redskins were a "romanticized" team; the Dolphins were all business. Thus did Don Shula, who once carried the romance of the old NFL, stamp "final" the parity the old guard feared, and was in fact the leader of the new guard, far more so now than even Joe Namath.

Nothing, it seemed, could dampen Shula's ascendance to the top. On the bus ride to the airport, Dorothy told him about clocking the fan. "Don," she told him, genuinely worried, "I've blown the whole thing. All the years, all the frustration . . . and now we're going to get sued!" He just smiled, serenely unconcerned, knowing he was untouchable.[18]

Even George Wilson now wanted to share in Shula's aura. While dining out in July, he saw Shula come into the restaurant. He went over to his table and congratulated him, then made a golf date. "I'm glad to be associated with him again," said Shula, who also made a rapprochement, such as it was, with Carroll Rosenbloom.[19] At the spring meetings, where C.R. had snubbed him the last time they met up, Shula put his hand out first, and this time Rosenbloom shook it.

"Don," he said, "let bygones be bygones."

Even so, Shula's success seemed to stoke some questionable judgment. For one thing, it led him to let his guard down to cash in on his good fortune. Seeking investments, he had recently become a limited partner in a real estate venture called the Saratoga Development Corporation, run by Allen Glick, a San Diego lawyer and land developer. Glick also was rumored to be tight with mobsters who had control of Las Vegas casinos. But he was an Ohio guy, and Shula always had a soft spot for those. It's also possible that he began listening to Al Davis more than he should have. Davis had formed the limited partnership, called Red Dog Investors, and sold Shula on coming in, as did some other very high-profile NFL figures, including Bills owner Ralph Wilson—and none other than Carroll Rosenbloom. Later, when it was prudent to separate himself from the deal, Shula would clarify that "I never met Glick. I just knew of a Mr. Glick by name."[20] Partnering up with Glick would be a far bigger problem for Davis down the road, but for Shula, a smaller fish in that stew, it would soon become clear that becoming involved with Glick was an unforced error.

Still, the halo over Shula's head following the Super Bowl proved that everyone loves a winner, and that being one has its perks. He quickly signed for an advance to co-write his autobiography with writer Lou Sahadi. Cleaning up on their own, Csonka and Kiick signed to write their riff-heavy, jokey dual memoir with *New York Times* sports columnist Dave Anderson; Griese also penned a surprisingly candid book about the season. Shula couldn't have been ecstatic that Butch and Sundance had taken public their private griping about his "childish" rules and how Shula had "stuck it" to Kiick, but it was the price of success in the new generation.

Garo Yepremian didn't write a book; rather, as jokes abounded about his historic bumble, he would grow more depressed, too ashamed to even leave his home for weeks, then worry he'd be cut from the team. His fear was allayed when he received a letter from Shula, assuring him of his place on the roster. It helped him come out of his shell. Years later, at a golf tournament with Shula, he told someone that his old coach "wrote the most important letter I ever received." Shula, though, didn't remember writing the letter—and for good reason. It had been written by Dorothy, who frequently signed letters to fans for him, and took it on herself to ease the kicker's worried mind. It worked. Soon, Yepremian himself was making jokes; one went, "President Nixon made me throw the pass."

Dorothy could indeed speak for her husband, knowing him better than anyone. But even she was surprised by his transformation in the wake of winning it all. That winter, in a *Sports Illustrated* profile of Shula titled SITTING ON TOP OF THE WORLD, she told of "watch[ing] the peace on his face. He'd light up a big cigar, and sit there, and I'm thinking, 'Happy at last.' For so long he'd been so sensitive. Small, petty things would bother him." They still would, of course. But as if perfection was a thematic imperative off the field as well, after decades of arising before him and making his breakfast—without variation, black coffee, grapefruit, eggs, and sausage—she said after the Super Bowl, "I'd get up and he'd already have the coffee made. And sometimes he'd even be cutting his own grapefruit."[21]

Inevitably, given that all boats were buoyed by the perfect season, Shula's staff was raided. The first target was Schnellenberger. Joe Thomas had taken a real liking to him in Miami, and when Thomas requested permission to approach the mustached assistant about becoming the Colts' head coach, Shula quickly assented when Schnellenberger told him he would accept the offer. "Hell, they even threw a party for me," said Schnellenberger. It seemed like a minor shuffle as the Dolphins received their championship rings, designed by Shula himself, with 17 encrusted diamond stones and the engraved slogans "Winning Edge" and "Perfect Season." Shula replaced Schnellenberger with Bill McPeak, who had coached the Redskins in the '60s and for the last five years was an assistant with the Lions.

At the draft, the most important draft picks made by Shula and Bobby Beathard were linemen, but Shula also took a QB, Virginia Tech's Don Strock, a six-foot-five, 220-pound specimen of the new generation of linebacker-sized quarterbacks. He would ride the taxi squad as a rookie, but was in Shula's future plans.

The schedule finally gave Shula a home game to begin a season. Against the 49ers, the Dolphins trailed 13–6 entering the fourth quarter, when Griese, who had been off all day, hit Warfield with a 10-yard touchdown. Yepremian booted two field goals, the defense rang up a safety, and the Dolphins prevailed, 21–13, for their 18th straight victory.

The streak finally ended the next game, at the hands of the Raiders in Oakland. The Dolphins kept it close, their stifling zone blitzes and tight coverage disrupting the Raiders' normal air circus. However, John Madden's runners gained 187 yards on 46 carries, and the Raiders' four field goals put them up 12–0 before a late 28-yard touchdown pass to Mandich made the final score 12–7. Over the next two games at home, Miami blew out the Patriots 44–23 and the Jets 31–3. It was in the former that Shula and Bill Arnsparger saw firsthand the new era of NFL defenses. Pats coach Chuck Fairbanks, who had walked on the Oklahoma Sooners, leaving the stink of recruiting violations behind him, installed his Sooner 3–4 gap-two alignment. The set itself was nothing new, but Fairbanks applied his fourth linebacker mainly to stopping the run, and while his team would go 5–9 that season, the idea spread around the league.

Shula's team, meanwhile, never really stopped winning. A Monday night affair in Cleveland—before which Csonka, encountering Howard Cosell in the same hotel the team was staying in, merrily ripped the broadcaster's signature toupee off his head and flung it down the hallway—produced a gritty 17–9 win. They then cranked out 10 straight wins. Again, the schedule was on the soft side, and in consecutive November games, they shut out the Colts and Bills. The closest calls came in the next two weeks. On Thanksgiving in Dallas, they went up 14–0 in the first quarter, the second TD a 45-yard laser from Griese to Warfield, and won 14–7. Next came the Steelers, who played arguably the worst first half ever, falling behind 27–0, with Dick Anderson running back *two* interceptions for touchdowns. By game's end, Miami had picked seven, three off Bradshaw, three off Joe Gilliam, Anderson tying a record with four. Chuck Noll's boys then staged a furious comeback attempt, but fell short, 30–26.

The only real stumble was the penultimate game, the return match with the Colts, in Baltimore. Schnellenberger, who at 2–10 was going through hell, vowed that his team would get even with the Dolphins and not punt a single time. He made it stand up, too, thanks to a lackadaisical effort by Miami, who rested Griese. Behind Marty Domres, the Colts won it 16–3. After being glad-handed by Shula, Schnellenberger recalled, the Dolphin players "ran down the field to congratulate me." That was the sole bright moment he would have. After finishing 4–10, Bob Irsay canned him and Joe Thomas made himself the new coach. Schnellenberger would sit out the next season before Shula asked him to return to the Dolphins sideline. "He said, 'Howard, I need you.' That's all it took."

Fans and reporters knew nothing of the clubhouse "cocktails" and painkilling shots being given to the players, nor the recreational drugs used by Mercury Morris. Headed for another 1,000-yard season, which would make him and Csonka the first pair of backs to each go over 1,000 twice, in that Steelers game he was hit hard by Mel Blount and came up screaming. "I think I've got a broken arm," he told Shula, feeling like "someone had taken a blow torch to my shoulder and opened it wide." In blinding pain, he crawled under the sideline bench. After the game, he was taken to a hospital for x-rays, which were negative; Dr. Herbert Virgin said he had no more than a neck sprain. Months later, when he was at the Pro Bowl, more x-rays were taken, showing fractures of his fifth and sixth cervical vertebrae—a broken neck. He would require delicate surgery, after which he would say, "I will have trouble the rest of my life."

Morris, looking back, took Virgin to task, asserting that he had doled out those "mood pills" and either "blew the diagnosis" or even "diagnosed the fracture from the beginning and then withheld that diagnosis from me." Given the team's desire to see him in the lineup, he said, "a 'misdiagnosis' would have been most advantageous."[22]

Virgin dismissed the allegations. The subject of hiding an injury, he said that year, "never came up." The players, he went on, "trust the medical staff. . . . The players are considered to be my private patients, and the coach backs me up."[23]

As it was, Morris's relationship with the team brass was poisonous. During a Jets game, as Morris was running out of bounds, he barreled right into Virgin, who was knocked violently to the ground. While it was clearly an accident, under the circumstances, it made people wonder. Morris was so peevish that, as he would say, "I was more than pissed off. I was obsessed." Once, practically jumping out of his skin due to dexies, he fumbled for a third time in one game. Wild-eyed, he hurled his helmet 50 yards. "I think you better sit down," Shula suggested. After dashing for a 71-yard TD against the Pats, he recalled, "I came off the field wanting to shove the ball in Shula's face."[24]

Even without a drive for a perfect season hanging over them, the team was high-strung. But they were still winning, and finished 12–2. When they met Paul Brown's 10–4 Bengals in the first playoff round, they tore it up, running 52 times, third-most in playoff history at the time, and gaining 241 yards. The 34–16 blowout sent them into another AFC title tilt, at home, against the always-tempestuous Raiders. This time, Al Davis couldn't mush up the field with water hoses.

The Raider defense came out mouthy, taunting the Dolphins, but was quickly silenced. Shula's intricate trap and misdirection blocking schemes cleared the way for Csonka to amass 117 yards, many on a play called "18 Straight," off-tackle to the right. He scored thrice on short runs, the first two putting Miami ahead 14–0. "We had some success to the right," Shula would say, grinning, of the Dolphins' 266-yard rushing avalanche.[25] The defense, meanwhile, swarmed the gimpy Snake Stabler and ganged up to stop the Raiders' tendency to run to the left side behind All-Pros Art Shell and Gene Upshaw. The Dolphins coasted to a 27–10 victory, Griese needing to throw a mere six passes.

With Shula calling it "a great win against a fine team," Ed Pope was convinced the Super Bowl was a formality, yipping that the Dolphins "may as well brace for that 'dynasty' tag people will want to pin on them." Csonka and Griese's numbers (39 and 12), he suggested, should both be retired "this minute," and that if "Don Shula wore a number, I'd vote for that number to go on the wall, too."[26]

The NFL decided to go ahead with Super Bowl VIII anyway. It would take place on January 13 in Houston's Rice Stadium; the enemy would be Bud Grant's Minnesota Vikings. It was a shot for the Purple People Eaters to avenge their defeat in the final premerger Super Bowl, and for 33-year-old Fran Tarkenton to prove he was more than a mad scrambler. He had done so during an 11–3 regular season before disposing of Allen's Redskins and Landry's Cowboys, aided by a running game led by All-Pro fullback Chuck Foreman. Receiver John Gilliam was also an All-Pro. Minnesota also had arguably the best offensive tackle in the game, Ron Yary. But, as always, the team's bedrock was its aging defense, which gave up the second-fewest points in the league and more than 21 points only once.

They seemed daunting, but as Hank Stram had exposed in Super Bowl IV, Grant's teams were on the light and slow side, and the headline-grabbing studs up front were vulnerable to trap blocking. Still, the Dolphins, whom Csonka called "a lot of quiet, hard-working players that like to go to the bank after the Super Bowl," had learned to say only flattering things about any given foe. This time, there was no George Allen to unnerve them. But, taking no chances, Shula would again conduct practices on an isolated field—and there was an Allen-like interlude when Rev. Brennan Dalton, one of Shula's travel-ing priests, saw "suspicious characters loitering near the practice field," and "two men with long-lensed cameras" in a building across the street.[27] Shula called the cops, but the men had fled, said one report, "in a brown Oldsmobile."

Shula was worried more about injuries to Buoniconti (hip), Kuechenberg (arm fracture), and Fernandez (hamstring). They would play hurt, but the pain was felt by the Vikings. Miami was favored by six and a half points, and on a cool, foggy afternoon, covered the spread within five minutes, when a grinding drive led to Csonka scoring on a five-yard run. As Grant would admit afterward, "I knew we were in trouble after their first drive." And their next drive was a near carbon copy: 10 plays, four minutes, two passes, Kiick banging it in from the one. Grant overplayed his linebackers outside to contain Morris sweeps, but his men were suckers for the Dolphins' array of traps, misdirection plays, and cutbacks—which, Tex Maule wrote, "shunt[ed] aside the Minnesota defenders, especially Middle Linebacker Jeff Siemon, who was attacked by a bewildering variety of blockers."[28]

Running 53 times, many through holes as wide as Minnesota, the Dolphins gained 196 yards. Csonka took by far the most handoffs of his career—33—ringing up a then-Super Bowl record 145 yards. Almost sheepishly, Griese called it arguably the best game of his career, throw-ing just seven times, completing six for 73 yards. Tarkenton did all he could, but Arnspager's wrinkle was to line up Tim Foley as a linebacker, and he and Larry Ball came tearing through the line on blitzes. With Tarkenton having to pass—he would go 18-for-28 for 182 yards and a pick—the Dolphins went with three linemen and a nickel back, smothering the deep lanes, but neither did short or medium passing do any good. When the Vikes, trailing 17–0, did reach the goal line just before the half ended, Buoniconti slammed into running back Oscar Reed, causing a fumble recovered by Scott.

Several times, Griese asked Csonka, whose forehead was cut and bloodied, what play he wanted to run, and in the second half, after a 27-yard pass to Warfield—Griese's sole pass of that half—Csonka notched his second touchdown on a two-yard run in the third quarter—a "roll right, trap left." That made it 24–0, the game effectively over. Tarkenton's touchdown on a four-yard keeper with 12 minutes left averted the shutout, and when a Seiple punt hit the turf, bounced up, and was downed on the three, wrote Maule, "a Minneapolis sportswriter threw his pencil on the floor and tore up his notebook." On the field, a frustrated Alan Page drew a penalty for a late hit on Griese. After Csonka's last carry, he was so spent he could barely stagger off the field, showered by an ovation from the crowd of mostly Dolphin fans. By then, the players were getting ready for another convoy of Shula. Paying homage to the line he had run behind, Csonka said, "You read about me saying I like to run over people, but that's not true. Sometimes it works out that way, but if you look I'm sliding off a lot of tackles because the line has cleared people out so they don't get a clean shot."

Tex Maule, no longer shilling for the old guard, wrote that the game "had all the excitement and suspense of a master butcher quartering a steer," echoing the common syllogism that Shula's team was too good and too mechanical, and therefore a snooze. The Dolphin method, he sniffed, had a "certain esthetic appeal for serious students of the science of football, but left devotees of drama more than a little bored." Not in Miami. The next day, with the *Herald* rhapsodizing the victory, its banner headline IT WAS THE DAY OF THE DOLPHINS, they came home to another victory party set up at the airport.

Shula, always the good son, had flown his parents to the game, and when he mounted a platform erected in the parking lot, he lifted the Lombardi Trophy, then introduced an elderly Mary Shula, the woman whose signature he once forged to keep playing football. She and Dan would soon be able to spend winters in a vacation home in Miami bought by their son, but Mary, frail as she was, smiled wanly, perhaps still not entirely happy that her son had disobeyed her and Dan's orders to bag football for the priesthood.

He also brought to the platform Dorothy, who joshed the crowd that the Shula family had a dynasty ahead of it—and she might be the first woman coach. With the Shulas, anything seemed possible. Theirs was a world owned by the son of Hungarian immigrants, their generation having bred the most popular and profitable American sport.

Ed Pope slavishly anointed the coach he had recommended. In 10 years, he wrote, every team would "have the Shula imprimatur. Shula will still be coaching the Dolphins at age 54, and 25 of his former disciples will be in command of other teams. . . . Instead of being compared with Vince Lombardi, they will be measured against Don Shula."[29] Pope actually was not far off. The truth was that one couldn't, and wouldn't, be able to get very far in discussions of NFL team building and coaching without the Shula brand defining those parameters, long after the Super Bowl celebrations stopped.

16

"CAMELOT DISAPPEARED"

Turning 44 just nine days before the Super Bowl, Don Shula seemed such a natural winner that it was almost jejune to honor him for it. When he lost out to the Rams' Chuck Knox as Coach of the Year, he could live with that. However, the afterglow of 1972 and '73 would dim too soon, the first ominous sign coming when Bill Arnsparger rode his trail of success as Shula's Sancho Panza into being hired by the New York Giants as their head coach. As with Schnellenberger's leap, he had Shula's blessing. But this loss, which Shula dealt with by hiring Vince Costello, Paul Brown's former linebackers coach in Cincinnati, was trivial compared with the convulsion that came next.

That winter, a new pro circuit, the World Football League, began. Its founder and commissioner, Gary Davidson, had announced it the previous October, calling the NFL "arrogant and fat," two things the sport's new owners craved. Well-heeled fatcats could pay low entry fees to the league and spend millions to raid NFL players, though almost all the big names, unavailable until their NFL contracts ran out, could only sign future contracts. Although the lineup of teams had yet to be set, even into the winter, the elder league watched warily as the effort got off the ground, shuddering at the impact it could have on salaries by giving players leverage. But no one knew how big the impact would be until the league made its biggest score of all, hitting Shula like a tack-filled sock.

At first, like most NFL poobahs, he didn't think he needed to fear the threat. But the new league's most ambitious owner was John Bassett, a former championship tennis player and the son of one of Canada's wealthiest sports and entertainment nabobs. Bassett owned a team in the rebel World Hockey Association and bought into the WFL in order to place a team in Toronto, to be called the Northmen. He immediately set out to woo Ed Keating and offer a package deal for Csonka, Kiick, and Warfield. The notion that the three Americans would deep-six the Dolphins after winning two straight titles must have seemed laughable to Keating. For one thing, they each had a year left on their contracts, so even if they jumped leagues, they would have to play an awkward final season in Miami. And Csonka seemed more interested in politics. In early March, he said he might run that fall for a seat in the Florida state legislature, something Keating said was a "complete surprise to me, but he's full of surprises."

But Bassett was relentless, and he had the green, having paid a good bit of it to hire former Dayton head coach John McVay. When Bassett made his offer, it made Keating's head spin: $3.5 million to be split by the trio, as well as a cut for each player of the league's merchandising, a no-cut/no-trade contract, a new luxury car every year, and a rent-free apartment in one of Toronto's choicest neighborhoods. What's more, the contracts were classified as "personal service" agreements, meaning that if the league went under, they would still be paid, something no NFL owner would ever have done, or could have, under league rules.

Ed Pope broke the story, reporting on March 13 that the three would be meeting with Bassett in Toronto 15 days later. He quoted Csonka as saying he was not eager to leave the Dolphins—"Especially Don Shula, the best coach in the world"—but the snowball rolled fast. A week before the meeting, the WFL held a draft, and two other Dolphins— Jim Mandich, who was among 14 unsigned Dolphins, and Don Strock—were chosen. The Birmingham team also would come after

Tim Foley and Bob Kuechenberg, whose older brother Rudy signed with the Chicago team coached by Jack Pardee. This put Joe Robbie in a bind. He needed to move on re-signing the in-limbo players, but the deal offered Csonka, Kiick, and Warfield was more than the entire Dolphins' payroll, and one-sixth of the team's overall value.

As it was, Robbie had kept Mercury Morris from the WFL by tearing up his three-year, $190,000 contract after a season and signing him to a new five-year deal for $675,000—his annual salary of $135,000 a barometer of a new era of untethered spending. He also re-signed Mandich, who had played the entire '73 season without a contract. But if he was hoping this would convince the would-be jumpers that they'd be paid well, he couldn't see any math that would work. As the Bassett contracts were structured, each player would have a three-year deal, Csonka's for $1.4 million (eight times his Dolphin salary), Warfield $900,000, Kiick $700,000. Bonuses worth another million drove the total tab to $3.84 million, a breathtaking figure.

Still, Csonka wouldn't sign until he could talk to Shula, feeling he owed it to a man he was so close to that, whenever the coach would call him on the phone, Kiick would say, "Your dad called." The would-be defectors didn't expect Robbie to match the WFL offer, but they did expect him to at least say he wanted them to stay.[1] Csonka said as much to Shula, who relayed the message to Robbie. But the next day, the owner chose to call not Csonka, but Keating, scolding the agent for having "spirited off" the players and "held them for ransom."[2] Frustrated, Keating issued an ultimatum: Robbie would need to immediately deposit $3.3 million in a bank of Keating's choosing and match the bonus and personal services clauses in the Bassett contracts, an obvious overreach and an impossibility in the NFL. Spitting profanity, Robbie slammed down the phone and shut down any further contact. As much as Shula blamed Robbie for his intransigence, as management, he couldn't publicly criticize the owner—not with his own mercenary past.

On Sunday, March 31, the deal was announced when the three runaways had a joint afternoon appearance on Howard Cosell's ABC television show. While Bassett was thrilled, the players were oddly dour, seeming unsure even now. In Miami, and around the NFL, the news hit like a bomb. Foreseeing that he, more than the defecting players, would be blamed by the team's fan base, Robbie held a press conference in his office, Shula by his side, during which he sputtered, "We were torpedoed" and promised to push back in court against the hijacking of players still under contract to him. Looking as sad as a man can look, Shula merely said he was "disappointed, shocked, sick."

Robbie—who had made it possible for Shula to jump from his old team—also dashed off an open letter in the *Herald*. He said he "deeply regretted" the defections and insisted "we did everything under the circumstances that were contrived," claiming falsely that both he and Shula were kept from speaking with the players by Keating. He insisted he made attractive offers that included outside "business opportunities."

Robbie clearly hoped to save face with the fans, but the fact that the letter ran on April Fool's Day seemed all too appropriate.

The other Dolphin players were sympathetic to the jumpers. "Everybody has their price," said Bob Kuechenberg. Larry Little thought it was good for the NFL, as it would cause a spike in salaries. Others voiced willingness to hear out WFL offers too. Nick Buoniconti wasn't sure that *Shula* wouldn't be in that crowd of possible defectors, saying, "Shula may be the next coach in Toronto. He's got to be looking for greener pastures now, too. Shula's done everything he can in Miami except win three Super Bowls in a row and he'll probably get that done this year."[3]

Although the wild projections of the WFL's influence were far too optimistic, these were heady days for a league that hadn't played a down yet. Pete Rozelle had to put up a brave front, saying the deals would never stand up, that Bassett wouldn't be able to even pay the tax on the deals, much less the salaries. But nationwide headlines were blaring about the NFL losing these valuable assets, leaving league owners and general managers gasping for breath; reflecting the general tone of the reporting, *Time* called it "the deal that astonished sports."[4] Al Davis, though he would lose Daryle Lamonica to the new league and see Ken Stabler sign a future deal with it, wasn't upset as much as envious that the WFL had done in a few months what it took the AFL six years to do: reach parity. It was another highly premature take, but anything seemed possible now.

As for Shula, losing Csonka in particular was, he said, "a bitter pill." Dorothy went further, saying it was like "losing a son," and "we had pictures of Larry and Jim hanging all over the living room, but the day I heard they signed with the WFL, I took them down."[5]

But Shula could be soothed by his own success. During the '73 season, Robbie had given him a five-year contract extension—his existing deal had been due to expire after the '74 season—bumping his salary to over $100,000, more than any Dolphin player at the time. But, according to people who knew him, Robbie believed he was not getting proper credit for the team's astounding rise to prominence, not with all the kudos directed at Shula. To his credit, Robbie always kept his distance, literally; his office was located 13 miles from the Dolphins' team office and facilities. But when they did have contact, Robbie seemed to want to pick arguments over failed drafts and trades and continued to pinch pennies with even the stars of the team. John Underwood would write in *Sports Illustrated*:

> [Robbie] is an enigmatic man, a case study of the type of guy who would pick a fight with Bo Derek on their wedding night. Robbie isn't happy unless the sparks are flying. He has been known to say terrible things to people in the privacy of public barrooms. He has had disputes with community leaders, the press, businesses that dunned him for nonpayments, Pete Rozelle, NFL owners and, of course, coaches, players and agents. The "little people" who work for Robbie complain the loudest, but usually behind his back. There he is roundly rebuked as a "skinflint."[6]

According to Dick Young, the acerbic columnist for the *New York Daily News*, whenever Shula referred to Robbie privately, he called him "that ass——."

Already reeling from the defections, Shula's tipping point came on the night of April 26, at the team's annual awards banquet at Miami's Fontainebleau Hotel. A stickler for punctuality—as was Shula—Robbie became angered when the coach lingered outside the hall, waiting for Dorothy, who was running late. Robbie walked toward him, and as Shula said later, he expected "some kind of greeting." Instead, Robbie expressed his impatience. "We've got a thousand people waiting on you," he bellowed. "Let's get up there!" Jaw tensing, neck vein bulging, Shula snapped.

"Don't ever yell at me in public again or I'll knock you on your ass!"[7]

Robbie wisely backed off and went inside. Dorothy arrived soon after, and they sat on the dais, Shula avoiding eye contact with Robbie. The chill lasted through the evening, and was the talk of the team. Bill Braucher filed a story about it on May 15, reporting that it had taken the intervention of Archbishop Carroll to bring the two men together over lunch. "If we have not been behaving like champions," said Shula, "I regret it," admitting he was "embarrassed about losing my poise," though he made sure to add that "it was very evident he had been drinking." Robbie chose to say nothing publicly about the whole ugly business. Extrapolating from the incident, Underwood wrote, "Under normal circumstances, it would seem too long ago to worry about, an incident one might even laugh over in time. Shula himself is famous for flying off the handle, but once the irritation is off his chest, he forgets it. His relationship with Robbie, however, has never warmed; they aren't even close to being good friends."

Rumors even flew that Shula would leave Miami. When *People* interviewed him and Dorothy during the season, broad hints were dropped: "In spite of the lavish palms and patio Miami living," wrote Ronald B. Scott, "Dorothy longs for the colonial home she left in Baltimore. Both she and Don are wondering what they will do after this season, even though his contract has three more years."

Things had certainly become hairy in Miami. Right after the Super Bowl, Shula had received death threats that he reported to the FBI; that winter, bureau agents guarded his home. He was in good company;

around the same time, both baseball's Reggie Jackson and golf's Jack Nicklaus were also given protection after threats.

Scott averred that "prospects for coaching the Jets creep into his handsome, massive head," and Shula threw in, "I do love the change of seasons—and Dorothy loves Connecticut." Still, the bottom line, wrote Scott, was that "If he leaves he must sell his share in the team." And, as Shula concluded, "I plan to honor my contract with Miami."[8]

He did just that. But during the summer of '74, there was more frustration. Yet another player strike derailed camp and two preseason games, players' union head John Mackey believing he could use the leverage of the WFL raids to gain looser rules for free agency. That limited freedom was a key selling point for the WFL when it went after players. When that league's 12-team season began a 20-game schedule on July 10—moved up from the fall to capitalize on the strike and fueled by a syndicated TV deal for Wednesday and Thursday night games—the teams were filled mostly with obscure names, but had a few established NFL stars. The season was meant to whet the appetite for ensuing years when names like Calvin Hill, Craig Morton, Danny White, Don Maynard, John Gilliam, Duane Thomas, both Raider quarterbacks, Lamonica and Stabler—and, of course, Butch, Sundance, and Warfield—would be free to join the league.

While the WFL hogged the summer spotlight, Shula could again only work with rookies and free agents, giving a boost to draft picks who would play important roles, such as the Dolphins' first-rounder, Jackson State defensive end Don Reese. "You're in the big time now, baby," Shula told him on the phone after making the pick, suggesting he go out on the town and "order anything you like." As Reese recalled, "I ordered a vodka and orange juice. Then a gin and orange juice. Then a bourbon and an orange juice. I was flying high."[9] Other top picks included Arizona State halfback Benny Malone, Hawaii cornerback Jeris White, Texas Tech tight end Andre Tillman, Florida receiver Nat Moore, and Penn State defensive lineman Randy Crowder. But two others, offensive tackle Bill Stevenson and linebacker Bob Lally, signed with the WFL.

The walkout would stretch on for 41 days, coinciding with the fall of Richard Nixon, whom the House Judiciary Committee voted to impeach on July 27 for obstruction of justice in the Watergate cover-up. He resigned on August 8, handing the presidency to former Michigan All-American Gerald Ford. As that convulsion rocked America, and a new one began when Ford pardoned Nixon, the strike ended two days later, when the players predictably caved—seven Dolphins had already crossed the picket line—and reported to camp without a new collective bargaining agreement, union leaders deciding to bank everything on the antitrust lawsuit Mackey filed.

Shula could now get busy defending his second title—which would be tested severely by Chuck Noll and his Steelers, who boasted four 1974 draft picks to become Hall of Famers: Lynn Swann, Jack Lambert, John Stallworth, and Mike Webster. Shula also had to deal with more melodrama from Morris. That summer, a cheaply made blaxploitation flick Morris had "acted" in called *The Black Six*, with costars that included Mean Joe Greene of the Steelers and Carl Eller of the Vikings, hit theaters. If Morris felt like a star, he came to camp as Shula, needing to reconsider his backfield once Csonka and Kiick were gone, planned on working in Benny Malone and Don Nottingham, the latter having come in a trade from the Colts the year before. From day one, Morris was moaning about seeing less time in a revamped Dolphin cast that would also include Nat Moore, who was so fast and slithery that he became the go-to receiver early on, leading the team with 37 catches as well as returning kickoffs and punts.

Meanwhile, the WFL got off to a fast start, with teams in most big-market cities, and some smaller ones like Orlando, Portland, Birmingham, and Honolulu. Playing in stadiums both big-league and comically inadequate, there were big crowds at first, until the NFL strike ended and the novelty gave way to the tedium of low-grade football and headlines about scarce crowds and failing franchises. Players who committed to the league soon had reason to believe they'd erred. The Dolphins' big three, who hadn't even put on their WFL stripes yet, wondered what they'd gotten into. As it turned out, they would not be playing in Toronto after all, but in Dixie. After the Canadian government introduced a law that would bar American players from competing in Canada in any league but the Canadian Football League, John Bassett moved his Northmen to Memphis, to play as the Southmen. By then, the defectors perhaps hoped the league would fold before their time came.

In the meantime, the Dolphins managed to keep ahead of rising teams in the AFC East. The Patriots, their opening game opponent, had added 18 rookies, including future Hall of Fame guard John Hannah, though the team that rose fastest was the Bills, who rode O. J. Simpson's rushing to finish 9–5 that season. Still, when the Dolphins met the Pats in Foxborough, Fairbanks's team ran out to a 24–7 lead and won 34–24. The Pats would win five of their first six games before collapsing. And Shula's boys? They won the next three, but after dropping a close one, 20–17, to Allen's Redskins, at 3–2 Shula was moaning, "Our defense hasn't stopped anybody, and offensively we haven't been consistent."[10]

Then, as if flipping a switch, they won eight of the last nine, dropping only a meaningless season finale to the Jets. Games panned out with the usual mechanical dispatch, the Dolphins scoring the third-most points and giving up the sixth-least despite injuries that cost Csonka two games, Warfield five, Griese one, and Morris nine. The latter's absence, as he feared, opened the door for Benny Malone, a mini-Csonka whom Morris called "a wild man," running straight into defenders instead of around them and frequently getting banged up. Carrying more than anyone but Csonka, he netted 479 yards, and Nottingham 273 with eight rushing touchdowns.

But, in keeping with the team's habit of finding turmoil in victory, Morris became a migraine, his fat paychecks buying no peace for Shula. Having injured his left knee in the third preseason game, he played sporadically. After he made a sensational catch in the win against the Chargers, he was scheduled to come to the team facility for whirlpool treatment, but chose to work out on his own at a local gym. Steamed, Shula sent Larry Little to fetch him. When Morris arrived, Shula told him, "I ought to fine you and suspend you." Sulking, Morris stayed home the next day, and Shula sent him a telegram saying he was suspending him "for good" and fining him $9,000.

"For good" turned out to be exactly one day. After Morris admitted he was wrong in a TV interview, Shula reinstated him. But the trouble went on. Morris recalled that he "allowed them to give me an injection to my knee when I didn't even need one."[11] He would sit out the next six games, even though Dr. Herbert Virgin pronounced him healthy enough to play. Pressed by Shula, Morris did return for two games late in the season, but ran carefully, not with his usual abandon. Meanwhile, both Csonka and Jim Mandich played through significant injuries. Other than Doug Swift, who broke his arm in game eight, replaced at starting outside linebacker by Bob Matheson, everyone but Morris was prepared to play, no matter what.

The season ended at 11–3, another division crown in Shula's pocket. The contretemps with Morris was mostly kept from the fans, though Bill Braucher at one point referred obliquely to the team's "internal strife." Within the Dolphin family, however, players had to choose who to believe: a fellow player who'd always given his all, or management, who said he was a slacker. It was an undercurrent nobody needed, and it would only get worse.

The first playoff round offered up the most compelling game of the season, against the 12–2 Raiders in Oakland, where it rained all week and the field, intentionally left uncovered by Al Davis, would be a bog expected to slow the Dolphins' elephantine running game. The Raiders were the highest-scoring team in football, as Stabler—who had another year before his WFL commitment would kick in—threw 26 touchdowns versus 12 interceptions, making first-team All-Pro. Yet the Raiders seemed to win mainly with their vicious defense, especially their defensive backs—one of whom, free safety Jack Tatum, nicknamed "The Assassin," would leave a receiver a paraplegic after a legal hit in 1978. The strong safety, George Atkinson, left Lynn Swann with a concussion in '76, with Noll impugning the Raiders' "criminal element." Shula, who might have privately admired them for doing much the same thing he had done himself on killing fields in the '50s, now had to find a way around them.

Dan Jenkins ventured in *Sports Illustrated* that "the real Super Bowl will be played in the mud of Oakland this Saturday." It also pitted the two best coaches, John Madden—called "Pinky" for his big-top-elephant appearance and pulpy Irish skin that glowed in the cold—having proven himself to Davis after he got the top job in '69 at age 32.

Shula hoped against hope that Morris could make it, but the latter seemed more intent on retribution against his own coach. Before the team left for Oakland, Morris recalled, "I went to see this Haitian root man, King Solomon, on 54th and 12th . . . you'd go down to his place, and you'd see lawyers there and people like that waiting for him to put some roots on somebody. . . . I told him, 'Shula's trying to kill me. I don't want him hurt, but I want him off me.'" The night before the Dolphins left for Oakland, "I was out in the backyard at 2 a.m., saying chants," and "I made a Shula doll and put it in a box and buried it."

During the game, Morris sat sullen, as if in a trance, in a Dolphin parka on the bench. On the opening kickoff, Moore left Raiders grabbing at air as he streaked 89 yards for a touchdown. The rabid, biker-gang Raider fans, who held semiliterate signs like SHULA + FLIPPER R ROOMMATES, were stunned. The Dolphins also rattled Snake Stabler into an early interception. But Stabler, whose left arm was the only non-cadaverous part of his body, tied it with a 31-yard bullet to halfback Charlie Smith. The game then swung back and forth, Yepremian's second field goal putting Miami up 19–14 with just under five minutes left. Stabler, on his own 28, then hit Cliff Branch, who slipped in the mud and went down. Henry Stuckey, who came in at cornerback after Foley and Lloyd Mumphord were hurt, went to pin him, but he also slipped and Branch got up and scampered for a 72-yard TD.

The Dolphins charged right back down the field. Malone sprung free on a sweep, bounced off a couple of tackles, and ran for a 23-yard touchdown and a 26–21 lead. Stabler had 2:08 left. Burning all his timeouts, completing short, pinpoint passes, he led the Raiders to the Miami eight with 35 seconds left. On the snap, he saw Fred Biletnikoff was covered and began to scramble right. Vern Den Herder grabbed him by the ankles, but Stabler managed to let a pass go as he fell to the ground. The ball floated end over end—a "wounded duck," as Den Herder called it—to the left front of the end zone, aiming for halfback Clarence Davis. Three Dolphins were there, and Mike Kolen got a hand on it—"I thought I had a clear interception," he said later—but the five-foot, nine-inch Davis somehow wrestled it away, tumbling to the turf with it, scoring the lead TD with 27 seconds left. In the NBC booth, Curt Gowdy kept shouting, "Unbelievable!"

Dubbed the "Sea of Hands Play," it was the yin to the yang of the Immaculate Reception that had destroyed the Raiders two years before. Davis's explanation was that it was "by a little luck and the grace of God." Manny Fernandez wasn't as poetic. "I mean, this guy couldn't catch a cold," he said of Davis years later. "It was probably the only pass he caught in his career. It was a lousy pass, a lucky reception [and] I've never forgotten it."[12]

Shula made the walk to midfield to dutifully congratulate Madden, whose team would be trampled 32–14 on the same field the next week by Noll's Steelers. Grim-faced, Shula strode off the field, many fans swearing they'd seen the best game ever. For Shula, who had seen a few on that level, the defeat was the worst to bear—at least Super Bowl III didn't come down to two fluke plays. Losing on that soggy day, he must have known, had knocked him back down a peg below Lombardi.

In the locker room, reported Pope, Shula was "as close to tears as he ever will be as a coach," and "his voice quivered although his chin never dropped." Hiding behind sentiments recycled from past failures, Shula said it was "the toughest defeat I've ever experienced" and that "we went down fighting and that's all you could ask."[13] Shula had to submerge his anger. At Al Davis. At Morris. At the inch more of Stabler's ankle that Den Herder couldn't grab in time. And at himself, for not compensating for it all. Far more emotionally consumed in defeat than they ever were in victory, his players barely moved from their stools.

Foley sat with his head hung between his legs, back facing the room, shoulders heaving as he sobbed. When a TV man held a microphone near Griese, he snapped, "Don't put that thing in my face."

The three now-ex-Dolphins all testified to the joy of playing on "the greatest dynasty ever." Csonka, who had rumbled for 114 yards, insisted, "Until I get back to Miami, I'm still very much a Dolphin."[14] Morris, meanwhile, was shaken, actually believing his voodoo ritual against Shula had worked, and backfired, sinking the team; he would still believe it far into the future. Yet not until the late '80s was he ready to admit his attitude toward Shula had been immature all along, and that "it was only after growing up that I understood Don Shula and saw the contribution he has made to the game."[15]

The game stories the next day carried headlines like "WOUNDED DUCK" FELLS A FOOTBALL DYNASTY. It could have been a metaphor for Shula falling from grace that soggy day, dragged from the throne by Al Davis, when, as Pope codified it, "Camelot disappeared." The plane ride home, wrote Pope, felt like "six continents long," and in that time, the best coach in football could only replay in his mind what he had told the press when he lost some of his shining armor. "When you lose like that," he said, "your dreams go down the drain."

As the '75 season began, it was just plain weird to see Csonka—the 10th-best rusher in NFL history, with over 5,900 yards—Kiick, and Warfield in their garish brown Memphis uniforms, letters peeling off the back, wondering what in the world they had done as their league crumbled all around them. Rozelle was right: the WFL's owners found themselves owing so much in taxes that when the league had held its first championship game, it was played only because the IRS—to which the league owed $237,000—agreed to take a part of the gate, and the winners' jerseys, as payment. The circuit somehow managed to survive even though some teams moved or folded. One coach, Jack Pardee, whose D.C. team moved twice before going under, was able to escape, leaping at the chance to become head coach of the Chicago Bears.

Ironically, now that the bloom was off the orange in Miami, Shula himself again seemed itchy to test the waters. When the Chiefs fired Hank Stram after the '74 season, rumors leaked that Lamar Hunt might do what Robbie had: induce Shula to jump with time on his contract. That, of course, never happened. For one thing, Shula had lucrative commercial endorsement deals in Miami. He would also have been required to sell his interest in the Dolphins—which now stood at 10 percent—the value of which was far above that of the Chiefs. Besides, running out at the first sign of a downturn would be a sure way to regurgitate old notions of betrayal.

That winter, he took Dorothy and the kids on a skiing vacation in North Carolina with Bob Matheson, a departure from the distance he normally kept from his players. He also went on a family pilgrimage to the old country—he, Dorothy, and Dan and Mary Shula taking a long flight to Hungary. They rented a car in Budapest, looking for Mulenshook. "It didn't show on the map," the son recalled, "but Papa inquired and they pointed us in the right direction." When they found it, Dan recognized the house he'd grown up in; when the door opened, there stood a cousin he hadn't seen for 65 years. Inside, over a bed, hung a tattered picture of Dan and Mary on their wedding day, which Dan had mailed to the house, not knowing if it would ever get there.[16] Before they came home, they detoured to the Vatican and had an audience with Pope Paul VI.

Shula returned from this idyll less morose, eager to get to work plugging the holes in the Dolphin ship. He talked George Young into leaving his job with the Colts to become the Dolphins' director of player personnel and scouting. But it would soon seem like he was bailing out water. Once summer camp and preseason games began, Buoniconti broke his right thumb in seven places and was out for the season, and other players kept coming up lame; one, defensive tackle Bob Heinz, tore up a knee and he too was lost for the season. Only one holdover on the defensive line would start: Den Herder. A WFL refugee, John Andrews, was at defensive end.

Griese, Little, Scott, and left offensive tackle Wayne Moore, an undrafted free agent in '69 who had elevated himself to the Pro Bowl, all turned 30 that year, Twilley 32. But the fruit of the previous year's draft crop paid off. Don Reese and Randy Crowder started on the defensive line, and Andre Tillman at tight end. Kolen replaced Buoniconti, but only until a rookie, middle linebacker Steve Towle, moved into the position after eight games and made the most tackles on the team. Matheson took Kolen's outside linebacker slot. Another rookie, five-foot-eleven stringbean receiver Freddie Solomon, who played quarterback in college but was projected as a receiver to help fill the Warfield void, helped do that as well as becoming one of the league's best kick returners. Among the old names, Mercury Morris, through voodoo or not, would stop bitching for a while when he finally got his wish to start consistently in the backfield. Adding a fullback, Shula traded with Joe Thomas for the stumpy Norm Bulaich, his last first-round pick with the Colts.

Shula would start the season against the Raiders in the Orange Bowl, booked by the league as the first Monday night showcase. Al Davis had cemented the last piece of a championship puzzle by sticking it to Shula—acquiring his prototypical linebacker/lineman with the Colts, Ted Hendricks. And he stuck it to Shula again on the field. The game was a mess. Each team turned it over five times. Stabler threw three picks—all to Charlie Babb—and, almost inconceivably, Griese threw four. After the Dolphins fell behind 17–0 early, Griese had to air it out 32 times, completing just 15. The Raiders' Harold Hart returned a Dolphin kickoff 102 yards. Final score: 31–21, Oakland.

Things looked even bleaker the next week in Foxborough. Against a team that would go 3–11, they were down 14–0 at halftime. But in the second half, Don Nottingham, who had carried just four times against the Raiders, came in for a struggling Bulaich and kept breaking big gains, one for 40 yards, racking up 120 in all on 16 runs and scoring a touchdown. Bulaich came back for a short TD run, and two Yepremian field goals put it out of reach—a 22–14 win that *Sports Illustrated* qualified as "uneasy." Still, again confirming the premise that Shula did his best coaching when against the wall, the Dolphins not only were jelling, but it seemed possible that Shula's prodigal sons would return to him.

The WFL could only make it through 12 games of its 18-game schedule before closing up shop, with no champion declared. This spared players like Stabler, who had signed future deals, from playing peewee-league football for uncertain money. For Csonka, Kiick, and Warfield, all of whom struggled, none making the league's All-Star team, it threw into doubt their guaranteed personal-services contracts and whether they even still worked for Bassett. His team, renamed the Grizzlies during the aborted season, had drawn well and Bassett wanted to hold on to his prize trio. After the league drowned, he and the owner of the Birmingham team would apply for entry into the NFL. The Dolphin renegades would still be paid their king's ransom, and were precluded from signing with the NFL again until the courts could rule on whether their personal services contracts were still valid. Adding more confusion, the Dolphins still retained NFL rights to Csonka, Kiick, and Warfield, though this, too, was uncertain because the Mackey lawsuit was moving toward a conclusion in a Minnesota circuit court, the ruling on which would determine whether the Rozelle Rule's oppressive compensation realities applied to the current crop of free agents, including the WFL survivors.

Things sat in limbo for the rest of 1975, though in Miami there was an expectation that the wandering triad would come back home. The *Herald* ran a headline reading, WFL IS DEAD—CSONKA EYEING RETURN TO DOLPHINS. Csonka said he was open to the idea, but there were complications. For one, Robbie was no more forgiving of their betrayal, nor the players of him for saying they had held the Dolphins for "ransom." And the Dolphins were doing fine without them; as Csonka said, "I can see that Shoes has no bleeding ulcers where running backs are concerned." Shula agreed, saying Nottingham and Bulaich were doing "excellent jobs."[17] He also raved about Solomon and the other receivers, a message to Warfield. If the three, and especially Csonka, were like sons to him, it seemed Shula's attitude was that once fish swam, they were on their own.

Bassett's attempt to keep the Memphis team in business would also take months to play out, and he advised Csonka, Kiick, and Warfield to sit tight, that he would continue to pay them to do nothing. That sounded good to Csonka, who seemed more eager to relax on his Ohio farm than play. Kiick, though, began to openly petition for employment, not on the Dolphins but his native team, the New York Giants, coached by Bill Arnsparger. Warfield spoke of finishing out his career with a final year back in Cleveland. Pending the resolution of the Mackey suit, Keating still had to deal with the Dolphins. And Robbie was no more open to paying any of the "traitors" what they wanted. When Csonka got hungry to play again, he called Shula, only to find his old coach and father figure standoffish, unwilling to do anything until the courts had their say. He also worried about Csonka's health after years of punishment.

Csonka spent the autumn on his ranch, his only appearance being with Kiick and Warfield when they went to New York and were called out of the audience of Howard Cosell's new, ill-fated Saturday night variety show. They rose, smiled, waved, then went back to playing the waiting game. In Miami, meanwhile, Shula would win seven in a row. With two games left, they were 9–3, a game ahead of the resurgent Colts. Even without Arnsparger, the defense under Vince Costello would surrender the fourth-fewest points in the NFL. With Howard Schnellenberger back running the offense, they would rack up the sixth-highest scoring attack. Morris, by midseason, was the NFL's second-leading rusher behind O. J. Simpson. But when Shula started alternating his starts with Benny Malone, he once again violated Shula's public-bitching rule, saying he wanted to be traded. Shula said he would try to accommodate him. But for now, he needed Morris to get him through the playoffs.

A win against the Colts in week 13 would clinch the AFC East. Ominously, Griese was out injured, replaced by Don Strock. As impressive as the Dolphins had been, so were the Colts under coach Ted

Marchibroda, whose big weapons were Bert Jones's strong arm, Lydell Mitchell's jitterbugging feet, and the "Looney Tunes" defensive line led by Joe Ehrmann and John Dutton. The game was a slog for both teams under a low fog of what seemed like pea soup in a funereal Memorial Stadium, but the Dolphins' running attack was in high gear. Dutton would say the Miami line "conducted a clinic out there. I never knew where their blockers were coming from next."[18]

In the third quarter, Morris, who skirted for 96 yards on 21 carries, scored the game's first touchdown on a three-yard jaunt. Mitchell tied it with a six-yard TD in the fourth. The Dolphins had chances to ice it, but it ended up in overtime, whereupon Jones conducted a long drive from his own four and the Colts kicked the winning field goal. "Miami was on top for a long time," said Mitchell, pronouncing his team the new kings of the division—big words from a team that would be crushed the next week by the Steelers.

On the Dolphins' team bus back to the hotel, Morris, who led the team with 875 yards rushing over the season, was seated behind Shula, who Morris said was in a "particularly bad mood." Seeing Lloyd Mumphord, who had been his roommate in Miami until traded to the Colts after a run-in with Shula, waving to him to get off and "party with him," Morris did, knowing full well that, by leaving the bus, he would break the rules again. As he recalled, "Shula stared at me, and I knew that was it,"[19] meaning his time as a Dolphin.

At 9–4, Miami still could draw an inside straight for a playoff berth. The Colts needed only to win their final game to cop the AFC East. But if Baltimore lost, and the Dolphins won the finale on Saturday at home against the Broncos, they'd sneak in. They did their part—barely. Spotting Denver a 10–0 halftime lead, they had to rally behind Earl Morrall, whose 10-yard TD pass to Howard Twilley cut it to 10–7 before a late drive capped by a short Bulaich run stole the game, 14–13. Shula may have thrown in an extra Hail Mary at Mass on Sunday morning, and more as he watched on TV as the Colts trailed the Patriots 14–10 at halftime. But the Colts pulled away and won 34–21. That was more bitter fruit for Shula, who had nonetheless done quite likely his best coaching job yet, going 10–4 with a sundered team held together by Scotch tape and spit. Those who had been expecting him to fall on his craggy face had to give him renewed props. Still, he felt cheated being out of the playoff picture for the first time in five years, just as his protégé Chuck Noll rose to eminence by winning consecutive Super Bowls. Indeed, Shula would have to preserve his reputation by winning more games than anyone could have foreseen, within a continuing maelstrom of discontent.

17

"IT'S ALMOST BIZARRE"

In 1976, when the Nixon years were purged by the election of a smiling Georgia peanut farmer, the NFL was forced to accept that its players could begin to share in the exploding profits previously hoarded by the owners. That year, the players' union's gamble paid off when a district court judge handed down a verdict in John Mackey's suit, ruling that the Rozelle Rule violated antitrust laws. Rozelle vowed to fight the decision all the way to the Supreme Court, but for the time being, he wrangled the union into accepting "Plan B" free agency, giving owners the right of first refusal on 37 of their players, a policy that still exists for one chosen veteran player per team since the rule was rewritten in 1992, when unrestricted free agency became a reality.

The ruling, which Joe Robbie swore would make the NFL an "endangered species," had an immediate effect on the WFL refugees, who still belonged to their old NFL teams but only owed them the right of first refusal, after which they could sign elsewhere without compensation. Csonka, Kiick, and Warfield were also freed from John Bassett when, rebuffed from entering the NFL, he released them, meaning he wouldn't have to pay them after all. The three were so intertwined that there was still the possibility they could again swing a package deal, though this was complicated by Ed Keating having branched out on his own. While he still represented Butch and Sundance, Warfield stuck with IMG, where he was being represented by ex-Browns fullback Ernie Green. He did sign with Cleveland, while Csonka dallied with returning to Miami.

In truth, Shula missed Csonka in the two losses to the Colts in '75. Now the coach arranged a "summit" in Miami between himself, Csonka, and Robbie, which Bill Braucher believed would prove that "Shula has an edge. His personality and methods hold a compelling fascination for Csonka," having made Csonka "a durable wonder . . . almost in spite of himself." However, when Robbie's offer got back to Csonka, he felt insulted and canceled the meeting, saying, "I was made out to be a fool" and "what he [Robbie] did hurt me deep down."[1] The next day, April 7, Csonka signed a fat, three-year, $1 million deal with the Giants, who would move that season into a new stadium in the New Jersey swamps and hoped for a revival after two dolorous seasons under Arnsparger. To help lure him, the team hired John McVay, Csonka's Memphis coach, as an offensive assistant, though the deciding factor may have been the personal enrichment of playing in the Big Apple.

Kiick, meanwhile, had to settle for a far less lucrative deal from the Denver Broncos as a backfield backup, to be released during the '77 season and play out his career with the Redskins. Thus ended the short-lived football buddy movie, the aging urban cowboys riding off toward different sunsets, though Csonka would still have another scene to play out with Sheriff Shula down his dusty road.

Shula had less regret about losing his "sons" the second time. As Howard Schnellenberger saw him, Shula "wasn't gonna get that close to any players again. He'd tell 'em all the same thing: 'You'll know when I'm damn ready to play you—or damn ready to trade you.' "[2] That spring, several aging players found that out. Norm Evans, left unprotected in the expansion draft, was taken by the new Seattle Seahawks. Doug Swift, facing a crossroads, retired. These moves alone saved the team $150,000 in salary. Nick Buoniconti announced his retirement in July after Shula said he would only have a backup role, but injuries to other linebackers led Shula to talk him into returning for one more season. Then there were the usual fandangos with Mercury Morris and Jake Scott.

Shula hung on to both, despite Morris's feeling that he was a goner and Scott's habitual trade demands, and despite them having the highest salaries on the roster. But Braucher wrote that Scott and Shula had "bickered" all through the '75 season, and it continued into training camp. Shula had seemingly defused it, grinning that the All-Pro safety hadn't repeated his trade demand since camp began. But in mid-August, Scott cursed out an assistant coach. When Shula interceded, Scott barked, "I wasn't talking to you."

Still, Shula let it go. A photo of them on the practice field ran in the paper, Scott, in thick muttonchop sideburns and dark shades glaring at Shula, who was holding his head as if he had a splitting migraine. Then, after injuring a shoulder, Scott refused a painkilling injection before a preseason game, sitting out instead. Shula, of course, had gone through this with Morris, though Scott went further, threatening to sue Dr. Herbert Virgin for malpractice, and Shula suspended him. He was reinstated a week later, whereupon he blew off the team's annual awards banquet benefiting the Boy Scouts, at which attendance was mandatory. After Shula fined him $500, Scott laughed that he had come out ahead, since he'd won $700 at the track that day.[3] Ed Pope, taking Shula's side as usual, foamed that Scott, who had been called "Big Play Jake," had lost his hunger with a big contract, was an "old" 31, and had been given "exceptional personal latitude." Concluding that Scott was a "burr," Pope asked, "Who needs it?"[4]

As for Morris, he went on mouthing off, saying he felt like "the odd man out" again in the backfield. At the same banquet, the team award for best offensive back went to Morris, Nottingham, *and* Bulaich. Morris took this as another sign that he was about to be shipped out, and even said he'd be happy to go anywhere except the moribund San Diego Chargers. And Shula was finally "damn ready" to trade both problem children. In late August, saying Scott had "refused to play,"

Shula dealt him to the Redskins for safety Bryant Salter and a second-round draft pick. Morris was sent packing hours later—to San Diego, for a mid-level draft choice.

Morris assumed the destination was intentional, a case of Shula spite. Decades later, he said, "I'm still bitter about it."[5] Scott, on the other hand, left skid marks getting away from Shula. Weeks later, after intercepting two passes in a game, he rebutted Shula by saying, "I never did refuse to play, at any time. But I will take no Xylocaine in a preseason game. That's ridiculous." Unlike Shula, he said that, under George Allen, "you're respected like a man." He went on, "The system here relates to the intelligent ball player. In Miami it was more of a robot-type system."[6]

He didn't say anything about winning two rings playing in Shula's system. Nor would he win any more under Allen in Washington, who after another three fruitless seasons left to coach again for the Rams. Scott, still effective but never to make All-Pro again, would be gone from the game a year later. As for Mercury, he reported to the Chargers, intermingling uninspiring play with pot shots at Shula. But, given that the broken-down Morris was a second-stringer in San Diego and gone from football after one more season, the corroborative lesson of these purges was that Shula usually made such moves after he had wrung all he could out of his players. And then, they weren't set free as much as they were disowned.

Only weeks before the '76 season would begin, Shula maintained his usual stoic calm and clenched-jaw resoluteness, even as the papers were writing about the Dolphins' "upheaval." He said he didn't consider their situation to be such, but rather the plight of any team in transition. And he had some good fortune. Among the new pieces were draftees like Arizona State linebacker Larry Gordon. He fell into Shula's lap when Joe Theismann decided to leave Canada and play in the NFL with the Redskins, who had to give Miami their first pick, at No. 17. Two slots later, with their regular pick, Shula took San Jose State linebacker Kim Bokamper. Later picks brought

New Mexico State receiver Duriel Harris and Cal Poly running back Gary Davis.

Shula also shuffled his assistants. After Bill McPeak suffered a mild stroke, he took a leave. Shula had also let go of Vince Costello, and then Monte Clark when the 49ers offered him the head coaching job in '76. Shula filled that hole by hiring John Sandusky away from the Eagles staff to coach the offensive line—for what would be the next 18 years. Schnellenberger concentrated on the receivers. Carl Taseff was given double duty with the runners and special teams, Tom Keane with the defensive backs and punters. Don Doll, who had replaced Shula as the Lions' defensive backs coach and had been doing the same job in Green Bay, came to Miami as linebackers coach for two seasons. But there was no actual offensive or defensive coordinator. Shula regarded himself as both.

He also was his own general manager, and he made a fortuitous trade by acquiring linebacker Rusty Chambers from the Saints. When the season started, the Dolphins won two of their first three games, then lost three, including another to the Colts and one in overtime to the decaying Chiefs. With passing yardage exploding around the league, Shula wanted a real passing attack, and though it was not his forte, Griese made it work. In early November, he went 16-for-21 with two touchdowns in a 27–7 rout of the Jets, putting the Dolphins at 5–4. But now they had to play three straight powerhouses—Pittsburgh, Baltimore, and Cleveland—and lost them all.

The three defeats killed the season, which ended at 6–8, third in the division, Shula's first of what would be only two sub -.500 seasons. He had an excuse: 10 of his players had surgery during the season, but he blamed himself for staying too loyal to the old dogs. "Maybe," he said, "I felt too strongly that people like Mike Kolen and Manny Fernandez and Dick Anderson would be able to come back and play. I can't let that happen again. If they come back next season healthy, fine, but I can't accept it as guaranteed until it happens."[7]

He was fortunate to be able to get back the guy he was most loyal to: Bill Arnsparger. Entering the '76 season, Arnsparger had won 7 of 21 games overseeing the Giants. Then, in the stadium in the Meadowlands, playing before enormous crowds of 80,000, the team imploded, Csonka debilitated by numerous injuries. Winless after seven games, Arnsparger was axed and replaced by John McVay. He would never again hold a head coaching job, but he always would have a sanctuary with Shula, who rehired him as defensive coordinator. It was Csonka's sad fate, however, to remain the center of attention on a lousy team, running only around a dozen times a game and insisting pitifully, "I'm not an old man." Casting his gaze southward, he was tantalized by the fact that Shula had finally gotten natural grass put in the Orange Bowl, while in Giants Stadium he was running on the artificial turf he had hated during his Dolphin years. Suddenly, the thought of playing again in Shula's backfield before he crumbled seemed appealing.

With the Dolphins' 1976 season ending early, Shula had time to ponder what had gone right and wrong. They'd come in 15th in points, for and against, losing only eight fumbles, best in the league, but while Benny Malone ran for nearly 800 yards, Griese threw 11 touchdowns and 12 interceptions. Jim Langer was the team's sole All-Pro. The Colts did displace the Dolphins at the top of the division, going 11–3 before being slammed by the Steelers in the first playoff round—costing Joe Thomas his job. With the Patriots also highly competitive, Shula seemed on the side of the road as the Raiders finally slew Noll's Steel Curtain in the AFC title game, earning them the right to trash the Vikings in the Super Bowl.

Worse for Shula, his team—and he—were suddenly tainted by scandal and legal woes. In late January of '77, a story broke that the arrest and trial of a former golf pro and gambler named J. Lance Cooper on bookmaking charges had "prompted an investigation" of the Dolphins by the NFL—which was requested as a cautionary measure by Shula, who was called a "friend" of Cooper, as were Bob Griese and other players. The NFL cleared them of any wrongdoing; Cooper pleaded guilty and was given probation.[8] Then, offensive tackle Darryl Carlton— Shula's first-round pick the year before, who was busted for marijuana possession but was kept on the team while he served in an "inter-vention" program—"went berserk," beating up a bouncer in a strip club. He tore a door off its hinges before fleeing in his car, which he then wrecked in a fiery five-car crash that left him with serious burns. Carlton plea-bargained down to careless driving and was handed one year of probation—a common dispensation for athletes at the time.[9] Shula eventually traded Carlton to the Redskins.

Finally, the ominous news broke on May 4, the second day of the '77 draft, that Don Reese and Randy Crowder had been arrested on felony charges for selling cocaine to undercover Miami cops in a sting operation. Also arrested was a 23-year-old flight attendant, Camille Richardson, for having arranged the $3,000 sale. She told the *Herald* she'd partied and snorted coke with nine NFL players—six of them Dolphins, though only Reese and Crowder were named and charged. Caught with more than a pound of cocaine, the pair nonetheless pleaded innocent. Shula seemed shell-shocked. "It's almost bizarre," he said. Acting decisively, he suspended the two, saying "their futures hinge on what a judge and jury decide. If they're guilty, naturally, I don't want them around." That went for any other of his men who were involved with drugs—at least, the drugs not prescribed routinely by the team doctor. "I would like to know [who they are] as soon as possible," he said, vowing: "I wouldn't want someone to get special treatment because he's a football player. If a guy's guilty, he should pay the penalty just like anybody else."[10]

This raised the question of why he *didn't* know what was going on right under his own nose, an ignorance that had likely shortened the career of Mercury Morris and perhaps others. Shula was no different than other coaches, even the toughest of them, who were perhaps will-fully ignorant of the burgeoning problem. Indeed, despots like Chuck Noll and Tom Landry had nothing on Shula when it came to cultural tunnel vision—or perhaps just looking the other way. Both of them ducked blame for some hellish behavior by their players. Noll, for example, had put up with Ernie Holmes, who in 1976 had been busted for coke possession but whose trial was postponed so he could play the season, and who was eventually acquitted.[11] Noll's backup quarterback, Joe Gilliam, was addicted to cocaine and heroin, and was sent to rehab, but he never got clean and would die at age 49.[12]

To coaches, these were "isolated incidents," as Shula himself said. However, that was of small solace when the *Herald* ran a page one headline like SIX DOLPHINS USED COCAINE, DEFENDANT IN DRUG CASE SAYS. Shula's longtime bootlickers in the press corps didn't cede him any safe space; headlines like CLOUDS OVER DOLPHINS GROWING DARKER and ARRESTS LEAVE TEAM IN DISARRAY seemed to indict him for losing control. For whatever reason, Shula never did get to the bottom of the drug problem, nor did he ever say if he knew who the other cokeheads were. He also took a lenient position, hinting he might take Reese and Crowder back, even if they were convicted. But Robbie had already made up his mind, summarily waiving them while blustering about protecting "our legal rights," not the players'. That prompted the *Herald*'s Bob Rubin to opine that, "in Robbie's eyes, they are guilty no matter what a jury finds."[13]

Reese and Crowder were convicted weeks later, sentenced to a year in the Dade County Stockade, then given probation and told to keep their noses clean. When they got out in August '78, Shula said they "should not be condemned for all time," arguing—like the liberal he once was—that they had paid their societal debt. He took flak for that in the papers, and was shot down again by Robbie, who not only said they would "never play for the Dolphins again," but called for Pete Rozelle to ban them from the league. Rozelle, foreseeing the legal tangle of doing so, left the door open for any team to sign them. Quickly, both were picked up, Reese by New Orleans, Crowder by Tampa Bay. After a final year in San Diego, Reese would retire in 1981 and write a landmark exposé of the league's drug plague in *Sports Illustrated*, in which he violated his parole by admitting to continued cocaine use.

Reese's anecdotes about playing for Shula were damning. He said cocaine had been "pushed on players, often from the edge of the practice field. Sometimes it's pushed by players. Prominent players." He said Lloyd Mumphord had brought it into the team's training camp dorm, and that he was snorting at least once a week, as were "half the players on the Dolphins—whites as well as blacks." On the team plane, he recalled, "we'd be in the back where it was dark, with our little brown bottles that held about a gram, and we'd sit and sniff right out of the bottle. Or if we were being extra cautious, we'd slip into the bathroom and sniff it there." Shula passed off the sensational revelations as the product of Reese's imagination. "I just refuse to believe [it]," he said. "I realize now there had to be some [cocaine] involvement. . . . But I wasn't ever conscious of [it]. [And] I'd be the first to notice it." As proud as he was of his players, he concluded, "I would not accuse or indict them on what Reese says."[14]

Reese—whose return to prison coincided with Mercury Morris being sent to jail for cocaine trafficking with a 27-year sentence (he was released after three, on a technicality)—would insist Shula knew more than he let on. Still, Shula kept things from blowing up the way they had with other teams, including the Saints teams Reese played on, as white powder swept through the NFL with no real response by the league office. Though there would be still more problems in this area, and some would judge Shula as weak and even clueless, Reese acknowledged that, despite the coach's lapses, "[T]he best thing we had going for us in Miami was Don Shula. He's smart, and he's been around players too long not to see things. Everybody always had to be on their toes. That kept the lid on." Even if not on those little brown bottles.

Shula dealt with the loss of two starting defensive linemen by drafting LSU defensive end A. J. Duhe and Alabama defensive tackle Bob Baumhower with his first two picks. As the purge of old-timers went on, Shula gave Jake Scott's old free safety slot to an undrafted walk-on, Grambling's Vern Roberson; a ninth-rounder, Norris Thomas, would soon start at left corner. Earl Morrall, at 42, could finally quit, Don Strock having paid enough dues to qualify as Griese's backup. Garo Yepremian would join him in retirement after the season, going out as an All-Pro. And Nick Buoniconti agreed to return for the final season of his Hall of Fame career. The fourth round pick, Texas A&M halfback

Leroy Harris, would get as many carries as Norm Bulaich. This flurry of change was rare for Shula, but becoming less so. Rick Volk, who at 32 was signed as a free agent that year, said he was a coach "trying to get control of a team a lot of people assumed was a mess."[15]

As if Shula needed any more uncertainty, Griese's vision was now an issue. The year before, having double vision in his right eye—he later would say he was actually legally blind in the eye—he began wearing contact lenses, then glasses. Up in New York, when Larry Csonka was asked about it, he said his old teammate "could play with one eye" and, "if they put braille on a football, he could play blind." If Griese had any vanity issues, he put them aside, becoming the first bespectacled QB, even if it meant he would look more like Buddy Holly than Bart Starr. In the season opener in Buffalo, the Dolphins slogged to a 13–0 win in a driving rain. "Sometimes I had to throw through bubbles," he smiled, "but I could see." He appeared on Shula's TV show wearing battery-powered specs with tiny windshield wipers.

The Dolphins won their first three, the last a 27–7 rout of the Oilers in which Griese rang up 21 first-quarter points for the first time in seven years. Dan Jenkins jived in *Sports Illustrated*, "It is still too early to know for sure, but it now appears that the city of Miami will be saved by Bob Griese's four eyes—and not by legalized gambling or nude beaches or [orange juice pitchwoman] Anita Bryant." He noted that "Miami has gone from a grind-it-out team to a 'get the ball into the hands of Nat Moore or Duriel Harris or Freddie Solomon if you don't mind' type of franchise."[16]

Griese would indeed throw for 2,252 yards, his most with Shula, his 22 touchdowns (against just 14 picks) the most in the league, and he was first-team All-Pro for the first time since '71. His big target, Nat Moore, also made the first team with 12 touchdowns. Almost with no one noticing, the rushing game was the league's fifth-best, Malone clearing 600 yards, halfback Gary Davis 500, Bulaich and Leroy Harris 400, and Nottingham 200.

Tied for the lead in the AFC East at 9–3, they had to go to Foxborough to play the Patriots, who were 8–4 and an elite bunch that, but for a horrific call in the playoffs the previous year, would have scuttled the Raiders' march to the title. However, Chuck Fairbanks had managed to make enemies all around, with the Sullivan family that owned the team overruling his inflated contract promises to key players. But Fairbanks motivated them. On an icy field, the Dolphins fell behind 14–0, forcing Griese to throw 38 times, completing 22 for 260 yards. In the third quarter, his arm was hit as he passed and the fluttering ball was intercepted. The next drive, he seemed to throw a TD to Moore, who was ruled down short, and on the following play, he overthrew Tillman in the end zone, kicking the turf in anger. He did hit Moore with a 23-yard TD later in the quarter, but the Dolphins lost 14–10.

However, quite helpfully, the Colts managed to lose later that day, too, creating a three-way tie. Shula had to win the finale against the lowly Bills in Miami on Saturday and hope the Pats beat the Colts on Sunday, letting the Dolphins sneak in. There were only around 40,000 in the Orange Bowl, most fans having given up hope, but Shula had his men growling. Griese went 10-for-14 for 210 yards and two touchdowns, Moore reeling in five passes for 144 yards, one on which he followed Larry Little on a flare pass all the way to the end zone for a 67-yard score. Buffalo's Joe Ferguson threw for 331 yards, but was picked thrice. It was 21–0 Miami at the half, 31–14 at the end. The next day, Shula had a premature tingle when the Pats took a 21–3 lead on the Colts. Then Bert Jones's third straight touchdown pass made it 24–23 Pats, and with Shula sitting on a folding chair at the training facility, watching a TV, can of beer in his hand, Baltimore took it down the field and ran it in, winning 30–24.

Frozen out again at 10–4, he went home cursing that the refs had screwed the Pats. The Colts' win did them no good; beaten once more by the Raiders in the playoffs, they would finish no higher than fourth over the next decade. But Al Davis, too, would stumble, losing the AFC title game to the Broncos, who fell victim to Tom Landry's resurrected Cowboys in the Super Bowl.

To be sure, Shula and Landry had proved through the most trying of circumstances that they could keep a team in the pack at the home stretch most every year. Their greatness was certified. But living with defeat, and making excuses for it, would claim large portions of their careers. Neither would ever be able to accept it, but as Shula had learned long ago, it was the nature of the business he had chosen. And the thrill now seemed not to be in the kill, but rather the hunt.

18

SUBPLOTS AND COUNTERPLOTS

The winter before the 1978 season, Shula's real estate partnership with the shadowy Allen Glick belatedly bit him. In the years since they became partners, Glick had been the subject of an FBI investigation dealing with the Mob's control of Las Vegas casinos. When that hit the papers, Shula suddenly ended the partnership, saying "it wasn't a good idea" for "a guy in my position" to be involved with someone like that. By contrast, Al Davis defiantly increased his involvement with Glick, giving the NFL ammunition in its escalating war with Davis, which would ignite when league owners rejected his bid to move the Raiders to LA two years hence. While Glick did neither Shula nor Davis any good, in the end all three of them escaped serious repercussions from the partnership, and Glick rehabilitated his image when he became a cooperating witness against Vegas wiseguys. Still, for Shula, the headlines about being somehow associated with a Mob type were an embarrassment, the worst implication being that he was anything like Al Davis.

Even so, Shula had bigger problems with his owner. For one thing, Joe Robbie had cost him his draft guru. Fed up with Robbie's penury, Bobby Beathard parlayed his relationship with Shula into a cushy job when George Allen quit the Redskins to go back to the Rams for the third time—only to be canned in preseason amid open rebellion by the players—and Edward Bennett Williams hired Jack Pardee as head coach and Beathard as general manager. This would prove to be the jumping-off point for the aging whiz kid to become a Hall of Fame executive, though it didn't happen in earnest until Joe Gibbs replaced Pardee in 1981. As John Underwood wrote of Beathard's falling out with Robbie, "his swan song was acid rock. He said his scouts had gotten one raise each in four years, and that Robbie wouldn't even pay their way to the Super Bowl. He said Robbie was 'just not an honorable person.' Nice knowing you, Joe. See you around, Bobby."[1]

The irony was, Robbie was sitting on a franchise now valued at $30 million to $40 million, and like all NFL owners, he profited hand-somely from the league's $140 million-a-year contracts with the TV networks. Robbie, wrote Underwood, was "a rich man with a flair for flashy spending (a $10,000 party for the cast and crew of *Black Sunday* in Miami; an $80,000-a-year contribution to his favorite university, Notre Dame, both accounted for under Miami Dolphins, Ltd.)." How-ever, he had gotten himself into hot water with the IRS for back taxes, a festering boil that would soon rupture. Amid this darkness behind the team's glowing brand, Shula's purge of veterans could be under-stood as a consequence of Robbie's henpecking about the bottom line. As Shula would say, paying guaranteed contracts "had an effect on the caliber of play. It hurt us."[2]

As management, Shula toed the company line as the balance of power shifted to the players, a shift that would accelerate in the '90s. No matter the caliber of his players, however, Shula kept the team in contention, adapting his sights to Robbie's outdated, priggish ways, as Underwood wrote, "despite front-office turmoil that would rival the court of Louis XVI in quirks and intrigue, in divisive subplots and counterplots that would have done in or driven out a lesser man."

Shula certainly deserved his props. Ever since his "I'll knock you on your ass" tongue-lashing of Robbie, they had coexisted peace-fully, if uneasily, the chilly discomfort between them palpable. When Shula had signed his most recent contract, he insisted on a clause that officially stated that Robbie would not interfere in coaching and personnel decisions. But Robbie could still criticize, and he had reason to do so about most of Shula's drafts—in the '78 edition, he had no first-round pick, and only three players would stick beyond a few seasons.

However, Shula came up a winner, thanks to the newest gamble gone bad by Joe Thomas. His next stop on his revolving-door tour of the NFL was in San Francisco, hired by the 49ers' new owner, Ed DeBartolo Jr. as his general manager. In '78, Thomas was determined to bring an aging O. J. Simpson to his native Bay Area. He traded five draft picks to get him, leaving the 49ers' top rusher, Delvin Williams, disposable. Williams, a former champion sprinter, had rushed for over 1,200 yards in '75, and Shula leaped, offering in exchange Freddie Solomon, safety Vern Roberson, and Miami's No. 1 and No. 5 picks. Not incidentally, the Colts were also after Williams, and agreeing to send Williams to Miami may well have been Thomas's way of flipping off Bob Irsay.[3] Even though Shula had to explain why he was giving up so much for one man, he considered it a favor, and he wouldn't forget it.

It was on the eve of the season that this writer met up with Don Shula for an interview that grew into a day-long sojourn with a man known to shun journalists beyond the locker room. It might have been the writer's engaging personality (not likely) that eased Shula's wariness, or the fact that, back then, there was little national exposure for athletes or coaches beyond *Monday Night Football* and the sports magazines. If so, this set Shula apart from Tom Landry, who was also a gracious man, but one who limited interview time and seemed not to care a whit about exposure, hating the Cowboys' branding as America's Team. Shula, more relaxed by the minute once away from team business, ferried the visitor around Miami in his sensible station wagon and to his home on the 16th fairway of the Miami Lakes Country Club. There, he poured himself a scotch and soda, then took a call from his son David, who was a sophomore receiver at Dartmouth. "Know all your plays?" he asked.

His other four kids were out, as they usually were, with friends, playing sports, hitting the beach, doing things their old man didn't have much of a yen to do; indeed, he had never played the golf course he lived on. Dorothy Shula, an ample, engaging woman with a neon smile, whom he still looked at with the googly eyes of a teen, did not seem much of a Miamian either. Both of them would drop hints, unprompted, about leaving for an old-guard, big-city NFL town someday, which made it natural to ask him about his prickly relationship with Robbie.

"Our relationship hasn't gotten any better," he said, "but it hasn't gotten any worse."[4]

He seemed to know that was the best he could hope for, especially in light of the fact that Robbie, as if wanting to meddle by proxy, named his 35-year-old son Mike the Dolphins' assistant general manager. But Shula would have to face losing a top adjutant, Howard Schnellenberger, for the second time. He had taken the head coaching job down the road at Miami University, where he would resurrect a moribund program and win the national title in 1983. Shula once more carried out the offensive coordinator duties himself, and there would be no quarterback or receivers coach until the next season, when he hired Dan Henning away from the Jets.

When the '78 season began, he again kept the team in contention despite the injuries, such as Griese's bruised ribs that kept him out of seven games of the new 16-game NFL schedule. Even missing so much action, Griese was All-Pro again, and when he was out, Don Strock ably handled the position. Del Williams ran for a career-high 1,258 yards and eight touchdowns, earning first-team All-Pro honors. Nat Moore, whom Shula sometimes lined up in the backfield to mask his routes, caught 48 passes and had 10 touchdowns.

At 8–5 with three games left, they blasted the Redskins 16–0 and then the Raiders 23–6. Now came the finale at home against the Pats, the last of three Monday night affairs. The latter had clinched the AFC East at 11–4; a Dolphin win would square the records, but not overcome the Pats' advantage in tiebreakers. Still, Shula could take the wild card, and as it happened, Chuck Fairbanks practically gift-wrapped it for him. Detested by the Sullivans and most of his players, Fairbanks had secretly cut a deal with Colorado University to become their head coach in 1979, breaking his New England contract with four years left. A day before the finale, Billy Sullivan and his son Chuck—neither of whom had objected to Fairbanks breaking his Oklahoma contract to come to New England—suspended him. On game day, the Dolphins came out before 72,000 Orange Bowl fans to engage a dazed and confused opponent. Griese methodically went 12-for-13 for 171 yards with two touchdowns. He called a flea-flicker that produced a 38-yard completion. The final was 23–3, the late-season rally getting Shula into the playoffs at 11–5.

It was a job well done. Thin as they were, the Dolphins had scored the second-most points in the league and given up the sixth-fewest. They forced the most turnovers (53, with 32 interceptions) and suffered the fewest (30). The wild-card playoff game would pit them against the Oilers again on Christmas Eve, at home. It was no secret that Shula's game plan was to not let Earl Campbell, the league's top rusher for the first of three straight years, grind his team into dust. He would take his chances on Dan Pastorini's passing, which often ended with interceptions. Pastorini would be playing with a sprained knee and bruised ribs, but so, too, would Williams and Davis play hurt.

The Dolphins would jam the rushing lanes, tracking Campbell with two linebackers. While he carried 26 times, he never broke free, gaining a very hard 84 yards. But provoking Pastorini backfired. He amassed 261 yards in the first half alone, while Griese—who took two pain-dulling shots for his ribs before the game—struggled. He went just 11-for-28 for 114 yards and was picked twice—the second after Houston went up 10–7 in the fourth quarter, preceding Campbell's one-yard TD run that put it out of reach, 17–7. The final indignity was when Shula yanked Griese with under two minutes, and then Strock threw a concluding pick. It was, understated Shula, "a tough way to end the year," words that had already begun to sound like a dirge.

It was Chuck Noll who was left standing at the end this time, nipping Landry's Cowboys in the Super Bowl. Survival in the league was always a crapshoot among a few elite teams and coaches. The best teams and the best minds were offered no guarantees. As Shula had learned, the best any coach could do was stay at the water's edge, waiting for the right tide to come in. Even when it seemed to, it could leave you drowning.

Youthful and pug-faced as he neared his 50th birthday, he still seemed like a man cruising for a fight. The coaches he invited comparisons with—Paul Brown, Papa Bear Halas, and Vince Lombardi—were gone or in retirement. The two men responsible for his ascent into pro coaching—George Wilson and Carroll Rosenbloom—died within a year of each other. The scabrous C.R. had just announced the Rams would move to Anaheim in '81. He had been wintering at his Miami Beach home not far from Shula's when he went for a swim in the ocean, apparently suffered a heart attack, and drowned. (*Apparently* because people began pushing conspiracy theories that he had been murdered, that wiseguys to whom he owed gambling debts had somehow pulled off an aquatic whacking—speculation that the LA coroner had to officially dispute even four years later.)[5] He was given a VIP send-off, his funeral attended by Hollywood big shots and NFL figures, some crying a few crocodile tears. Shula may have shed some of those himself, his detente with C.R. never really free of the foulness of their breakup.

On the eve of the '79 season, he had two years left on his Dolphins contract, and there would be the usual speculation about his intentions regarding staying in Miami. He had kept his value high by overachieving with middling squads and constant melodrama. The latest of that quotient was provided by his number one "son" returning to the family. That off-season, the Giants refused to pick up the option year of Larry Csonka's contract, making him a free agent. By then, Csonka felt tainted by his New York detour, with reason. He helped create the most epic screw-up in the team's long history—the late-game handoff he fumbled, which the Eagles' Herm Edwards picked up and ran back for the winning touchdown. That play—"The Miracle of the Meadowlands"—cost both Csonka and John McVay their jobs, though McVay would go on to serve nearly two decades in the 49ers front office.

Csonka's landing was less cushy. Now 33 and gimpy, he wanted to quit on a high, and suddenly he had a newfound appreciation for the benevolent dictator in Miami. And Shula now thought it a good idea to bring him home for a last hurrah in the sun. He talked Robbie into letting bygones be and set up a meeting between the old combatants. As Shula recalled, "Once Zonk and Robbie got in the same room together, things went pretty smooth. It's hard to be mad at a guy that's meant so much, that's been such a part of the success."[6] Neither did Robbie have a problem forking over $125,000 for Csonka's valedictory contract, though Shula had to dispute that it was an act of sentimentality rather than sound football logic.

"I have a good memory for guys that really put it on the line for me," he said, "but if I ever let emotion enter into it, I wouldn't be doing my job as a football coach." Throwing in some Shula brine, he added, "He still has to win a job on the football team."

Csonka was so serious about doing so that he even came to the rookie camp sanguine about the drills, gassers and 12-minute runs, or the rules he'd once chided as "childish." He wasn't Sundance now; he was dancing in the dusk. "I've had a mood change," he said. "I still think Shula's training camp is a bunch of hooey—his curfew and all that. But for the first time in my life I'm ready to cooperate in every instance." Having ballooned to 264 pounds, he didn't need Shula to hound him into losing nearly 30, eating one meal a day and subjecting himself to the torture of a medieval device called an Orthotron, built by the trainer Bob Lundy; strapped in, he would lift his brace-covered leg in endless repetitions. Once, the retired Jim Kiick visited the camp and heard him screaming.

"What's all this moanin'?" Kiick asked.

"Go to hell," a sweating Csonka replied.

"Zonk," Butch warned him, "this is only the beginning."

Actually, it was the beginning of the end. But it allowed Dorothy to put the old pictures back on the wall. Shula named his new collie Zonk, merrily saying the pup "was always banging into things, knocking things over. And he was the kind of dog if he ran away I knew he would come back."[7] In Shula's merit system, there could be no higher praise than when he said, "The guy has immense pride."

Around the team, Csonka, who felt like he was more of a dad than a teammate, was revered, a role he was not always comfortable with. A writer from *Sports Illustrated*, Tom Archdeacon, found him in the Miami bar he owned, Stagger Lee's, where he "has been minding his own business, picking up bar tabs for his Dolphin teammates, including several rookies he doesn't even know by name. . . . All eyes are on him, and although he relishes the attention, he doesn't know what to do."

Still, that he could turn back the clock was something even Mercury Morris envied. Now retired, and in cocaine hell, Morris also realized that Shula had his own voodoo. In San Diego, Morris said, "I could take my helmet off, get a drink of Kool-Aid, and relax," but under Shula, "I never had a drink of water on the practice field. A player like me needs that regimentation."[8] Another Dolphin who had demanded a trade, Marlin Briscoe, now admitted that he "bitterly regretted" it. "It was in Miami that I learned how to win," he said. Kiick, for his part, spoke of Shula as a man of subtle distinctions he couldn't see back then. "Voicing your opinion doesn't get you in trouble [with Shula]," he said, "but complaining gets you in the doghouse." He admitted he did the latter more than the former.

Csonka didn't complain. Prepared to be a third-down, short-yardage guy and blocker for Davis and Williams, he passed by Leroy Harris at fullback early on. He was now younger only than Griese and Little on a roster getting younger all the time. Yet he was the story of the season. He would carry 220 times—more than anyone, and one more than his previous high for a season—and gaining more yards per game than at any time since '74. He put up 837 yards and 12 touchdowns, and caught 16 passes, his most ever under Shula. The Dolphins didn't score a ton of points, nor did they need to with a defense that yielded the fourth-fewest yards and points.

The Dolphins started the season 4–0, but this was no joy ride. There-after, they couldn't win two in a row again until November, along the way dropping a Monday night showdown in Oakland, 13–3, and another in overtime to the Browns. The key game was the Thanksgiving night match at home against the Patriots, each team sitting at 8–5. The Pats, coached now by Ron Erhardt, had ripped up the Dolphins 28–13 in week eight, and led this one 17–13 at the half. Then Miami wiped them out, scoring 29 unanswered points and winning 39–24.

After splitting the final two games to end the season at 10–6, another AFC East crown in the bank, a harder task awaited them in Pittsburgh, in what John Underwood described as a meeting of "football's best team against football's best coach," confirming the remarkable reality that, even with Shula six years removed from a playoff win and Noll owning three rings to Shula's two, "even today, when two or more foot-ball people get together, chances are the consensus will be that Shula is the NFL's top coach."[9] Noll wouldn't have argued; indeed, his own reign wasn't built for long-term perpetuation, but for domination until inevitable burnout. At the tail end of that reign, the 12–4 Steel Cur-tain came in as nine-and-a-half-point favorites, the largest spread ever against a Shula team.

The game, on a cold and raw December 30, confirmed the spread. In the first quarter, the Steelers ahead 7–0, Miami safety Neal Colzie muffed an interception in the end zone and Terry Bradshaw then threw one for John Stallworth. Closing in on him, the mobile Vern Den Herder and cornerbacks Gerald Small and Norris Thomas all collided with each other, and Stallworth took it in for a 17-yard TD. Bradshaw then hit Lynn Swann from 20 yards out, and it was 21–0. The Steelers ran 40 times for 159 yards, Franco Harris gaining 83, and Bradshaw was 21-for-31 for 230 yards. In a hole early, Griese went 14-for-26 for 118 yards and a TD to Duriel Harris, but he also overthrew tight end Bruce Hardy in the end zone and later threw a killer pick at the Steeler two. The final: 34–14.

There was no soothing syrup from Shula this time. Looking sick and no doubt feeling, as Ed Pope put it, "how Napoleon felt trying to take Moscow," he bemoaned, "I can't be proud of the way we came here and did not challenge them in a game that meant so much." Offensive guard Ed Newman said, "We never had a shot to express ourselves." Pope's take on Griese was like an elegy: "He has had a grand and glorious career but . . . he has shown a sharply diminishing ability to make the big play."[10] Griese had been given a new multiyear contract that season, but now he was talking about retirement. He would give it another go, but prepared himself to ride it out on the bench, a symbolic turn of the page as the new decade would begin with almost nothing left of Shula's title teams, and a whole new challenge of settling on a new quarterback.

Shula was so low about how the '70s were ending that he was dripping with self-pity. The league was about to name a ceremonial Team of the Decade, and Shula was already conceding that "I don't think we will be given any consideration." Someone asked him if he thought that honor would go to Chuck Noll's team. "That's obvious," he said.[11]

He could take losing. He couldn't take pity from others, which is what the Steelers' faint praise for the Dolphins seemed to be after the game. Joe Greene, meeting up with some of the Dolphins as the teams left the field, told them, "Nice try, guys" and "You guys hung in there"—condescendingly, some believed. Nonetheless, the end of the '70s would mark just the halfway point in Shula's reign as a head coach. And Noll? After beating the Rams in the Super Bowl, he would win his division four more times, but never return to the Super Bowl— nor would the team until 1995, under his successor, Bill Cowher.

The holy trinity of Shula, Noll, and Landry, who had lost to the Rams in the playoffs, would carry on—still in eminence, but fading. Of the three dinosaurs, though, Shula would avoid extinction the longest. Impressive indeed was his seeming ability to shed his skin and reinvent himself year after year, young and swaggering all over again.

19

"THIS IS STILL MY PRODUCT"

Despite Shula's preemptive concession, his Dolphins did win the contrived Team of the Decade designation—the deciding factor being his 104–39–1 regular-season record in the '70s, bettering Noll's 99–44–1. Naturally, it was cold comfort for his less-than-sublime record in the playoffs. And it meant little in the ongoing tug of war Shula seemed to always be having with the man who had brought the team into the world, Joe Robbie. The first order of business for Shula in 1980 was to obtain a new contract before his current one expired after the season. The problem was that Robbie was in hot water with the IRS, which in the spring of '80 dunned him for what was reported to be $600,000 to $700,000 in back taxes. That meant Robbie had to secure huge loans, putting up the Dolphins' bottom line as collateral, subject to collection if he didn't make his IRS payments.[1]

Robbie's stalling on a new Shula deal exacerbated their latent personal feud. Frustrated, Shula seemed to send up a smoke signal that he was through with Miami. He decided to sell his 10 percent of the team's stock back to Robbie for $750,000 and give up his title as vice-president. This was something Landry had also done in Dallas, to loosen the tethers the Cowboys had on him; in both cases, it meant the coaches were underselling themselves—Shula's interest in the Dolphins was probably worth around $3 million.

It appeared Shula might even wind up at Notre Dame, a perfect job for him. He went to South Bend to meet with the school's athletic director, Moose Krause, who held informal negotiations on the golf course. As Shula recalled wryly, "Moose said there was no hurry. He'd accept my decision after we finished the front nine." Shula could appreciate Krause's impatience. His coach, Dan Devine, who had replaced Ara Parseghian in 1975 and won the national title in '77, would soon announce he planned to retire after the '80 season. Krause wanted a seamless transition to the next head man, and if Shula came to terms, it would mean both he and Devine would be lame ducks that year. It would also mean Shula, as coach-in-waiting, would invite the same sticky situation Chuck Fairbanks had.

The point became moot, however. There was no chance Shula could commit to this or any job based on an afternoon of golf, if in fact he had serious interest to begin with. He was, after all, hugely popular in Miami, and he knew he could leverage that popularity with Robbie. So he let the Notre Dame fable die, whereupon Krause would hire Gerry Faust, whose five-year reign would be unsuccessful. Shula continued negotiations with Robbie, in a process that took what one writer later called "an excruciatingly long time coming to terms," which hardly helped the relationship any.

In the meantime, there were other contracts Shula and Robbie had to tie up, and Shula had to go about that task without George Young, upon whom he had relied to keep track of the contract minutiae. Wellington Mara had offered Young the general manager's position with the moribund Giants—a job he would hold for the next 18 years, reaping two championships and, like Bobby Beathard, going to the Hall of Fame. (He was also the NFL's senior vice-president of operations until his death in 2001.) The priority for Shula was Don Strock, whom he expected to be ready to replace Bob Griese. Strock was given a multiyear deal at $100,000 per season. As insurance, Shula drafted LSU quarterback David Woodley in the eighth round.

Besides Griese, the only championship Dolphins left were Larry Little, Vern Den Herder, and Bob Kuechenberg, all on borrowed time. And then there was Larry Csonka. Feeling young again after his comeback season, for which his teammates voted him the team's MVP, he wanted more loot to keep going. When summer camp began, Robbie offered him a $100,000 raise, but Csonka held out for another $300,000, to be on the same level as Del Williams. Instead, Robbie said publicly, "We did more for Larry Csonka by a hell of a lot last year than Larry Csonka did for us." When Csonka met with Shula in his office—where the coach kept a signed Csonka helmet on his desktop—he asked the coach if he agreed with the owner. Shula wimped out, saying, "I can't comment on that." Soon after, Shula did admit, "I totally disagree with the way that it was handled by Joe Robbie." But if he tried to change the owner's mind in private, it didn't work.

Indeed, Robbie hadn't even allowed Ed Keating, whom he detested, to enter the talks. "It's all supposed to be family and team spirit," Csonka said, "but when I try to talk to them, they make it sound like money, money, money." He gave a little, dropping his demand to $250,000. Robbie made his final offer of $230,000 in early August, yet Csonka remained a holdout. Miffed, Shula felt he had gone as far as he could for his "son." He announced, "The door is no longer open. It has been slammed shut."[2]

Csonka was waived, feeling "bewildered" and "betrayed" after he had "busted my rear" for the team. Yet, Shula's timing was right again. Csonka, who then retired, popped up in the news the following spring as the subject of a federal investigation into a "major marijuana smuggling operation." He was said to have had discussions with undercover agents about transporting large amounts of weed between Louisiana and Miami.[3] Csonka's first response was "I've never smuggled anything." Shula's was a familiar "I find it hard to believe." But when called before a grand jury, Csonka took the Fifth. In the end, he got off easy. Authorities concluded he was a "casual acquaintance" of one of the prime smugglers, and he had gotten suspicious and backed out of the deal. But if he hoped to come back to the Dolphins, that misadventure killed off Sundance for good.

Shula had no compunction about making his own demands. When the preseason ended and he still hadn't gotten his contract, he said he would break off negotiations if not signed by opening day. Robbie took until the Saturday before the opener to give Shula another three years at $450,000 a year, then the highest salary paid to a head coach in the history of the game—though Ed Pope posited that "at least a half-dozen clubs" would have given him "upward of three-quarters of a million dollars" in '81. "So," concluded Pope, "it was more than money."[4] Presumably, that meant loyalty to a team owned by a guy he could barely stand. Perhaps it was just that he could see clearly down the road and liked what he saw. John Underwood, quoting a Dolphin insider, wrote that Csonka's final exit "may have been good for Shula. It finally forced him to quit looking to old solutions." Still, Underwood added, "the ugly, stupid dispute [with Csonka] opened at least the memories of old wounds and exposed the realities of life in wonderful, whimsical Robbieland."[5]

Shula went into camp with his usual optimistic front. Underwood noted that the coach "has high hopes for some of the Dolphins' recent acquisitions. That Jon Giesler [his first-round pick] and Eric Laakso have helped solidify the offensive line. That Alabama All-America Don McNeal is already a star in the secondary." Armed with his new contract, Shula marched onto the field in Buffalo, where he had won 21 games in a row—and left it beaten, 17–7. Hobbling and brittle, Griese started, launching his farewell season by throwing two picks before being relieved by Strock, who threw two of his own.

But the Dolphins then won three straight, Griese rifling the Saints with 241 yards and a TD, going 16-for-23. He followed that up with 272 yards in a loss to the Colts. However, Griese came away with his right shoulder injured and Shula, playing a hunch, went with the rookie David Woodley in the next game, against the Patriots. Woodley couldn't have been much worse, going 11-for-28 for 48 yards in a 34–0 loss, which exposed the Dolphin running game as anemic, more so because Shula didn't start Del Williams in six games because of unspecified disciplinary issues. The workload went to Tony Nathan, the third-round draft pick in '79 who had gone to the Pro Bowl that year as one of the league's top punt- and kickoff-return men, and veteran Terry Robiskie, acquired from the Raiders.

Shula decided to stick with Woodley, who for all his flaws usually kept games close enough to win, reaching his acme when he threw three touchdowns and ran for another in a 35–14 blowout of the Rams. A week later, they beat the 49ers. That ran the Dolphins' record to 6–5. The next game was a Thanksgiving night national TV showcase against the 7–4 Chargers in the Orange Bowl, pulling a record crowd of 83,013. They saw an instant classic. It swung wildly back and forth, the teams compiling nearly 700 total yards between them. In the fourth quarter, Don Coryell, whose high-flying offense, dubbed "Air Coryell," relied on Dan Fouts's arm, turned Fouts loose and he put the Chargers up 24–17 with his third TD pass. Then, with time running out, Woodley hit key passes, and on a fourth down, Williams plunged in from a yard out to send it to overtime.

The Chargers had gotten to Miami at 2 a.m. because of plane trouble, but seemed the fresher team. Halfway through the OT, Woodley aimed a pass for Nat Moore. Linebacker Woody Lowe smelled it out, grabbed it at the Miami 40, and ran it to the 12. A field goal ended it at 27–24; Shula called it "one of the toughest losses we've had around here in a long, long time."

Still reeling, they were decked by Noll's Steelers a week later, 23–10. The season now seemed meaningless, but they went on to beat the Patriots on Monday night, December 8, 1980. It turned out to be a historic game, not for anything that happened on the field, but for the stunning moment in the fourth quarter when Howard Cosell broke away from commenting on the game to solemnly reveal to the nation that the biggest avatar of his generation, John Lennon, had been murdered in the courtyard of his Manhattan apartment building.

The Dolphins finished 8–8, the soft spots obvious. The offense had the fourth-fewest points and third-fewest yards in the league. And yet, a play here or there, and who knows what might have been. Even though Woodley threw more picks than touchdowns, he won six of his

11 starts and nimbly evaded pressure with his scrambles, sacked just 10 times. Shula saw enough to be able to tell Griese he was free to retire at 35. He would punch his Hall of Fame ticket in 1990.

Shula again burned that there was no postseason for his team, but seemed somewhat relieved that he had almost no lingering ties and loyalties to the past. His young defense, ranked ninth, was stocked with ferocious hitters. He and Arnsparger had decided to go to a permanent 3–4 set, anchored by Bob Baumhower at nose tackle, left end Kim Bokamper, and inside linebacker A. J. Duhe, whom Shula had switched from defensive end because of his range and speed. His totally recast secondary had 28 interceptions, fourth-most in the NFL. Shula had staked his reputation and status on the kids, and they were about to roll.

In the crazy quilt of the Dolphins' front office, however, things weren't as calm. There still was no official general manager, the title being held by Robbie's son Mike, with the understanding that Shula had the final say on all decisions. No one really knew who was supposed to be signing players—the one area Shula kept a distance from—and while he noted that personnel director Chuck Connor had helped him draft 22 players still on the roster, he said he was "understandably appalled" about losing Oklahoma halfback David Overstreet, the first-round draft pick in '81 who, feeling stiffed by Robbie, signed with the Canadian league.

He also saw tragedy take another player. On July 1, Rusty Chambers, the roving linebacker and the team's leading tackler in '78 and '79, was killed in a car accident. That, of course, jolted the team beyond words, and their grieving only added to the uncertainty surrounding the Dolphins' future. The team, wrote one scribe, "lacks in so many areas it will be the miracle of the century if [Shula] breaks even again" in '81.[6] Robbie had gotten so frustrated that he began to hint that he might be willing to call a truce and rehire Joe Thomas, who had been run out of San Francisco after two galling seasons. Few could make sense of Robbie reclaiming Thomas. Speculating, John Underwood wondered if the owner was preemptively "cushioning himself for a fall if Shula finally calls it a career" and "doesn't rebound from last year."

But as long as he was in power, Shula wouldn't be steamrolled. He'd had a cordial relationship with Thomas in the past, but he had watched him become a despot who created chaos wherever he went. A friend of both men said that Shula saw the irascible Thomas now as a "non person" for "doing in" some Shula allies, the latest being Monte Clark (who wound up coaching the Lions and would return to the Dolphins' front office in the '90s). Still, Shula owed Thomas for Del Williams and was willing to have him back, though he made it clear that there was "no room" for Thomas in player personnel, a function Shula would now conscript.

Given Shula's all-encompassing leverage, Robbie could only offer Thomas an administrative position, with no say in drafting or trades. At least, that was the original arrangement, with Thomas as vice-president for special projects, such as being a liaison with the Miami Sports Authority, the city's newly created sports bureaucracy with which Robbie would need to reach an agreement for a new stadium. Thomas, it was said, was conducting "how-to-watch-football classes for women," to which Underwood jibed, "If that is the case, then Robbie hired Rembrandt to paint the mailbox."

All this was meant to mollify Shula, and Thomas paid him the respect of calling him in order to "set the record straight" on his duties. Although Shula made it clear he believed "Monte got the short end," he averred that he bore Thomas no ill will. But he did clarify, "This is still my product. I'm in charge of decisions that affect this team." In a move apparently designed to install another buffer against Thomas encroaching on him, Shula got Robbie to hire Charley Winner—the former St. Louis Cardinal and New York Jet coach, and Weeb Ewbank's son-in-law—to fill the role of personnel director. Only then did he agree to allow Thomas the leeway to help sign players.

But Thomas may have taken that concession as an inch he could stretch into a mile. While he confirmed he would not be involved in personnel matters, he would attend practice now and then. When he did, Shula would get his back up. Things were tenser than ever, the troika of executives rarely speaking and casting suspicious sidelong glances at each other.

Of course, it wouldn't be a Dolphin summer without contract drama. In the run-up to the '81 season, Williams held out. Shula had no patience for such vanity; already a problem child, Williams was 30 and prone to nodding off in team meetings, which he claimed was due to narcolepsy. Shula dealt him to Green Bay, where he would be injured and retire. His place would be taken by 23-year-old Andra Franklin, the second-round draft pick out of Nebraska the year before, who had mainly sat during the season. In '81, he was a workhorse in the Csonka mold, a pulverizing blocker in addition to carrying 201 times for 711 yards, second to Tony Nathan's 782. This balanced backfield allowed the jittery Woodley to sit in the pocket, though he was prone to panic and tearing off on scrambles.

Shula, in fact, had put together another of his autopilot teams, the kind few regarded very highly but looked up to find at the top of the division all season. Without much notice, and with Woodley so unreliable that Shula often yanked him for Don Strock—the two known in tandem as "Woodstrock"—they finished 11–4–1. It was another little Shula miracle by a team that boasted exactly one All-Pro, Baumhower, yet gave up the fifth-fewest points.

It got them a home game in the first round of the playoffs—a break for Shula, who had not won a postseason game since 1973. The divisional-round matchup on January 2 brought another edition of the Air Coryell Chargers. That year, Dan Fouts had come within 200 yards of being the first QB to break 5,000 passing yards. Fouts's targets were terrifying: future Hall of Famers Charlie Joiner and tight end Kellen Winslow—the league's top receiver for the second year in a row—and All-Pros John Jefferson and Wes Chandler. Fullback Chuck Muncie, a great athlete with a checkered past and a festering cocaine habit, led the NFL with 19 rushing touchdowns. Coryell, who with his crooked beak and beady eyes rivaled Shula for owning the best coaching face in the business, notched a 10–6 record, his offense ranked No. 1, while his defense was the polar opposite—No. 26, dead last, against the pass.

The Dolphins brought out Miami's Archbishop Edward McCarthy before kickoff. "May the best team win," he said to the crowd, concluding his prayer with "and you know which one that is." But the Chargers were slight favorites, and they seemed an easy bet as they screamed to a 24–0 lead after one quarter. When Woodley was picked off to set up a Fouts TD pass, he was benched—"ignominiously," wrote Paul Zimmerman—for Strock, and the tough kid from the Pennsylvania coal country threw quick touchdowns to Joe Rose and Tony Nathan.

With six seconds left in the half, Shula got funky and called a "hook and lateral," a schoolyard play that began when Strock fired a pass to Duriel Harris at the Charger 25. As he was going down, Harris shoveled the ball two-handed to Nathan, who ran in untouched for an electric 40-yard touchdown. No team had ever been behind by 24 in a playoff game and won. But the Dolphins surged, and with the crowd edging toward insanity, the comeback was complete on the first drive of the third quarter. Shula, seeing the Charger linebackers laying off his tight ends, called passes for Rose and Bruce Hardy. Another to Rose, a 15-yard dart, tied it at 24. But Fouts had Winslow, who was so talented, Coryell left him to his own devices; as John Underwood wrote in *Sports Illustrated*, "Winslow plays just about wherever Winslow wants to play: tight end, wide receiver, fullback, wingback, slotback," as well as—fatefully—on special teams.

Fouts found Winslow for a 25-yard TD. Strock countered with a rare deep route for Hardy, who reeled in a stunning 50-yard bomb. After Lyle Blackwood picked off Fouts, Nathan ran one in for a 38–31 lead early in the fourth quarter. Things were looking good for Shula and grim for Coryell, who once said it took him months to "get over the depression" of losing, something Shula could relate to. Now, observed Underwood, Coryell was "hunched over, hands on knees, his eyes looking despairingly at the scoreboard, as if a new depression had already begun."[7] But he got a gift. With time running down, Franklin fumbled. Fouts took his team 82 yards to the Dolphins 10, and on a busted play, scrambled and floated one to tailback James Brooks in the end zone, tying it with the extra point.

Strock did get the Dolphins into long field goal range with seconds left, but at the snap, Winslow exploded straight up and batted down Uwe von Schamann's kick. Players and fans were already limp in the muggy night, the vibe much like the Colts–Giants "greatest game ever" and the Christmas double-overtime win over the Chiefs. In this overtime, both kickers, first Rolf Benirschke then von Schamann, missed—*again* blocked by Winslow. A second extra session loomed when Fouts squared up and hit Joiner with an enormous pass to the Miami 12.

To that point, Fouts had rung up 433 yards, completing 33 of 53; Strock was 29-for-43 for 403 yards. Three Charger receivers had gained over 100 yards, as had two Dolphins. But it came down to Benirschke, a wafer of a man who'd nearly died two years earlier from Crohn's disease. This time, from 29 yards out, he put it through. After four hours and a combined 1,000 yards and 10 touchdowns, the players seemed like they had survived the siege at Bastogne. Winslow was so spent, he fell to the earth and needed to be helped off by two teammates. Shula greeted Coryell, barely able to keep from imploding. No hyperbole seemed out of place, not even Winslow channeling Martin Luther King by saying, "I feel like I've been to the mountaintop."

Ed Pope, in adjective overdrive, wrote an ode declaring it "the finest football game ever . . . a dizzying, dazzling, kaleidoscopic spectacular." Fouts called it "the greatest game I ever played in." *Sports Illustrated* dubbed it A GAME NO ONE SHOULD HAVE LOST. Most media types would settle on "The Epic in Miami."

For Shula, it went beyond frustrating. "It's going to be a tough one to live with," he said yet again. "But our guys are men. They proved it."[8] So had he. Unlike Coryell, whose team was destroyed the next week by the Bengals, who went to the Super Bowl and lost to the 49ers, Shula had actually been to the mountaintop, twice. But all that meant a decade later was that his own success seemed to be mocking him.

In the '82 draft, Shula's top pick was an All-American guard out of USC: Roy Foster, a six-foot, four-inch, 280-pound man-mountain who would make All-Pro twice over the next eight seasons. He also added another wide receiver, Northwestern State's Mark Duper, who was also a champion sprinter. The All-Pro team would make room for him, too, three times. The third- and fourth-rounders were also blue-chip prospects: Penn State cornerback Paul Lankford and Duke linebacker Charles Bowser. Indeed, this was perhaps Shula's best draft of all, and it kept Joe Thomas at bay. Shula now had the league's youngest team, with only two starters over 30, Kuechenberg and Ed Newman. Roster turnover had been so thorough that when Don Reese's cocaine confessions ran in *Sports Illustrated* in June, they seemed almost irrelevant.

Shula had put to bed the negative vibe surrounding the Dolphins' drug subplot far better than had Tom Landry and other coaches who still wallowed in the problem. As Mercury Morris observed, Shula had at least put a lid on it better, a truly remarkable thing, with the team situated in the hub of America's drug trade, a status reflected in pop culture by hysterical movies like *Scarface* and glitz-and-grime TV takes like *Miami Vice*. While the Dolphins were still a prime attraction, a virtual stamp on the city's identity, they also reflected Shula's blue-nosed sensibilities, even as the team was no longer an outsider tweaking the establishment; they *were* the establishment, and Shula had no objection to that.

His timing was right, too. In '82, fate seemed to give him a mulligan, the result of a sport cheapened by a game of chicken between the league and the players' union. The latter, seeing the owners fattened even more by a flood of TV money, demanded a higher cut of revenues for salaries. Unable to make headway, the union played its hand by walking off the job during the season, after two games. For Shula, who publicly said the players deserved more—but, reflecting his latter-day elitism, added they didn't have the right to "change the system"—it stopped a roll the Dolphins had started the season on, beating the Jets and Colts. For the next two months, the sport went dark, resulting in a $275 million drain in revenue and wages.

During the interrupted season, on October 9, Mary Shula called her son with the news that Dan Shula, who had been ill for months, had died of respiratory failure at 80. The son who had made their immigrant family a household name flew to Painesville to bury the quiet, stalwart man who had put aside his reluctance and let his son play sports instead of studying the sacraments. The son spent a week in his native grounds, eulogizing his father at the funeral and greeting old friends. He worried that his mother would lose her will to live, and found himself giving her the sort of pep talks he wished he could have given his striking players. Growing restless, he returned to Miami and, like other management, held firm against the players' demands. He could see that the union would have to fold. And it did, in mid-November, accepting a token raise but vowing to continue the fight. Salvaging the season, a nine-game schedule would determine seeding for a nearly all-inclusive playoff scheme.

The Dolphins' return game against the Bills on November 21 was unsightly. With no real practice time, the teams were rusty, creating a nine-turnover mess. Buffalo led 7–6 in the last quarter, but Uwe von Schamann saved it, hitting a 21-yard field goal to win 9–7. The next week, in Tampa Bay, Woodley was still in a funk, so Shula went with Strock, who threw two touchdowns but four picks in a 23–17 loss. They beat the Vikings, then played the Patriots in Foxborough in a blinding snowstorm. With 4:45 left in a scoreless game, the Pats got into field-goal range and their coach, Ron Meyer, directed a plow driver on the sideline to go clear the snow for kicker John Smith, who booted the winner, sending Shula into one of his neck-bulging rants. Seeing the plow as an unfair advantage, he bellowed to the referee Bob Frederic, "Why would you let that happen?"

Frederic himself didn't know if it was legal or not, which angered Shula even more. Ironically, Shula then had a shot to tie on a long field goal, and Frederic assured him he could have the plow clear the snow for him too. But he passed it up, opting to go for it on fourth down, whereupon Woodley was intercepted, ending the game. Shula was steaming in the locker room. "I don't know about illegal," he seethed, "but it will certainly be in my report to the commissioner."[9] Most everyone had fun with the "Snowplow Caper," even more so when it emerged that the plow driver was a convict on a work-release program. For Dolphins beat writer Larry Dorman, the defeat was a "crime," but "the Miami offense should be picked up for vagrancy."

Shula indeed took his grievance to Pete Rozelle, claiming that the defeat should be overturned because, under a broad interpretation of the rules, the use of the plow was an "unfair act." The commissioner refused to make that radical call, instead banning the use of snowplows during games. Burned again that he never seemed to get proper respect from Rozelle, Shula was calmed a bit when von Schamann bailed out the Dolphins with another field goal the next week against the Jets. He finished atop the division at 7–2, gaining the No. 2 seed. They also had a defense that led the league and gave up the second-fewest points, including just seven touchdowns. The writers, looking to inject a little pizzazz to another workmanlike Shula team, took to calling the defense the "Killer Bees," with Bokamper, Baumhower, and Doug Betters up front, Bob Brudzinski (obtained from the Cowboys) at left outside linebacker, and the Blackwood boys deep.

Actually, they were much like the No Names of yore. Only Baumhower went to the Pro Bowl. Paul Zimmerman wondered if their stats were "a statistical mirage." What's more, Woodley was inept much of the season, throwing five touchdowns to eight picks. But having the home field was a salve. In the first round, when they played the Patriots, someone in the Dolphins PR department thought it would be hilarious to hire an actor in prison garb to drive a snowplow onto the field before the game. Shula, not amused, said, "I don't know anything about it. I don't want to be associated with it." His men then laid 460 yards of offense on the Pats, winning 28–13.

Next were the Chargers, who expected to break Shula's heart again on his home turf. Said Bokamper later, "I read newspaper stories out of San Diego that the Chargers didn't respect us too much. They thought we were a fluke or something." The Chargers were indeed favored, but Shula's team was merciless, winning 34–13, holding Kellen Winslow to one catch. That put the Dolphins back in the AFC championship game.

Bokamper, sounding a lot like his coach, said, "Today we went out and showed the country what kind of defense we are when it comes to the real serious situations." Dan Fouts, who was picked three times, agreed. "Miami didn't give us anything," he acknowledged. "Its defense is the best we've seen."[10] Zimmerman's game story in *Sports Illustrated*, the cover of which was emblazoned DAY OF THE DOLPHINS, hailed THE REVENGE OF THE KILLER BEES, though it seemed more like the revenge of Don Shula.

Many regarded the '82 playoff tournament as the route toward a cheapened title. Indeed, not only were the Dolphins an unlikely contender, but their opponents were the Jets, making their first AFC title game appearance ever, a reward for the long-suffering Richard Todd, who'd succeeded Joe Namath and had once thrown 30 picks in a season. While still erratic, he had the luxury of the league's leading rusher, Freeman McNeil. The Jets' defensive front four, the New York Sack Exchange, got most of the attention, led by end Mark Gastineau, the NFL's Defensive Player of the Year, who punctuated sacks with seizure-like dance moves.

As always with the Jets and Shula, there were degrees of separation from Super Bowl III. The Jets were coached by Walt Michaels, whose older brother Lou had baited Joe Namath into his "guarantee." But Shula didn't need anyone to bait Todd. All he needed was some rain. And Miami got a lot of it on January 23. Shula may have learned something from Al Davis when it came to wet fields. Loathe to spend $4,000 on a tarp to protect the field, per league rules, the Dolphins claimed their grass surface, technically called Prescription Athletic Turf, made one unnecessary, as pumps below the surface were designed to clear the field of excess water. On this day, the amount of water bailed could have fit in a thimble. Before the game, Jets president Jim Kensil saw the field and bitched the same way Shula always did in Oakland.[11]

As it happened, the Jets had just come from Oakland, where they had beaten the Raiders in the previous round and the prickly Michaels was convinced that Davis had bugged their locker room. He was also miffed at Shula, misconstruing the latter's remark during the week that the Jets had a "Swoyersville mentality," referring to Michaels's Pennsylvania hometown, which was meant as a compliment. Already melting down when he saw the Orange Bowl quagmire, Michaels needed to be calmed by Kensil.

During the game, he only grew more overwrought. The contest devolved into what one reporter called a "three-hour mud wrestling match." Neither team did much with the ball, Todd and Woodley combining for eight picks. But the Dolphins were bailed out by A. J. Duhe, who in one report, displayed "the best defense since Clarence Darrow."[12] In the third quarter, his pick set up a touchdown and 7–0 lead. In the fourth, he grabbed another; then, two minutes later, he lined up as a down lineman, spun outside in midplay to cover halfback Bruce Harper in the flat, and when the ball glanced off Harper's hand, Duhe took his AFC playoff-record third interception into the end zone for a 35-yard touchdown. Final score: Duhe 14, Jets 0.

In the mud, the Jets had only managed 139 total yards, the fewest ever in an AFC title game, and beyond the field conditions, some wondered if the Dolphins might again have all the answers. In his game story, no longer seeing mirages, Zimmerman asked, "Has Arnsparger finally come up with the perfect coverage scheme to combat the football of the '80s?" He noted that Shula's great defenses of the past had funneled coverage to the middle of the field, where the safeties roamed free and made the big steals. "Todd was made to believe the inside was open," wrote Zimmerman, "and then it was taken away from him."[13]

If ever Shula was given a free ride, this year was it. His offense on this day had only managed 198 yards, and Woodley was slapped back into reality. Michaels certainly wasn't impressed. On the plane home, he had a near breakdown, screaming that he would demand an investigation of Shula. A day later, he was fired.[14] Whatever one thought of

Shula and his dubious season, he had done what he had to in order to find his way back to another Super Bowl.

Shula's opponent at the less than lofty summit would be the Redskins, who beat Tom Landry's Cowboys in the NFC title game, setting up a delayed rematch of the Super Bowl that capped the Dolphins' perfect season. George Allen was long gone, now coaching in yet another fledgling football league challenging the NFL, the United States Football League. Still, there was a history between the two teams, and Bobby Beathard had made himself an elite general manager, building the 'Skins back into a force; when the head coaching job came open the year before, he recommended that owner Jack Kent Cooke sign Joe Gibbs, the best move the franchise ever made. Of course, there was also Joe Theismann, now entrenched in the NFL 12 years after snubbing Shula.

The meek-looking, soft-spoken Gibbs had been an assistant for 17 years, mostly as offensive coordinator under Don Coryell. Canny as Gibbs was, he knew the undersized, mercurial Theismann was no Dan Fouts. His system had the QB roll out to utilize his speed and scrambling ability and rely heavily on fullback John Riggins, the ex-Jet and a Csonka clone with speed, running behind the most massive offensive line in the game, known as The Hogs. The biggest of those linemen was 300-pound tackle Joe Jacoby, who with his fellow sows opened up passing lanes for Art Monk, Charlie Brown, and tight end Don Warren. Gibbs also stocked his defensive line with cattle, such as veteran tackle Dave Butz, another three bills of brawn.

That defense, anchored in the secondary by veteran all-Pro strong safety Tony Peters, was ranked No. 1, giving up just 14 points a game. Even the kicker, Mark Moseley, was something special; he won the NFC's MVP award that year, making 20 of 21 field goals. The 'Skins had gone 8–1, then destroyed the Lions, Vikings, and Cowboys, looking like Shula's '68 Colts. Yet Shula had made believers out of the bettors; the 'Skins came in favored by only three and a half points for the game, played on January 30, 1983, in the Rose Bowl in Pasadena.

Shula later admitted he was spooked by how good the Redskins looked on film. Gibbs had outdone Landry with funky, arcane formations, such as using three tight ends and an "I" stack of three receivers on the line. The scariest specter, though, was the 33-year-old Riggins, an insatiable runner who had carried 36 times against the Cowboys and wanted more. He was a slightly daft farm boy, one day impish, the next glowering. As a Jet, he had worn a Mohawk hairdo. During Super Bowl week, he showed up at one press confab in camouflage pants with an elephant gun belt buckle, at another in a white top hat and tails. Speaking less about football than killing coyotes, he dominated media coverage the way Namath had in '69.

Shula hoped he could defuse Riggins, if Woodley would rejuvenate in the warm California sun. Abandoning his usual Super Bowl shell game, he would let Woodley come out flinging, hoping to catch the 'Skins off guard and force Theismann to play catch-up. He drummed this into his men for two weeks while sealing them off from the outside world, strictly enforcing curfews, and ringing the practice field with security.

Gibbs, who was so relaxed, it seemed he could nod off in midsentence, gave his boys a looser rein, no doubt partly because there was no way to rein in Riggins, on or off the field.

On game day, it was a relatively cool 54 degrees, but Woodley came out hot. On Miami's second possession, he hit undersized receiver Jimmy Cefalo on the sideline between the short and deep zone, and Cefalo beat Peters in a footrace—76 yards, the biggest play of the season. But the most impressive thing they did was to somehow avoid being blown away. From the start, the Dolphins could not brake Riggins or keep from being suckered by the same kind of cut-back, misdirection trap plays, Shula had used to cream the Vikings in the Super Bowl. Gibbs even shifted all five eligible receivers back and forth before a snap, creating a vertiginous effect on the defense. The 'Skins built a huge surfeit in rushing and total yardage, and their defense recovered and kept Woodley under control with waves of blitzes and stunts.

And yet, they could not not break it open. When it was 10-all in the second quarter, Miami second-year return man Fulton Walker returned a kickoff 98 yards for a touchdown, the first in Super Bowl history and at the time the longest. The Dolphins were making big plays—interceptions by Bokamper and then Lyle Blackwood at his own one-yard line on, of all things, a flea flicker—and 'Skins screwups helped them keep the lead, 17–13, entering the fourth quarter. But Shula's defense was gassed; later, Jacoby would say "their chests were heaving and the steam was coming off them." With under 12 minutes left, on a fourth-and-one at the Miami 43, Gibbs went for it. Riggins, behind a running back and a tight end, went left, off tackle. As Shula recalled, "We were in a short-yardage defense, and he went off the left corner, and we had a man slip and a man miss an arm-tackle on him, and it didn't work."[15]

Riggins cleared the line, broke outside, and kept running, mainly untouched. Don McNeal tried arm-tackling him and bounced off like a pinball. Riggins's 43-yard run claimed the lead. And here, many observers would criticize Shula for sending Woodley back in. He had gone 4-for-13 for 97 yards, just 21 since the Cefalo bomb. "I thought I'd give David one more series," he would explain. Two runs and a penalty left Woodley with a critical third-and-11, and he missed on a pass to Harris. Riggins then ran eight of the next 12 plays, padding his numbers to 38 carries and 166 yards, still Super Bowl records. That took seven minutes off the clock, and a short TD pass made it 27–16 with two minutes left.

Only now did Shula go to Strock, who in an impossible situation threw three incomplete passes before the 'Skins ran out the clock. Over the second half, as Washington rolled up a then-record 276 rushing yards, Shula's offense had two first downs and 34 total yards. A good many thought Gibbs had outcoached Shula, but most came away praising the latter for keeping it so close despite the avalanche of yardage against his team. Gibbs—who had beaten, in succession, Bud Grant, Landry, and Shula—backed off any suggestion he was in their league. "The truly great people in this profession are great for years and years," he said, prophetically. "Let's see how I am in 10 years"—by which time he had won as many rings as the latter two combined.

Afterward, reported Ed Pope, "Shula came off the phone from telling President Reagan that he was 'proud' of the Dolphins, then stood tall in Miami's funereal dressing room and spoke without a quiver of how the Redskins had smashed his [team]. 'Give them all the credit. They deserve to be champions.' " Really, what else could he say? He had to admit that "they manhandled us" and that Riggins was a "tremendously dominating force," but then he turned to the broader, familiar themes of personal defeat, pity, endless redemption and fate. "It could have been a great story," Shula said. "But now it will only be on the Redskins. I realize better than anyone else that after a Super Bowl they're only going to be talking about one team, and it won't be the Dolphins." Then, by rote, "We had a fine season, and we have to turn this loss into a learning experience, which is the only positive thing I can possibly say about it."[16]

The next day, on the flight home, he tried putting it out of his mind with the comforting thought that the last time he'd lost a Super Bowl, he won the next two. With the vagaries of the college draft, he might take that one step further if he could somehow get a quarterback with the next-to-last draft pick of the first round.

20

NEW KID IN TOWN

With his customary good timing, Don Shula's personal stock index had risen during the wave of unfettered corporate greed that accompanied the installation of Ronald Reagan, the fifth president to take office during his coaching career. Establishment icon that he now was, Shula had no objection as Reagan railed with equal force against both an "Evil Empire" in Russia and domestic blue-collar labor unions (even the players' union of extant and would-be millionaires couldn't escape being tarred), though the union movement was the very backbone of the Shula family's assimilation in working-class Ohio.

But he had his own challenges and complications. As he aged, mortality began to enter his worldview. One front-office man had died in his arms. One of his players had died in his prime. And on February 10, Joe Thomas collapsed in his Coral Gables home and died of a heart attack at 61, leaving a wife and daughter. Robbie eulogized his first hire as "the keenest judge of talent I have ever encountered." Shula, as distant and wary as he had become with Thomas, said he was "in shock" and "we'll miss him."[1]

There was also another challenge to the NFL for Shula to deal with. At first, the USFL avoided direct competition, commencing in '83 as a spring-summer circuit with 12 teams in mainly big markets, playing in whatever stadiums they could find. Rebuffed in his attempt to crash the NFL, John Bassett owned a team in Tampa Bay. (A second Florida team would be placed in Jacksonville in '84, playing in the Gator Bowl.) While the well-heeled dilettantes who bought into the league's owner-ship held off raiding top-shelf NFL talent, a big splash was made when Georgia's Heisman Trophy–winning halfback, junior Herschel Walker, took advantage of the USFL's policy of allowing underclassmen to be drafted and signed a fat deal with the New Jersey Generals, who played in Giants Stadium. Their owner, Oklahoma oil baron Walter Duncan, had given Chuck Fairbanks a pass back to the pros as coach, GM, and minority partner. The biggest name among ownership was George Allen, part-owner/coach of the Chicago Blitz. Longtime NFL assistant Jim Mora became head coach of the Philadelphia Stars. Sig-nificantly, the USFL secured a TV contract with ABC and the year-old cable sports network ESPN, whose president, Chet Simmons, was named its commissioner. While Shula was unconcerned by the threat, he was more than a little intrigued how much money the new league was willing to pay its coaches.

Shula, aware that collegians were in the new league's crosshairs, confined his picks to those who personally pledged to play for him. Convinced he could no longer continue the Woodstrock era, his focus was a quarterback with a big arm who was a natural leader. Getting that with the No. 27 pick seemed impossible. And it would have been in any other year, but this was the so-called "great quarterback draft." Not tipping his hand, Shula told reporters, "We're looking for big, strong defensive linemen . . . offensive linemen and defensive backs," hoping it might leave a good arm free that some teams might assume would still be there in the second round.

The draft was now a real PR vehicle for the NFL; ESPN began televis-ing it in 1980 from a ballroom in the New York Sheraton Hotel, where it was again held, with draft junkies watching Pete Rozelle announce the continuing picks. On April 26, the first day of the two-day event, the quarterbacks fell like bowling pins. Stanford's John Elway was, predictably, taken first overall by the Colts, despite Elway's vow that he wouldn't play for them. At No. 7 went Penn State's Todd Blackledge, then Miami's Jim Kelly (No. 14), and Illinois's Tony Eason (No. 15). When No. 24 came up, it seemed a given that the Jets would take Pitt's Dan Marino.

Shula had watched the parade pass, knowing Marino was the best QB left, and maybe the best of the whole field. To many, he was the reincarnation of Joe Namath, born and raised in Pittsburgh, a dropback guy with a cannon for an arm and a hair-trigger release. He was somewhat of a Shula clone, too: blue-collar, Catholic school–educated, a natural athlete who'd also been drafted by baseball's Kansas City Royals. While breaking passing records on Jackie Sherrill's highly-ranked Pitt teams that went 33–3 over his first three seasons, he left pass rushers baffled that he'd whistled one right past them. He was big (at six foot four), not fast but mobile, with a missile launcher of a right arm, boyishly hunky, and gregarious. He was also a bit of a jerk, going at it with writers he thought maligned him.

As a junior, he threw for nearly 3,000 yards with 37 touchdowns, so productive that even with 23 picks—he liked to throw, a *lot*—his passer rating was a gaudy 143.1. After that season, the USFL's Los Angeles Express had made him the No. 1 pick in the league's first college draft and offered $800,000 for four years. He stayed in college, thinking he would reap a lot more. But he hit a pothole. Having been Sherill's pet, after the coach left for Texas A&M, Marino was rudderless under Foge Fazio. He threw 17 touchdowns, but the same 27 interceptions, his passer rating dropping to 115.2. He fell from fourth to eighth in the Heisman vote, fifth among quarterbacks. Pitt, which had beaten No. 2 Georgia the year before in the Sugar Bowl, went down to Eric Dickerson's SMU team in the Cotton Bowl, after which Marino got into a tiff with a writer, telling him with a sinister tone, "Don't worry, I'll see you somewhere down the road."[2]

His play was suspect enough, but as one NFL writer put it in euphemistic terms, "His off-field reputation also hit a slump," a reference to rumors of partying and pot smoking. Marino denied it—the whole team, he said, had been tested and passed. Still, the rumors persisted, Fazio insisting they came from disgruntled gamblers. "A lot of it was disappointment we didn't beat the point spread," he said. "That's where the viciousness came out." [3]

Marino thought none of this would matter. He'd been the MVP of the Senior Bowl and figured he'd go within the top three. It didn't happen. Even later, Chuck Noll, who had the 21st pick and knew Marino was a perfect candidate to succeed Terry Bradshaw, was scared off by the rumors. [4] When the Jets' turn came, their fans chanted Marino's name, but Rozelle strode to the podium and announced that they had chosen Ken O'Brien, of Division II Cal-Davis. Shula must have wanted to kiss Jim Kensil for that.

Not that Shula didn't harbor some reservations of his own. He had seen Marino go through his paces at the NFL scouting combine and came away saying the quarterback was a "stand-up guy" who took the blame for bad throws. But, figuring he'd never get him, he had not spoken with Marino, nor had he fact-checked the rumors. While the clock ticked on the pick, he placed an urgent call to Fazio, who vouched for the kid's character. He then called Marino. He asked if he wanted to be a Dolphin. "I'm ready to go," Marino said. "See you in Miami." The pick was announced to joyous screams from Dolphins fans in the gallery.

The following day, Ed Pope's page one *Herald* column was headed DOLPHINS MAKE LUCKY CATCH: DAN MARINO. Pope ventured, "I suspect he could pan out as the [team's] handiest offensive choice since Larry Csonka in '68." Not everyone agreed. Paul Zimmerman was skeptical that, even under Shula, Marino could "overcome the problems he's had." [5] Shula himself tried to discourage hype, saying he wanted a guy who could "possibly come into this league and do a fine job," which prompted another scribe to point out, "Note the use of the word *possibly*." [6]

Marino, professing humility, nonetheless took a jab at the last quarterback to go before him, asking, "Who's Ken O'Brien?" Shula himself couldn't resist doing the same, biting his lip as he said, "Apparently, the Jets thought O'Brien was better." Years later, he would swear that Marino's pride was so hurt at being picked so low that he played every game wanting to prove how wrong all those teams were. A few days after the draft, Art Rooney sent Shula a letter, congratulating him for doing what Chuck Noll wouldn't.

Shula had reason to be giddy. By going so late, Marino had little leverage. (He certainly had less than Elway, who bluffed the Colts by insisting he would rather play baseball than with them, won a trade to the Denver Broncos, and pocketed a four-year, $600,000-a-year deal and a million-dollar bonus, vaulting him ahead of Buffalo's Joe Ferguson as the highest-paid NFL quarterback.) Marino had the same agent as Elway, Marvin Demoff, but after two months of dickering with Robbie, the best Demoff could do was a four-year package: $150,000 the first year, $200,000 the second, $300,000 the third, and $350,000 the fourth, with no bonuses. Marino took it, putting him on the lower end of the salary scale for the first-rounders, which was between $150,000 and $200,000. (Jim Kelly made out the best, signing with the USFL's Houston Gamblers for four years at $500,000 a year, plus bonuses and low-interest loans.)

The USFL's influence on all this was tangible, albeit the opposite of what the NFL had feared. Despite the coin lavished on Walker and Kelly, the league's median player salary was just $50,000. Like most NFL executives, Shula had vowed not to make the same mistake he had when the WFL waved its money around, when he gave out long-term contracts, some to men he would otherwise have cut loose. But not only would the salary structure of the game explode before long, Shula himself, in no mood to take a vow of poverty, was about to shatter a symbolic economic ceiling.

Weeks after the draft, Marino came to the Dolphins' mini-camp and was startled to find himself scrimmaging with the starting unit and learning the offense on the fly, not just poring over films and blackboard schemata. He guessed that Shula "had confidence in me." But Shula couldn't risk hurting the feelings of his Super Bowl quarterback,

David Woodley, who, like Don Strock, was being courted by the USFL. Shula appeased him, saying that starting Marino would be "far fetched for a rookie" and "I still like David. He's had only three years with us and is still in the learning process."[7] Quarterback emeritus Bob Griese piped in that Shula "didn't draft Marino to be its starting quarterback in 1983."[8]

When summer camp began, Woodley was signed, but not Strock, and Marino got more snaps, sharing time on the first unit with Woodley. No one doubted Marino needed work. He held the football too long, resulting in sacks and fumbles. He also needed to raise the angle of his release. But when he was behind center, with the iconoclastic number 13 on his uniform and wearing Namath-style alabaster shoes, he gave the stodgy Dolphins a livelier pulse. The drama was palpable. There were other new faces around. Shula had added a couple of defensive studs in the draft, the best being Syracuse's 300-pound nose tackle Mike Charles. He also took back David Overstreet, who after his years in the Canadian league was willing to play for Shula as a backup runner.

The defense, however, was beset with bad luck. While Betters and Baumhower would be first-team All-Pros, tragedy dealt another devastating blow in July, when linebacker Larry Gordon collapsed while jogging in Texas and died of a heart attack at 28. Shula would start second-year man Charles Bowser at his outside right linebacker slot. Then Don McNeal ripped his Achilles tendon and would miss the season, replaced at left corner by unproven William Judson.

As for Marino, Shula was cautious, even saying he would give Jim Jensen, the utility backfield plug-in listed as the third-string quarterback, a shot. In the preseason games, he kept Marino taking second-half snaps, and when Strock finally re-signed in early September, it seemed Marino would mainly be a spectator. But Marino quickly developed an innate connection with the receivers, whose speed suddenly made every passing play a potential touchdown, epecially for eighth-round pick Mark Clayton, a five-foot, nine-inch gnat drafted as a punt returner.

Shula stuck with Woodley, even after a poor performance in the season opener in Buffalo, a 12–0 Dolphin win. In week two, he threw two touchdowns in beating the Patriots 34–24. Then came a trip to LA to play the Raiders on Monday night, when Al Davis's team, in its second year since leaving Oakland, seemed never to lose. Woodley couldn't get a point on the board, and, down 27–0 in the fourth quarter, Shula threw Marino to the hounds. With 2:29 left, he threw a six-yard touchdown pass to Joe Rose; then, with time running out, another to Mark Duper from two yards out. In Miami, despite the loss—Shula's 11th in 14 games against Davis—that two and half minutes was the future, a cloudburst of 11 completions for 90 yards.

Still, Shula again kept faith with Woodley, starting him against the Chiefs, though the Dolphins had to run 47 times to create any kind of offense in the 14–6 win. The next game, they trailed 7–0 in New Orleans with 2:51 to go in the half. Woodley had gone 4-for-12 with a pick. Bypassing Strock, Shula went with Marino. He wasn't great—12-for-22, 150 yards, one touchdown, and one pick that was returned for a touchdown—and didn't get his team on the board until a late 10-yard TD to Duper that made the final score 17–7.

Afterward, Shula was noncommittal about who he'd start the next game, but there was a pall around him, one reporter writing there was a sense the season was "beginning to unravel." Woodley was the most despondent. "I don't know where we go from here," he said. "I don't know. I just don't know."[9]

Shula announced on Tuesday that Marino would get the start in the return game against the Bills, who had lost 17 straight in the Orange Bowl. In a game reminiscent of the madcap Epic against the Chargers, the Bills raced to a 14–0 lead before Marino, firing away, connected with Duper, whom Shula had started in place of Duriel Harris for Marino's benefit, on a 63-yard touchdown. Then Clayton took it on an apparent reverse, squared up, and flung one to a solitary Duper for a tricky 48-yard TD. The Bills led 28–21 in the fourth quarter, but Marino finished two drives with short touchdown passes to Moore and

Clayton, and the Dolphins now led 35–28. With time running short, on fourth-and-goal from the Miami one, Joe Ferguson threw the tying TD to force overtime, which again ended in agony for Shula after von Schamann missed two long field goals and the Bills kicked the winner to make the final score 38–35.

If Shula was desperate for offense, he got it—485 yards of it. Marino was 19-for-29, 322 yards, three touchdowns, two picks. Duper had seven catches for a massive 202 yards. But the Dolphins' knotty defense seemed to wilt, as if playing fast and loose was the price for the new go-go offense. Shula and Arnsparger wouldn't tolerate a repeat; another defensive collapse would cost people their jobs. And in the next game, against the Jets, the new Dolphin symbiosis was born. Marino threw three more touchdowns, but this time the defense stole six passes, one taken back by Bokamper for a 24-yard touchdown. The 32–14 rout raised their record to 4–3. They had their future, right now.

And then, just when things were starting to congeal, Shula was thrown off stride by his fleeting brush with Donald Trump.

Back in September, Walter Duncan sold the USFL's New Jersey Generals to the social-climbing, playboy son of a shady real estate developer for $6 million. Trump was 37 then, in the process of building a house of cards in real estate, hotels, casinos, and golf courses—most all of which, bankrolled by his old man, would wind up in debt and bankruptcy—and his big plans matched his sense of self-promotion and endless bullshit. A fixture in the tabloids, he instantly became the face of the renegade USFL as it became bolder, soon to expand to more cities, beating the NFL to college stars like Reggie White and Steve Young (who received a $40 million deal from the LA Express, the team Marino had passed on). Trump came in spending other people's money and set his sights on a coach for the next season, 1984, that was worthy of him. That meant the biggest coach of all. His offer to Shula: $1 million a year.

The details of their tango are still murky, subject to the claims of each. In context, it seems preposterous that Shula, who had just gotten his dream quarterback, could have seriously considered jumping to the ersatz league. But then, in '83 he was working for half that amount, and was without a new contract this late for the first time in his 14-year coaching career. Like anyone else, he had a price—and Trump was willing to meet it, for five years, with a 20 percent ownership stake in the Generals and in some Trump properties. So Shula listened, in a series of phone calls, then followed up by sending his lawyer to New York to meet Trump.

Shula could legally do that, since tampering did not apply to teams outside the NFL. Still, he wanted it kept secret so as not to disrupt the Dolphins' evolving season. However, it didn't take long for Trump to shoot off his mouth. In mid-October, Larry Dorman reported on the offer, quoting Trump as calling Shula "a wonderful man and a wonderful coach" who would "fit in with the new league." Shula, trying to have it both ways, said he'd only spoken with Trump after hours and that it didn't "distract me from preparations for the next game." But he had soon cooled on Trump, taken aback when, during halftime of the Dolphins' October 23 game in Baltimore, Trump went on national TV and said the deal had been "all set and ready to go" until a sticking point arose—Shula's demand for a rent-free flat in Trump Tower, which had recently opened its gilt-edged doors on Fifth Avenue.

Shula, besieged with questions about it after the game—a tidy 21–7 win—acted highly offended by the story. "It really has developed into a huge distraction," he said. "When the third question at my press conference after the ball game is about my personal contract and not about our football team. I don't think it's fair to the people I'm responsible to." As a result, he huffed, he was "no longer interested." With some verbal gymnastics, he tried to walk the whole thing back. "I've never felt that I in any way have ever committed myself to that extent," referring to the alleged contract.[10]

That was debatable. Jerry Magee, a longtime football writer in San

Diego, reported that, up until Trump went on TV, "Persons close to Shula say he was leaning strongly to leaving Miami for the [USFL]."[11] For his part, Trump unctuously said, "Don is a good man, an excellent guy really. . . . But I could not have given him an apartment in Trump Tower. Money is one thing. Gold is another." But how serious had Shula been about living in that glass tower? Could he really have believed Trump would have ever handed over free space there? Indeed, Magee added, "Shula was never interested in a Fifth Avenue apartment. What interested him was the $1 million for five years." If Shula did make such a demand for property, it might well have been to offend Trump when he needed an escape hatch. If so, it was the smartest thing he ever did.

Joe Robbie never thought Shula was going, saying Trump "engaged more in ballyhoo than in a serious effort to build a franchise completely by sound professional management."[12] But just knowing Shula had an itch to jump started the negotiations. In the interim, the Dolphins had won three of four, Marino rising to the top of the NFL quarterback ratings. In early November, he bested Joe Montana in a tense 30–27 win over the 49ers, with two more touchdowns and zero picks—he had gone 139 throws without an interception. Paul Zimmerman, no longer doubtful, now raved about him, pushing him as a Pro Bowler: "The highest completion percentage for a rookie passer in NFL history is Jim McMahon's 57.1 last year with the Chicago Bears. Marino is currently at 60.1%."[13]

The reason for his instant maturation, Marino said, was that "I've got Coach Shula working with me." From afar, Bobby Beathard agreed: "There are not a lot of great quarterback coaches around. Shula happens to be one of them. He took that kid down there right after the draft and really prepared him. He handled him just right. He didn't throw him in to sink or swim; he put him in when he thought he was ready."[14]

Shula had not named another quarterback coach after Wally English, who got the job in '81, but left after the '82 season to be head coach at

Tulane. And it is fair to wonder what the lesser quarterbacks drafted ahead of Marino might have amounted to had they played for Shula. As it was, only Kelly was thriving, albeit in the inferior league, and Elway was benched in Denver after five games. And Woodley had gone to a Super Bowl.

At 7–4, the team was, said Zimmerman, "the class of their class." After they blanked the Colts 37–0, Robbie chose the day of the next game, a Monday night contest against the Bengals, to announce Shula's new five-year agreement. Matching Trump's offer, he made Shula the NFL's first million-dollar-a-year coach. At Shula's insistence, he also gave the assistant coaches raises. The key to the deal, Shula deadpanned, was "a one-bedroom efficiency on Biscayne Boulevard."[15] In truth, he would sink $575,000 into a new, bigger home, right next door in Miami Lakes at 7345 Gleneagle Drive.

He went on to win that night, 38–14, and closed the season with five straight wins and, at 12–4, another East title, tying the Raiders for best conference record. However, Marino sprained his knee late in the season and Shula gave him the last two games off, going to his "long reliever," Strock. But Marino was already an All-Pro and a strong candidate for Rookie of the Year (though he would lose out to the Rams' Eric Dickerson, who led the league with 1,808 rushing yards). He had eye-popping numbers: 2,210 yards in 11 starts, 58.4 completion percentage, 20 touchdowns, 6 interceptions, a 96 passer rating, overshadowing two other QBs who threw for over 4,000 yards: Lynn Dickey, who led the NFL with 32 TD passes, and Bill Kenney, a Pro Bowler. His 7.39 yards per pass attempt, 6.8 touchdown percentage, and 3.27 sack percentage led the league, his 2.0 interception percentage second-best. Duper bloomed as his leading target, becoming the first Dolphin receiver to go over 1,000 yards, hauling in 51 balls and 10 touchdowns, sending him to the Pro Bowl.

In Marino, Shula had something he hadn't had since Johnny Unitas. As great as Bob Griese was, Marino gave Shula the ability to make short work of any defense, in one killing strike, not 10 grinding ones.

His team fed off the buzz that swelled on the downbeat to the snap. But all this was moving just a little too fast.

Marino's knee seemed healed for the Dolphins' first playoff game, on New Year's Eve day against the heavily underdog Seattle Seahawks. Going 9–7 under Chuck Knox, they had made the playoffs for the first time in their seven-year history, beating the Broncos in the wild-card playoff. Their marquee player was rookie Curt Warner, who rushed for over 1,400 yards to lead the AFC and went to the Pro Bowl. But they had the 24th-worst defense.

The pregame hype was all about Marino, who in one story was dubbed, admiringly, a "QB Terrorist."[16] But to Knox, he was a rookie quarterback who hadn't won a high-pressure game, while the Seahawks had had to beat the Raiders twice over the season to cop a playoff berth, behind quarterback David Krieg, a walk-on in 1980 but a budding All-Pro. And now, he would outplay the hyped rookie.

Marino did get off fast, zipping touchdowns to tight end Dan Johnson and Duper to go ahead 13–7. But, rushed hard, his knee hurting, he was stumped by Knox's seven-deep prevent defense. As Barry McDermott wrote in *Sports Illutrated*, he seemed to be "looking through the trees all day," throwing several tipped balls and two interceptions. Down 14–13 in the third quarter, he seemed lost. The Seahawks had stopped his running game and he threw for only 58 yards in the second half. As Seahawk fullback Dan Doornink would say, "Before the game, we could tell they were a little cocky. [But] I didn't feel they had the intensity they've had in the past."[17]

Miami led 20–17 with 4:43 to go, but were out of gas, allowing the Seahawks to come away with a 27–20 win. For Knox, who was carried off on his players' shoulders, it was an exhilarating moment that, like Coryell after the Epic, would last just a week before his team was mauled by the Raiders in the AFC title match.

For Marino, and Shula, on the other hand, it was "Midnight for Cinderella," penned McDermott. Still, it seemed this was one Shula could concede, even if he did so with his jaw tight enough to crack a walnut. As poised as Marino was, no rookie quarterback had ever started a Super Bowl. The bigger picture for Shula to consider was that his men again seemed to choke in a big one. He didn't think it would happen much longer. Looking ahead, he was prepared to turn Marino loose in a big way. This was to be Shula's gamble, one he would strap himself to for the rest of his time on the sideline.

21

"SHULA IS GOD"

D on Shula was still just 53, but he was breeding a football family tree. He had been grooming his eldest son, David, since the kid was a teenager, when he spent time on the sideline, charting the plays. Dave played receiver in high school and at Dolphin practices was allowed to run pass patterns with Paul Warfield. "He was happy that I was so fascinated by the thing he did for a living," he said of his father. "A lot of nights after dinner I'd take out one of his diagram pads to draw up plays and pass routes. He taught me a million things."[1] Though slow and smallish, Dave won his scholarship to Dartmouth and broke school records catching passes from another fortunate son—Jeff Kemp, whose father, Jack, was one of the earliest AFL star quarterbacks, and later a Republican congressman and Bob Dole's vice-presidential running mate in 1996.

Despite his surname, Dave was not drafted and was signed as a walk-on by the Colts. The old man pulled no strings for him, but when his son was released after a year, his paternal instinct kicked in. He made Dave an assistant receivers coach. This was one of many ways Shula used his staff to dispense favors; when Bob Matheson was diagnosed with Hodgkin's disease, Shula hired him as special teams coach. Shula's second son, Mike, meanwhile, played quarterback for Alabama in '84. Before Archie Manning's sons Peyton and Eli became football's first family, the Shulas had been injected into the game's DNA. And while Archie only had a decade in the pro game, the Shulas' patriarch was working on his fourth, a young elder statesman.

Unlike his younger, brasher days, he was insulated from criticism, permitted his sanctimoniousness and self-pity in bad times. As Larry Dorman, who had moved on to the *New York Times*, recalled in 1995:

> During the early 1980's at the Orange Bowl, a sign was affixed each Sunday to a spot in the upper deck. In large block letters, it proclaimed "Shula is god," and about the only argument it ever generated around town concerned whether the letter "g" should be upper or lower case. [Shula] owned South Florida. He was omnipresent, if not omnipotent. His face, with the trademark jutting jaw, was on billboards all over town. He had an expressway named after him. There were serious suggestions that he could not be defeated if he ran for governor.[2]

Shula never claimed he was either a god or God. Life never dealt him an easy hand. In 1983, he was cut to his knees when Dorothy was diagnosed with breast cancer. She took the news with her usual optimism and resolve, throwing herself into chemotherapy and other treatments. She kept it relatively quiet while embarking on a crusade to cheat the odds with a tenacious, almost metaphysical display of will. If Don Shula was calling in every chit with his God to help will Dorothy to health, he nonetheless felt small and inconsequential as reality intruded on the relative triviality of football. During her battle, he would not have recognized himself as a tough guy. In his eyes, he was nowhere near as strong as Dorothy Bartish Shula.

Marino's extraordinary ascension made David Woodley so forgotten that, when Shula traded him to the Steelers, it seemed minor news, though ironically, Chuck Noll thought so much of him that he was given the biggest contract on the roster. Don Strock was also irrelevant now, but would stick around as Marino's backup for four more seasons before finishing his career with the Browns.

That Marino would need to carry the team was made evident by another mediocre draft, with none of Shula's picks doing much except for linebacker Jay Brophy. With Bob Kuechenberg retired, Roy Foster, the first-round pick in '82, was rolled in at left guard, where he would stay for the next seven years. Shula, who had gone without a defensive coordinator since the elevation of Bill Arnsparger to assistant head coach, now hired Chuck Studley, who'd been the interim head coach for the Oilers in '83. But Shula would still be his own offensive coordinator, and if there was a tell coming into the season, it was that he again neither drafted nor traded for a big running back to make Marino's job easier, believing Andra Franklin was good enough.

However, Franklin tore up a knee in September and was gone for the season. With no reliable backup, Shula made a move out of desperation, trading a second-round pick in '85 for Chuck Muncie, who had gotten on Don Coryell's last nerve in San Diego. Muncie passed a physical, but failed a urine test, indicating he was still using cocaine—which killed both the deal and Muncie's career. (In 1989, he was sentenced to 18 months for selling cocaine.)[3] Shula dodged that bullet, but he was stuck with an anemic ground game.

Meanwhile, Marino's star treatment only escalated. *Sports Illustrated* put him on the cover of its 1984 football preview issue, and he deserved it. Opening day was in D.C., a very tough task. Joe Gibbs's Redskins would win 11 games that year, and while Marino had missed most of the preseason with a broken finger, he hit Duper for two touchdowns, the second a 74-yard missile that put Miami up 14–10 at the half. He then added TD strikes to Jim Jensen, Mark Clayton, and Jensen again. The final was 35–17 and Marino's numbers were dizzying—21-for-28, 311 yards, no picks, no sacks, his passer rating 150.4. The defense contained John Riggins and intercepted Joe Theismann twice.

"That was pretty good football," Shula allowed.

The media's infatuation with Marino fed into a new trope for Shula as the ultimate molder of talent as the Dolphins decimated teams week after week, not necessarily dependent on Marino, but certainly riding his success. Shula even used his thin running game to effect. Victimized twice that season, the Pats' dazed defensive coordinator, Rod Rust, explained what he'd been up against:

> One thing Shula's offense does is make you defend the entire field, both the length and width of it. The Dolphins won't let you shrink the field on them. They'll run a screen, and when you try to rush to it, they'll run a double-screen off it and fake it and go downfield. They have a big collection of special plays and gimmicks, and they use 'em well. They're a big-play team, but you've got to play the run honest, because they'll use it as a platform for the big play.[4]

Indeed, while Marino was making a shambles of defenses, the disruption was subtler than most people realized. When secondaries dropped deep against Duper and Clayton—whose cyclonic presence led writers to call them the "Marks Brothers" or "Twain Marks"—Marino cleaned up on short and medium passes. He was as gifted as Unitas at play faking, and he didn't need to square up to pump one 50 yards down the field. Shula refined him, further cutting his drop in half and having him move laterally and throw sooner, the way Bill Walsh did with Montana in the 49ers' West Coast offense. If under pressure, a slip of the hip would buy time. To his guard Ed Newman, Marino was "the definitive wonder boy. Nothing awes him out there. . . . [G]ive us credit for blocking. But Marino is the magic."

Howard Schnellenberger—who coached the Miami Hurricanes to the national title in '83, then was made coach and part owner of an intended third USFL Florida franchise, to begin in '85 and to be called the Spirit of Miami—said Shula recognized that the game had sped up. "That was the trend, and the key was the linebackers. The quarterbacks had to see if they were coming in, because they all blitzed now. You needed a little time to see that, and react, throw to the vacated area. And if Shula was on to something, he was gonna wring the hell out of it."[5]

The stats tell the story. The record for most touchdown passes of 40 or more yards is shared by Johnny Unitas and Peyton Manning, their eras bookending that of Marino, who would retire as the record holder for TD passes under 40 yards (he's now fifth, as football reaps massive passing numbers both long and short). He was hardly a mad bomber, but with an outburst against the Patriots, Marino was just 84 yards short of Griese's club record for single-season passing yardage and on pace to obliterate the single-season NFL record for passing touchdowns—36, shared by George Blanda in '61 (in the old AFL) and Y. A. Tittle in '63. The rushing game wasn't Butch, Sundance, and Merc, but it confused defenses with intricate trap and sucker blocking. As Newman explained, "We batted 'em—that's our term for an outside trap, with me trapping on the other side." Newman, the only player left from the last Dolphin title team, was doing much the same as he did then, on the run and pass blocking.

Some underrated the attack as "all whoosh and no muscle," and some coaches groused that Shula got an inordinate number of pass interference calls, on his reputation and power. "That's what it means having the coach on the NFL Competition Committee," said one anonymous coach that October.[6] "Sour grapes" was Shula's reply. For the media, a team that had been as exciting as watching paint dry was not only winning now, but was fun to watch. To Paul Zimmerman, who took to doting on them in *Sports Illustrated*, Shula's men wore "a look of greatness. . . . And the best is yet to come."

The Dolphins took an 11–0 record (with 16 straight regular-season victories over two years, one shy of Papa Bear Halas's 1933–34 Bears record) to the coast to play the Chargers. For three quarters, Shula seemed on safe ground. Though Don Coryell, needing to keep pace with the Dolphins' newfound air circus, had freed Dan Fouts even more that year, the Dolphins defense held him down. Marino did his thing, going 28-for-41 for 338 yards, throwing touchdowns to Clayton and Bennett. But Fouts, the real mad bomber of the league, hit Charlie Joiner for one touchdown, then led a 19-play, 10-minute, 91-yard drive that ended with a short pass to Eric Sievers to tie it. Von Schamann was set up for a winning field goal but missed from 44 yards, resulting in yet another overtime. It ended when Buford McGee ran in a 15-yard touchdown—repeating the agony of the Epic, with the same scars for the Dolphins, who wound up surrendering 537 yards, Fouts amassing 380 and setting team records for pass attempts and completions, going 37-for-56.

If this was a warning sign, the Dolphins sped past it. In the next game, against the Jets, Marino tied the Tittle/Blanda touchdown record in an easy win. However, going up against Al Davis's 9–4 chain gang the next week brought them back down to earth. Marino threw 57 times, completing 35, for 470 yards and four touchdowns, breaking the record, but the team lost 45–34, Miami squandering 515 total yards. The final two games, though, were impressive wins over the Colts and Cowboys. The reward was a 14–2 record, a division crown, and all kinds of Marino highlights. Some were already classics, such as Nat Moore's "helicopter" catch in the first Jets game, when he was hit by two defenders and twirled around twice in midair before coming down.

Marino's final tallies were 48 touchdowns and 5,084 yards (which still rank fourth and seventh-best in history, the former record not broken until Peyton Manning in 2004, the latter not until Drew Brees in 2011). Marino's other records, all since broken or tied, included nine 300-yard games, four straight games with four or more touchdown passes, and 12 straight games with two or more. In his shadow, it seemed almost quaint that the Giants' Phil Simms and the Cardinals' Neil Lomax each had more than 4,000 passing yards that season. Amazingly, Marino threw all those touchdowns, even though he averaged fewer passes per game than Fouts, 35.3 to 39. Some of Marino's stats weren't exceptional. He had 17 picks. His completion percentage of 64.2 was lower than what Joe Montana and Steve Bartkowski rang up. His 108.9 passer rating, the fourth-best ever at the time, is now 23rd. His 317.8 passing yards per game were less than Fouts's 320.3 two years before. His 8.5 touchdown percentage was inferior to that of numerous quarterbacks from earlier eras. And, beside the touchdowns and yardage, the most important stat might have been that he was sacked just 13 times—a microscopic 2.25 percent of his pass attempts. For the coach, of course, this was a sacred trust: a missed block letting someone get to Marino would mean incurring the wrath of Shula.

If anything redefined the outer limits of the passing game, it was Marino's efficiency and nose for the end zone. And he had these instincts at the age of 23, even before the league made passing easier with rule changes protecting the receivers downfield. But Marino had his kryptonite. And it was the same as Shula's in his later years: the big game.

Marino was the runaway MVP, but Shula had four other All-Pros on offense: center Dwight Stephenson and Newman made the first team, while Clayton (with a league-high 18 touchdowns) and Duper (8 TDs) the second team, as did Baumhower and Duhe on defense. As vital as the running game was to the offense's balance, it could not have won games on its own, ranking 16th and featuring no real game breaker. While the offense rang up 513 points, the defense gave up 298, seventh-best in the league, but perhaps a few too many for comfort. With Duhe never completely healthy, Shula had to go with a rookie and a second-year man, Jay Brophy and Mark Brown, as his inside linebackers, holding his breath each game.

Any quibbles, though, were buried in the first playoff game, a revenge match with the Seahawks, whom they paid back for the year before with Marino throwing a 34-yard touchdown to Cefalo in the first half, then breaking it open in the third quarter with two more to Hardy and Clayton. Shula walked off with a 31–10 win. The next round—the AFC championship game at home against Noll's Steelers—figured to be a lot tougher. But these weren't the Steel Curtain Steelers any more. They had sneaked into the postseason at 9–7 after a season that saw David Woodley losing his job again, to Mark Malone. The Dolphins were a 10-point favorite, and acted like it before the match. Marino came out for warm-ups, noted Ralph Wiley in *Sports Illustrated*, "in shorts and a T-shirt, his belly already beginning to take on some of the spreading opulence of a Sonny Jurgensen," laughing and cutting up with other Dolphins—with the tacit approval of the coach who once would have blown a fuse over such horsing around.

"Clearly," wrote Wiley, "Marino was enjoying the feel of the day; he wore his confidence like a tuxedo."[7]

Noll's boys were tough nuts at first. After Marino threw an early 40-yard touchdown to Clayton, Malone sailed a 65-yard bomb to John Stallworth to go ahead 14–10. From then on, though, it was party time for Marino. His 41-yard pass to Duper took back the lead, then a 36-yard shot to Clayton made it 31–14 and a six-yard scoring flip to Bennett left the Steelers for dead. It ended at 45–28, Marino's 421 yards just missing the playoff-yardage record. The defense cracked, giving up 455 yards, but didn't break, making three picks.

Noll was tart about his own assistants failing to properly get to the bottom of Shula's strategies. "Scouts aren't perfect," he said. "They make mistakes." As had he. The QB he had passed on, he agreed, was the "best we've seen, no question." Steeler cornerback Dwayne Woodruff seemed dazed. "We were all over them sometimes," he said, "but Marino was right on, as right on as a man can be." To *Sports Illustrated*, the game was SUNDAY IN THE PARK WITH DAN.

So, Shula came into another Super Bowl, his fifth, on a high. No quarterback had ever had a season like Marino had, and perhaps no other quarterback except the one that altered the social context of football had ever entered a Super Bowl as cocky as he was. After the Steelers win, Marino had no use for humility. "We knew we could go upfield," he said. "It was there. It's always there." Little wonder that comparisons between Marino and Namath were inevitable, because of their flair, ego, and shared quick release. However, that induction overlooked a crucial difference: Namath beat Shula because of his backfield, Snell and Boozer. Against Pittsburgh, Shula had struck as much of a balance between the pass and run as he could while letting Marino dominate. But in Super Bowl XIX, coach and quarterback would face a team that knew how to systematically deconstruct another team trying to hide a weakness.

Bill Walsh's 49ers were a team without flaw. They were carved in the image of their own super quarterback, Joe Montana, who at 28 was at his peak. The team had gone through the season like cold-blooded assassins. They lost only once, to the Steelers in week seven. Five times, they gave up fewer than 10 points, never more than 17 in the last eight games. Montana threw for 3,630 yards with 28 touchdowns and 10 picks, and was first-team All-Pro, but threw 132 fewer times than Marino within a classic balanced offense—halfback Wendell Tyler rushed for 1,262 yards, fullback Roger Craig for 649 while also catching 71 passes out of the backfield. Running the archetypical West Coast offense, Montana had sure-handed targets: Dwight Clark, Freddie Solomon, and tight ends Earl Cooper and Russ Francis. Across the line, George Seifert's 3–4 defense was a thresher. Walsh had five All-Pros on offense, five on defense—37-year-old linebacker Hacksaw Reynolds had been an All-Pro twice.

San Francisco was second to Miami in points scored, first in least points allowed, and in the playoffs had plundered the Giants 21–10 and the Bears 23–0. Montana, with his wide smile and marriage to a model providing fodder for the tabloids, would have been the focus during Super Bowl week if not for the precocious kid. Paul Zimmerman observed that the "pregame hype . . . relegated [Montana] to something less than a spear carrier to . . . the dazzling young Dan Marino."[8] He and his 49er teammates, who had won it all in '81, were still bristling over the previous year's 24–21 loss to the Redskins in the NFC title game. As the Super Bowl approached, they were salivating about cutting Marino down to size.

Other players around the league wondered if Marino needed a lesson in dues paying. The Steelers' longtime center Mike Webster, who had snapped the ball to Bradshaw in four Super Bowls, said, "It takes time [for a quarterback]. You don't win four Super Bowls in one year." But Marino could look around and see only glitter. He was on the cover of the January 14 *Sports Illustrated*, beneath the words DANGEROUS DAN, the story inside puffing him up as "unstoppable." A week later, in the pre–Super Bowl issue, Paul Zimmerman similarly wondered, "Can Marino be stopped?" Asked about the pressure, the quarterback coolly responded, "I think I can handle it."

To be fair, he had acted the same way before the Steeler game, which he treated as a sort of frat party. Not even Namath was that arrogant. "From a team standpoint the hype bothered me a little," Montana admitted. "Deep down we all felt it. All we heard was 'Miami, Miami, how are you going to stop Miami?' Yeah, yeah, we were overlooked a little." Even Shula seemed to be taking a lot for granted. Bragging about his main man, he dropped his usual humility, saying, "Teams have tried all kinds of schemes against him—drop eight men and rush only three, or blitz everybody, or combinations. Pittsburgh tried the combinations [but] Dan had the answers."

The game, on January 20, 1985, would be played on virtual home grounds for the Niners, in nearby Palo Alto at Stanford Stadium. The Dolphins had to make a 3,000-mile trek to play a great team in its own backyard. Shula's game plan was formulated on getting out to a quick lead, defusing the Niners' intensity and morale. As Tom Landry, who'd seen them plenty, noted, the Niners were "a ball-control team. You have to strike fast against them."[9]

The game, which began in a dense fog, provided some false hope. On their first drive, the Dolphins moved effortlessly. Marino's swing pass to Nathan broke for 25 yards when the Niners blew a tackle. They got a field goal out of it. Then, after Montana found scrub running back Carl Monroe for a 33-yard touchdown, Shula unveiled his surprise, going no-huddle. At a hastened pace, the team gained 70 yards in six plays, capped by a two-yard touchdown pass to Dan Johnson for a 10–7 lead. In response, Walsh made a modification. He began switching from the 3–4 to a 4–3 and even a 4–2, to get more heat on Marino. It was more than the highly praised Dolphin line could handle—or Marino. Walsh didn't blitz much, keeping his linebackers and secondary back in coverage, blocking Marino's sight lines. And his linemen were on fire.

The Dolphins stopped moving, and when Montana controlled the ball, he engineered touchdowns on three straight drives, running one in from six yards. It was 28–16 at the half. Trying somehow to slow the momentum, Shula junked the no-huddle and all but bagged the run. He called for long, increasingly desperate passes—that is, when Marino could get them off. Under attack, he was sacked four times, twice by right end Dwaine Board, and hounded by an extra lineman, Gary Johnson. He would throw 50 times, completing 29 for 318 yards, but he threw two interceptions and never got into the end zone again. Montana, a 38–16 winner, took back his sovereignty, going 24-for-35, with 331 yards, three touchdowns, and a 127.8 passer rating, all Super Bowl records at the time.

Before the game had even ended, the league announced Montana as the game's MVP, which Ed Pope considered "a classless act." Shula then walked through the gloom to midfield for the ritual he despised, shaking Walsh's hand, then several 49er players sought him out to shake his. In the locker room, he was glowering but graceful in defeat.

"It's going to be tough to live with this one," he said. "I'm so disappointed. Montana kept us off balance the entire game. He's a great, great athlete."[10]

Ashen, the gray at his temples and lines on his forehead in contrast to his bright orange sweater, defeat seemed to age him on the spot. "You can't get dragged down, you've got to think about all the good things that happened this year," he went on. But, by now, it seemed too habitual even to old retainers like Pope, who, like everyone else in Miami, thought the winning would never end. Pope, seeming offended, wrote in his postmortem, "The fog also spread like virus through the Dolphin coaching brain trust. . . . [W]hy did the Dolphins abandon the no-huddle system that worked so well on their only touchdown drive?" Shula had to explain why his entire ground game was nine rushes, for just 25 yards—the first still a Super Bowl record for fewest carries. No explanation was good enough for Pope, who saw an alarming pattern:

> I don't know what it is with the Dolphins in Super Bowls. If you should figure it out, give them a buzz. The fact is, even winning at the ends of the 1972 and 1973 seasons, in five Super Bowls now they have gotten steadily worse in each quarter:
> First quarter—Dolphins 38, opponents 10.
> Second quarter—Dolphins 29, opponents 38.
> Third quarter—Dolphins 7, opponents 20.
> Fourth quarter—Dolphins 0, opponents 35.

Shula's methods were proven to develop tough, smart, highly conditioned men who were fortunate to play for him. But, for whatever reason, they left too much intensity against the best of opponents inside the locker room. Maybe the All-Pro punter Reggie Roby cut to the heart of the problem in explaining his awful punting that day. "I was trying to kill the ball, and I kicked it bad." he said. "I didn't hit one well. I was scared—scared to make a mistake."

There was still time to alter this pattern, but Shula was infatuated with having a quarterback like Marino, and it became his crutch. Rick Volk, who had been there when Shula fell into the unrelieved hell of the Jets loss, said, "Look, no one knew better than Don that you couldn't win it all without a running game. He knew that with Unitas. He had it with Csonka, Kiick, and Morris. But when he got Marino, he didn't want to waste that arm. He became a different kind of coach."[11] Marino was willing to take the hit, saying, "I didn't play as well as I could have. Sometimes I had a chance to move, and I didn't." But Shula felt no apologies were necessary. Altered reality or not, he believed that all he needed was for Marino to gain some more experience, and that both of them were sitting on top of the future of the game in yet another era of change.

Marino's hard fall set an unfortunate precedent and future trope: the "curse" of the great quarterback class of '83. Of those who made it to a Super Bowl, only Elway would win—twice, in the last two years of his career. Other than that, they collectively lost all nine of their Super Bowls, four of which were the most lopsided Super Bowl losses in history. As their careers played out, Marino had already risen highest, although Kelly made a small ripple in the USFL by passing for 44 touchdowns and over 5,200 yards, winning Rookie of the Year and MVP honors. Given Kelly's fat contract, Marino was not about to accept the contract he had signed as a 27th pick—especially when Bernie Kosar gave up his remaining eligibility at Miami and, taken in a supplemental draft by the Browns, was lavished with a $5.2 million deal. Having paid his dues smashing all those records, Marino wanted a new deal, on a par with Montana's $1.3 million salary, which made him the highest-paid quarterback. Robbie made an offer of $6 million over six years. Marino, livid, walked out of the '84 summer camp.

Robbie and Shula huffed that he would be fined $500 for every day he missed. Shula—who, with Strock also a holdout, began camp with no established quarterbacks—said the situation was "as disruptive as [anything] I've encountered in my coaching career,"[12] somehow forgetting Csonka, Kiick, Warfield, and Morris. Marino wouldn't budge, and began taking hits in the press as the preseason began. He seemed selfish, and a *Herald* readers' poll favored Robbie. Marvin Demoff said Marino would report if Robbie agreed to binding arbitration; Robbie said no. Demoff said he'd come in if Robbie took out an insurance policy on Marino; Robbie said no. The holdout stretched for 38 days, Marino incurring over $7,500 in fines.

He finally buckled a week before the season opener in Houston, his only recourse to play out the original deal and take Robbie at his word that one more year of excellence would get him his top-shelf salary. Days later, he was in the starting lineup, having arguably his worst game as a pro. Rusty and indecisive, his right elbow slightly injured, he was intercepted twice and came out in the fourth quarter for Strock, who got the lead before the Oilers won it on a late touchdown, 26–23. Marino was revived the next week, laying 329 yards and two touchdowns on the Colts in a 30–13 win. The Dolphins won four in a row, had a midseason slump, then won their last seven. Marino didn't come close to his record-setting numbers; his passer rating fell to 84.1, his picks ticking up to 21. But he turned in another first-team All-Pro season with 4,137 yards and 30 touchdowns.

Shula had made an attempt to cultivate a powerful ground game. However, his first draft pick, Florida running back Lorenzo Hampton, carried just 105 times for 369 yards, which even so was second on the team to Nathan's 667. Despite the criticisms of imbalance, the Dolphins ran *less*, dropping in yardage from 16th to 18th. The defense also fell to 12th, leading Shula to acquire Tampa Bay's former All-Pro outside linebacker Hugh Green in midseason. But the team was defined by Danny the Wonder Boy. Three-time All-Pro Dwight Stephenson wore the honor of the man who "keeps Danny off his fanny."[13] That would earn him a new deal, too, Robbie tearing up his contract in '85 and raising him to $300,000 a year.

The sole drama of the season came when Mike Ditka's Bears, en route to a championship chiseled by defense, won their first 12 games, then, as if on cue, came to Miami on a Monday night. On that evening, before a huge national audience, Shula motivated his men by loading up the sideline with players from the '72 team, whose honor they would defend. Stoked, the Dolphins stopped the Bears like the Romans repelling the Etruscans on the Tiber bridge. Marino riddled the Bears' historically stingy 46 Defense with touchdown passes to Moore and Clayton, filing away a 38–24 win. It was a statement game, and it allowed Shula to walk off every bit a Caesar, if for but one night.

The Dolphins finished an impressive 12–4, and Marino, unlike the precocious frat boy of the previous two years, wore a lean, hungry look. His ability to keep his cool in the clutch was obvious; even while throwing three picks against the Steelers, he led a late drive to pull out a win. But the Dolphins were walking on a razor's edge. The first playoff match was against the Browns, an 8–8 team that was 21st in offense despite the arrival of Kosar, two 1,000-yard rushers in Earnest Byner and Kevin Mack, the wondrous tight end Ozzie Newsome, and three All-Pros on defense. By the third quarter, with Byner having run for 21- and 66-yard touchdowns, leading a 251-yard rushing avalanche, Cleveland was ahead 21–3. Still, the Dolphins stole it with three straight touchdowns, lifting Shula to yet another AFC championship game by the skin of his teeth.

He had made it back to that game again with a chasm between the pass and run—the Dolphins only ran the ball 19 times against the Browns. The conference title match brought in the Patriots, a wild-card team that had beaten the Jets and Raiders. Ironically, under Shula's old Hall of Fame receiver Ray Berry, they were a pound-it-out bunch, a throwback to Shula's pre-Marino Dolphins. In fact, the success in '85 of the Pats and Bears would reflect a brief reincarnation of Stone Age football. Berry had Tony Eason do little but hand off to All-Pro fullback Craig James (1,227 yards) and halfback Tony Collins, passing only when needed. The defense was sixth-best in the league, outside linebacker Andre Tippett a first-team All-Pro, while inside linebacker Steve Nelson and cornerback Ray Clayborn made the second team.

The Dolphins were five-and-a-half-point favorites and had beaten the Pats 18 consecutive times in the Orange Bowl. But even amid the usual frenzied pregame rituals, they came out of the tunnel with the same puzzling lack of four-quarter intensity that had crippled them in the last two Super Bowls. The normal oven-like conditions in Miami, which almost always gave Shula a definitive home-field advantage, were cooled by rain, and the turf was muddy. And it was the Dolphins who floundered. Nathan fumbled on the first drive, setting up a Pats field goal. Marino did grab the lead with a 10-yard strike to Dan Johnson in the second quarter. But thereafter, he made errant passes, two of them picked off. Five times the Dolphins fumbled, losing four, one by Marino deep in Pat territory. Another by Hampton on the second-half kickoff led to a Patriots touchdown. Yet another, by Joe Carter, did the same. Dolphin kicker Fuad Reveiz, who had dependably replaced von Schamann this season, missed a 31-yard field goal.

The year before, Rod Rust admitted his defense couldn't stop Marino. Now, they smothered him and his receivers. Marino could do no better than 20-for-48, his 248 yards mostly in his own territory. Shula's neglected runners ran 13 times for 68 yards. By contrast, the Pats owned the ball, doubling the Dolphins in possession time. During the week, New England's All-Pro wideout Irving Fryar was stabbed in the hand by his pregnant wife (an accident, he insisted), taking him out of the game. But Eason needed to throw only 12 times, completing 10 for 71 yards, his passer rating a superb 130.9 (to Marino's 54.9). He threw three short touchdowns to go ahead 24–7 after three quarters. Marino could only shave it to 24–14 with a 10-yard pass to Nathan, but another Pat drive iced it at 31–14.

"They made the big play, I'm disappointed we didn't," Shula lamented. "We never did the things we needed to do to win a game of this caliber."

Coming from the highest-paid, highest-regarded coach in the game, words like these had become much too familiar. Once, a home play-off defeat would have been stunning, almost unthinkable, requiring an "epic" performance. Now, it seemed a replay of the same dreary episode, with Shula in his teeth-gritted pose, wondering aloud where his team's heart and soul had gone, but vowing they would be back, with the proper corrections. Perhaps no other coach could have sold this menu for long. But for Shula, it was as if his players were mortal, not him, and what he promised to deliver was always just another season away.

22

NO NEED TO RUSH

These kinds of gut punches paled before the biggest blows Don Shula ever suffered—the thinning out of his family. On April 1, 1986, the intrepid Mary Miller Shula died in Painesville at age 83, three years after her husband, Dan. Their children laid her to rest next to him in St. Mary's Cemetery. For their famous son, life at age 56 was no longer open-ended, and certainly not carefree. But, still made of equal parts brick, piss, and brine, he put the same long hours into his team, constantly adapting young men in his image. Trying in vain to hold the line on exploding player salaries—but not his own—was making his life as an executive less dictatorial year by year. Indeed, in 1986, his 24-year-old quarterback, only three years of service under his pads, was owed a mint.

At least the USFL was no longer a threat. Its slow death was made final that year after Donald Trump persuaded his fellow owners to go directly against the NFL that fall, only to see the league crumble before any games were played. Howard Schnellenberger's Miami team never came to be. (The vanquished league would launch an antitrust suit against the NFL and "win," but because its woes were its own fault, it was awarded damages of one dollar, trebled under antitrust law to three). That sent its highest-paid stars into the NFL. Jim Kelly had already signed with the Bills in '85 for eight years and $5 million, his starting salary a cool million. Steve Young, whose $10 million USFL contract guaranteed him deferred payments for the next 40 years, pocketed a six-year, $5 million deal from Tampa Bay, two years before he was traded to the 49ers.

Watching this gravy train of inflated quarterback salaries, in early September Marino and Marvin Demoff collected Robbie's IOU, his new deal for six years and a guaranteed $9 million, with a $2 million signing bonus and $850,000 roster bonus. His salary would climb from $500,000 to $1.45 million, $1.5 million, and $1.6 million, with incentives adding another $100,000 per year. That lifted him above Joe Montana, but not Kelly. On a team molded by Shula to strip away individualism, Marino's star power was a justifiable exception, a boon to the Dolphins' stock value, which made Shula pine for the shares he'd sold back to Robbie on the cheap.

The Marino era certainly helped Robbie prosper more, though he sank most of the bottom line into getting his vanity stadium built. In '86, construction on the futuristic site was rising out of swampland in Miami Gardens, a still-unincorporated tract just north of downtown off the Florida Turnpike, ahead of schedule, the project eating just about every spare penny Robbie had after paying his players, his coach, and the IRS. One reporter wrote that Robbie "had to hock the Dolphins, right down to their last jersey and pair of cleats, to keep construction going. At the Super Bowl game in Palo Alto, Robbie offered tickets to the game and transportation on a chartered plane for anyone buying a suite in his new stadium. . . . Robbie is such a salesman that before the 160-acre site had even been cleared, using only architect's renderings, he had persuaded the NFL's brass to put the 1989 Super Bowl in his stadium."[1]

The problem was, the '86 season interrupted Shula's streak of staying in contention. Adhering to his new formula, Marino put the ball in the air the most he ever would—623 times. He would complete the most passes of his career, too, 378 with 44 touchdowns to 23 picks, amassing 4,746 yards. He was first-team All-Pro for a third straight season. And for all that, Shula lost four of the first five games, one in a raucous 51–45 shootout to the Jets.

With two years left on his own historic contract, Shula had begun making his case for an extension to protect his status as the top-paid coach. Slathering Robbie like butter on a baked potato, he said that, given the "good relationship" they had, Robbie "continues to support me in every way and I'm going to be loyal to him in every way." It worked. After the team had typically battled back to 6–6, he got his extension, another five years at $1.2 million per. However, the season ended at 8–8, in third place, out of the playoffs. It almost seemed a mockery that the Giants won it all that year, their quarterback, Phil Simms, an unassuming, conservative fellow who, in Bill Parcells's game plan, threw mainly high-percentage passes, besting John Elway's Broncos.

Not making the playoff was a rarity for Shula. But in what was playing out as a Groundhog Day, each season was coming down to the same ending: just short of something good.

The '87 season was momentous for the Shula clan. For one, Mike had been drafted out of Alabama by the Tampa Bay Buccaneers (his last college game was the Senior Bowl, coached by his father, with his brother, Dave, the offensive coordinator). Tough like his old man, but not as talented, he had taken the Crimson Tide to a couple of bowl games but never really had a shot as a pro quarterback. Taken in the 13th round, he washed out early, then took an offer from coach Ray Perkins to become a Bucs assistant in '88, then following the path of his brother, Dave, onto the Dolphins' staff.

As for the Dolphins family, that '87 season brought the fruition of what Joe Robbie had promised, to snickers, when the humbly named Joe Robbie Stadium opened. To the former nonbelievers, this was the "Miracle of Miami." Robbie hadn't shorted himself or the fans. The 216 executive suites were peddled for up to $65,000 a year, fitted with air conditioning, two TV monitors, refrigerator, and catered buffet and liquor cabinet. These would raise $9 million a year in lease payments, securing more loans from the banks that had financed the project. The two looming scoreboards, 140 feet wide and 56 feet high, would project nonstop highlights of Marino and of Shula's perfect season. Six years later, when the expansion Florida Marlins were born, they would play baseball there as well, making for year-round revenue.

The first regular-season game in the place was set for September 27, week three, against the Giants. However, in late September, after the Dolphins had split their first two games, the Players Association's collective bargaining agreement with the owners expired and it called a sudden strike, reminiscent of the in-season walkout of '82. Catching the owners off guard, it forced the NFL to cancel the next week's games—including Robbie's long-awaited home opener at his stadium. This time, not wanting to lose TV capital, the NFL went with a grab bag of replacement players. Predictably, this was a disaster, the fans rejecting this bottom-of-the-barrel product. During the interlude, Shula's quarterback was one Kyle Mackey, a discarded 11th-round pick of the Cardinals in '84 who, after losing to the faux Seahawks, was the leader for what was now the opening of Robbie Stadium, against the Chiefs. The ersatz Dolphins won 42–0, witnessed by 25,000 curiosity seekers, few of whom would brag about being there. The next week, Mackey threw five interceptions in an overtime loss on the road to the replacement Jets.

Shula got his men back a week later, after the union crumbled once again, ending the walkout without a new CBA, the union instead filing another antitrust suit against the league. In the interim, the two sides agreed on a compromise that would permit looser Plan B free agency in return for a team salary cap. And so, the "real" opening of Robbie Stadium came on October 25 against the Bills, pitting Marino against Kelly. It drew a gate-busting crowd of over 74,000, and it was worth waiting for. Each of them threw for over 300 yards, Marino for four touchdowns, Kelly two, and neither had an interception. After Marino hit Clayton to tie it in the fourth quarter, the Bills won on a field goal in the OT, 34–31. At 2–4, it seemed the season was headed for another no-show in the playoffs.

But Shula kept them afloat, finding critical pieces. Fourth-round pick Troy Stradford would lead the team with 619 yards rushing and catch 48 passes in the abbreviated 15-game season. The second-round pick from '84, inside linebacker John Offerdahl, was an All-Pro. The three down linemen—T. J. Turner, Brian Sochia, and John Bosa, his first-round pick that year—were young and hungry. Shula also hired a defensive coordinator, Tom Olivadotti, Howard Schnellenberger's former defensive line coach with the Miami Hurricanes. But the team was still squarely on Marino's shoulders. Don Strock had become such a forgotten man that, when he demanded to be paid the same salary as the 37-year-old Ron Jaworski, who had been signed as an additional backup for Marino, it was hardly noticed that Shula summarily let Strock go, to join the Browns and rip into his old coach for not appreciating him.[2]

Marino, who was on the same wavelength as Shula and called nearly all his own plays, made second-team All-Pro in '87 with 3,245 passing yards and 26 touchdowns; the Dolphins were No. 1 in yards and attempts. Keeping the team in the race, Shula had given himself a chance by the season finale against the Patriots. Both teams were 8–6, and a win might have gotten him a wild-card berth, but the Dolphins were run out of their new home. Down 24–3 at the half, they lost 24–10, with Marino picked off twice. At 8–7, they again ended stuck in third place, another also-ran season, out in the cold for the sixth time in Shula's 18 years in Miami. But again, he had believable excuses and he had Marino. That, and his reputation, were all he needed to keep the hounds off him for another year . . . or three.

Needing to keep Marino upright at any cost, Shula had to perform radical surgery on his offensive line. Dwight Stephenson had blown out his knee in '86 and retired. That enormous gap was filled by six-foot, six-inch, 290-pound Jeff Dellenbach, the fourth-round pick in '85. Other injuries gave the right guard spot to low-drafted rookie Harry Galbreath. Another rookie, third-rounder Ferrell Edmunds, replaced Bruce Hardy at tight end. But the going got rougher in '88, putting Shula in crisis. Starting out being crushed by the Bears 34–7, and then losing a field-goal battle to the Bills, the Dolphins clawed back to 5–4, then lost five in a row and six of the last seven—three by four points or less—to finish 6–10, last in the five-team AFC East. It was Shula's lowest finish of all, and only sub-.500 season other than the 6–8 slip in '76.

In one game, Marino threw for 521 yards against the Jets, the second-most ever to Norm Van Brocklin's 554 in 1951—and lost 44–30. There was also the game against Tampa Bay, when Don Shula coached with one son on his sideline and another on the opposite one, with Dorothy watching and keeping to a stolid impartiality. The old man just barely got by the gruesome Bucs 17–14. Marino's regular insistence that "we're a better team than what our record is, we just haven't put it together" became a mantra, although it was a hard sell watching quality time being given to names like Scott Schwedes, Brian Kinchen and Weegie Thompson.

Shula did get a rare top-10 draft pick out of this dreadful season and finally tried to repair the broken running game by taking Florida State running back Sammie Smith, who in '89 would slog a team-high 659 yards on 200 carries, then over 800 yards in '90. But he had an alarming tendency to fumble, usually at the worst times—15 of them over those two seasons. Shula also gave in to hiring an offensive coordinator, Gary Stevens, who'd held that job under Schnellenberger with the Hurricanes. But what may have been just as relevant to Shula in '89 was that Tom Landry was fired before the season after the oafish Jerry Jones bought the Cowboys and installed his own coach, Jimmy Johnson. That Landry was axed after 29 years without so much as a thank you no doubt made Shula, who was about to coach his 26th year, far more sensitive to criticism, and to the reality that even he could be displaced.

When the Cowboys were still owned by Bum Bright, a Dallas sportswriter guessed that the team's next coach might be Shula, who was said to be "best friends" with Cowboys team president Tex Schramm.[3] But even though Shula's contract was due to expire in '89, he would never have embarrassed Landry by taking his job. They were the lions of the NFL, epoxied in mutual respect. During the '88 season, they had sat for a joint interview with NBC, displaying different reactions to criticism. While Landry humbly said it "hurts a little bit," but that "it won't take a toll on me," the pit bull in Shula railed at "innuendos and half-truths," particularly public scapegoating of his son Dave as if by proxy to criticize him—which the old man took personally. With a bitter laugh, he noted that the team had gone to two Super Bowls "and won more games in the '80s than anyone" with Dave as an assistant.[4]

Whether by coincidence or not, by the time the '89 season rolled around, Dave Shula had left to become Landry's intended offensive coordinator in Dallas, and was kept on when Johnson took over. But the elder Shula was still dodging bullets. The year before, Mark Duper had been suspended for the last two games after testing positive for an unnamed substance. Shula was forced to deny he had ignored the problem when *Sports Illustrated* reported in December that he and Robbie had been warned as far back as 1986 that Duper and former Dolphin Nat Moore had been photographed by police partying with Nelson Aguilar, a Miami dealer later convicted of drug trafficking.[5]

For Shula, it was an uncomfortable flashback to the Reese–Crowder mishigas, and his response was just as tepid. He admitted being so warned, being "very disturbed," and notifying the NFL security department. He also called in the pair to discuss it, insisting, "That was the extent of what I could do," even though the team continued Duper's suspension pending a league investigation. Indeed, Shula seemed more intent on saving his own reputation, decrying the article as "an insult to my integrity and to the discipline that I demand from myself and my players." Some in the media didn't buy it; SHULA IGNORES DUPER CASE, read one headline.[6] Coming to his aid, the league's communications director, Joe Browne, said it was "ludicrous" to question Shula's credibility.

Then, in February 1989, *Sports Illustrated* alleged that Duper had snorted cocaine for the last six seasons, based on the testimony of a driver at Duper's limousine business who said he supplied both Duper and Mark Clayton, a prominent anti-drug crusader.[7] Duper's agent called the story "entirely false, shameless yellow journalism," and no further action was taken by the team or the league against either player.[8] After Duper passed a lie detector test, he and Clayton were cleared of any wrongdoing by the league. Thus spared, a year later, Duper would become the second Dolphin receiver to gain over 7,000 career yards. Clayton also excelled, making his fifth Pro Bowl in '91 before both Marks Brothers retired a year later. Yet it might have been Shula who felt the most relieved, and vindicated.

His Teflon indeed seemed undisturbed during the '89 season. The Dolphins lost two of their first three games, but they were 7–4 after beating the Cowboys 17–14 right before Thanksgiving. The only happier person than Shula that day might have been the exiled Landry, whose bad blood with Jones made him root against the team he had ruled since its inception. He had a lot to smile about that year, when Johnson went 1–15. And Shula, perhaps learning from Landry's fall, seemed prepared to steel himself to keep from seeming vulnerable. He was also ready to bend a bit on the passing game. Marino threw less, just missing 4,000 yards, his 24 touchdowns putting him past 200 in his career faster than anyone ever had done it, though his somewhat toned-down game may have cost him another All-Pro designation.

The offense ran more, but the defense was a mishmash of odds and ends surrounding Offerdahl and the aging Hugh Green. For Shula, it ended with one more 8–8 record, one more third-place finish. He was on a treadmill, to be sure, but, as always, trusted to sprint ahead any day now.

Entrenched in a tropical market fueled by a culture of excess, Shula had his big contract—which had been bettered when Bill Walsh was raised to $1.3 million in '88—and his prophylaxis with the fans and the press. He seemed too big, too permanent, to fail. However, as if underlining the uncertainty of the future, right after the new decade rang in, Joe Robbie checked out. He had been in poor health for months, suffering from a respiratory illness resulting from heavy smoking. Unable to breathe without aid, he sat in his owner's box, sucking oxygen from a tank. Knowing he had scant time, he had placed the team under a living trust for one more generation, keeping in place his wife, Elizabeth Ann, as a paper vice-president and three sons, vice-president/GM Mike Robbie, vice-president of public affairs Tim Robbie, and director of sales Dan Robbie.

Two weeks after he saw the Dolphins lose their season finale on Christmas Eve to the Chiefs, Robbie died in a Miami hospital on January 7, 1990, at 73. His legacy was deserved, the investment for which he had to scrounge around to raise 100 grand now worth $120 million. One of the first people his widow called to inform of his death was Shula, who, for all his ambivalence about a man he had once wanted to punch in the mouth, knew his career had been salvaged by Robbie in 1970.

"I've never been around a guy who was more dedicated or wanted to win more than Joe," he said. "His accomplishments made sports history. I'm just sorry to see him pass away after . . . we came so close but just didn't get there."⁹

As the tributes flowed for the "tough and tenacious" Robbie, for Shula there would be the hard-eyed matter of courting loyalty with a new majority owner once the Robbies chose to sell the controlling interest to Wayne Huizenga. Balding and moon-faced, the 53-year-old Huizenga had made his fortune in the garbage collection business, founding Waste Management Inc., before adding another future Fortune 500 company, Blockbuster Entertainment. The Robbies sold him 15 percent of the team and 50 percent of the Robbie Stadium Corporation—the latter non-negotiable as they had racked up $88 million in debt on Robbie's "miracle" stadium, killing any chance that the family could afford to retain majority ownership. The tab for Huizenga to take control was around $75 million, and he was prepared to reach deeper into his pocket to buy the Robbies out altogether.

Shula could read Huizenga's mind. While the Robbie family had his back now, they were on borrowed time. Huizenga would surely want want to name his own coach at some point. Shula wasn't even 60 yet, hardly geriatric by NFL standards, but his permanence, his familiarity, and of course his salary were not to his advantage. Only getting back to the top could preserve him as the enduring face of the team.

Before he died, Robbie had promoted Eddie Jones, the vice-president of finance, to the position of executive vice-president and general manager. A highly respected career NFL executive, Jones was a gracious, solicitous type, and Shula felt a lot better about sharing power with him than he would have with Joe Thomas. But subtle moves like this were a small sign that the Dolphin bosses knew they needed to become less mom-and-pop in nature. And Shula was still in the long shadow of Vince Lombardi, certainly not immortal. When the 1990 edition of *Who's Who in America* came out, Shula had been dropped from its pages. As Rick Reilly caustically wrote in *Sports Illustrated*, "A guy has a couple of 8–8 years and they're filling out death certificates."[10]

Not just yet. Partly with a win-one-for-Joe motivation—something he had never used before—Shula turned the last decade of the outgoing millennium into a personal renaissance. Not coincidentally, this was also Marino's contract play-out season, and with Elway up to $1.5 million a year and Jim Kelly signing a new deal paying him $1.4 million with a $3 million bonus, the incentive for Marino to perform was high. To shield him more, in the first round of the 1990 draft, Shula picked Texas A&M's massive offensive tackle Richmond Webb, who would start at left tackle. Another rookie 300-pounder, Keith Sims, the second-round pick, started at left guard. Webb would hold his position for seven years, Sims eight, each a periodic All-Pro. With a new center, Jeff Uhlenhake, a fifth-round pick in '89, and Jeff Dellenbach backing them up, the line resembled a herd of circus elephants, with two still-growing kids, Galbreath and tackle Mark Dennis, on the right side.

But the real surprise of '90 was the defense. Two years earlier, Shula had found a wild man with his ninth-round pick in Jeff Cross, who now won the job at right end and made All-Pro, leading the team with 11½ sacks. The two young safeties, Jarvis Williams and Louis Oliver split 10 interceptions. A free agent walk-on from '88, David Griggs, made it as an outside linebacker; a trade pickup, Shawn Lee, got his shot at nose tackle. A graybeard pickup from the Colts, Cliff Odom, held down an inside linebacker slot. As Marino rang up the fourth-most passing yardage in the league, the defense gave up the fourth-least.

Marino had to survive three interceptions in the opener at Foxborough, his second touchdown pass, seven yards to fullback Tony Paige, lifting the Dolphins to a gutty 27–24 win, with Sammie Smith going for 159 yards and the defense sacking Steve Grogan four times. Thereafter, the defense went on an amazing streak, giving up fewer than 10 points five times, and as many as 20 only once. The team won seven of eight, had a critical overtime win over the Eagles, and waltzed home with a 12–4 record, a game behind the Bills in the division, but enough to grab a wild card. It was all very Shula-like, circa 1973. Marino threw the fewest passes in his career in a 16-game schedule (531), for the fewest yards (3,563), with the fewest picks (11), and the second-fewest touchdowns (21).

This time around, the media didn't go overboard. The prevailing attitude was to wait and see whether Shula had come upon the right formula. In the wild-card playoff game against the Chiefs, he fell behind 16–3 and Marino had to save them with late touchdowns to Paige and Clayton, pulling out of the fire an uncomfortably close 17–16 win. That got Shula the unenviable task of going to the divisional title game with the Bills. On a blustery 30-degree day in Buffalo, it was Kelly who could throw economically, 29 times, because he had an accomplished running game, the name of which was Thurman Thomas, the All-Pro fullback and the league's second-best rusher. Thomas pounded Shula's defense with 32 carries for 117 yards and two touchdowns.

Again behind, 20–3, Marino would let it rip 49 times and complete 29. He connected with Duper on a 64-yard TD, and later, there were short scoring passes to spare halfbacks Roy Foster and Tony Martin. But Kelly would parry him each time, tossing three scores, outpassing him, 339 yards to 323. Buffalo won 44–34, carving another dubious distinction for Shula—who with this game had coached in the two highest-scoring playoff games ever, in four quarters (at the time) and overall (the Epic), losing both. Kelly went on to wreck the Raiders 51–3 and get to the Super Bowl, where reality would always set in for him. This time, he tasted the first of his three Super Bowl defeats, on a blown field goal against the Giants, played at the height of the mercifully brief Gulf War.

But the fact that Shula had made it to two playoff games was a win for him. He had bought himself time to make more history.

However, 1991 began with another tragedy, the harshest realities of life and mortality stealing the last mercy he asked his God for. Dorothy Bartish Shula's inspiring fight against breast cancer had been intense and beyond courageous, and he had let himself believe that she—they—had beaten it. But after a series of remissions and relapses, it had metastasized to her lungs and she was pronounced terminal. She fought on, and in truth, the family had been preparing for her death for eight years, living with an enormous burden. In 1987, when the Broward Booster Club held a tribute dinner for her, David Shula told the teary-eyed audience, "We haven't had to fight the battle she has had to fight." He addressed her, saying, "When I feel down and sorry for myself, I think of your fight with cancer. I don't think I could have matched it."[11]

Unable to attend Dolphins games and sit in her box, she was last seen in public at an American Cancer Society dinner the previous August. Weakening and wasting away, but smiling widely, she rose to give a speech urging no one to feel sorry for her, but to instead contribute to the charity. Her husband followed her on the stage and said, "Talk about courage." He still looked at her the way he did when they were kids, deeply in love. Their friends openly wondered how he could survive without her.

"There were days he lost it, he'd come apart at the seams, which was very unlike him," said Howard Schnellenberger. "He's a very sensitive man, with feelings the world never sees because he hides them. That was why he stuck around so long in the game. He needed football to get him through it. The game was his salvation."[12]

On February 25, 1991, the beating heart of the Shula clan finally lost her long battle at age 57, a week after her family began keeping vigil at her bedside. Her husband made the announcement the next day, saying, "She went peacefully, thank God. It was about as peaceful as it could be. She went into a coma and just drifted away. Thank God everybody was here, all the five children. That's what she wanted."[13] The funeral was two days later at Our Lady of the Lake Catholic Church in Miami Lakes, and she was buried in Our Lady of Mercy Cemetery. Dozens of players past and present attended the service, where Shula stood beside the coffin and, voice shaking, harked back to the long-ago days in Painesville, when he wore his letterman sweater.

"We were known as a sexy couple and a guy who couldn't hold a job," he said. "We never thought anything about having kids or picking up and moving." Then, with a snap of his fingers, he added, "It just went like that." It was too much for many in the church to hear without their throats tightening. In the days after, he found himself deeply depressed, sitting in a suddenly empty seven-bedroom house, staring almost in a catatonic trance at her now-empty place in their bed. His friends and the children had never seen him like that. When he did get out of the house, he would wander about, telling people, "This is going to be my first year in coaching that Dorothy hasn't been around." Bob Griese, who had recently lost his wife to cancer as well, understood. "Everybody sees him on the sideline with that stern jaw sticking out," he said. "Everybody thinks he's so much in control, and he is. But we all have to go home in the evening. Dorothy was a big support for him."[14]

That year, he hired his son Mike as a Dolphins assistant. Mike moved back into the house, getting his father's mind on football, dragging him out to play some golf, or just talking out their grief. But Shula couldn't help sitting at a desk in the office where Dorothy, by the light of a Dolphin-helmet lamp and under pictures of their wedding day, had organized her volunteer work, paid the bills, written and signed his return letters to fans. He made an effort to grow closer to his five grandchildren, having said at the funeral that Dorothy's greatest joy was looking forward to them growing up. "He's really made an effort to take over a lot of the things my mother used to do," said his daughter Donna, who was 30 then and the mother of two. "Things that we never used to talk to him about, we talk to him about now. I see him as more vulnerable. I used to see him as this almighty person. I don't think he used to like to let anyone see that he was vulnerable or hurt or scared. He comes to me a lot of times with things to talk about. It feels good."

He launched a foundation to raise money for breast cancer research, planning celebrity golf tournaments and fund-raisers. He had moved on well enough to resume his job in time for the '91 draft. When spring camp opened, he was back at his own mahogany desk, checking waiver lists, taking meetings with Eddie Jones and Mike Robbie, stalking practices, yelling himself red-faced, conducting his chalk talks with the old vigor. Often, he spoke of having an epiphany.

"What I learned from Dorothy more than anything is always take the necessary time," he said. "She always had time for people, to say or do things to help make their lives more pleasant, to feel better about themselves. At this stage in my life, that's something I want to do. I don't need to rush anymore."

One of his old warthogs, Bob Kuechenberg, noticed the change in the old pit bull:

> Maybe [Dorothy's] death had something to do with it, the slow and tragic way it happened. I saw him at a dinner after that. He hugged me. He said, 'I love you, Bob.' When he walked away, I said to my wife, 'Did you just hear what I think I heard?' It's something he never would have said in the old days. The Lombardi in him wouldn't have let him. Now he can say something like that. He isn't afraid to show that kind of emotion.[15]

The '91 season surely tested his new sense of tolerance. Although Shula persuaded Mean Joe Greene to come to the Dolphins as defensive line coach after five years in that job with his old Steelers team, the defense was anything but mean; they crashed back to earth, falling

to 24th, ranking 27th against the run. This crash was evident on opening day, when Marino lost another shootout to Kelly, mainly because
Kelly again had Thurman Thomas, who ran for 165 yards. Buffalo laid
582 total yards on them, and while Marino put them ahead with a short
pass to Clayton in the fourth quarter, Thomas's subsequent seven-yard
TD clinched it.

Shula did get an astonishing performance that day from Mark
Higgs, a five-foot, seven-inch kick-return man he obtained in a trade
in '90. In what looked like a misprint in the box score, *only* Higgs carried the ball for Miami the entire game—30 times, for 146 yards—one
of the strangest anomalies in the Shula era. Higgs would virtually be
the entire running game that year, gaining over 900 yards. Meanwhile,
Sammie Smith fumbled his way off the team and out of the league,
his finale prompting chants of "Sammie Sucks" in Robbie Stadium
and Smith needing a police escort from the park. Whatever was ailing
Smith seemed to be evident three years later, when he was convicted
of selling cocaine and spent seven years in prison.[16]

Marino—who, as a product of this bizarre turn, was actually the
team's third-leading *rusher* that season, with all of 32 yards—never
heard chants like that. In '91, he rang up 3,970 passing yards, 25 touchdowns, and just 13 picks, elevating Clayton into the Pro Bowl with him
by throwing him 12 touchdowns. And Shula, who won his 300th game
early in the season, 13–3 over the Packers, again kept the team in contention. The Bills ran away with the division, but after 14 weeks, the
Dolphins were 8–6, a win away from a wild card. But now they had to
make another nightmarish trip to San Diego. Although Coryell and
Fouts were gone and the Chargers were rebuilding, it was downright
eerie how much pain they could cause Shula. This time, after Miami
took a 23–10 lead, Marino, on the Chargers nine, threw behind Duper
and was intercepted. The Chargers stormed back and won 38–30.

Shula still had a shot at the playoffs. He was a game ahead of the
Jets, who were the opponents in the season finale in Robbie Stadium.
Late in the game, Marino came up clutch, finding Edmunds with a
one-yard scoring pass to go ahead 20–17. But now the much-maligned

Ken O'Brien, who might have remembered Marino's slight on draft day, led a drive that produced a game-tying field goal, sending it to overtime, where another Jets field goal won it 23–20. It was another routinely demoralizing failure for Shula, who tried to get by with Higgs carrying the ball on 15 of 16 Dolphins running plays, to little effect, while the Jets' Johnny Hector rumbled for 132 yards. Marino, with no help, threw an ill-timed interception. The Jets snared the wild card, leaving Shula out in the cold, again.

"We had control of it in San Diego and couldn't do the job, and then we had control again here and couldn't do the job," was his latest lament. "This one will last a long time, for me and for us."[17] These were words he had used too often to count. But leave it to the old bulldog, he could still make them sound fresh each time he uttered them. He was safe, but for how long?

23

DON VOYAGE

The Shula family became a wider brand in 1992. Dave Shula, given credit for the development of Troy Aikman as the Cowboys improved from 1–15 to 7–9, was offered the job of receivers coach by the Cincinnati Bengals, who had won their division but needed better work from Boomer Esiason's receivers. Dave took the job, but things went bad fast. The team went 3–13 and head coach Sam Wyche was fired by Mike Brown, Paul Brown's son and the team president. To replace Wyche, Brown took a chance on the Shula pedigree, passing over Chiefs defensive coordinator Bill Cowher—perhaps, it was speculated, in solidarity with another fortunate son overshadowed by a legendary father. At 32, Dave was a year younger than his old man when he got the Colts job in '63. Meanwhile, Mike Shula would remain on the Dolphins sideline through that year before moving on to become Dave Wannstedt's tight ends coach with the Bears.

As for the patriarch, Shula *pere* would begin his 30th year as a head coach, safe enough that Wayne Huizenga, whom he had aggrandized, was on board with making him the top-paid coach again. Jimmy Johnson, having turned the Cowboys around, had gotten an extension the year before at $3 million a year, which no other owner beside Jerry Jones would have even considered. Keeping up with Jones as best he could, Huizenga gave Shula a two-year extension, to take effect in '93, when Shula's salary would zoom to $1.7 million. In '94, he would be paid $2 million. The extension was announced at a presser at Shula's Golf Resort in Miami Lakes. Relieved that things had gone so smoothly, Shula said after signing in mid-July, "We had two meetings in the last three days. One of them lasted 6 minutes, and the other one I think took 12 minutes."[1]

While Johnson would earn his meed by winning NFL titles in '92 and '93, even as he bridled under Jones's meddling thumb, Shula, left alone by his owner, earned his with another magic carpet ride with Marino and borderline talent. The Dolphins won their first six games in '92, including a 37–10 massacre of the 10-point-favorite Bills in Rich Stadium, when Marino hit on three touchdown passes and the suddenly revitalized defense intercepted Jim Kelly four times and held Thurman Thomas to 33 yards. The running game was still weird. Higgs would carry 256 times for 915 yards that season; the next in line, Bobby Humphrey, a former 1,000-yard rusher with Denver, but barely used by Shula, had 102 carries for 471 yards. Third-highest again was Marino . . . with 20 carries, 66 yards.

But Marino could turn games in an instant. Shrugging off losses to the Colts and Jets, he then faced the Colts again and went 22-for-28 for 245 yards and two touchdowns in a 28–0 rout. Then, after losing three of four, one a close loss in the return match with Buffalo, the Dolphins baked the Raiders 20–7, Marino going 16-for-26 with a 62-yard touchdown heave to Duper. The Dolphins finished strong at 11–5, their overtime win over the Patriots in the finale banking another division crown for Shula, Marino depositing over 4,000 passing yards again.

Their first playoff game was the divisional shakeout against the revitalized Chargers, Shula's personal tormentors. Worse, Higgs hurt his knee in the finale and was done for the postseason. Shula patched up the already famished backfield by starting a third-round pick from '91, Aaron Craver, who had run three times for nine yards over the season. This time, at Robbie Stadium, everything went right. Marino pumped three touchdowns, Craver ran for 72 yards, one more than Humphrey, in a rare 157-yard rushing day, and Miami won 31–0. However, while this ushered Shula into the AFC championship game in style, he would need to dispose of the Bills to get back to the Super Bowl.

He was at home, but never had a chance. Kelly had a low-key 177 passing yards and two picks. But his 17-yard scoring pass to Thurman Thomas put the Bills ahead 10–3, and their 182 yards on the ground burned the clock and kept adding points, aided by egregious Dolphin giveaways. They fumbled the second-half kickoff. Minutes later, Thomas fumbled, too; rookie defensive end Marco Coleman tried to scoop it and run, but he fumbled it right back. Marino, his ground game back to being a non-factor—11 carries, 33 yards—choked the air with 45 balls, completing 22 passes for 268 yards, with two picks. Clayton and Tony Martin dropped long completions. Harassed and chased by Bruce Smith and linebackers Cornelius Bennett and Phil Hansen, Marino was sacked four times and fumbled once. His late scoring pass to Duper was moot, making the score 26–10. The final was 29–10, with Bills coach Marv Levy punching his ticket to another losing Super Bowl, to be cut down this time by the Cowboys.

For the Dolphins and the fans, it was all too routine. The 71,224 at Joe Robbie Stadium, who were deafening when the team took the field, seemed too inured to failures like this to boo or make much noise at all once the outcome was clear. The same went for Shula. Wooden and blank-faced, the familiar tight jaw a bit slack, he repeated his old script. "It's a real disappointment that we didn't play better in a game that meant so much," he said. By now, what else was there to say? No analysis of what went wrong mattered on a cellular level as much as the continuation of big-game failure with no real answers.

Shula could still make the case that he alone could have gotten within one win of a Super Bowl with the cast he had. But an argument could also be made that leaving the running game so thin rendered eventual failure almost a self-fulfilling prophecy. The old bugaboo about the team coming out flat for those summit games had grown into one of the great mysteries in sports. On balance, the pros and cons still weighed on his side, at least in the view of Wayne Huizenga, the only one who really counted. Then, too, he was always the biggest celebrity of his team, his off-field businesses sunk into the loam of South Florida, the events of his life major news.

That off-season, the latest news was that he had a new love in his life.

As prudish as he was, at least on the surface, he had mourned enough after two years. Always a man who needed a woman to come home to, and to whom to turn over matters of domestic responsibility, as he prepared for the new season, a headline appeared that read, WHO IS THE WOMAN ON DON SHULA'S ARM? The answer was Mary Anne Stephens, the thrice-married, 48-year-old ex-wife of, most recently, Jackson T. Stephens, a filthy-rich financier from Little Rock, Arkansas, who had a piece of Walmart and Tyson Foods and was a major donor to the Republican Party. Stephens had made Mary Anne co-chair of George Bush's 1988 and 1992 presidential campaigns in the state.

Beautiful and magnetic, she became a high-society figure in Miami after Stephens bought a mansion on Indian Creek Island for $8.9 million in 1989, the most expensive home sale in Dade County that year. In '91, the house was given to Mary Anne in a divorce settlement, in addition to $1 million a year in alimony. As a society matron, she threw dazzling parties, one at the Fontainebleau Hotel that raised half a million dollars for the Miami Heart Fund. Raven-haired with ruby lips, sparks flying from her fingertips, she certainly wove a spell on the dashing widower the moment they met in 1992 at a New Year's party at pro golfer Ray Floyd's home near hers on the island. There were even rumors in the ensuing months that they had secretly eloped, and clucking from her tony friends that a football coach, even one who was a millionaire, wasn't up to her standards. One such "friend" was quoted as saying, "I just hope Don Shula is worthy of that woman."[2] Of course, *his* friends had the same reservations about *her*. As they were seen in public more often, arm in arm, beaming at each other like lovebirds, Howard Schnellenberger's take was that "she chased him and he didn't fight it. It wasn't love at first sight for him. He already had that.

You only get it once in your life. But Don needed a woman around him. And he got a damn good one."³

Others simply took Mary Anne for a gold digger and social climber. But he was too much in love to care, and as the pair inexorably neared marriage, not even the obsessive work he put into a football season would get in the way.

That work had different parameters now, making his life as an executive both less and more complicated. In 1993, the players' union won an enormous victory in court, as a result of which free agents could be signed without restrictions. While many owners insisted they wouldn't break the bank for available stars, Shula no longer needed to pinch pennies as he had for Joe Robbie. Huizenga, who that year bought out the Robbie family for $115 million, giving him total control of the franchise, was obviously a free spender, and he jumped at the big free agents. The Dolphins nailed the biggest, Philadelphia Eagles tight end Keith Jackson, who'd been first-team All-Pro in his first three seasons. He signed with the Dolphins for four years and $5.9 million. Shula also harvested Eagles fullback Keith Byars, a tremendous receiver out of the backfield, and Irving Fryar from the Patriots. They would earn their fortune; the latter two would make All-Pro that year as Dolphins, Fryar with 64 receptions, Byars with 61, eight touchdown receptions between them. Jackson added 39 catches and six touchdowns. Shula also acquired Giants receiver Mark Ingram, that team's first-round pick of '87.

The '93 season panned out as another manic-depressive carousel ride. After a 3–1 start, in the Dolphins' game in Cleveland, Marino began to feel pain in his right heel. He tried to take a step and nearly buckled, needing help to be lifted up and taken off the field, foot dangling. Shula sent in backup Scott Mitchell, whose first pass was intercepted by Browns cornerback Najee Mustafaa and run back 97 yards for a touchdown, the longest such return in Browns history. Mitchell settled in, his third-quarter touchdown passes to Tony Martin and Jackson taking back the lead and clinching a 24–14 win. Shula had faint hope that Marino might not be seriously hurt. But a day later, it was confirmed that he'd ripped his Achilles tendon and was through for the season. For the first time since he became a starter, he would miss games (not counting the strike), ending a run of 145, the longest streak by any quarterback then in the league.

But even an injury to Marino couldn't derail the wedding. Shula and Mary Anne had agreed to tie the knot on October 19, during a bye week. They made no announcement, and the ceremony was private, held before a small party at St. Joseph's Catholic Church. On that blessed day, he put on his best suit and stood at the altar with his best man, his son Mike, who took a day off from the Bears—Dave couldn't do that with his Bengals team. Mary Anne was walked down the aisle by her debutante daughter. After the vows, a reception was held at Mary Anne's mansion, which would now be Shula's primary residence. The honeymoon would be delayed until after Shula's latest quest to find his lost glory. Most of South Florida didn't learn of the nuptials until he returned to the Dolphins office three days later, "flashed a sly grin and said, 'What's new?'" before revealing the news.[4] Even the skeptics could see that he needed that wedding band on his finger. For many, it was the first time he looked happy since Dorothy died.

During the week off, he had begun to duly scour rosters for a serviceable arm, bringing in Tampa's backup, 39-year-old Steve DeBerg, the league's oldest player. But he held off signing him when the Browns suddenly released the once-overhyped Kosar. While Shula went about wooing Kosar, he let Mitchell start the next game, against the Chiefs, and he went 22-for-33 with 344 yards and four touchdowns in a 30–10 blowout. It was Shula's 324th career victory, tying him with Papa Bear Halas as the NFL's winningest coach.

Kosar subsequently signed as a backup for Troy Aikman in Dallas, so DeBerg became a Dolphin, but he had no practice time before Shula had his first try at beating Halas, against the Jets. With Mitchell under center, he lost 27–10. The next try was in Philadelphia on November 14. DeBerg still wasn't ready, and Shula was snakebitten again when Mitchell separated his shoulder early in the third quarter. Rather than rushing in DeBerg, he swallowed hard and went with Doug Pederson, a third-string scrub who hadn't thrown a single pro pass. But Pederson did not need to do much. The Dolphins were aided all game by Eagles fumbles, two of which came on strips by Shula's slightly crazed outside linebacker Bryan Cox, the second setting up a Pete Stoyanovich field goal that put them ahead. Pederson then led a long drive, leading to another field goal with 3:36 left that made it 19–14. Shula had to sweat it out when the Eagles got the ball back and Ken O'Brien, who had landed in Philadelphia after the Jets gave up on him, heaved a long one to an open James Lofton, who dropped it.

Some of the Dolphins began to pick up the Gatorade bucket to dump on Shula's head, but Mike Westhoff, the special teams coach, told them it would piss Shula off. Instead, Sims and defensive tackle Larry Webster hoisted him on their shoulders. He enjoyed being on that metaphorical top of the world, pumping his fist in the air. Someone dug up the fact that Shula's record with backup quarterbacks was 29–8, a better percentage than his overall 325–153–6. Said Pederson, who would, far in the future, enjoy the same glory Shula had as a Super Bowl coach, with the very team he had just defeated, "He just kept telling me I could do it."

Shula called it a "special" win, given its makeshift nature, and waxed thoughtful and melancholic, rewinding his life. "You take a job at age 33 and you go out every day, every week, to do as good a job as you can," he said, relaxed in a postgame setting perhaps for the first time since winning his second championship. "You hope the second year will be better than the first, and the third better than the second."[5] Now, he only needed to be better than he was in the 29th year.

The front page of the *Herald* was etched with "325" and carried factoids of the Shula reign—such as him now having more wins than 17 other franchises, and that 187 other head coaches had been employed during his tenure. There were sidebars about his rise from a "Grand River boy into the King of Miami," and a whimsical Dave Barry column ruminating that Shula had to win the most games, because, "With that GLARE, how did he ever lose?"

But Pederson, after being regaled in the media for a week, was said to be "crushed" when Shula told him DeBerg would be taking the snaps now. In his first start, against the Patriots, he nailed two fourth-quarter touchdowns to win 17–13. Then, on Thanksgiving, the Dolphins, their 8–2 record notwithstanding, went to Dallas as 10-point underdogs to the 7–3 Cowboys. In a surreal sight, heavy snow came down through the signature hole in the roof of Texas Stadium. Even on the slippery turf, Byars took a handoff, broke two tackles, and streaked 77 yards— tying the team record—for a touchdown. After an Aikman touchdown pass and Kevin Williams's returned punt for a 64-yard touchdown, Dallas had the lead, 14–7. Shula crept closer on two Stoyanovich field goals. With 15 seconds left, down a point, the Dolphins had a third down on the Dallas 24. Not risking a run or pass, Shula sent Stoyanovich out again for a 41-yard attempt, but it was blocked, the ball squibbing down the field and spinning like a top at around the 10-yard line, though the yard markers were obscured by snow.

The shivering crowd erupted. Cowboys on the sideline celebrated. Jerry Jones went into some sort of spasmic victory jig. But down near the goal line, as Cowboys kept away from the ball, their hulking lineman Leon Lett, thinking it was a free ball, sliced in and tried to recover it. Sliding in the snow, he inadvertently kneed the ball, nudging it a few yards toward the end zone. That set off a mad scramble, and Jeff Dellenbach emerged with it somewhere near the goal line. The baffled officials discussed what had happened, then gave the Dolphins possession at the one (though it should have been ruled dead where Lett touched it at around the seven), with three seconds left. Dolphin players now began kicking and clawing chunks of snow and ice, some bloodying their frozen fingers, from where Stoyanovich would again kick—the 19-yard line. The field goal sailed through and the game was over, 16–14 Miami.

Shula later cracked that he wished he'd had a snowplow available to him, and for once he could crow about winning a "miracle" game, one that ended, wrote Ed Pope, as if "the gentle rain of mercy droppeth from heaven."[6] Bemoaning his cruel fate, Jimmy Johnson said, "It was the most disappointing loss I've ever been around."

He'd get over it, the loss not deterring him from his first ring. For Shula, though, the "miracle" in Dallas seemed a good example of the magic he could spin and his ability to re-create himself. Next, against the 8–3 Giants, DeBerg put up 365 yards, but was intercepted twice in a tough 19–14 loss. Then the Dolphins went to Pittsburgh for a Monday night game against Bill Cowher's Steelers, who would win their division for the first of four straight years and played like it. They went out to a 21–6 lead. Then DeBerg, who would throw for 344 yards, cut it to 21–13 with a short touchdown pass to Jackson, and O. J. McDuffie returned a punt 72 yards for another, forcing the Steelers to hang on for dear life, winning by a point.

With Mitchell's shoulder healed, Shula now gave DeBerg the Pederson treatment. He went back to Mitchell for the fourth killer game in a row, against the Bills at Joe Robbie Stadium. His two early touchdown passes put Miami up 17–9, but then they imploded. An interception was returned for one touchdown, a fumble for another— "We played Santa Claus," said Shula—and it was 47–20 in the third quarter, the final to be 47–34. At 9–5, with three losses in a row, the last two games would be on the road, the first a Monday night showcase in their personal snakepit, San Diego's Jack Murphy Stadium—where, for all intents and purposes, the Dolphins' season died. They were never in it, and by the third quarter were down 31–13, the Chargers in the process of laying 220 rushing yards on them and Stan Humphries throwing three touchdowns.

Entering the finale in Foxborough, they really did need a miracle to claim a wild card. The game went back and forth. The Pats' rookie quarterback, Drew Bledsoe, got a 17–10 lead with a touchdown pass, but Mitchell got even with one of his own to Ingram early in the fourth quarter. Down the stretch, Bledsoe threw another touchdown to go up 27–24, but Stoyanovich kicked a clutch field goal to send the game into overtime, only prolonging the agony until Bledsoe's fourth touchdown pass ended it, 33–27. For Shula, finishing 9–7 seemed pallid, given the five straight losses that added up to disaster.

In mid-December, before the collapse was complete, *Sports Illustrated* named him its 1993 Sportsman of the Year, and the honor was still valid. On the cover, Shula was presented as Lincolnesque, in black and white, using an intaglio print style like that on a dollar bill, his face turned to a three-quarter view, his jaw jutting. Paul Zimmerman wrote that Shula had managed to keep winning while down to his fourth quarterback. In truth, the selection felt more like a lifetime achievement award, Zimmerman noting that the honor was for Shula's "unparalleled success and pursuit of excellence."[7]

Of that, there was no doubt. But pertinent now was that he had failed in spectacular fashion more than a Lombardi would. If he had any self-doubt, he kept it to himself. The season crumbling, he allowed, was something "we're going to have to live with"—the emphasis on the editorial *we*—"and that's something that's going to be tough to handle."[8] Still, with two years left on his contract, the echoes of Landry's sad demise—not to mention Paul Brown's in Cleveland—were unmistakably trenchant, the precedent having been set for a lion winding up as a sacrificial lamb. Objectively, he had to be next, but when?

Flexing his power, Wayne Huizenga would soon have Robbie's name scraped off the stadium, having made a 10-year, $20 million deal with Fruit of the Loom to call the grounds Pro Player Stadium, after one of the underwear company's sub-brands. Tacky or not—and short-sighted, as the brand would go belly-up in 1999—it showed that Huizenga wanted a quick return on his investment.

For now, he kept faith with the coach, who still had a base of support. Indeed, Shula had every right to believe he was safe. Before the '94 season, Huizenga, no doubt wanting to avoid the obloquy Jones invited by firing Landry, gave Shula a two-year extension through the '96 season, putting him over $2 million a year—the top coaching salary by default after Jimmy Johnson reached the breaking point with the meddling Jerry Jones, who, after their second straight title, bought out his contract and let him go, blasting Johnson as "disloyal." Shula also was given the sop of a renewed ownership stake: 3 percent of the team.

That way, Huizenga need not respond to inquiries about Shula's job status. However, what the owner kept quiet was that, just before he extended Shula, he had one of his adjutants call Johnson's Miami attorney, Nick Christin, to assay Johnson's interest in coaching the Dolphins. This, of course, was a minefield for both Huizenga and Johnson; if word got out, it would be a monumental insult to Shula. Johnson would not dismiss the notion outright, claiming he would only consider the job if Shula voluntarily retired. Knowing Shula would never quit, thereby forfeiting his stock, Huizenga's only recourse was to commit to him for those two years, leaving himself wiggle room to accommodate Shula with a payoff deal if he wanted to ease the coach out before then.

To be certain, the end was near. As if that was a given, Shula was being sanctified now for his past rather than being put in context as a contemporary of such men as Bill Parcells and Bill Cowher. One could look in the paper at any given time and see him being given something like the Jim Thorpe Pro Sports Award along with Wayne Gretzky and Hank Aaron. When the '94 season began, it was almost as if a de facto farewell tour had begun, not that Shula would have acknowledged that. The season's fifth game, against the Bengals in Cincinnati on Sunday night, October 2, would match Shula against his own spawn, marking the first time a father would coach in the NFL against his son.

People had been waiting for that since Dave became a head coach, and the senior Shula took the occasion to sell 100 commemorative "Shula vs. Shula" autographed footballs for $500 each, to benefit his breast cancer research foundation. That week, 40 members of the extended Shula clan gathered in the Queen City as guests of Dave, whom his father allowed to handle most of the interviews, keeping himself and the Dolphins sequestered in a Marriott hotel 15 miles outside the city. Early in the week, Dave tried a little prank. He called the hotel manager and told him to treat his father "like a king," with instructions to "make sure there's plenty of Heineken and butter-pecan ice cream. That's what he loves."[9] Luckily, the manager checked with the Dolphins, because he found out that Shula *hated* Heineken and butter-pecan ice cream.

The Dolphins had won three of their first four, while the Bengals—a grotesque 8–28 in Dave's reign until then—were winless. The "king" admitted to being uneasy at perhaps hastening his boy's firing by dealing him another loss, appealing to Mike Brown to "give David a chance to work his way out of this thing." Sympathizing with Dave, whose team was an eight-point underdog, Shula's daughter Donna said, "We love Dad, but I think just about all of us are rooting for David." But the old man took no pity; the Bengals scored first on a 51-yard pass, but Marino threw a touchdown to take a halftime lead, and another to go up 17–7. The Bengals turned it over five times and lost 23–7. They met at midfield, embracing, the father tousling the son's hair and draping an arm over his shoulder before going his own way. In the locker room, he said the Bengals "came out looking like a good team" until the parade of turnovers. He added, "I looked over at their sideline during the national anthem and I felt proud seeing David across the way. Then the game started, and it was just football."

For the son, it was the only love he would get over the season, going 3–13. But the old man called it: Mike Brown would keep Dave as coach another year, and when he got another shot at the Dolphins in '95, it would be the patriarch who needed to worry as much about staying employed.

Joe Robbie Stadium would host the Super Bowl for the second time to cap the '94 season, and Shula's team put the league on notice, racing to a 7–2 start. Ominously, he did this again with a hash of a run game. Byars and Terry Kirby were lost for the season with knee injuries, and the load fell to former scrub Bernie Parmalee, who ground out 868 yards. For now, it was good enough.

And Marino was plenty good. Just in case, before the season, Shula had belatedly signed Bernie Kosar. During camp, there were suggestions that Marino was slower afoot, more vulnerable to the pass rush. Hearing the flak, Marino seemed bitter. "It's like, 'What have you done for me lately?'" he said. But that year, he would take almost every snap and return to the Pro Bowl, passing for 4,453 yards and 30 touchdowns and compiling a 62.6 completion percentage and an 89.2 passer rating, while going down only 17 times. None of these numbers led the league, but his four comeback drives did.

Against the Jets in Giants Stadium on November 27 came the pièce de résistance of Shula flimflammery. With just over three minutes left, trailing 24–21, third down, no timeouts, ball on the Jet eight, Marino came to the line pointing to the ground, the common hand signal for spiking the ball, which would have stopped the clock so that the field goal unit could come in. But Shula had a play in his quiver that he'd had his team practice without using—until now. At the snap, Marino—who was a monster that day, 31-for-44 for 359 yards and four touchdowns—seemed to stop moving. Expecting him to spike, the Jets also stopped. Then, in an eye blink, he shifted into gear and popped a pass to Ingram in the end zone.

Thus did the "fake spike" enter football lore, lifting the Dolphins to a 27–24 win and an 8–4 record—a critical margin that eased the pain when Shula himself became a casualty in early December, ripping *his* Achilles while taking a wrong step. Undergoing surgery, he took no time off, instead plopping into a golf cart on the sideline during practices and games. He finished 10–6, ruling the AFC East again. He did this with a defense ranked 17th, with Bryan Cox its lone All-Pro. But Marino was so locked in that it seemed he alone could get Shula up that last step. His prime target, Irving Fryar, with 73 receptions and seven touchdowns, went to the Pro Bowl, as did Webb and Sims on the line.

The first playoff round brought the wild-card Chiefs to Miami on New Year's Eve day. With the Dolphins tilling 132 yards rushing, Marino threw a modest 29 times, completing 22, including consecutive short touchdown passes to backup tight end Ronnie Williams and Fryar to tie the game and then take the lead in the eventual 27–17 victory. It was neat and clean, unspectacular in the pre-Marino manner, and it got them to the divisional round. But that would be played in—

good Lord, no—San Diego, the Chargers having finished one game better in winning the AFC West. Coached now by Bobby Ross, and rebuilt by Bobby Beathard as their general manager, they were a conservative bunch reliant on fullback Natrone Means, who ran for 1,350 yards and 12 touchdowns.

Despite the misery they had laid on the Dolphins in Jack Murphy Stadium, the attitude among the Chargers was that Shula had never given them due credit, his postmortems leaning toward themes of self-destruction. Even Beathard, whose career was made by Shula, had a run-in with him before the game, for a familiar reason. A rare rainstorm in San Diego had drenched the field the previous day, and in a reverse take of Shula's spat with the Jets before the Mud Bowl, the issue became the tarp that covered the grounds. Beathard refused to take it off the field, preventing the Dolphins from working out in the park. Rather, Beathard told his former boss to take his men to a practice field outside the stadium, and he ordered guards to keep the gates closed to the Dolphins. Shula, neck veins bulging, appealed to Jerry Seeman, the league's director of officials, who ruled the visitors could use the field, upon which Shula smugly laid down tracks in his golf cart, leaving Beathard to sputter a grievance heard often around front office circles: "Anything he wants, he gets! He runs the goddamn league!"[10]

When the three-point-underdog Dolphins took a 21–6 halftime lead in the game on three Marino touchdowns, they repaired to the locker room, whereupon they found the lights and air conditioning not working. Players sweated through their uniforms in the darkened room, bitching about Beathard presumably acting like Al Davis. Still, the lead looked secure. Midway through the third quarter, Marco Coleman stopped Means one on one on a fourth-and goal. However, one play later, Bernie Parmalee was tackled in his end zone for a safety. Means, who shredded the Shula defense with a career-high 139 yards, then ran one in from the 24, cutting the lead to 21–15. The Chargers would get the ball with three minutes left, same score, Shula one more stop from a glorious win.

Riding the fate that had so often cursed Shula, Stan Humphries took his team on a 10-play journey, cashing in four first downs. From the Miami eight, he floated a pass in the flat to receiver Mark Seay. Troy Vincent was late covering him, and Seay took it in with 35 seconds on the clock. The extra point made it 22–21, San Diego. But Marino was a dangerous man with 35 seconds and three timeouts. He got a 32-yard pass-interference call on a long ball, putting the ball on the Charger 30—no doubt confirming for Beathard his conspiracy theories about Shula's deep-state control of the sport. The Dolphins were in long-field-goal range. Marino tried getting closer, but misfired twice. On third down, five seconds left, Stoyanovich trotted on for a 48-yard shot for the win and a berth in the AFC title game. The snap was high, forcing the holder, John Kidd, to stretch for it, messing up Stoyanov-ich's precise timing. As the kick went up, Shula rose from his cart. As it slid wide right, he slumped back down, cursing. Beathard had the last laugh.

As agonizing failures went, this one was particularly brutal, as it all but slipped a noose around Shula's neck. For his part, Marino would never let go of it. Months after, he said, "I had two downs to put Pete at least 10 yards closer. . . . I'll be driving in my car somewhere, and all of a sudden I'll just start thinking about it. These things are harder for me to take than they were years ago." [11]

The Chargers reacted much like the Dolphins had in the Dallas "miracle." They danced off the field to blaring rock music piped through the PA system. Shula, who had to thread his way through gyrating Chargers to shake Ross's hand, could only repeat once again the chronic ritual he had come to detest, saying, "That's about as tough a loss as I've ever been around," yet another "bitter disappointment." But had he done more to bring it about than he would admit?

For one thing, he had worked the team hard, in full pads, during the week, while the Chargers, coming off a bye week, were fresh. There was also the usual disappearing running game; the Dolphins ran all of eight times for 26 yards, the fewest runs in club history—this, even when they had a big lead. One reporter also noted that the team had wilted during the season, and had a critical loss in the penultimate week, when a win would have given them the playoff bye; that loss, to the Colts, occurred because, inside the enemy 10 late in the game, they ran seven plays and failed to ram it in. Shula remained oblivious to the criticisms, assuming he was still on safe ground and that he'd fight any suggestion that he step aside.

But, in the broader frame, his biggest loss wasn't to the Chargers, who would ride the momentum through the AFC title game against the Steelers but be routed by the 49ers in the Super Bowl at Robbie Stadium. Rather, it was the exit of the Robbie family from the Dolphins' power structure, and the unfortunate timing—for Shula—that Jimmy Johnson was idle. The acrid reality was that, for Shula, a quarter century of loyalty now counted for little in a world where a Jimmy Johnson was a coaching get. In Miami, where Johnson had also coached a winner, and still lived, the forces of a cheapened culture were ganging up against Don Shula.

Huizenga was subject to these forces when he bought the Robbies out. And even without the public aware of his secret feeler to Johnson, the latter was lurking over Shula's shoulder, seemingly from the day of his split from Jerry Jones. That only heightened any criticism directed at Shula and his men, which was happening far more easily all the time, even from within. During the summer of '95, *Sports Illustrated* writer Johnette Howard found that, around the team's summer camp, the players and coaches were "tired of making excuses. Fed up with having to make allowances for injuries. Sick of starting each season with talk about going to the Super Bowl, only to flame out by year's end." Then, repeating the growing speculation about the coach-in-waiting who had already replaced one fallen legend, "for the past 15 months," Jimmy Johnson "has been biding his time in the nearby Florida Keys, waiting for the 'right opportunity'—hint, hint—to lure him back to coaching in the NFL." The title of the story, referring to Shula, was IT MAY BE 1995 OR NEVER.

That trope was no longer verboten now that a younger cohort of outspoken sportswriters, brazenly indifferent to yellowing history, had claimed spots in the media. The prickliest, Dan Le Batard, openly beat the drum for Johnson in his *Herald* column, writing that he had "better results than Shula" and was "a coach who won as many Super Bowls in five years as Shula did in 25," and that, "If you are going to fire Shula, Johnson is just about the only man you do it for."[12]

References to the overly tanned and lacquered Johnson were like hornet stings to Shula, worse because Johnson never really tried to quiet the speculation that he would lead a palace coup for the second time. Hoping to head that off, Shula went on another shopping spree over the off-season, signing free agents like tight end Eric Green and receivers Gary Clark and Randal Hill, lavishing a six-year, $12 million deal on Green. He traded for Bears defensive end Trace Armstrong and Packer cornerback Terrell Buckley, using Keith Jackson and Mark Ingram as the trade bait. When Byars and Higgs couldn't make it back from their knee injuries, Shula traded them, too, freeing up more money to spend and luring defensive tackle Steve Emtman with a $5 million deal and $750,000 signing bonus—which was doubly satisfying as payback to the 49ers, who had beaten Shula to Deion Sanders the year before. Their general manager, Dwight Clark, who was also hot for Emtman, reacted with magnificent hypocrisy. Shula, he moaned, was "trying to buy a Super Bowl."

Huizenga had to pay $18 million in signing bonuses alone, for Shula the price for proving wrong the critics and people he now deemed enemies. But, knowing that Johnson was looming over him, Howard noted, "irk[ed] him considerably. The irritation shows in Shula's occasionally curt answers and in the way his famous jutting jaw clenches when the subject of his future is broached." Ed Pope wondered why Shula was subjecting himself to it—why, at 65, he didn't just walk away from the grubby, ego-driven jungle the game had become and enjoy his life.

There were times when Shula had to ask himself the same thing. In the spring that year, he and Mary Anne took off for a month of globetrotting, during which they made the scene at Wimbledon, did Paris, and cruised the Mediterranean. It was a hell of a lifestyle. But if he was going to walk away from the game, he didn't want to look back with regret. Thus did he head into another season with his array of shiny new toys on a roster that included 19 former first-round draft picks. Huizenga was so impressed, he forgot about Jimmy Johnson for a while and all but claimed the Lombardi Trophy in advance, joking, "Welcome to the Super Bowl."

Huizenga's boast seemed prescient on opening day, when the Dolphins lost a 14-0 lead, took it back on a 50-yard Marino touchdown to Irving Fryar, and put it away 35–14 on Troy Vincent's 69-yard interception. The final—52–14—was a message to Shula's tormentors. So, too, was his perfect record after four weeks, the last of these wins coming on another ambivalent afternoon, coaching against his No. 1 son. Dave's Bengals played it tough, requiring Marino to throw 48 times, completing 33, for 450 yards and a late 16-yard touchdown to provide the winning edge in the Dolphins' 26–23 victory. Again showing his soft side, the patriarch bragged more about his boy's coaching than his own team's performance.

But now the optimism began to die a slow death. The Dolphins then dropped three straight, one in overtime, the last two with Kosar at quarterback after Marino sustained hip and knee injuries, undergoing arthroscopic surgery for the knee. By the end of November, they were 6–6, and talk had resumed about the silver-haired beachcomber needing to come to the rescue. The *Herald, Palm Beach Post,* and *Sun-Sentinel* ran polls as to whether Shula should be replaced by Johnson. All were landslides for Johnson, the *Sun-Sentinel* taunting Shula with the headline DON VOYAGE. At Pro Player Stadium, he was now hearing scattered chants of Johnson's name. During one game, a small plane flew overhead with a trailing banner riffing on Jimi Hendrix's "Fire": "Move Over Rover, and Let Jimmy Take Over."

Part of this thirst for change was due to the parallel rise of the NBA's Heat, whose pulse was quickened by the slicked-back, Rodeo Drive–bred image of their coach, Pat Riley, who made Shula seem as dated as the 1970s movie that had given his two super teams their élan. *Sports Illustrated,* which only recently had all but sung hymns to his grandeur, split-shot the two men's faces on the cover of the December 11 issue, Shula looking like an aging blowfish, beneath the line HOT & NOT: MIAMI LOVES PAT RILEY BUT WANTS TO GIVE DON SHULA THE BOOT. Huizenga still clung to his mantra that he had "all the confidence in the world in Don," and called the polls "a vocal minority," though he explicitly refused to rule out firing Shula. For his part, Johnson unctuously said during his regular gig on the Fox pregame show that he was a "non-story in this situation." Despite his stated respect for Shula, however, he had no qualms about writing in his syndicated column that the Dolphins, with all their talent, "have a group of individuals. They don't have a team."[13] That was about the most unflattering thing anyone could say about any coach.

Worse, Shula was again being weakened from within. Ever since Dorothy's death, and with Mary Anne further softening his edges, players were challenging him in ways Csonka and Kiick never would have dared. Some claimed that his age was an issue, that discipline had broken down. The AP's Steven Wine pronounced the team "in a shambles," and that an "ugly backlash" had developed, with players "shouting at coaches and literally pointing fingers on the sideline." The mouthiest of them, Bryan Cox, had screamed at Shula during one game. Safety Gene Atkins, who also had roughed up a reporter without being disciplined, said he would quit if Shula didn't play his buddy, safety Mike Stewart. Upset about not getting enough passes, Eric Green said, "I'm so down. Sometimes I feel like just giving back the money."[14] Players openly ragged the coaches' play calling, mainly that of Tom Olivadotti, who, even with his defense 10th best in the league, admitted, "I'm dead in this town."

Old rivals, who might have been rankled by Shula but had held their peace about him, piled on. Ron Meyer airily concluded that Shula had "lost control of his team." Mike Ditka said in one breath that "Shula is entitled to write his own ticket as to when he retires. I don't think he'd necessarily want to do another 10 years, but I'd bet he'd want to do it for another five years"; in the next, "You can't win without order. The head coach is the boss. The inmates don't run the asylum."[15] Shula, clearly feeling the heat, said, "I'm upset [too]," but "I can't let it drag me down. I've got hard work to do . . . the buck stops here. I take full responsibility." But he also offered some rare introspection about living within the pincers of discontent:

> You try to shut the criticism out, but it's pretty hard to do. You see people on the street, friends, people that you know are in your corner, and they come and tell you how bad they feel, and that's not the kind of conversation you want. I don't want anyone to feel bad for me.[16]

Shula, as always, had his defenders. To many, the mob mentality of the once-protective Dolphin fans was the sorriest part of the nightmare. *Detroit News* columnist George Puscas's New Year's resolution for Shula was: "Forgive the Dolphins fans, Don Shula. But you have some real idiots there."[17] And Shula did forgive. He neither called out the fans nor any players, even though most of the high-tag free agents were underperforming. Seeing him take crap from players with impunity, Kim Bokamper said, "He used to get right in your face if you screwed up. And now players get in his face? And he's patting guys on the butt when they mess up?"[18]

All of this came to a head the week of the December 3 game against the Falcons. Shula, saying it had been "the toughest week I've ever spent in my coaching career," called a team meeting the day before, during which everyone was free to spout off. On Sunday, they went out all riled up, then seemed to forget why. Early in the fourth quarter, they were losing 20–9. A Parmalee TD run got them closer, but the extra point failed and it looked bleak when Marino subsequently threw his second pick. Then, with time running down, the score 20–15 Atlanta, the Falcons had a fourth-and-one at the Miami 27, but coach June Jones passed up a game-clinching field goal try to go for it. Ironhead Heyward took the handoff, but Cox wrapped him up—no gain. With 1:49 left, Marino—who threw 50 times, completing 35 for 343 yards—connected on three quick passes. He then took off and ran one for 12 yards to the Falcon 21, with 11 seconds left. Now he dropped back and zipped one to Irving Fryar for the lead, 21–20, which, after the two-point conversion failed, was the final score.

That was winning ugly, but Shula was ecstatic, dancing through the end zone to wave at Mary Anne, later saying, "It was such a tough week on her." She said the same of him: "Boy, my coach is tough."[19] Pointedly, he gave the game ball to Olivadotti, the object of so much scorn. The following week, he had another gritty win, getting by the Chiefs 13–7. And though he fell to the Bills 23–20 on a fourth-quarter field goal, he was 8–7 and still in it when the team went to St. Louis for the season closer against the mediocre Rams on Christmas Eve. Though outpassed by Mark Rypien and picked twice, Marino broke it open with short TD passes to Fryar and O. J. McDuffie in the second quarter, greasing the way to a comfy 42–22 win that delivered the 9–7 Dolphins a wild card—Shula's 20th year in the postseason, and one of his most satisfying seasons of all, considering that, with all the static, one could reasonably ask: *How?*

Shula's Christmas was merry, but the reward for success was a trip to Rich Stadium, on December 30. "I never thought I'd be happy going to Buffalo this time of year," he said. He was confident that the Dolphins had closed the gap with Marv Levy's team, which was only a three-and-a-half-point favorite. But one could only imagine Shula's helplessness as it just kept getting worse. Down 24–0 halfway into the second quarter, his defense ripped to bits by Thurman Thomas barging through gaping holes and Cox nullified by gang blocking, Shula quickly bagged his running game and let Marino wing it, 64 times, tying Bernie Kosar's then playoff record and five shy of Drew Bledsoe's overall record. His 33 completions were just three fewer than Warren Moon in a '93 playoff game, his 422 yards third to Kosar and Fouts—all that with 10 of his passes being muffed by stone-fingered receivers.

But nothing slowed down the Buffalo run on the other side, the Bills ringing up an AFC playoff record 341 yards, Thomas with 158 of them. On one schoolyard play, Kelly faked *two* double reverse plays, handed it to halfback Bill Brooks, and he broke for a 41-yard touchdown, leaving Louis Oliver to ask later, "How can we let that happen? I mean, a fake double reverse? C'mon!"[20] The carnage ended, mercifully, at 37–22. Few Bills took pity on Shula's team, who seemed wholly unprepared. Troy Vincent even used the dreaded "Q-word." He said, "It was an attitude game. They had it. A lot of guys today just quit. We brought in a lot of players to get us to the promised land, and some of them didn't show up." Jeff Cross was so disillusioned, he said, "I wouldn't be surprised if nobody around here came back next year."[21]

While a front-page *Herald* story was titled FOR MARINO, A FAMILIAR, HOLLOW RING, the recriminations were mainly saved for the old coach. Indeed, the numbers had become grim for Shula. He was now 5–17 head-to-head against Levy, his 22-year streak without a title tying him with Chuck Knox for second all-time, in all pro sports. An AP photo of Shula in the closing seconds of the game showed him alone, hands in pockets, looking up at the clock, or perhaps the heavens. Still a compelling figure, he was now also a pitiable one as he stood for the umpteenth time at attention in the hallway, regurgitating the well-practiced banalities of losing—"We didn't compete, and all of us have to live with that."

He had, of course, said that before, ad nauseam, but he had never needed to address whether he would have the chance to get it right the next time. Because never before did anyone ask if he would; it was implicit. Now, someone asked if he would be there for the '96 season.

"I intend to fulfill the last year of my contract."

What if Huizenga had other ideas?

"I'm not going to address that now."

The general assumption was that he was already gone, one game story assuming that the defeat was "a terrible way for Shula to go out." The *Los Angeles Times*'s Bill Plaschke painted him as worse than inef-

fectual, "a legend who never looked so small, shaking a bared fist that
has never seemed so harmless. . . . On the sidelines, Dolphins either
argued or huddled underneath capes and avoided each other. The more
Shula shook that fist, the more they seemed to ignore him." Plaschke
added by rote that Jimmy Johnson was "available . . . and he wants to
come home to Miami. Why would Huizenga want to make Johnson
wait one more year—thereby risk losing him to another team—in
exchange for a tired and very lame duck? And why would Shula . . .
want to be in that situation?"[22]

Huizenga's only public comment that day was, "I have nothing to
say today. It's just a very disappointing day," though Plaschke, either
using ESP or reading body language, believed that "The way Huizenga
glared at his team as it passed by the locker room afterward left little
doubt about what he didn't have to say." To be sure, the owner was
under heavy pressure from season-ticket holders, especially younger
ones who wanted a new, bold face for the team. And Johnson, by playing coy, had only put himself in greater demand.

For three days, nothing happened. Then, on Thursday, as Shula celebrated his 66th birthday at a party at Indian Creek Country Club,
the *Herald*'s Armando Salguero reported, "Word of Shula's imminent
departure from the sideline [has] spread like an unchecked epidemic."
Hours later, Huizenga had him over to the team office and dropped
the ax. Having rehearsed this scenario for months, he eased the sting
by presenting Shula with a face-saving way out. And he needed one,
because Shula would not have gracefully accepted being kicked to the
curb as Jones had done to Landry. Besides paying him his remaining year, Huizenga would allow Shula to keep his Dolphins stock and
remain with the organization. That apparently convinced Shula to
swallow his pride and say he was leaving voluntarily. That sticky situation dealt with, Huizenga could turn to signing Johnson as soon as
Shula made an official retirement announcement.

As leaks were fed to the press, ESPN's Chris Mortensen reported
that Shula was out, followed by confirmations by three South Florida

TV stations. Salguero wrote that Shula would "remain with the organization one more year in the figurehead role of vice-president and director of football operations." Shula would say nothing until the next day, Friday, January 5, at a press conference hastily arranged at a downtown hotel. That morning, he dutifully arrived and entered a ballroom crawling with reporters and TV cameras that would beam his announcement live throughout the state. A cadre of some of his '70s players was there, jointly holding a sign reading, "Thanks, coach." Groups of fans still loyal to him stood on the street outside.

Huizenga, looking much relieved, if a tad guilty, bathed Shula with sincere praise and confirmed the happy ending that kept Shula a Dolphin executive for a year, not as football operations director but "vice-chairman of the board of directors," an intentionally nebulous term delineating no responsibilities. It was good enough for the owner to say, "This is not goodbye" and "We love you, Don." Shula, in an immaculately tailored dark blue suit, pinstriped shirt, and silk print tie, took to the podium, Mary Anne and his children standing behind him, all with damp eyes. He began by saying it was "the day you thought was never going to happen. Now it's here." Then, turning to Mary Anne, "Today is the first day of the rest of our lives."

The decision to step down, he said, was "soul-searching and gut-wrenching." But he insisted, more than once, that he had not been fired or forced out, pointing instead to the timeworn shibboleth about "family considerations." In fact, he said, Huizenga had actually offered him an extra year as coach—two more seasons—if he would fire his staff and bring new ones in, but he had declined because he could not have found people who'd take a job, only to be ousted in a year or two. Besides, he said, staying on as coach for two years was "the last thing I want to do."[23]

Although he made all this sound convincing, the more hard-boiled writers had a hard time believing it. For one thing, they knew him as a man who never would have obeyed an order to sack his trusted assistants. For another, given the massive turn of public opinion against him—and knowing of Huizenga's infatuation with Johnson and the heat he was getting from the season-ticket holders—how could the owner have offered him even one more hour as a coach? Then, too, was Shula really adverse to a two-year extension at top-shelf money? As he admitted that day, "This is the first time in 43 years that I haven't been on the sideline [and] I'd be lying to you if I didn't say it's going to be gut-wrenching the first time a football is kicked off," and that "we felt were a football team that was building."

But this was not a day for scrutiny. He had the stage to himself and he was feeling it. At times, he was the old bulldog, not able to keep from calling some of the flak he took "mean, dirty criticism." But he withheld most recrimination. "We're going to make this a happy day," he said. "I'm at peace with myself and am looking forward to spending time with my lovely wife," a sentiment that led one ESPN commentator to say he sounded less a coach than a " 66-year-old grandfather wanting to get on with his life." His remarks, wrote Salguero, were "filled with one-liners and love."[24] Maybe a tad too ebullient, he stopped at one point and said, "I'm putting on a helluva front."

To Ed Pope, who knew all of his moods, Shula seemed "relieved."[25] Not that Shula would ever be able to look back at this exercise easily. Five years later, he would say, "I didn't go out as I would have liked," in part because he had gone out losing, but possibly also because he believed he had been manipulated, the farewell a sham.[26] As Greg Cote observed of the staged event in the *Herald*, "I've heard of putting the best face on something, but this makeover was a masterwork. The technical adviser must have been Maybelline."[27]

In the end, he was a good company man. In his heart, he believed he still had a place in the game, but he readily accepted that he wasn't made for the new trend of coaches subjugated by management. As Howard Schnellenberger said, "The game was going to hell with these coaches hired and fired in a year. In his day, our day, great coaches were all around. But how many teams now are molded by their coach? Belichick. Who else? Nobody. Because the loyalty factor is gone. Don saw that coming, and he didn't want to be a part of it. He didn't want to be on trial anymore. And he went out with class because that was the only way he knew how to do it."

Questions would linger about the sincerity of the event, but not Shula's character. Marino's benediction was, "Everybody should appreciate what this man has done for all of us in South Florida." Huizenga promised that the famous "jutting jaw" would be on that landscape "for many years to come." When a reporter asked the owner if he really would have given Shula two more years, he turned it up a notch. If Shula woke up the next day and changed his mind, he insisted, somehow keeping a straight face, "he can coach as long as he wants for the Miami Dolphins."[28]

The next day, Huizenga sent a helicopter to take Shula and his goombah Ray Floyd to Huizenga's golf course for a round, just the two of them. Shula also sat for an interview in his palatial home with Jimmy Cefalo, now a broadcaster with a local TV station, the show including Mary Anne and his two coaching sons. But he did not make a side trip to the Dolphins' facility, where his current players were packing for the off-season. Shula hadn't spoken with many of them since they left Buffalo. "There was absolutely no warning" about the retirement announcement, Trace Armstrong said.

But that was Don Shula. In the job, he sucked up all the oxygen, a virtual puppet master for the players. Now, much like when he quit Kentucky and the Colts, he was gone, smoke through a keyhole. He would return in time to remove his belongings and mementos. But all he really needed to remember about the glory days was safely in his head. The locker room wasn't his anymore.

Shula could finally bask in fustian but well-deserved elegies. Carolina Panthers general manager Bill Polian said of his retirement, "It's tragic. It's a loss for the NFL, it's a loss for America."[29] Marv Levy wrote in *Sports Illustrated*: "What the Babe was to baseball, Shula is to football coaching. . . . This was a man who didn't just like coaching; he liked coaches. He never got too big for the other guys in the game." He called Shula "the last of the legends."[30] Paul Tagliabue, keeping him in the league's inner sanctum, extended him a place on the league's competition committee.

As for Huizenga, he now admitted what he knew all along: Jimmy Johnson, he said, was "at the top of the list" to replace Shula. But a complication arose in Shula's undefined role with the Dolphins, with Johnson bridling at the thought of Shula looming over *his* shoulder. Whatever Huizenga may have promised Shula—who only said he would be "making recommendations" and "give input" to the new coach, if asked—Huizenga told Johnson that Shula would have no part in player or management decisions. That was fine by Shula, who wanted as little to do with Johnson as Johnson wanted to do with him. It was good enough for Johnson. He agreed to a five-year deal at $2.2 million a year—a pay cut from his Cowboy days, but with stock options and numerous perks and bonuses, as well as inheriting Shula's lucrative weekly TV shows. He would have Shula's old title of coach/director of player personnel.

Huizenga introduced him at another press conference on January 11, the TV ratings for which dwarfed Shula's final bow. Having gotten their wish, the Johnson whisperers in the Miami media celebrated, not aware or not caring that Johnson's success in Dallas was due to an abundance of stockpiled high draft picks that the Dolphins lacked. As a sop to Shula's pride, Johnson would retain two assistant coaches, Gary Stevens and Mike Westhoff. (Carl Taseff, anticipating Shula's retirement, had left after the '93 season after nearly a quarter century; Tony Nathan, who, after he retired, became running backs coach, was one of the coaches fired.) Eddie Jones remained as the titular GM.

Privately, Shula burned at the thought of leaving his team to the Judas of the coaching profession. He held his tongue for now, saying only nice things about the new man, and Johnson about him, each sounding like hostages. Keeping his distance, Shula would spend almost all of his time as a Dolphin "executive" on the golf course, notching a hole in one on one round. The encomiums came on a semi-permanent conveyor belt. One of Ed Pope's columns about him was titled TESTAMENT TO HONOR.[31] In another, Pope, who was on the Hall of Fame's board of selectors, wrote, "I have to present Shula, and after merely mentioning his name what could I possibly add other than, 'What could I possibly add?' "[32]

For a time, it seemed as if he might change his mind about his "voluntary" retirement, and he seemed to revel in the speculation. When he was sighted in the Dallas airport a few days later, a writer asked where he was going. Knowing that what he said would be in the papers, he kibbitzed, "On my way to see Jerry Jones."

One serious offer did come in. Only days after Shula bowed out, Bill Belichick was canned from his first pro head coaching job by Art Modell after five trying seasons with the Browns. Modell was so eager to be rid of Belichick that he ate the last two years of his $1.3 million-a-year contract. Modell then went after Shula, inviting him to his Palm Beach home, portending that Don Shula might soon be walking in the historic footsteps of Paul Brown. However, it wasn't so easy. Modell had announced that he was moving the team to Baltimore, and he would be enjoined legally from using the Browns' name and team colors. Even so, there was another circle-closing angle to coaching again in Baltimore, and Modell would have given him full authority and equity. But Shula's gut told him he didn't need to uproot his life and start over at his age, and so he shut the door, saying he "wasn't interested at this time."

Then, with the Shula smirk, he added, "But you never know."[33]

An undercurrent of that decision was that he could have stuck it to Belichick by taking the job, and with cause. Shula had known Belichick for decades, having been close with his father, Steve, an assistant coach at the United States Naval Academy in the late '60s. Back then, Shula had allowed Steve's teenaged son to hang around the Colts' camp as a ballboy and gofer, sucking up the game the way Shula had at the same age. He liked the kid's moxie. When the kid grew up and became a head coach, however, he apparently promised Mike Shula a job as an assistant coach, only to renege. Taking Belichick's job would have been the family's payback. Instead, Shula was the bigger man, not letting it enter into his decision. But it would not be long before he had a more personal reason to want to sully Belichick, for even better cause: coming dangerously close to treading on Shula's most prized historical turf.

24

A GRANITE-JAWED DEITY, STILL

Professor Bonnie Mann was right: humans will always fail in one way or another, even the sovereign males. One of the most sovereign of them all, Donald Francis Shula, learned early in his rise that failure was a partner of success, and its most enduring artifact. He could live with it, if uneasily. And now, in retirement, if there was any relief to watching and not doing, it was because he could observe other coaches absorbing the same education, riding the same roller-coaster ride of jubilant heights followed by deadly curves of descent.

The hardest one to watch was his own flesh and blood, as Dave Shula's misery only deepened in Cincinnati. After somehow making it through two more laborious losing seasons, he was freed after the '96 season by Mike Brown, though Peter King noted, "It is unlikely whether Vince Lombardi or, yes, Don Shula could have won many more games with this bunch."[1] The numbers were gruesome; Dave's winning percentage of .268 was the worst ever for a coach who lasted that many games. Not once did he beat the Dolphins, losing six times as a player, head coach, and assistant coach. Understandably chapped, he turned to the off-field business of being a Shula, running the Shula's Steak House/Shula Burger chain, which would grow to have franchises in 15 states.

On the other end of the scale, the patriarch more than enjoyed the eclipse of Jimmy Johnson, who, after his red-carpet entrance, won just 55 percent of his games in Miami, far below Shula's 66 percent. His cop-out was that he would also have needed to coach 26 years to be fairly compared to the man he replaced. "This is my sixth year," he said before his Miami debut. "I don't think I'll make it that long." He only fell 22 years short. Making the postseason thrice in his four years, he made it no farther than Shula, bricked by Elway's Broncos 38–3 in '98 and, incredibly, 62–7 by the Jacksonville Jaguars in '99. Shula felt no pity for him, only for Marino, who, in Johnson's contained, defensive-oriented system, never again made All-Pro.

Debates still rage about whether Marino should be bronzed or docked for being so dominant while the team failed so much—his backers make the case that he never played with a Hall of Famer in the backfield or among his receiving corps (which, in turn, sparks other debates, such as whether the Dolphins' all-time leading receiver, Mark Duper, with 511 receptions and 59 touchdowns, deserves to be one). That would shift the blame to Shula for his personnel decisions. Marino surely left pieces of himself all around the league. After the '99 season, when his body was shot and he missed five games, he limped away at 38—his last play a touchdown pass. That came days after Johnson quit, with no sham retirement ceremony, having fallen so far that he only made Shula look nobler.

In retirement, Marino and Shula—a coach/quarterback tandem that had won more games than any other (116, since surpassed by Belichick and Brady's 207 through 2018)—were again joined as permanent avatars within the football culture. Shula went into the Hall of Fame in 1997, after the minimum one-year waiting period. At the Canton festivities, wearing the hall's ceremonial yellow jacket, suntanned, designer shades over his eyes, he laughed easily as Dave Shula preceded him by playfully reviewing the litany of defeat that came before his arrival in Miami, which, Dave said, "fueled the fire of an intensely competitive man." Mike Shula then spoke of his father's "tender side—you just have to find it."

After the three of them embraced, the patriarch had his moment in the August sun. Mary Anne and the grandchildren were in the first row, along with his surviving siblings, the triplets whose births had been such a big story. So was his coach at Harvey High, Don Martin, and a Catholic school coach, Joe Jenkins. Of course, Carl Taseff was there. Bill Arnsparger was, too, with a dozen of the greatest Dolphins, four of them in the Hall, with Nick Buoniconti, Dwight Stephenson, and Marino yet to be. Earl Morrall made it there. Perhaps pointedly, Johnny Unitas managed not to.

"It's 50 miles from Grand River to Canton," Shula began, the eyes of the bronzed bust of him seemingly staring right into his, "and it took me 67 years to travel that distance."

He hailed Dan and Mary Shula for teaching him there were "no free lunches," and even lauded a logic professor he had at John Carroll, whose theories he said he used as a coach. He curdled his mouth in jest as he recalled his blackest day, needing only to say "the Jets," but gave a nod to Weeb Ewbank, who was there, two years before his death at 91. He praised his nemeses Pete Rozelle and Al Davis. He singled out Paul Brown, Tex Schramm, Chuck Noll, Howard Schnellenberger, and other assistant coaches, though neither George Wilson nor Blanton Collier. He thanked his three owners. The fans, he said, were "the best," the writers "true professionals."

The speech nearly over, he admitted, "I would've liked to have ridden off into the sunset," adding sadly, "but it didn't happen." That was something he knew he would have to live with; that he had done something unprecedented, yet it could have been better. *Should* have been better.

He lived not entirely uneasily, retirement never blissful but easy enough, a peripatetic figure in the city he often fantasized about leaving. He did consider straying from the Dolphin family in 1998, when he joined in a group of investors angling to bring a new Browns team to Cleveland the following year—as with Modell's previous entreaty, perhaps the only other one he would have made an exception for. In the end, though, the group was outbid by bank magnate Al Lerner. But Shula would have been an absentee owner. Unlike Dorothy, Mary Anne had no affinity for cold-weather climates, and so it was in South Florida that he would enjoy his post-career life.

He became so unimpeachable in his later years that he could freely abhor the decline of civilization bred by the drug culture and not have to answer for the coked-up players he had selectively excused. In 2001, Don Strock wrote an autobiography in which he wrote that Shula was the best coach in creation, but that he "didn't stick up for me" and "doesn't stick up for anybody other than himself and his son, maybe. . . . Special tantrums, wild rages, veiled threats—all have always been part of the Don Shula package." He also wrote of widespread use by Dolphin players of Ritalin, which is today classified as a performance-enhancing drug. Players, he said, had "private pillboxes and bottles." He confirmed the shots of Xylocaine and Novocain; and that when Glenn Blackwood broke his nose, he was given an injection "right between the eyes." Once, in the Superdome, Strock wrote, the doctor "slipped [the needle] under the carpet . . . and that damn thing might still be there, rusting away." Asked if he meant Herb Virgin, who retired in 1983, and his son Charles, the team doctor until 1988, he said, "You could assume that."[2]

There would always be whispers, intimations, winks about being complicit in the drug accounts. The trainer who replaced the Virgins, Bob Lundy, once said that drug usage on Shula's Dolphins "wasn't done recklessly or anything," but that "it's like how they used to send people into coal mines; the consequences weren't known at the time." Jim Langer, in retrospect, called it "part of the dark side of the NFL," but said that, at the time, it was "just the way it was with our team."[3]

Shula's resolute defense is: "The only way pain-killers were used is if they thought it wouldn't be long-term harmful. I would never want them used if they'd jeopardize a player's career." It was all he had to say to rise above it all.

In the brutal heat of Miami, he eased the aches in his bones and settled comfortably into the business of being Don Shula, maintaining his restaurants and golf resort. He kept himself in remarkably good shape, still doing gassers in his backyard. As for his old team, he didn't stray far. In 1996, his name went up on the Dolphins' Honor Roll in Pro Player Stadium. Once Johnson's palace coup was itself overthrown, he began, with no title or official attachment—nor the stock that had been bought back—acting like a team spokesman, even a *consigliere*—not in board meetings, but through his periodic remarks in the media. In this capacity, he seemed to enjoy riling things up, saying what the coaches couldn't.

In 2007, when Nick Saban quit as the Dolphins' coach with three years left on his contract to take the same job at Alabama University, Shula saw it as no less than sedition—no matter that Shula himself had once walked out on a team to take a better job. Saban, he fumed, had "run away from the challenge . . . That tells you a bit about the guy. [He] likes to hear himself talk and then doesn't follow up what he says." Not incidentally, there was another factor involved: Mike Shula, who, after being stiffed by Belichick in Cleveland, had done quite well, hired by the Tampa Bay Buccaneers as offensive coordinator, then back to the Dolphins as quarterback coach. In 2003, he was hired as the Crimson Tide's head coach. The school was under sanctions for recruiting violations, yet by his third year, they won 10 games and were ranked No. 10, earning him a new million-dollar contract and a six-year extension. But when Saban became available a year later, another Shula was out in the cold.[4]

The same family tie might also help explain why, beyond pride, Shula pricked Belichick during the Patriots' 16-game, undefeated regular season in 2007. While the old coach acknowledged that Belichick had done "a tremendous job," he averred that "the Spygate thing has diminished what they've accomplished," referring to Belichick's illegal videotaping escapade, which cost the Pats its No. 1 draft pick—the same penalty Shula himself had once cost the Colts.[5] Shula even did a guest shot during a Monday night game that fall, openly rooting against the Patriots, something that seemed tacky to many fans; one Boston writer, even a decade later, judged him to be "an angry old man."[6] When "Beli-Cheat," as he called him, was upset in the Super Bowl by the Giants, Shula lavished praise on Tom Brady, but added, "I can't say anything nice about Belichick." Even when that game faded and Shula's perfect record stood, he wouldn't let go of Belichick's ankle, reminding anyone who would listen, "We didn't deflate any balls." His achievements, he said, overlooking his own ethical lapses, were "always done with a lot of class, a lot of dignity. Always done the right way."[7]

Once, he kept those sort of grudges quiet. Now he didn't need to play nice. He always believed Marino had been misused by Johnson, virtually shoved out the door. When Marino was elected to the Hall of Fame in 2005—Shula's 14th and last player to go in, and the eighth Dolphin—he claimed proprietary rights to him. Before heading to Canton for the ceremonies, at which Marino called him "the greatest coach ever" and, "other than my father, the most significant influence" on his life, Shula said Marino "had one coach" in his career. That was Shula's revenge on Jimmy Johnson.[8] And as for Belichick, Shula could savor another big-game loss by the Patriots, to the Eagles in Super Bowl LII. The winning coach was Doug Pederson, the third-stringer who had fleetingly tasted glory in 1993 before Shula forgot about him. As tenuous as that proxy was, to Shula, it was justice being served.

He had enough commercial and banquet appearances to keep himself occupied. In 2000 he was paid handsomely as a "financial coach" for Shochet Securities, a discount brokerage house in Boca Raton. He had his golf tournaments, the burgeoning empire of his restaurants, and charities—when the former Dolphin team dentist's son died of cystic fibrosis, Shula began a fund in the son's name. He avidly participated in nostalgic documentaries about the perfect season, Marino, and himself. He was, to be certain, a peripatetic figure, hovering around the Dolphins, getting together with his old players at reunions. After the Dolphins retired Marino's number in 2000, Shula took the microphone at Pro Player Stadium. "Before I start," he said, "I want to thank all of the general managers in the National Football League who passed on Dan Marino. Otherwise, we wouldn't have tonight."

He seemed the picture of health, a swinging, suntanned senior, handsome as ever, trophy wife on his arm. He and Mary Anne were often seen together on the golf or tennis court, and in numerous TV commercials. As much as people rolled their eyes about the marriage, she kept him young and rich and was a ferocious protector of their mutual interests—and definitely her own. Still receiving $1 million a year in alimony from her late former husband, she sued her former stepson for having "drained the assets" of the Stephens estate. She sued the city, also in vain, to roll back their property taxes, saying that Shula was "on the back nine of his life. . . . If our taxes go up, he'll suffer. What gives you the right to do that?"

Such melodrama created openings for the media to poke some fun at the aggressive, magnolia-drawling belle who had bagged the legendary coach. "Are the Shulas broke?" asked one article. "Or is football demigod Don's wife just a cheapskate?"[9] If they were broke, they had a funny way of showing it. In 2004, they paid $2 million for a second home, a Mediterranean-style villa they called their summer retreat, in Palm Beach Gardens—inside Old Palm Golf Club, whose course was designed by Ray Floyd. The two-story, 6,087-square-foot lakefront home features four master suites, four full baths and one half bath, a gourmet kitchen, vaulted ceilings, and a summer kitchen in the backyard.

Even without Mary Anne's fortune. Shula, at a net worth of $30 million, ranked fourth in a 2017 *Money* magazine list of the richest coaches of all time. (Jimmy Johnson was first, at $40 million, Belichick next, at $35 million.)[10] As with many of his generation, great wealth moved him from FDR Democrat to Reagan Republican, but his only official political endorsement was for Charlie Crist, a moderate Republican later turned Democrat. He also hosted a fundraiser for Democrat Bob Graham, the Florida senator and former governor, in 2003 when the latter announced a short-lived presidential run. He always did know when to go out on a limb for someone, and when to make a statement by saying nothing at all. The latter seemed to be his approach to his old foil, who, to his astonishment, somehow became president of the United States, proving that some things in life simply cannot be explained on any logical basis. But then, he knew that to be reality the day he lost Super Bowl III.

Living like a king, he appeared immune to age as his contemporaries began to drop. Bill Braucher died in 2014, Ed Pope in 2017, a year before Wayne Huizenga. His oldest football confrere, Carl Taseff, went in 2005. He has outlived some of his players, such as Johnny Unitas, Earl Morrall, and Garo Yepremian. Others suffered in uneasy retirement—David Woodley, for one. While he and Hall of Famer Ken Stabler were the only quarterbacks to win over 60 percent of their games and throw at least 10 more career touchdowns than interceptions, few remembered the lanky Dolphin quarterback. After becoming a heavy drinker, in 1992 he underwent a kidney transplant, and in 2003, he died of kidney and liver failure at the age of 44.[11]

Others had to cope with a living death, the result of something no one in football paid much attention to in the old days: the cumulative effects of head trauma. Nick Buoniconti, Shula's only defensive player on the Dolphins to be elected to the Hall of Fame, had lived well in retirement, doing much TV work. But in 1985, his life took a cruel turn when his son Marc, a linebacker for the Citadel, injured his spinal cord, and was rendered quadriplegic.[12] Buoniconti sued the school, settled for $800,000, and began raising funds to find a cure for paralysis, with Shula joining in the effort. Then his own health began to deteriorate, with symptoms that only in recent times became familiar indications of traumatic encephalopathy, or CTE, the condition found in the autopsies of many NFL players. "At 55 I was very normal," he said in 2017. "I'm not normal anymore. I can't remember how to lace my shoes. My left arm won't do what my brain tells it to do."[13]

Jim Kiick went through the same hell. As "Butch" hit his 60s, his mind began to fail, and in 2011, he was diagnosed with dementia/ early-onset Alzheimer's and possible CTE; five years later, his finances drained, living in squalor, he was placed in an assisted living facility. Looking back in anger, he blamed an easy target: the coach who had told him so often, "Just get back in there."[14] Mark Duper disclosed in 2013 that he, too, had tested positive for signs of CTE.[15] Bill Stanfill underwent hip replacement and three spinal fusion surgeries and had crippling neck pain and the loss of feeling in his hand and arm. Possibly suffering as well from CTE, he was diagnosed with dementia before dying in 2016.[16] "Sundance" Csonka suffered from spine damage.

There were also those with self-inflicted wounds. Similar to Mercury Morris, Mark Ingram was convicted of money laundering and fraud in 2008 and was sent to prison for seven years.[17]

Shula hurt for them all, but he refused to believe that anything he had ever done contributed to their woes. Football, he said, was not a game for the weak of heart or limb. He could give thanks during his daily Mass that his mind was nimble, what with the hits he took as a player. But he had his own health issues. In his 80s, his speech grew slow and slurred, his famous ramrod posture stooped, but after brushing off minor problems, he awoke one night gasping for breath, frightening him and Mary Anne when they learned he had sleep apnea, the condition that had caused the premature death of the Packers' Hall of Fame defensive end Reggie White. He began wearing a ventilator to sleep without disruption, and as his legs weakened, he began using a motorized cart to zip around in.

"He invited me to come and play in one of his celebrity golf tournaments," said Rick Volk, "and when I got there, I saw him in a wheelchair and I was shocked. He always seemed indestructible, ageless, to me. I said, 'What're you doin' in that thing?' He just smiled and said, 'Rick, we all get old.'"[18]

He still likes to drive, usually too fast, sometimes on the Don Shula Expressway. Those sorts of monuments were all around him. One exception was the stadium Robbie built for himself, which was never renamed Don Shula Stadium. Bouncing from one sponsor to another, it was renovated and rechristened five times; after Huizenga sold the team in 2009 to real estate magnate Steven Ross for $2.2 billion, it became Land Shark Stadium, then Sun Life Stadium, then Hard Rock Stadium, the address of which is 347 Don Shula Drive. It has a 10-foot statue of Shula on the sidewalk and a huge mural of him on the outside wall; in many ways, it *is* Don Shula Stadium.

In the wreckage of a once-haughty team that has had 10 coaches since he left, only his name and image can evoke phantasms of better days ahead, mirroring the better days past. Not that he became less crotchety about the "kids" he had to put up with and never really understood, and the changes in the game that had caused him complications. As Ed Pope wrote, Shula "revered and reveled in his game so much, worked at it so passionately, so honorably, he could not even begin to understand why Eric Green did not gather in passes as hungrily as Raymond Berry and Howard Twilley and Nat Moore had. Couldn't see why paying someone $3.5 million in advance should not have the slightest effect."[19] Such old-world sensibility seemed quaint, but it was why Greg Cote could write dreamily in 2018, "How long has this franchise, my team, been riding the fumes of Shula's early successes? We forgive that he spent his last 22 seasons wanting nothing more than to win a third Super Bowl but failing to do so. Shula is our granite-jawed deity, still."[20]

The family continues to annex turf within the sport. Mike Shula, who fashioned Cam Newton's whirlwind offense that took the Carolina Panthers to a nearly perfect regular season—with the patriarch saying he "would love" for Mike's team to go undefeated—and one game short of a title, was fired when the team collapsed. He then went to the Giants as offensive coordinator in 2018. And now there was a third generation. Dave's son Dan—named for his great-grandfather—landed with Florida Atlantic University, where Howard Schnellenberger had founded the football program. Dave's middle son Chris crept up as an assistant at Indiana, Ball State, and, in 2014, as defensive coordinator at John Carroll, where his grandfather had taken him as a teenager a decade earlier, when the new football field was dedicated—Don Shula Stadium. Chris made history by becoming the Blue Streaks' head coach, then advanced as an assistant coach with the Chargers and the Rams. Even Dave Shula began to get itchy again, and in 2018, he returned after 20 years to become head coach at his alma mater, Dartmouth.

The patriarch, meanwhile, remained content not to haunt any sidelines, and is sympathetic with those who followed in his footsteps in Miami, without success. When Adam Gase became the Dolphins' coach in 2016, Shula pronounced him a "good guy" and asked the fans to give him a "fair chance," as he had done with the previous coach, Joe Philbin. At that point, he was engaging simply in boosterism, but he clearly enjoyed being asked to lend his support (not that it spared Gase from the gallows after the 2018 season). Just as he enjoyed being asked to play himself in a cameo role in the pilot episode of *Ballers*, the Miami-based HBO football series starring Dwayne "The Rock" Johnson. The script had him lounging in the back of a yacht with a fictitious Dolphins coach. He had one line, telling a new player, "You're an asshole." He did it, perfectly.

In April 2018, the swells gathered at the Fontainebleau Hotel to see Joe Namath be presented with something called the Don Shula Sports Legend Award. Namath, at 73, was nearly half a century removed from the day he caused Shula's heart to break. When he rose to accept the award, he walked slowly and painfully, at the mercy of his prosthetic knees. Shula, at 88, sat waiting for him in his cart, puckish grin on his kisser.

"I can't believe I'm presenting Joe Namath an award," he said, still gritting but able to laugh about it. But what was hardest to believe was that both of them were relics of a sport they had, by turns, defined by their youth.

Shula, at a still-spunky 88, was no longer youthful, but he has left his mark, particularly around South Florida. Over the summer of 2018, the writer who had interviewed him so long ago was in one of those too-quickly constructed bar/eateries along the slinky Intracoastal

Waterway, yachts and sailboats floating lazily by. Shula, he had learned, had been to seemingly all of these places at one time or another, signing autographs between bites and digressing into battle stories, some of them literally so—such as the one about how he and Mary Anne visited the troops in Afghanistan, wearing 40-pound bulletproof vests as they rode in an army helicopter, squirming as machine-gun fire was aimed at it from the ground. When they landed safely, he said, you could smell the gunpowder from a suicide bomb that had gone off only hours before. He would tell this story, and then, when asked to take a selfie, he would laugh and say, "Thirty-five dollars, two for seventy."

One need not have an interest in football to feel as if they know him. At the bar this night, an underdressed woman in her mid-60s, sipping a margarita, heard a man utter the name Don Shula.

"Oh, yes, I know him," she said, confidently. "Shula Burger."

Where brands are concerned, other sporting legends have had eponymous restaurants, but in Shula's case, being synonymous with a slab of ground beef just fits the contours of his being. He knew that when he began the chain. Because, in his self-awareness, it was clear that what sustained him for so long wasn't the sizzle, but the meat.

NOTES

Introduction: Shula Pride

1. "Don Shula Net Worth Is $30 Million," GetNetWorth.com, http://www.getnetworth .com/tag/don-shula-coaching-tree/.
2. Darfin Gantt, "Don Shula Learned an Early Lesson about Business with Donald Trump," NBC Sports.com, July 2, 2015, https://profootballtalk.nbcsports .com/2015/07/02/don-shula-learned-an-early-lesson-about-business-with-donald -trump/.
3. Mark Ribowsky, "Shula Pride," *Sport*, December 1978.
4. Paul Zimmerman, "Don Shula: Sportsman of the Year," *Sports Illustrated*, December 20, 1993.
5. John Underwood, "His Eyes Have Seen the Glory," *Sports Illustrated*, July 27, 1981.
6. Brandon Schlager, "Don Shula Refers to Bill Belichick as 'Beli-Cheat,'" *Sporting News*, January 8, 2015.
7. "Backstory: Don Shula," *A Football Life*, aired September 10, 2013 on NFL Network.
8. Ken Blanchard and Don Shula, *Everyone's a Coach* (New York: Harper Business/ Zondervan, 1995), p. 37.
9. Zimmerman, "Sportsman of the Year."
10. Art Donovan, *Fatso* (New York: William Morrow, 1987), p. 7.
11. Ribowsky, "Shula Pride."
12. Underwood, "His Eyes."
13. Zimmerman, "Sportsman of the Year."
14. Dave Hyde, "It's Up to Gase, Not the Players, to Set Dolphins Culture," *South Florida Sun-Sentinel* (Deerfield Beach, FL), August 4, 2018.
15. Ed Pope, "Shula, Chargers' Beathard Clash," *Miami Herald*, January 9, 1995.

Chapter 1: A Sovereign Masculinity

1. Carly Cundiff, "Shula Chair Discusses Masculinity," *Carroll News*, February 25, 2016.
2. "Shula's Roots—A Rock Foundation," *Sun-Sentinel* (Fort Lauderdale, FL), November 15, 1993.
3. Don Shula and Lou Sahadi, *The Winning Edge* (New York: Dutton, 1973), p. 29.
4. Ken Blanchard and Don Shula, *Everyone's a Coach* (Grand Rapids, MI: Zondervan), p. 36.
5. Jeff Schudel, "Don Shula at 80: From Harvey to Hall," *News-Herald* (Willoughby, OH), July 18, 2010.
6. "They're the Talk of Lake County Village," *Cleveland Plain Dealer*, August 23, 1936.
7. Schudel, "Don Shula at 80."
8. Zimmerman, "Don Shula."
9. Shula and Sahadi, *Winning Edge*, p. 33.

Chapter 2: Catechism

1. "Shula's Roots."
2. Don Martin, "A Coach's Memories of Don Shula at Painesville," *Cleveland Plain Dealer*, December 16, 1964.
3. *The Anvil*, Harvey High School, 1946.
4. *The Anvil*, Harvey High School, 1947.
5. Shula and Sahadi, *Winning Edge*, p. 33.
6. Ibid., p. 39.

Chapter 3: "Who Is John Carroll?"

1. Marvin L. Krier Mich, *Catholic Social Teaching and Movements* (New London, CT: Twenty-Third Publications, 1998).
2. Shula and Sahadi, *Winning Edge*, p. 40.
3. Charles Heaton, "Shula, Carroll's Sophomore Backfield Find, Starts against B.-W. Saturday," *Cleveland Plain Dealer*, October 14, 1948.
4. Charles Heaton, "Schaffer Hurls 5 Touchdown Passes as Carroll Beats Bee Gees, 38–24," *Cleveland Plain Dealer*, October 29, 1949.
5. Charles Heaton, "Shula Is Leader of Ground Attack," *Cleveland Plain Dealer*, November 6, 1950.
6. "Carroll's Streaks Whip Dayton, 24–12," Associated Press, November 4, 1950.
7. Shula and Sahadi, *Winning Edge*, p. 42.

Chapter 4: The Cleveland Caliph

1. Shula and Sahadi, *Winning Edge*, p. 45.
2. Bill Cobbledick, "37th Takes Mock Warfare in Serious and Alert Stride," *Cleveland Plain Dealer*, July 19, 1951.

3. Shula and Sahadi, *Winning Edge*, p. 45.

4. Ibid., p. 40.

5. Ibid., p. 48.

6. "Team Fight in Browns' Training Camp Would Convert Diehards," United Press International, August 12, 1951.

7. Shula and Sahadi, *Winning Edge*, p. 55.

8. Paul Zimmerman, "Sportsman of the Year."

9. Charles Heaton, "Paul Brown Has 'Red-Letter' Day," *Cleveland Plain Dealer*, August 6, 1967.

10. George Cantor, *Paul Brown: The Man Who Invented Modern Football* (Chicago: Triumph, 2008), p. 96.

11. Ribowsky, "Shula Pride."

12. John G. Blair, "Summer Greets Last Units of 37th Arriving at Camp," *Cleveland Plain Dealer*, January 26, 1952.

13. "Football Talk," *Cleveland Plain Dealer*, November 17, 1952.

14. "Browns Vote to Cut Team Aides' Share," Associated Press, December 29, 1952.

Chapter 5: One Tough Sonofabitch

1. Paul Hornung, "Bruney Counted in Brown's Plans," *Columbus (OH) Dispatch*, March 29, 1953.

2. Associated Press, August 27, 1953.

3. Shula and Sahadi, *Winning Edge*, p. 59.

4. Tom Davidson and Ray Lynch, "Obituary: Dorothy Shula, Wife of Dolphins' Coach," *Sun-Sentinel* (Fort Lauderdale, FL), February 26, 1991.

5. Jill Young Miller, "Without Dorothy," *Sun-Sentinel* (Fort Lauderdale, FL), July 1, 1991.

6. Shula and Sahadi, *Winning Edge*, p. 61.

7. Donovan, *Fatso*, p. 143.

8. Zimmerman, "Sportsman of the Year."

9. Shula and Sahadi, *Winning Edge*, p. 62.

10. Zimmerman, "Sportsman of the Year."

11. Donovan, *Fatso*, p. 177.

12. Tom Callahan, *Johnny U: The Life and Times of John Unitas* (New York: Random House, 2006), p. 68.

13. Donovan, *Fatso*, p. 8.

14. Edmon J. Rodman, "The Call of the Rams to Jewish Fans," *Jewish Journal*, January 14, 2016.

15. David Harris, *The League: The Rise and Decline of the NFL* (New York: Bantam, 1986), p. 45.

16. Donovan, *Fatso*, pp. 8 and 177.

17. Lou Sahadi, *Johnny Unitas: America's Quarterback* (Chicago: Triumph, 2004), p. 50.

18. Shula and Sahadi, *Winning Edge*, p. 64.

19. Ibid.

Chapter 6: Coach Shula

1. Young Miller, "Without Dorothy."
2. *Petersburg (VA) Progress-Index*, October 15, 1958.
3. Shula and Sahadi, *Winning Edge*, p. 73.
4. John Underwood, "Sitting on Top of the World," *Sports Illustrated*, September 17, 1973.
5. Author interview with Howard Schnellenberger.
6. "Shula Resigns as UK Grid Aide to Join Lions' Staff," *Lexington (KY) Herald*, March 21, 1960.
7. Donovan, *Fatso*, p. 170.
8. "Dolphin Aide Succumbs," *Palm Beach Post*, November 20, 1970; "His Drawl Wins Layne Freedom," *Detroit Free Press*, December 7, 1951.
9. Tim Rohan, "The Playoff Bowl: The Worst Kind of Garbage Time," *Sports Illustrated*, June 22, 2017.
10. Gordon Cobbledick, *Cleveland Plain Dealer*, September 7, 1961.

Chapter 7: Fly Me to the Moon

1. Shula and Sahadi, *Winning Edge*, p. 80.
2. Oscar Fraley, "Browns, Lions Represent Study in Contrast in Sideline Conduct," United Press International, January 9, 1961.
3. Shula and Sahadi, *Winning Edge*, p. 86.
4. Associated Press, December 18, 1962.
5. "Shula Heads Baltimore; Ewbank Out," United Press International, January 9, 1963.
6. "Ewbank Fired; Shula Gets Job," Associated Press, January 9, 1963.
7. Morris Siegel, "Brown Resented Being Bossed," *Washington Evening Star*, January 10, 1963.
8. Morris Siegel, "Rip's Fete Draw Only 'Select Few,'" *Washington Evening Star*, February 17, 1963.
9. Harris, *The League*, pp. 45–46.
10. Sahadi, *Johnny Unitas*, p. 172.
11. Ibid., and Harris, *The League*.
12. "Colt Coach Shula Praised by Owner," Associated Press, July 16, 1963.
13. Mike Klingaman, "Baltimore Athletes Remember Being 'Dazed,' 'Shaken' on Weekend of JFK's Death," *Baltimore Sun*, November 21, 2013.
14. "D-Day Comes for Coach Don Shula," *Baltimore Sun*, September 15, 1963.
15. Associated Press, December 10, 1963.
16. Tom Callahan, *Johnny U: The Life and Times of John Unitas* (New York: Random House, 2006), p. 199.
17. Hearst Headline Service, December 27, 1964.

18. "Baltimore Relies on Video Tape," *Associated Press*, December 22, 1964.
19. Sahadi, *Johnny Unitas*, p. 85.
20. Shula and Sahadi, *Winning Edge*, p. 87.

Chapter 8: National Frustration League

1. Chuck Johnson, "Green Bay's Defense Provides Equalizers," *Milwaukee Journal-Sentinel*, September 27, 1965.
2. Shula and Sahadi, *Winning Edge*, p. 90.
3. Callahan, *Johnny U*, p. 208.
4. Tex Maule, "The Point of Some Return," *Sports Illustrated*, January 3, 1966.
5. Ibid.
6. "Shula Somber after Defeat," *Associated Press*, December 27, 1965.
7. John Steadman, "Chandler's Admission Helps Take Sting Out of 31-Year-Old Bad Call," *Baltimore Sun*, November 3, 1996.
8. "Coach Is Upset over Colt Loss," *Associated Press*, December 27, 1965.
9. Bob Maisel, "Morning After," *Baltimore Sun*, December 27, 1965.
10. Callahan, *Johnny U*, p. 210.
11. "Baltimore Colts," *Sports Illustrated*, September 12, 1966.
12. Chuck Johnson, "'Come to Papa,' Says Robinson," *Milwaukee Journal*, December 11, 1966.
13. Cameron Snyder, *Baltimore Sun*, December 11, 1966.
14. Author interview with Rick Volk.
15. Sam Blair, "And 4 to Go," *Dallas Morning News*, December 18, 1967.
16. "Unitas Retains Cool amid Stunned Colts," *Los Angeles Times–Washington Post* Service, December 18, 1967.
17. Cameron Snyder, *Baltimore Sun*, December 18, 1967.
18. Bob Maisel, "The Morning After," *Baltimore Sun*, December 18, 1967.

Chapter 9: Sweet

1. "Streets of Fire: Governor Spiro Agnew and the Baltimore City Riots, April 1968," Maryland State Archives, http://teaching.msa.maryland.gov/000001/000000/000061/html/t61.html.
2. Author interview with Rick Volk.
3. Louis Chestnut, "The Sports Spectrum," *Charleston (SC) News and Courier*, August 25, 1968.
4. Shula and Sahadi, *Winning Edge*, p. 97.
5. Callahan, *Johnny U*, p. 213.
6. "Unitas May Miss Season Opener," *Associated Press*, September 10, 1968.
7. Cameron C. Snyder, "Unitas Quits Passing Drill in Pain," *Baltimore Star*, September 12, 1968.

8. Callahan, *Johnny U*, p. 213.

9. Shula and Sahadi, *Winning Edge*, p. 101.

10. Chuck Heaton, "Too Much, Too Soon," *Cleveland Plain Dealer*, October 22, 1968.

11. Cameron C. Snyder, "Win Puts Colts on Gravy Train," *Baltimore Sun*, December 23, 1968.

12. Mark Ribowsky, "Reading Keys: What You Need to Know to Play in the NFL," *Inside Sports*, October 31, 1980.

13. Tex Maule, "Baltimore Lowers the Boom," *Sports Illustrated*, January 6, 1969.

14. "Shula: Colts Deserved Title," United Press International, December 30, 1968.

15. Gordon Beard, "Matte Collapses after Title Tilt," Associated Press, December 30, 1968.

Chapter 10: Sour

1. Tex Maule, "Say It's So, Joe," *Sports Illustrated*, January 20, 1969.

2. "R.I.P. Lou Michaels, Who May Have Sparked Namath's Super Bowl Guarantee," Fox Sports.com, January 19, 2006, https://www.foxsports.com/nfl/story/baltimore -colts-new-york-jets-late-lou-michaels-may-have-sparked-joe-namath-s-guarantee -011916.

3. David Barron, "The Guarantee That Shocked, Changed Football," *Houston Chronicle*, January 29, 2004.

4. Zimmerman, "Sportsman of the Year."

5. Shula and Sahadi, *Winning Edge*, p. 103.

6. "Shula Lauds, Cut Jets' Jaunty Joe," United Press International, January 7, 1969.

7. Author interview with Rick Volk.

8. Shirley Povich, "Jets, Namath Take Spotlight," *Washington Post*, January 12, 1969.

9. Tex Maule, "A Go Pattern vs. a Stop Team," *Sports Illustrated*, January 13, 1969.

10. "Winter Will Be Long for Shula," *Cleveland Plain Dealer*, January 14, 1969.

11. Cameron Snyder, "Matte, Bubba Absent from Colt Drills," *Baltimore Sun*, January 4, 1969.

12. Bob Maisel, "Morning After," *Baltimore Sun*, January 11, 1969.

13. Shula and Sahadi, *Winning Edge*, p. 103.

14. Ogden Nash, "Prognostications Are for the Birds, Lay Off Me, Please, While I Eat My Words," *Life*, January 24, 1969.

15. William Wallace, "Billy Ray Smith: 'My Pride is Bent, We Let Teammates, NFL Down,'" *New York Times*, January 13, 1969.

16. Bob Maisel, "Morning After," *Baltimore Sun*, January 13, 1969.

17. Robert Lipsyte, "Broadway Joe Is No. 1," *New York Times*, January 13, 1969.

18. Tom Wicker, "Underdog-Lovers Rejoice with Jets," *New York Times*, January 14, 1969.

19. "Beating Colts in '69 Super Bowl Never Boring Topic with Namath," *Baltimore Sun*, September 30, 2004.

20. Shula and Sahadi, *Winning Edge*, p. 107.

21. "Colts Seek Vengeance," *Baltimore Sun*, January 18, 1969.

22. Shula and Sahadi, *Winning Edge*, p. 110.

23. Mike Klingaman, "Shula's Fateful Loss," *Baltimore Sun*, February 1, 2008.

24. "Baltimore Still 'Shock City USA,'" United Press International, January 15, 1969.

25. Dan Boone, "They Said What? All Time NFL Quotes," *Bleacher Report*, June 18, 2008, http://bleacherreport.com/articles/30484-they-said-what-all-time-nfl-quotes.

Chapter 11: "The Biggest Thing Since Bubble Gum"

1. Underwood, "Sitting on Top."

2. *Baltimore Sun*, January 18, 1969.

3. Author interview with Howard Schnellenberger.

4. Chuck Heaton, "Shula's Star Still Rising," *Cleveland Plain Dealer*, March 21, 1969.

5. Author interview with Rick Volk.

6. Cameron Snyder, "Shula Takes Exception to Davis's Statements," *Baltimore Sun*, August 21, 1969.

7. Cameron Snyder, "No Levity in Colt Locker Room after Beating," *Baltimore Sun*, September 29, 1969.

8. Cameron Snyder, "Shula Seeks Only Last Win amid Rumors of Leaving," *Baltimore Sun*, December 17, 1969.

9. Doug Brown, "An Exile from the Colts Office," *Baltimore Sun*, December 28, 1969.

10. Shula and Sahadi, *Winning Edge*, p. 112.

11. Ibid., p. 114.

12. Ibid., p. 119.

13. Ibid., pp. 121–23.

14. Bill Braucher, "Coach Shula Says He Has No 'Magic Formula,'" *Miami Herald*, February 19, 1970.

15. Ed Pope, "The 22 Days It Took to Land Don Shula," *Miami Herald*, February 19, 1970.

16. Luther Evans, "Firing Surprises Players," *Miami Herald*, February 19, 1970.

17. Bob Maisel, "The Morning After," *Baltimore Sun*, April 16, 1970.

18. Cameron Snyder, "Mackey Won't Miss Don Shula," *Baltimore Sun*, April 2, 1970.

19. Shula and Sahadi, *Winning Edge*, p. 131.

20. Brown, "Exile from the Colts Office."

21. Shula and Sahadi, *Winning Edge*, p. 241.

22. Cameron Snyder, "Owners Approve Stock for Shula," *Baltimore Sun*, May 28, 1970.

23. Shula and Sahadi, *Winning Edge*, p. 130.

24. "Dolphins Penalized—Colt Tampering," Associated Press, April 14, 1970.

25. Shula and Sahadi, *Winning Edge*, p. 131.

26. Bob Griese, *Perfection: The Inside Story of the 1972 Miami Dolphins' Perfect Season* (Hoboken, NJ: John Wiley, 2012), p. 170.

Chapter 12: Hired by the Man Who Fired Flipper

1. Mark Kram, "This Man Fired Flipper," *Sports Illustrated*, December 15, 1969.

2. Author interview with Howard Schnellenberger.

3. "Ready-Made Team," *Palm Beach Post*, January 12, 1972.

4. Eugene "Mercury" Morris with Steve Fiffer, *Against the Grain* (New York: McGraw-Hill, 1988), p. 56.

5. Griese, *Perfection*, p. 28.

6. *Tampa Tribune*, July 15, 1970.

7. Bill Cooke, "Remembering Miami Beach's Shameful History of Segregation and Racism," *Miami New Times*, March 10, 2016.

8. Eugene "Mercury" Morris, "Former Dolphin 'Mercury' Morris Recalls Good and Bad in Late '60s Miami," *Miami Herald*, September 15, 2016.

9. Morris, *Against the Grain*, p. 59.

10. Dave Anderson, "The Dolphins' Irresistible Force and Unmovable Object," *Sport*, January 1974.

11. "The Week in Sports," *Baltimore Sun*, July 5, 1970.

12. "Yepremian Gets Chance at Miami," Associated Press, August 19, 1970.

13. Anderson, "Dolphins' Irresistible Force."

14. Griese, *Perfection*, p. 65.

15. John Underwood, "The Blood and Thunder Boys," *Sports Illustrated*, August 7, 1972.

16. Larry Csonka and Jim Kiick with Dave Anderson, *Always on the Run* (New York: Bantam, 1973), p. 6.

17. Morris, *Against the Grain*, p. 70.

18. Griese, *Perfection*, p. 27.

19. Csonka and Kiick, *Always on the Run*, pp. 29–30.

20. David Wolf, "Mercury, Wings and All: Eugene Morris, the Country's Best Unknown Ground-Gainer," *Look*, October 18, 1968.

21. Csonka and Kiick, *Always on the Run*, p. 5.

22. Danny Perry, *Super Bowl: The Game of Their Lives* (New York: Macmillan, 1997), pp. 100–101.

23. "Bubba Smith Will Make Shula Sorry He Left Colts," *Florida Today*, August 28, 1970.

24. Tony Petrelli, "The Incredible Miami Dolphins Do It Again," *Palm Beach Post*, August 30, 1970.

25. George Sullivan, "Pats Hook Dolphins on Defense, 27–14," *Boston Herald*, September 21, 1970.

26. Bill Braucher, "Griese's Passing Carries Dolphins By Oilers 20–10," *Miami Herald*, September 28, 1970.

27. Bill Braucher, "Dolphins Shock Jets, 20–13," *Miami Herald*, October 11, 1970.

28. Bill Braucher, "Cleveland Shuts Out Dolphins," *Miami Herald*, October 26, 1970.

29. Cameron Snyder, "Shula's Dolphins Test Colts," *Baltimore Sun*, November 1, 1970.

30. Ed Storin, "35–0: A Not-So-Hot Time in Don Shula's Old Town," *Miami Herald*, November 2, 1970.

31. Bill Braucher, "Inept Dolphins End Philadelphia Futility," *Miami Herald*, November 9, 1970.

32. Zimmerman, "Sportsman of the Year."

33. Ed Pope, "Shula Wasn't Geared for 'Screeching Halt,'" *Miami Herald*, December 28, 1970.

Chapter 13: Butch, Sundance, and a Cuddly Cypriot

1. Bill Braucher, "Yepremian FGs Edge Jets, 16–10," *Miami Herald*, December 14, 1970.

2. Csonka and Kiick, *Always on the Run*, p. 8.

3. Harris, *The League*, pp. 50–51.

4. James Dudko, "Bill Arnsparger: Remembering the Godfather of the Zone Blitz and Hybrid Defense," *Bleacher Report*, July 19, 2015, http://bleacherreport.com/articles/2526034-bill-arnsparger-remembering-the-godfather-of-the-zone-blitz-and-hybrid-defense.

5. Bill Braucher, "Csonka, Kiick Contract Talks 'Get Nowhere,'" *Miami Herald*, July 24, 1971.

6. Csonka and Kiick, *Always on the Run*, p. 88.

7. Ed Pope, "In the Long Run, Dolphins Win by a Toe," *Miami Herald*, December 26, 1971.

8. John Underwood, "Up, Up, Up and Away," *Sports Illustrated*, January 3, 1972.

9. Robert Weintrab, "Endless Emotions over NFL's Longest Game," *New York Times*, December 26, 1971.

10. Shula and Sahadi, *Winning Edge*, p. 180.

11. Cameron Snyder, "Colts Plan Daily Drills in Tampa," *Baltimore Sun*, December 28, 1971.

12. John Underwood, "'They Kept Coming and Coming,'" *Sports Illustrated*, January 10, 1972.

13. Ed Pope, "Rainbow Arch Forecast Griese-Warfield Dazzler," *Miami Herald*, January 3, 1972.

14. Author interview with Rick Volk.

15. "Ready-Made Team," *Palm Beach Post*, January 12, 1972.

16. Ed Pope, "New Dolphin Battle Cry—Win One for the Doaker," *Miami Herald*, January 13, 1972.

17. Bill Braucher, "Scott Hopes Staubach Recognizes Old Face," *Miami Herald*, January 13, 1972.

18. Bill Braucher, "Tempting New Orleans Next Stop for Dolphins," *Miami Herald*, January 9, 1972.

19. Shula and Sahadi, *Winning Edge*, p. 189.

20. Ibid., pp. 197–98.

21. Ed Pope, "We Never Challenged—Shula," *Miami Herald*, January 17, 1972.

Chapter 14: "Stay Ready, Earl. Stay Ready"

1. "Thomas Indicted," United Press International, February 9, 1972.

2. Underwood, "His Eyes."

3. Ed Pope, "Joe Thomas Resigns from Dolphins," *Miami Herald*, February 19, 1972.

4. Ray Lynch, "A Man of Perfection: Joe Robbie Had a Fire That Warmed Many and Burned a Few, Says Danny Thomas," *Sun-Sentinel* (Fort Lauderdale, FL), January 9, 1990.

5. "Rams History (Long): 'Best Wishes, George Allen's Daughter,'" RamsOnDemand .com, July 4, 2017, http://ramsondemand.com/threads/rams-history-long-best-wishes -george-allens-daughter.50038/.

6. Morris, *Against the Grain*, p. 62.

7. Csonka and Kiick, *Always on the Run*, p. 22.

8. S. I. Price, "How Jim Kiick Fell through the Cracks," *Sports Illustrated*, May 9, 2017.

9. Bob Griese, *Perfection*, p. 62.

10. Csonka and Kiick, *Always on the Run*, p. 196.

11. Ed Pope, "'We Controlled Game,' Says Proud Shula," *Miami Herald*, September 18, 1972.

12. Csonka and Kiick, *Always on the Run*, p. 60.

13. Griese, *Perfection*, p. 64.

14. Terry Galvin, "Griese Belted High, Asserts the Deacon," *Miami Herald*, October 16, 1972.

15. Ed Pope, "Earl Tunes Hearing Aid," *Miami Herald*, October 16, 1972.

16. Dave Hyde, "Bill Stanfill, Defensive End on Dolphins' Super Bowl-Winning Teams, Dies at 69," *South Florida Sun-Sentinel* (Deerfield Beach, FL), November 11, 2016.

17. Morris, *Against the Grain*, p. 75.

18. Ed Pope, "Up-Tight Warfield Finally Gets Loose," *Miami Herald*, December 25, 1972.

19. Bill Braucher, "Annie Gets Own Horse," *Miami Herald*, December 26, 1972.

20. Bill Braucher, "Fourth-Down Conversions Set Up All Dolphin TDs," *Miami Herald*, January 1, 1973.

21. "'Best Wishes, George Allen's Daughter,'" RamsOnDemand.com.
22. Author interview with Howard Schnellenberger.

Chapter 15: Rapture

1. Tex Maule, "The Top-of-the-Hill Gang," *Sports Illustrated*, January 15, 1973.
2. "Miami's Unmiraculous Miracle Worker," *Time*, December 11, 1972.
3. Ed Pope, "Allen Wanted Morris but Lacked 'Bait,'" *Miami Herald*, January 10, 1973.
4. Csonka and Kiick, *Always on the Run*, p. 212.
5. Bill Braucher, "Allen Discussed Deal for Morris with Don Shula," *Miami Herald*, January 10, 1973.
6. Ed Pope, "Shula Hasn't Time to Worry About Rosenbloom," *Miami Herald*, January 13, 1973.
7. Csonka and Kiick, *Always on the Run*, p. 211.
8. Bill Braucher, "Rosenbloom Raps Both Allen, Shula," *Miami Herald*, January 12, 1973.
9. Shula and Sahadi, *Winning Edge*, p. 3.
10. Csonka and Kiick, *Always on the Run*, p. 199.
11. Griese, *Perfection*, p. 235.
12. Tex Maule, "17–0–0," *Sports Illustrated*, January 22, 1973.
13. Griese, *Perfection*, p. 49.
14. John Underwood, "Sitting on Top."
15. Maule, "17–0–0."
16. Ed Pope, "A Cake Walk, Dolphins Should Have Won, 24–0," *Miami Herald*, January 15, 1973.
17. Author interview with Howard Schnellenberger.
18. Underwood, "Sitting on Top."
19. "Ex-Dolphin Coach 'Buries Hatchet,'" *Palm Beach Post*, July 9, 1973.
20. William R. Amlong, "Investigation Mentions Don Shula," *Miami Herald*, July 27, 1978.
21. Underwood, "Sitting on Top."
22. Morris, *Against the Grain*, pp. 79–81.
23. *Miami Herald*, November 17, 1974.
24. Morris, *Against the Grain*, p. 77.
25. Bill Braucher, "It Was Lineman's Day for Shutting Up Raiders," *Miami Herald*, December 31, 1973.
26. Ed Pope, "Griese Called 'Em, Csonka Conked 'Em for Dolphins," *Miami Herald*, December 31, 1973.
27. Gene Miller, "The Eyes in Texas Were upon Them," *Miami Herald*, January 12, 1974.
28. Tex Maule, "It Was the Day of the Dolphins," January 21, 1974.
29. Ed Pope, "Dolphins a Prototype NFL Team," *Miami Herald*, January 15, 1974.

Chapter 16: "Camelot Disappeared"

1. Andrew Abramson, " 40 Years Ago Today: Csonka, Kiick, Warfield Shock Dolphins, NFL by Jumping to WFL," *Palm Beach Post*, March 31, 2014, http://dailydolphin.blog .palmbeachpost.com/2014/03/31/40-years-ago-today-csonka-kiick-warfield-shock -dolphins-nfl-by-jumping-to-wfl/.
2. Harris, *The League*, p 170.
3. "Three Big Dolphins Put WFL on Professional Football Map," *Palm Beach Post*, April 1, 1974.
4. "Sport: The Defection Deal," *Time*, April 15, 1974.
5. Ronald B. Scott, "Coach Don Shula, the Would-Be Priest Who Makes Miami Mean," *People*, December 2, 1974.
6. Underwood, "His Eyes."
7. Bob Braucher, "Archbishop Gets Shula, Robbie Together," *Miami Herald*, May 15, 1974.
8. Scott, "Coach Don Shula."
9. Don Reese, " 'I'm Not Worth a Damn,' " *Sports Illustrated*, June 14, 1982.
10. Gary Long, "People Expect Too Much, Shula Says," *Miami Herald*, October 1, 1974.
11. Morris, *Against the Grain*, p.85.
12. Paul Guttierez, "Raiders' Top Plays: The Sea of Hands," ESPN.com, July 8, 2014, http://www.espn.com/blog/oakland-raiders/post/_/id/4873/raiders-top-play-the -sea-of-hands.
13. Ed Pope, " 'Wounded Duck' Fells a Football Dynasty," *Miami Herald*, December 22, 1974.
14. Ed Pope, "Malone's Quick TD Left Enough Time to Lose," *Miami Herald*, December 22, 1974.
15. Morris, *Against the Grain*, p. 92.
16. "Shula Fame Spreads to Hungarian Village," *Boston Herald*, July 9, 1975.
17. Bill Braucher, "WFL Is Dead—Csonka Eyeing Dolphins," *Miami Herald*, October 23, 1975.
18. Mark Mulvoy, "The Colts Don't Horse Around," *Sports Illustrated*, December 22, 1975.
19. Morris, *Against the Grain*, p. 92.

Chapter 17: "It's Almost Bizarre"

1. Bill Braucher, "Shula, Csonka Near Summit," *Miami Herald*, April 3, 1976.
2. Author interview with Howard Schnellenberger.
3. Morris, *Against the Grain*, p. 94.
4. Ed Pope, "Jake the Great Saddle-Burn," *Miami Herald*, August 19, 1976.
5. Morris, *Against the Grain*, p. 94.

6. "'Big-Play' Scott Fulfilling Expectations of 'Skins' Allen," Associated Press, September 22, 1976.

7. Ed Pope, "Winning Coach Talks about a Losing Year," *Miami Herald*, December 12, 1976.

8. "Gambling Trial Put Off to March 21," *Miami Herald*, January 19, 1977.

9. Ray Kennedy, "Pittsburgh Fats Dodges a Silver Bullet," *Sports Illustrated*, May 7, 1977.

10. "Six Dolphins Used Cocaine, Defendant in Drug Case Says," *Miami Herald*, May 6, 1977.

11. Kennedy, "Pittsburgh Fats Dodges."

12. Richard Goldstein, "Joe Gilliam Is Dead at 49; Pioneer Black Quarterback," *New York Times*, December 27, 2000.

13. Bob Rubin, "Crowder, Reese Innocent Until . . . ," *Miami Herald*, August 3, 1977.

14. Kathy Blumenstock, "Reese: Probation Violation Inquiry," *Washington Post*, June 11, 1982.

15. Author interview with Rick Volk.

16. "Spectacles Make Him Spectacular," *Sports Illustrated*, October 10, 1977.

Chapter 18: Subplots and Counterplots

1. Underwood, "His Eyes."

2. Paul Attner, "Birth of USFL Wasn't Boon to NFL Salaries," *Washington Post*, March 29, 1983.

3. Dave Brady, "49ers Trade Williams for 2 Dolphins, 2 Picks," *Washington Post*, April 18, 1978.

4. Ribowsky, "Shula Pride."

5. "Rosenbloom Death Not Murder—Coroner," Associated Press, January 6, 1983.

6. Tom Archdeacon, "Last Call for Number 39," *Sports Illustrated*, July 29, 1979.

7. Underwood, "His Eyes."

8. Archdeacon, "Last Call."

9. Underwood, "His Eyes."

10. Ed Pope, "Steelers' Compassion Came after Game," *Miami Herald*, December 31, 1979.

11. Henry Seiden, "Dolphins Might Have Many New Faces," *Miami Herald*, December 31, 1979.

Chapter 19: "This Is Still My Product"

1. Underwood, "His Eyes."

2. Henry Seiden, "Dolphins 'Waive' Goodbye to Zonk," *Miami Herald*, August 6, 1980.

3. Eston Melton, "U.S. Drug Agents Investigate Csonka," *Miami Herald*, April 4, 1981.

4. Ed Pope, "Shula Staying for Super Goal, Not Just a Rich Dolphin Pact," *Miami Herald*, September 7, 1980.

5. Underwood, "His Eyes."

6. Ibid.

7. John Underwood, "A Game No One Should Have Lost," *Sports Illustrated*, January 11, 1982.

8. Ed Pope, "Dream Comeback Dies in OT," *Miami Herald*, January 2, 1982.

9. Larry Dorman, "Snowplow Helps Clear Pats' Path," *Miami Herald*, December 13, 1982.

10. Paul Zimmerman, "The Revenge of the Killer Bees," *Sports Illustrated*, January 24, 1983.

11. Christine Brennan, "Jet Officials Unhappy with Field Conditions," Knight-Ridder Newspapers, January 24, 1983.

12. Jere Longman, "Miami Defense Throttled Jets," Knight-Ridder Newspapers, January 24, 1983.

13. Paul Zimmerman, "Miami Was One Tough Mudder," *Sports Illustrated*, January 31, 1983.

14. George Usher, "Michaels' Departure Linked to Outburst Against Davis, Shula," *Newsday*, February 10, 1983.

15. Paul Zimmerman, "Hail to the Redskins!," *Sports Illustrated*, February 7, 1983.

16. Ed Pope, "Don Shula Knows Dolphins Were Manhandled as Redskins Run Away with Super Bowl XVII," *Miami Herald*, January 31, 1983.

Chapter 20: New Kid in Town

1. Dudley Martin, "Walker Issue Poses Problems," *Augusta Chronicle*, February 24, 1983.

2. John Sturbin, "Marino Stirs Memories of Unhappy New Year," *Fort Worth Star-Telegram*, August 7, 1983.

3. Mike Tanier, "NFL Urban Legends: Dan Marino, Drug Rumors and the Draft-Day Slide," *Bleacher Report*, August 11, 2015, http://bleacherreport.com/articles/2519683 -nfl-urban-legends-dan-marino-drug-rumors-and-the-draft-day-slide.

4. Associated Press, "Why Didn't Steelers Draft Marino? Noll Finally Answers the Question," *Observer-Reporter* (Washington, PA), May 12, 1992.

5. "Elway to Marino," *30 for 30*, directed by Ken Rodgers, aired on ESPN on April 23, 2013.

6. Art Brooks, "A Draft Review," *Dallas Morning News*, April 27, 1983.

7. Chuck Heaton, "Burnout? Shula Says No," *Cleveland Plain Dealer*, May 31, 1983.

8. Frank Dascenzo, "Griese: Dolphin Last Unbeaten Team," *Durham (NC) Sun*, May 23, 1983.

9. Fred Lankard, "Woodley's Showing in Dome May Cost Starting Job," *Baton Rouge Advocate*, October 3, 1983.

10. Dave George, "Shula Passes on Coaching Bid from Trump, USFL," *Palm Beach Post*, October 25, 1983.

11. Jerry Magee, "Inside Football," *San Diego Union*, October 30, 1983.

12. Will Hobson, "Donald Trump's Long, Stormy and Unrequited Romance with the NFL," *Washington Post*, September 23, 2017.

13. Paul Zimmerman, "The Class of Their Class," *Sports Illustrated*, November 14, 1983.

14. Ibid.

15. Associated Press, "Shula Signs Contract with Miami," *Augusta (GA) Chronicle*, November 29, 1984.

16. Steve Kelley, "QB Terrorist," *Seattle Daily Times*, December 29, 1983.

17. Anne S. Crowley, "Dolphins . . . 'Don't Know How It Happened,'" *Baton Rouge Advocate*, January 1, 1984.

Chapter 21: "Shula Is God"

1. Mike DelNagro, "The Sons Have Also Risen," *Sports Illustrated*, September 29, 1980.

2. Larry Dorman, "Suddenly a Minor Deity: Don Shula No Longer Owns Florida," *New York Times*, December 5, 1995.

3. Richard Goldstein, "Chuck Muncie, Troubled NFL Star, Dies at 60," *New York Times*, May 14, 2013.

4. Paul Zimmerman, "A Look of Greatness," *Sports Illustrated*, October 29, 1984.

5. Author interview with Howard Schnellenberger.

6. Zimmerman, "Look of Greatness."

7. Ralph Wiley, "Sunday in the Park with Dan," *Sports Illustrated*, January 14, 1985.

8. Paul Zimmerman, "The Niners Were Never Finer," *Sports Illustrated*, January 28, 1985.

9. Blackie Sherrod, "Irish QBs May Suffer from Water," *Dallas Morning News*, January 20, 1985.

10. Ed Pope, "Fog Loomed over the Dolphins in Their Super Bowl XIX Loss to San Francisco," *Miami Herald*, January 30, 1985.

11. Author interview with Rick Volk.

12. "Walkout by Marino Irks Shula," Associated Press, July 27, 1985.

13. Rick Telander, "He Keeps Danny Off His Fanny," *Sports Illustrated*, September 30, 1985.

Chapter 22: No Need to Rush

1. Shav Glick, "Miracle of Miami: They Said Joe Robbie Could Not Do It, but His Stadium Is Proof He Could—and Did," *Los Angeles Times*, August 16, 1987.

2. Greg Cote, "Strock: Pills, Shots, Common; QB's Book Tells of Painkillers, Stimulants," *Miami Herald*, May 5, 1991.

3. Mark Ribowsky, *The Last Cowboy: A Life of Tom Landry* (New York: Liveright, 2013), p. 296.

4. *NFL Pregame Show*, aired November 12, 1988, on NBC.

5. Craig Neff, "Cocaine Connections," *Sports Illustrated*, December 12, 1988.

6. Associated Press, "Shula Ignores Duper Case," *Los Angeles Times*, December 8, 1988.

7. Craig Neff, "Scorecard: Cocaine Connections II," *Sports Illustrated*, February 6, 1989.

8. "Duper Cleared, Reinstated by Miami," *Los Angeles Times*, April 13, 1989.

9. Donna Gehrke, "Dolphins' Owner Joe Robbie Dies at 73," Knight-Ridder Newspapers, January 8, 1990.

10. Rick Reilly, "A 'Who's Who' of Who-Wases," *Sports Illustrated*, December 17, 1990.

11. Greg Cote and Gary Long, "Dorothy Shula Was the True Coach in a Family of Them," *Baltimore Sun*, February 26, 1991.

12. Author interview with Howard Schnellenberger.

13. Jerry Greene, "Shula's Wife Dies of Cancer," *Orlando Sentinel*, February 26, 1991.

14. Jill Young Miller, "Shula Misses Staunchest Fan," *Sun-Sentinel* (Fort Lauderdale, FL), July 21, 1991.

15. Zimmerman, "Sportsman of the Year."

16. "Ex-Dolphin Sammie Smith Faces Life for Cocaine Charge," *Los Angeles Times*, September 16, 1995.

17. Steven Wine, "Allegre Keeps Jets' Playoff Hopes Alive," Associated Press, December 23, 1991.

Chapter 23: Don Voyage

1. "Fast Talk and Big Money for Shula," *New York Times*, July 18, 1992.

2. Jill Young Miller, "Who Is the Woman on Don Shula's Arm?" *Sun-Sentinel* (Fort Lauderdale, FL), August 8, 1993.

3. Author interview with Howard Schnellenberger.

4. Jason Cole, "Shula Won't Say Much about Small Wedding," *Sun-Sentinel* (Fort Lauderdale, FL), October 19, 1993.

5. Barry Wilner, "Miami's Shula Gets Record," Associated Press, November 15, 1993.

6. Ed Pope, "Dolphins Leave Cowboys Numb," *Miami Herald*, November 26, 1993.

7. Zimmerman, "Sportsman of the Year."

8. "Patriots Stun Dolphins in Overtime," Associated Press, January 3, 1994.

9. Paul Zimmerman, "Father's Day," *Sports Illustrated*, October 10, 1994.

10. Ed Pope, "Shula, Chargers' Beathard Clash," *Miami Herald*, January 9, 1995.

11. Johnette Howard, "Tightly Focused for Miami Dolphin Coach Don Shula and His Quarterback Dan Marino, It May Be 1995 or Never," *Sports Illustrated*, July 17, 1995.

12. Ibid.

13. Dorman, "Suddenly a Minor Deity."

14. Michael Silver, "The Waning of Legend," *Sports Illustrated*, December 11, 1995.

15. Mike Ditka, "Shula Takes Responsibility, but Miami Players Should Take Blame," *State Register* (Springfield, IL), November 30, 1995.

16. Dorman, "Suddenly a Minor Deity."

17. George Puscas, "Xmas Wishes of All Kinds," *Detroit News*, December 25, 1995.

18. Howard, "It May Be 1995 or Never."

19. Silver, "Waning of Legend."

20. Bucky Gleason, "Dolphins' D Takes Day Off," Associated Press, July 31, 1995.

21. Bill Plaschke, "Bills Batter Dolphins' Defense," *Los Angeles Times*, January 31, 1995.

22. Ibid.

23. Steven Wine, "Misty Farewell," Associated Press, January 6, 1996.

24. Armando Salguero, "Shula Spices Farewell with Love," *Miami Herald*, January 6, 1996.

25. Ed Pope, "J.J., Dolphins to Talk Soon; Shula Seems Relieved (And No Wonder)," *Miami Herald*, January 7, 1996.

26. Patrick Danner, "Shula Becomes 'Financial Coach,'" *Miami Herald*, November 22, 2000.

27. Greg Cote, "Wayne Gets What He Wants—A Change," *Miami Herald*, January 6, 1996.

28. "Tribute to a Legend," aired January 6, 1996, on WPLG-TV, Miami.

29. David Newton, "Panthers' Polian Gave Shula Words of Advice," (Columbia, South Carolina) *The State* (Columbia, SC), January 6, 1996.

30. Marv Levy, "The Last of the Legends," *Sports Illustrated*, January 15, 1996.

31. Ed Pope, "Testament to Honor," *Miami Herald*, January 28, 1996.

32. Ed Pope, "Shula Seems Relieved."

33. Bill Plaschke, "NFL Legend Shula Quits Dolphin Job," *Los Angeles Times*, January 5, 1996.

Chapter 24: A Granite-Jawed Deity, Still

1. Peter King, "The NFL," *Sports Illustrated*, November 29, 1993.

2. Greg Cote, "Strock: Pills, Shots, Common."

3. Dave Hyde, "Unbeaten Dolphins Pay Price," *South Florida Sun-Sentinel* (Fort Lauderdale, FL), April 1, 2001.

4. "As Saban Starts New Era, Don Shula Talks of 'Lies,'" *New York Times*, January 5, 2007.

5. Gary Myers, "Don Shula: Spygate Would Mar Pats' Undefeated Season," *New York Daily News*, November 6, 2007.

6. Tom E. Curran, "Shula Will Be Remembered in New England as an Angry Old Man," NBCSports.com, May 6, 2016, https://www.nbcsports.com/boston/new-england-patriots/don-shula-will-leave-imperfect-legacy-in-new-england.

7. Barry Jackson, "Shula: Miami Dolphins Were about Class, Didn't Deflate Any Balls," *Miami Herald*, May 9, 2015, https://www.miamiherald.com/sports/nfl/miami -dolphins/article20593530.html.

8. "Marino Finds Humor in Shula-Johnson Feud," *Houston Chronicle*, July 24, 2005, https://www.chron.com/sports/texans/article/Marino-finds-humor-in-Shula -Johnson-feud-1934854.php.

9. Gus Garcia-Roberts, "Mary Anne Shula Sues for Her Dead Husband's Alimony Millions," *Miami New Times*, May 12, 2010.

10. Nat Berman, "The 20 Richest NFL Coaches of All Time," *Money Inc.*, August 2017.

11. Elizabeth Merrill, "Super Bowl XVII Starter Woodley's Life Drifted after Football," ESPN.com, January 23, 2008, http://www.espn.com/nfl/playoffs07/news/ story?id=3209245.

12. Erik Brady, "Buoniconti Paralyzed on the Field, But Not in Life," *USA Today*, September 24, 2010.

13. S. L. Price, "'I Feel Lost. I Feel Like a Child': The Complicated Decline of Nick Buoniconti," *Sports Illustrated*, May 17, 2017.

14. S. L. Price, "How Jim Kiick Fell through the Cracks," *Sports Illustrated*, May 9, 2017.

15. Bruce Feldman, "Duper Latest Ex-NFL Star to Test Positive for Signs of CTE," CBSSports.com, November 8, 2013, https://www.cbssports.com/college-football/ news/duper-latest-ex-nfl-star-to-test-positive-for-signs-of-cte/.

16. Price, "'I Feel Lost,'" and Associated Press, "Bill Stanfill, Former Georgia and Dolphins DL, Dies at Age 69," ESPN.com, November 11, 2016, http://www.espn.com/ nfl/story/_/id/18021133/bill-stanfill-former-defensive-lineman-georgia-miami -dolphins-dies-age-69.

17. Kate Nocero and Helen Kennedy, "Ex-Giants Great Sentenced for Jumping Bail to Watch Heisman-Winning Son Play," *New York Daily News*, March 22, 2010.

18. Author interview with Rick Volk.

19. Ed Pope, "Testament to Honor," *Miami Herald*, January 28, 1996.

20. Greg Cote, "Confessions, Frustrations of a Lifelong Dolphins Fan Who Grew Up to Cover the Team," *Miami Herald*, May 12, 2018.

INDEX

Adderley, Herb, 81, 167
African Americans, 27, 55, 57, 74, 142–43, 144–45
Agnew, Spiro, 96, 125
Aikman, Troy, 309, 316
Ali, Muhammad, 116–17
All-America Football Conference (AAFC), 26–27
Allen, Ermal, 57
Allen, George, 89, 93, 101, 124, 260, 265
    as Rams head coach, 89, 93, 94, 101, 124, 126, 235–36
    as Redskins head coach, 185–86, 187–92, 200, 226, 235
Alworth, Lance "Bambi," 166–67, 169
Ameche, Alan, 46, 50, 56, 64, 65, 69, 90
American Cancer Society, 304
American Football League (AFL), 58, 87–88
Anderson, Bill, 84
Anderson, Dave, 196
Anderson, Dick, 141, 150, 153, 165, 177, 181, 182, 198, 227
Anderson, Edwin, 59
Andrews, John, 217
Archdeacon, Tom, 242
Armstrong, Trace, 325, 334
Arnsparger, Bill, xiv, xvi, 57–58, 340
    as Colts assistant coach, 76, 123, 129
    as Dolphins assistant coach, 139, 141, 157–58, 175, 190, 193, 198, 201, 228, 250, 271, 279
    as Giants head coach, 204, 220, 224, 227–28
Atkins, Gene, 327
Atkinson, George, 213
Atlanta Falcons, 99, 101, 114, 125, 149, 153, 173, 328–29

Babb, Charlie, xv, 172, 182, 218
Ball, Larry, 172, 202

Baltimore, Maryland, 74, 96, 97
Baltimore Colts, xiv, 52, 53–54, 69, 105–6, 149, 151, 153, 156, 159, 160, 162, 198, 220–21, 227, 228, 233, 255–56, 268, 274, 282, 309, 310, 324
    Ewbank as head coach of, 43–52, 61, 64–65
    1958 championship of, 56
    and 1962 draft, 67–68
    in 1971 AFC title loss to Dolphins, 163–65
    Shula as player on, 37–38, 39–52
Baltimore Colts, under Shula, 65–133, 136, 162
    1963 season of, 70–72
    and 1964 draft, 80
    1964 season of, 75–79
    1965 season of, 81–82, 84–87
    1966 season of, 88–89
    and 1967 draft, 91–92
    1968 season of, 99–104
    and 1969 draft, 122–23
    1969 season of, 124–26
    and 1970 draft, 128
    in Super Bowl III, x, xx, 105–17
Baltimore Sun, 73, 84, 87, 95, 99, 121–22, 133
Bartish, Dorothy, *see* Shula, Dorothy
Bartkowski, Steve, 282
Bass, Mike, 192
Bassett, John, 205, 206, 207, 212, 219–20, 223, 265
Baughman, Howard, 10, 14–15
Baumhower, Bob, 231, 250, 252, 257, 269, 283
Beathard, Bobby, xv, 172–73, 197, 235–36, 246, 260, 273, 322, 323
Belichick, Bill, xiii, xiv, 333, 336–37, 342–43, 344
Belichick, Steve, 336
Bell, Bert, 39, 40, 48, 49, 61, 69
Bell, Bert, Jr., 126–27
Bell, Bobby, 160
Bell, Upton, 91
Benirschke, Rolf, 254

Bennett, Cornelius, 311
Bennett, Leeman, 57, 281, 284
Berry, Raymond, 44, 50, 53, 68, 74, 81, 89, 92, 98, 291, 347
Betters, Doug, 257, 269
Beverly, Randy, 113, 115
Bielski, Dick, 81
Biggs, Verlon, 106
Biletnikoff, Fred, 215
Bingaman, Les, 60
Blackledge, Todd, 266
Blackwood, Glenn, 257, 341
Blackwood, Lyle, 253, 257, 262
Blanda, George, 281
Bledsoe, Drew, 317–18, 329
Blount, Mel, 183, 199
Board, Dwaine, 287
Bokamper, Kim, 226, 250, 257–58, 262, 271, 328
Boozer, Emerson, 106, 113
Bosa, John, 297
Bowser, Charles, 255, 269
Boyd, Bobby, 45, 83, 85, 86, 102, 123, 125
Braase, Ordell, 44, 81, 113, 116, 119, 123
Bradshaw, Terry, 128, 183, 184, 198, 243, 267, 285
Brady, Tom, 343
Branch, Cliff, 214
Bratkowski, Zeke, 81, 85, 89
Braucher, Bill, 129–30, 134, 151, 152, 155, 170, 209, 213, 224, 225, 345
Brees, Drew, 282
Brettschneider, Carl, 60
Briscoe, Marlin, 175, 242
Brodie, John, 125
Brokaw, Tom, x
Brooks, Bill, 330
Brophy, Jay, 279, 283
Brown, Charlie, 260
Brown, Ed, 82–83, 84
Brown, Jim, 53, 77, 78
Brown, Larry, 185, 188, 191, 192
Brown, Mark, 283
Brown, Mike, 309, 320, 338
Brown, Paul, xii, 18–19, 23, 25–27, 41, 43, 44, 49, 66, 106, 115, 149, 155, 200, 240, 340
    coaching style of, 29–30, 34–35
    as Shula's mentor, x, xiv, 33
    tactical system of, 25–26, 30, 31, 32, 41, 46
Brown, Roger, 60, 93
Brown, Willie, 154
Brudzinski, Bob, 257
Bryant, Bear, 57, 59, 130
Buckley, Terrell, 325
Buffalo Bills, 151, 153, 177–78, 198, 212, 233, 248, 256, 270–71, 293–94, 296, 298, 303, 307, 310, 311, 317, 329–30
Bulaich, Norm, 128, 218, 219, 221, 225, 232
Bumgardner, Rex, 30
Buoniconti, Nick, xiii–xiv, xv, xvi, 134, 141, 143, 147, 150, 161, 165, 168–69, 175, 190–91, 192, 201, 202, 207, 217, 218, 224–25, 231, 340, 345
Butz, Dave, 260
Byars, Keith, 313, 316, 320, 325
Byner, Earnest, 290–91

Caffey, Lee Roy, 68
Campanella, Joe, 90–91
Campbell, Earl, 239
Canadian Football League, 212
Carlton, Darryl, 228–29
Carolina Panthers, xx, 347
Carroll, John, Archbishop, 16
Carson, Bud, 183
Casey, Bernie, 93
Cefalo, Jimmy, 261, 283, 334
Chambers, Rusty, 227, 250
Chandler, Don, 85, 86, 89, 162
Chandler, Wes, 252
Charles, Mike, 269
Chestnut, Louis, 98
Chicago Bears, 42, 50, 71, 73, 76, 82, 92, 102, 180, 216, 290, 297
Chicago Cardinals, 58–59
Cincinnati Bengals, xx, 106, 149, 155, 200, 254, 274, 309, 319–20, 326
Clark, Dwight, 285, 325
Clark, Gary, 325
Clark, Monte, 140, 148, 227
Clayborn, Ray, 291
Clayton, Mark, 269–71, 279, 280, 281, 283–84, 290, 296, 300, 303, 307, 311
Cleveland Browns, xiv, 19, 27, 70, 77–78, 99–100, 102, 103–4, 105–6, 151, 162, 198, 224, 227, 243, 290–91, 313, 336
    Shula as player on, 29–37
Cleveland Plain Dealer, 19–20, 21, 23, 29, 31, 32, 33–34, 62
Cobbledick, Bill, 29
Cobbledick, Gordon, 62
Cogdill, Gail, 63
Cole, Terry, 102
Coleman, Marco, 311, 322
Collier, Blanton, 57, 58, 59, 67, 70, 77–78, 103–4, 140, 142, 151, 182, 340
Collins, Gary, 77, 78
Collins, Tony, 291
Colzie, Neal, 243
Commings, Bob, 57
Connor, Chuck, 250
Cooke, Jack Kent, 260
Cooper, Earl, 285
Coryell, Don, 249, 252–54, 260, 281
Cosell, Howard, 198, 206–7, 220, 249
Costello, Vince, 204, 220, 227
Cote, Greg, 333, 347
Cowher, Bill, 244, 309, 317
Cox, Bryan, 315, 321, 327, 328–29
Craig, Roger, 285
Craver, Aaron, 310
Croghan, Joe, 139
Cross, Jeff, 302, 330
Crowder, Randy, 210, 218, 229, 230, 299
Csonka, Larry, xii, xii, xviii, 10, 141, 143, 145, 155–56, 165, 223, 224, 232, 346
    defection to WFL, 205–6, 210, 211–12, 216, 219–20
    Dolphins' re-signing of, 241
    dual memoir by Kiick and, 174, 196
    as Giants player, 228, 240–41
    1970 season of, 150–51, 153–54

in 1971 contract dispute, 158–59
1971 season of, 160, 161, 164
1972 season of, 175–76, 178, 180, 181, 184
1973 season of, 199, 200
1974 season of, 212, 213, 216
retirement of, 247
Shula's relationship with, xv, 146, 147, 159,
     174, 206, 241–42
in Super Bowl VI, 168–70
in Super Bowl VII, 189, 191
in Super Bowl VIII, 201–2
CTE (traumatic encephalopathy), 345–46
Cuozzo, Gary, 76, 82, 89, 91
Curry, Bill, 91, 99, 109, 126
Curtis, Mike, 80, 97, 98, 102, 105, 123, 164

Dale, Carroll, 85
Dallas Cowboys, xii, 87, 90, 94, 126, 156, 198,
     233, 240, 260, 261, 282, 298, 300, 309–10,
     311, 316–17
in Super Bowl VI, 166–70
Darden, Colgate, 55
Davidson, Cotton, 44
Davidson, Gary, 204
Davis, Al, 47–48, 58, 62, 66, 88, 123–24, 131, 137,
     153–54, 195–96, 207–8, 218, 233, 235, 270,
     282, 340
Davis, Clarence, 215
Davis, Gary, 227, 232, 239, 242
Davis, Willie, 89
Dawson, Len, 160, 175
DeBartolo, Ed, Jr., 237
DeBerg, Steve, 314–15, 316, 317
Del Gaizo, Jim, 173, 177
Dellenbach, Jeff, 297, 302, 316
DeMarco, Bob, 161
Democratic Convention of 1968, 97
Demoff, Marvin, 268, 289, 294
Den Herder, Vern, 157, 192, 215, 217, 243, 247
Dennis, Mark, 302
Denver Broncos, 159, 221, 233, 268, 339
Detroit Lions, 58–59, 82, 98
Shula as assistant coach of, 59–61, 63–64
Detwiler, Jim, 91
Dickerson, Eric, 274
Ditka, Mike, 167, 169, 290, 327–28
Doll, Don, 227
Domres, Marty, 178, 198
Donovan, Art, xvii, 40, 41, 42, 44, 45, 46, 47,
     49, 60, 66, 68, 119
Doornink, Dan, 275
Dorman, Larry, 257, 278
Duhe, A. J., 231, 250, 259, 283
Duncan, Jim, 125
Duncan, Walter, 265, 271
Duper, Mark, 255, 299, 303, 311, 339, 346
allegations of drug use by, 299–300
1983 season of, 270, 271, 274, 275
1984 season of, 279, 280, 283, 284
Dutton, John, 221

Eason, Tony, 266, 291, 292
East, Ron, 176
Edmunds, Ferrell, 297, 307
Edwards, Glen, 184

Ehrmann, Joe, 221
Eisele, Herb, 14–15, 17, 18–19, 20, 21, 22, 23
Elliott, John, 106
Elway, John, 266, 268, 274, 289, 302
Emtman, Steve, 325
Erhardt, Ron, 243
Esiason, Boomer, 309
Evans, Luther, 134
Evans, Norm, 176, 224
Ewbank, Wilbur "Weeb," 98, 136, 340
     as Colts head coach, 43–52, 61, 64–65
     as Jets head coach, 105–7, 110–15, 151, 158

Fairbanks, Chuck, 198, 233, 239, 246, 265
Fears, Tom, 32, 35, 49, 91
Ferguson, Joe, 233, 271
Fernandez, Manny, 144, 150, 175, 190–91, 201,
     215, 227
Fischer, Pat, 190
Fleming, Marv, 143, 144, 157, 161, 173
Floyd, Ray, 334, 344
Foley, Tim, 157, 191, 201, 206, 214, 216
Ford, Gerald, 211
Ford, William Clay, 59
Foreman, Chuck, 200
Foster, Roy, 255, 279, 303
Fouts, Dan, 249, 252, 253–54, 258, 281–82, 329
Francis, Russ, 285
Franklin, Andra, 252, 253, 279
free agency, 135, 210, 223, 296, 313
Fryar, Irving, 292, 313, 321, 326, 329

Gabriel, Roman, 83, 93, 94, 124
Galbreath, Harry, 297, 302
Garrett, Mike, 177
Garrison, Walt, 168
Gase, Adam, 348
Gastineau, Mark, 258
Gaubatz, Dennis, 81, 85, 113
Gent, Pete, 178
George, Bill, 60
Gibbs, Joe, 236, 260–63, 279
Giesler, Jon, 248
Gilliam, Joe, 198, 230
Gilliam, John, 200
Gillman, Sid, 58, 62, 106
Glass, Bill, 60
Glick, Allen, 195–96, 235
Goode, Tom, 141
Gordon, David, 131, 132
Gordon, Larry, 226, 269
Gowdy, Curt, 114
Graham, Otto, 27, 31, 33, 35, 49, 52
Grand River, Ohio, 2–3
Grant, Bob, 124
Grant, Bud, 200, 201
Great Depression, 6, 7
Greatest Generation, x–xi, 96
Green, Eric, 325, 327, 347
Green, Ernie, 224
Green, Hugh, 290, 300
Green Bay Packers, 61, 71, 73, 76, 81–89, 93,
     100, 125, 149, 160, 307
Greene, "Mean" Joe, 183, 184, 211, 244, 306
Greenwood, L. C., 183

Gregg, Forrest, 86
Griese, Bob, xii, xiv, xv, 134, 141, 146, 148–49,
    178, 196, 212, 216, 232, 233, 242, 246, 247,
    269, 274, 281, 305
    1970 season of, 149, 150–51, 152, 153, 154
    in 1971 contract dispute, 159, 161
    1971 season of, 159, 160, 164–65
    1972 season of, 175–77, 180, 182, 184
    1973 season of, 197, 198, 200
    1975 season of, 217–18, 220
    1976 season of, 227, 228
    1978 season of, 238, 239
    1979 season of, 243, 244
    1980 season of, 248, 250
    in Super Bowl VI, 168, 169
    in Super Bowl VII, 186, 190, 191–92, 194
    in Super Bowl VIII, 201–2
Griggs, David, 302
Grogan, Steve, 303

Hadl, John, 62, 177
Halas, George, xi, xii, xiii, 41, 42, 76, 78, 101,
    102, 180, 240, 281, 314
Ham, Jack, 183
Hampton, Lorenzo, 290
Hannah, John, 212
Hanratty, Terry, 184
Hansen, Phil, 311
Hardy, Bruce, 243, 253, 297
Harper, Bruce, 259
Harris, Duriel, 227, 243, 253, 262, 270
Harris, Franco, 183, 243
Harris, Leroy, 231–32, 242
Harris, Wendell, 81–82
Hart, Harold, 218
Hauss, Lenny, 190
Hawkins, Alex, 69–70, 116
Hayes, Bob, 166–67
Hayes, Woody, 82
Heaton, Charles, 19–20, 21, 22–23, 122
Hector, Johnny, 308
Hendricks, Ted, 122–23, 124, 218
Henning, Dan, 238
Herman, Dave, 106
Heyward, Ironhead, 328–29
Higgs, Mark, 307, 308, 310, 325
Hill, Calvin, 167, 168, 169
Hill, Jerry, 70, 71, 83, 85, 103
Hill, Randal, 325
Hill, Winston, 106
Hilton, Roy, 81
Hinton, Eddie, 152
Holmes, Ernie, 229–30
Hornung, Paul, 68–69, 81, 82, 85, 86
Houston Oilers, 150, 176, 232, 239, 289
Howard, Johnette, 324, 325
Howley, Chuck, 169
Huff, Sam, 60
Huizenga, Wayne, 301, 312, 313, 325, 326, 327,
    330, 331, 347
    contract extensions given to Shula by, 309–
    10, 318–19
    death of, 345
    Johnson hired by, 335
    Johnson secretly approached by, 319, 324
    Shula's retirement and, 331–34

Hulmes, Harry, 91
Humphrey, Bobby, 310
Humphries, Stan, 317, 322–23
Hunt, Lamar, 88, 217

Ingram, Mark, 313, 317, 321, 325, 346
Irsay, Robert, 172, 198, 237
Ivy, Pop, 58, 59

Jackson, Keith, 313, 317, 325
Jacksonville Jaguars, 339
Jacoby, Joe, 260, 262
James, Craig, 291
James, Tommy, 33, 34, 36
Jaworski, Ron, 297
Jefferson, John, 252
Jefferson, Roy, 185
Jenkins, Al, 192
Jenkins, Dan, 214, 232
Jensen, Jim, 269, 279
Jeter, Bob, 89
John Carroll University, 1, 347–48
    Shula as student at, xviii, 16–24, 340
Johnson, Curtis, 141, 157, 165
Johnson, Dan, 275, 286, 291
Johnson, Gary, 287
Johnson, Jimmy, 298, 299, 300, 309–10, 317,
    318–19, 324, 335, 344
    as Dolphins head coach, 335, 339, 343
    as possible successor to Shula, 319, 324–25,
    326, 327, 331
Joiner, Charlie, 252, 281
Jones, Bert, 221
Jones, Deacon, 93, 176–77
Jones, Dub, 30, 33, 35, 36
Jones, Eddie, 302, 306, 335
Jones, Jerry, 298, 300, 309–10, 316, 318–19, 324, 336
Jones, June, 328
Josephson, Les, 93
Joyce, Don, 44, 45, 49
Judson, William, 269
Jurgensen, Sonny, 54

Kansas City Chiefs, 90, 105, 127, 160–62, 173,
    175, 217, 227, 270, 301, 321, 329
Kapp, "Indian Joe," 124
Karras, Alex, 60, 68–69, 144, 192
Keane, Tom, 42, 140, 227
Keating, Ed, 158, 205, 206, 220, 223–24, 247
Kellett, Don, 40, 43, 67, 80, 90
Kelly, Jim, 266, 268, 274, 289, 293–94, 296, 302,
    303–4, 307, 310, 311, 330
Kelly, Leroy, 103, 182
Kennedy, John F., 63, 72–73
Kennedy, Robert, 96
Kensil, Jim, 258, 259, 267
Kentucky, University of, Shula as assistant
    coach at, 57–58
Kern, Rex, 164–65
Kidd, John, 323
Kiick, Jim, xii, xviii, 141, 143, 145, 155–56, 160,
    164, 188, 223, 224, 241, 242
    defection to WFL, 205–6, 210, 211–12, 216,
    219–20
    dementia of, 345–46
    dual memoir by Csonka and, 174, 196

Morris's rivalry with, 153, 173–74, 190
1970 season of, 149, 150–51, 152, 154
in 1971 contract dispute, 158–59
1972 season of, 176, 178, 181, 182, 185
Shula's relationship with, xv, 146, 147, 159, 174–75
  in Super Bowl VI, 169, 170
  in Super Bowl VII, 191
  in Super Bowl VIII, 201
Kilmer, Billy, 185, 189, 190, 191, 192
King, Martin Luther, Jr., 96
King, Peter, 338
Kirby, Terry, 320
Klosterman, Don, 127–28, 134, 135
Knox, Chuck, 57, 204, 275, 330
Kolen, Mike, 150, 218, 227
Korean War, 29, 36, 37
Kosar, Bernie, 289, 290, 314, 320, 326, 329
Kram, Mark, 138–39
Kramer, Jerry, 85
Krause, Moose, 246
Krieg, David, 275
Kropac, Roy, 15
Kuechenberg, Bob, 192, 201, 206, 207, 247, 255, 279, 306
Kuechenberg, Rudy, 206
Kuharich, Joe, 53, 54

Laakso, Eric, 248
Lambeau, Curly, xii
Lambert, Jack, 211
Lamonica, Daryle, 151, 154, 207, 210
Landry, Tom, xi, xii, 46, 50, 74, 78, 87, 90, 94, 143, 156, 166–67, 168, 171, 185, 229, 233–34, 237, 240, 244, 245, 255, 298, 300
Lane, Dick "Night Train," 59–60, 61, 62, 63–64
Langer, Jim, xvi, 228
Lanier, Willie, 160
Lankford, Paul, 255
Lary, Yale, 60
Lauterbur, Frank, 54–55
Layne, Bobby, 36–37, 49, 59, 60
LeBaron, Eddie, 53
Le Batard, Dan, 325
LeBeau, Dick, 60
Lee, Shawn, 302–3
Lennon, John, murder of, 249
Lett, Leon, 316
Levy, Marv, 311, 329, 330, 334–35
Lilly, Bob, 167, 168
Lipsyte, Robert, 116
Little, Larry, 143, 148, 160, 184, 207, 212, 217–18, 233, 242, 247
Lofton, James, 315
Logan, Jerry, 68, 85, 94
Lomax, Neil, 282
Lombardi, Vince, xi, xiii, 50, 60, 61, 63, 77, 79, 82, 84–87, 95, 111, 117, 122, 131, 166, 203, 240
  death of, 132, 149
  Shula's rivalry with, 80, 84–85, 86, 87, 88, 89–90, 93, 94, 132
Lorick, Tony, 75
Los Angeles Chargers, see San Diego Chargers
Los Angeles Raiders, 270, 274, 282, 310
  see also Oakland Raiders
Los Angeles Rams, 32, 33, 35, 45, 46, 47, 72–73,

82–83, 89, 92, 93–94, 100, 101, 124, 126, 156, 185, 226, 235–36, 240, 244, 249
Lundy, Bob, 341
Lyles, Lenny, 81, 104
Lynch, Jim, 160

Mack, Kevin, 290
Mackey, Clarence, 10–12, 14
Mackey, John, 68, 69, 71, 74, 76, 81, 83, 92, 97, 98, 101, 102, 103, 111, 124, 125, 143
  as players' union head, 135, 141–42, 148, 210, 211, 219, 220, 223
  see also Rozelle Rule lawsuit
Madden, John, 197, 214, 215
Magee, Jerry, 272–73
Maisel, Bob, 84, 87, 95, 111, 134
Malone, Benny, 210, 211, 212, 214, 220, 228, 284
Mandich, Jim, 157, 173, 176, 191, 197, 205, 206, 213
Mann, Bonnie, 1–2, 338
Manning, Archie, 158, 278
Manning, Eli, 278
Manning, Peyton, 278, 281, 282
Mara, Wellington, 246
Marchetti, Gino, 41, 45, 64–65, 66, 67, 71, 72, 75, 78, 80–81, 90, 91, 140
Marchibroda, Ted, 220–21
Marino, Dan, xiv–xv, 278–79, 294, 340
  Dolphins' drafting of, 267–68
  Hall of Fame induction of, 343
  1983 season of, 268–69, 270–71, 273–76
  1984 season of, 279–80, 281–82
  in 1985 contract dispute, 289
  1985 season of, 289–92, 298
  1986 season of, 294–95
  1987 season of, 296–97
  1989 season of, 300
  1990 season of, 302–3
  1991 season of, 307–8
  1992 season of, 310–11
  1993 season-ending injury of, 313–14
  1994 season of, 320–23
  1995 season of, 326, 328–30
  personality of, 266–67
  post-Shula career of, 339, 343
  records held by, 281, 282, 289
  Shula's overreliance on, 288
  on Shula's retirement, 334
  in Super Bowl XIX, 286–87
Marshall, George Preston, 53
Martin, Don, 11–12
Martin, Tony, 303, 311, 313
Matheson, Bob, 103, 157, 191, 213, 217, 218, 277
Mathis, Bill, 113
Matte, Tom, 70, 71, 82, 83, 84, 85, 87, 89, 97, 98, 102, 103, 104, 105, 113, 114, 125, 147, 159
Maule, Tex, 104, 111, 116, 167, 169, 187, 188, 194, 201, 202
Maxwell, Tommy, 123, 124
Maynard, Don, 106, 110–11, 113
McBride, Arthur "Mickey," 27, 31, 35
McCafferty, Don, 67, 68, 76, 137, 151–52, 156, 165, 178
McCauley, Don, 157, 164
McCord, Darris, 60
McCormack, Mike, 39

McDermott, Barry, 275
McDuffie, O. J., 317, 329
McGee, Buford, 282
McGee, Max, 81–82, 89
McLean, Scooter, 60
McNeal, Don, 248, 262, 269
McNeil, Freeman, 258
McPeak, Bill, 197, 227
McVay, John, 205, 224, 228, 241
Means, Natrone, 322
Memphis Southmen (Grizzlies), 212, 216, 219–20
Meyer, Ron, 327
Miami Dolphins, 348
    Johnson as head coach of, 335, 339, 343
    Shula hired as head coach by, x, 129–33
    Shula's post-retirement role with, 332, 335
Miami Dolphins, under Shula:
    black players on, 142–43, 144–45
    drug use by, xvii, 178–79, 199, 229–31, 255, 299, 341
    "53 defense" of, 157–58, 175
    miserly salaries of, 171–72
    1970 season of, 149–54
    and 1971 draft, 157
    1971 season of, 159–62, 163–65
    and 1972 draft, 172–73
    1972 season of, x, xiii, xv, 175–85
    1973 season of, 197–200
    and 1974 draft, 210
    1974 season of, 212–16
    1975 season of, 217–19, 220–21
    and 1976 draft, 226–27
    1976 season of, 227–28
    and 1977 draft, 231
    1977 season of, 232
    1978 season of, 238–39
    1979 season of, 242–43
    1980 season of, 248, 249
    1981 season of, 250–54
    and 1982 draft, 255
    1982 season of, 255–56, 258–60
    and 1983 draft, 265–66, 267–68
    1983 season of, 268–71, 273–76
    1984 season of, 279–80, 281–84
    1985 season of, 289–92
    1986 season of, 294–95
    1987 season of, 296–97
    1988 season of, 297–98
    1989 season of, 300, 301
    1990 season of, 302–3
    1991 season of, 306–7
    1992 season of, 310–11
    1993 season of, 313–14
    1994 season of, 319–24
    1995 season of, 326–30
    in Super Bowl VI, 165–70
    in Super Bowl VII, 185–86, 187–95
    in Super Bowl VIII, 200–203
    in Super Bowl XVII, 260–63
    in Super Bowl XIX, 286–87
    Team of the Decade award of, 245
Miami Herald, 133–34, 170, 176, 194, 202, 207, 219, 229, 230, 267, 315, 325, 326, 330, 331, 333
Michaels, Lou, 80–81, 83, 86, 109, 113
Michaels, Walt, 258, 259

Miller, Fred, 81, 113, 164
Minnesota Vikings, 73, 76, 81, 92, 102, 124, 127, 139, 176, 200–201, 228, 256
Mira, George, 159, 173
Mitchell, Lydell, 221
Mitchell, Scott, 313, 317
Mitchell, Tom, 102, 113, 124, 152
Modell, Art, 66, 336
Molesworth, Keith, 41, 43
Monk, Art, 260
Monroe, Carl, 286
Montana, Joe, 273, 280, 282, 285, 286–87, 289, 294
Moon, Warren, 329
Moore, Lenny, 50, 69, 71, 72, 73, 74, 77, 81, 83, 85, 88, 92, 97
Moore, Nat, 210, 211, 214, 232, 233, 238, 249, 270, 282, 290, 299, 347
Moore, Wayne, 217–18
Mora, Jim, 265
Moran, Jim, 19, 20, 21
Morin, Milt, 103
Mormile, Dan "Zip," 19
Morrall, Earl, xv, 59, 98–99, 108, 121, 123, 125, 152, 173–74, 186, 190, 192, 221, 231, 340, 345
    1968 season of, 99–104
    1972 season of, 177, 181, 182–83, 184
    in Super Bowl III, 109, 111, 113, 114–15, 116, 120
Morris, Eugene "Mercury," 141, 142–43, 145, 146–47, 149, 160, 199, 242, 255
    in conflicts with Shula and Dolphins management, 212–13, 214, 216, 220, 221, 225, 226
    drug use and trafficking by, xviii, 179, 199, 229, 231
    Kiick's rivalry with, 153, 173–74, 190
    misdiagnosed neck injury of, 199
    new contract of, 206
    1970 season of, 152, 153, 154
    1972 season of, 175, 178, 180–81, 182, 184
    1974 season of, 212–13
    1975 season of, 218, 220, 221
    in Super Bowl VI, 169
    in Super Bowl VII, 191
    in Super Bowl VIII, 201
    in trade to Chargers, 226
Mortensen, Chris, 331
Moseley, Mark, 260
Motley, Marion, 26, 27, 30, 33, 35, 36
Mullins, Gerry, 184
Mumphord, Lloyd, xvii–xviii, 141, 191, 214, 221, 230–31
Muncie, Chuck, 252
Murphy, Russ, 41
Murray, Jim, 187
Mustafa, Najee, 313
Mutscheller, Jim, 51

Namath, Joe, x, 59, 97, 98, 105–17, 118, 151, 176, 258, 261, 266, 284, 348
Nash, Ogden, 114
Nathan, Tony, 249, 252, 253, 286, 290, 291, 292, 335
National Football League (NFL):
    AFL merger with, 87–88

drug use in, 178–79, 199, 229–31, 255, 299, 341
merger of AAFC and, 27
1974 player strike in, 210, 211
1982 player strike in, 255–56
1987 player strike in, 296
Neely, Ralph, 81
Nelsen, Bill, 103
Nelson, Steve, 291
New England (Boston) Patriots, xiv, 150, 153,
    159, 160, 197, 212, 218, 221, 228, 232–33,
    238–39, 243, 248, 249, 256–57, 270, 280,
    281–82, 291–92, 297, 303, 310, 316, 317,
    342–43
New Jersey Generals, ix, 265, 271
Newman, Ed, 244, 255, 280, 281, 283
New Orleans Saints, 91, 92, 125, 153, 248, 270
Newsome, Ozzie, 290
Newton, Cam, xx, 347
New York Giants, xiv, xx, 33, 71, 98, 180, 204,
    220, 224, 240, 295, 317
New York Jets, 65–66, 151, 153, 158, 159, 176, 178,
    197, 212, 227, 255, 257, 258–59, 271, 282,
    295, 298, 307–8, 310, 314, 321
    in Super Bowl III, x, xx, 105–17
NFL-AFL Championship Game:
    of 1966 (Super Bowl I), 88, 90
    of 1968 (Super Bowl II), 94
Ninowski, Jim, 61
Nixon, Richard, xi, 96, 110, 168, 189, 194, 211
Nolan, Dick, 149, 153
Noll, Chuck, xii, xiii, xiv, 92, 123, 149, 183, 198,
    211, 213, 222, 229–30, 239–40, 244, 267,
    278, 284, 340
Noonan, Karl, 149, 155
North, John, 57
North Dallas Forty (Gent), 178
Notre Dame University, 246
Nottingham, Don, 164, 165, 211, 212, 218, 219,
    225, 232
Nussbaumer, Bob, 59
Nutter, Buzz, 86

Oakland Raiders, 66, 88, 94, 105, 106, 151, 156,
    183, 197, 200, 213–16, 218, 228, 233, 238,
    243, 259
    see also Los Angeles Raiders
Oberst, Gene, 17, 19, 21
O'Brien, Ken, 267–68, 307–8, 315
Odom, Cliff, 303
Offerdahl, John, 297, 300
Ohio State University, 26
Olivadotti, Tom, 297, 327, 329
Oliver, Louis, 302, 330
Olsen, Merlin, 93
Orr, Jimmy, 66, 68, 73, 81, 92, 98, 103, 111, 114,
    115, 116, 124
Overstreet, David, 269
Owen, Steve, 33

Page, Alan, 202
Paige, Tony, 303
Painesville, Ohio, 2, 8, 42, 74
Parcells, Bill, 295
Pardee, Jack, 93, 185, 206, 216, 236
Parker, Buddy, 36
Parker, Jim, 66, 88

Parmalee, Bernie, 320, 322, 328
Parseghian, Ara, 26, 246
Pastorini, Dan, 239
Pederson, Doug, 315–16, 343
Pellington, Bill, 41, 45, 47, 49, 60, 64, 80, 81
Perkins, Ray, 98
Peters, Tony, 260, 261
Philadelphia Eagles, 70, 90, 125, 152, 303,
    314–15
Philbin, Gerry, 106
Philbin, Joe, 348
Phipps, Mike, 182
Pittsburgh Steelers, xii, 105–6, 123, 149, 183–85,
    198, 199, 211, 215, 221, 227, 228, 244, 249,
    283–84, 317
Plaschke, Bill, 330–31
Plum, Milt, 63
Podolak, Ed, 161
Polian, Bill, 334
Pope, Edwin, xviii, 130, 134, 154, 170, 181, 188,
    194, 200, 203, 205, 215, 216, 225, 244, 248,
    254, 263, 267, 287–88, 316–17, 325, 333, 336,
    345, 347
Povich, Shirley, 110
Puscas, George, 328

racism, 55, 57, 74, 142–43, 144–45
Randle, Sonny, 55–56
Reagan, Ronald, 263, 264
Reed, Oscar, 202
Reese, Don, 210, 218, 229, 230–31, 255, 299
Reilly, Rick, 302
Reynolds, Hacksaw, 285
Richardson, John, 150
Richardson, Willie, 68, 92, 98, 100, 103, 111,
    113, 149
Riggins, John, 260, 261–63, 279
Riley, Jim, 150
Riley, Pat, 326–27
Robbie, Joe, xiv, xvii, 153, 156, 157, 158, 171–72,
    193, 223, 224, 264, 268, 273, 274, 289, 290
    Dolphins coaching job offered to Shula by,
        130–32
    Dolphins drug scandal and, 230
    illness and death of, 300–301
    penuriousness of, 172, 208, 235–36
    personality of, 138–39
    personal tragedies and alcoholism of, 172
    Shula's relationship with, xviii, 208–9, 236–
        37, 238, 245–46, 248
    tax problems of, 236, 245
    WFL defections and, 206–7, 219, 220
Robbie, Mike, 238, 250, 301, 306
Roberson, Vern, 231, 237
Robinson, Dave, 89
Robinson, Jackie, 27
Robiskie, Terry, 249
Roby, Reggie, 288
Rooney, Art, 82–83, 183, 268
Rose, Joe, 253, 270
Rosenbloom, Carroll, xiv, 39, 40, 43, 48, 64–65,
    66, 67, 72, 82, 87, 89, 90, 91, 105, 126, 133,
    152, 156–57
    in Colts-Rams swap, 172
    death of, 240
    gambling by, 68–69, 119

Rosenbloom, Carroll (*continued*)
  and Shula's move to Dolphins, 132, 135–36
  Shula's relationship with, xviii, 78, 111–12,
    118–19, 123, 125, 127, 128–29, 135, 136, 189,
    195
Rosenbloom, Steve, 127–28, 131, 132, 133, 134, 156
Ross, Bobby, 322, 323
Ross, Steven, 347
Rozelle, Pete, 68–69, 72, 136, 185, 188, 189, 193,
    207, 216, 223, 257, 265, 340
Rozelle Rule lawsuit, 135, 211, 219, 220, 223
Rubin, Bob, 230
Russell, Andy, 183
Rust, Rod, 280, 291–92
Ryan, Frank, 77–78
Rypien, Mark, 329

Saban, Lou, 106
Saban, Nick, 342
Sahadi, Lou, 196
St. Louis Rams, 329
Salguero, Armando, 331, 332, 333
Salter, Bryant, 226
Sample, Johnny, 113
Sanders, Deion, 325
San Diego Chargers, 62, 176, 177, 212, 225–26,
    249, 252, 257–58, 281, 307, 310, 317, 321–23
Sandusky, Alex, 44
Sandusky, John, 67, 178, 227
San Francisco 49ers, 71, 83, 84, 99, 125, 149,
    166, 197, 237, 249, 254, 273, 280, 285, 294
Sauer, George, Jr., 110–11, 113, 115
Scarry, Mike, 140
Schmidt, Joe, 60, 64
Schnellenberger, Howard, 59, 64, 146, 179, 185,
    224, 280, 293, 298, 340
  as Colts head coach, 197, 198
  as Dolphins assistant coach, xiv, 140, 148,
    149, 177, 186, 194, 198, 220, 227
  as Miami University head coach, 238
  on Shula, 57–58, 122, 224, 304, 312–13, 333–34
Schramm, Tex, 88, 298, 340
Schupska, Charlie, 12, 13
Scott, Jake, 141, 142, 150, 153, 160, 184, 189, 190,
    191, 202, 217–18, 225–26
Scott, Ronald B., 209–10
Seattle Seahawks, 224, 275, 283
Seay, Mark, 323
Seifert, George, 285
Seiple, Larry, 152, 184
Shaw, Dennis, 128
Shaw, George, 46–47, 49, 50, 51
Shell, Art, 200
Sherman, Rod, 154
Shinnick, Don, 81, 84–85, 134–35
Shula, Anne, 74
Shula, Chris, xviii, 347–48
Shula, Dan (father), 2, 3–5, 6–7, 14, 23, 97, 203,
    340
  death of, 256
  factory job of, 8–9, 10
  marriage of Mary and, *see* Shula, Mary Miller
  in trip to Hungary, 217
Shula, Dan (grandson), 347
Shula, David, xvi, xix, 57, 162, 189, 237, 299,
    304, 314, 339

  coaching career of, xx, 277, 295, 299, 309,
    319–20, 326, 338, 348
Shula, Donald:
  Achilles tendon injury of, 321
  author's interviews with, 237–38, 348–49
  black players' negative views of, 143
  as Browns player, 28–37
  business ventures of, 310, 312, 338, 343, 349
  and Campanella's death, 90–91
  Catholicism of, xiv, xvi, 7
  character of, xv, xvii
  charities of, 343
  childhood of, 6–9
  coaching style of, 64, 68, 70, 73, 146, 147
  Coach of the Year awards of, 78, 102, 181
  college career of, 15, 16–24
  as Colts head coach, *see* Baltimore Colts,
    under Shula
  as Colts player, 40–52
  death threats received by, 209
  as Dolphins coach, *see* Miami Dolphins
  Dolphins coaching offer to, 129–32
  as Dolphins part owner, 132
  and Dorothy's death, 305–6
  emotional intensity of, xix
  and father's fishing business, 8
  favoritism shown by, xvii–xviii, 97
  as first generation American, xi
  Hall of Fame induction of, 339–40
  high school career of, 11–14
  as Kentucky assistant coach, 57–58
  lifetime wins of, xii
  as Lions assistant coach, 59–61, 63–64
  marriages of, *see* Shula, Dorothy; Shula,
    Mary Anne
  Miami TV show of, 139
  million-dollar contract of, 274
  motivational books by, xx
  Namath's award presented by, 348
  national guard service of, 29, 31, 35–36
  net worth of, ix, 344
  as 1970s Coach of the Decade, xiii
  1973 contract extension of, 208
  in 1980 contract negotiations, 245, 248
  1986 contract extension of, 295
  1992 contract extension of, 310
  1993 contract extension of, 318
  as 1993 Sportsman of the Year, 318
  Notre Dame job considered by, 246
  parents' ban on playing football defied by,
    10–11
  Paul Brown system adopted by, 55, 57
  players' open challenges to, 327–28
  political conservatism of, 97, 110
  post-career life of, 340–41, 342–49
  priesthood considered by, 9, 15, 17–18
  racial discrimination opposed by, 74–75,
    144–45
  as Redskins player, 52, 53–54
  in retirement as Dolphins coach, 331–34
  in sale of Dolphins stock to Robbie, 245–46
  sleep apnea of, 346
  tactical system of, 145
  total games coached by, xiii
  in trade to Colts, 37–38, 39–40
  in trip to Afghanistan, 349

in trip to Hungary, 217
as Virginia assistant coach, 54–56
and WFL defections, 205, 208
Shula, Donna, 59, 306, 320
Shula, Dorothy, 42, 55, 56, 90, 118, 122, 132, 139, 196–97, 208, 209, 217, 238, 242
cancer battle of, 278, 304
death of, xix, 304–5
Don's courtship of, 42–43, 54
in humanizing of Don's coaching demeanor, 73–74
pregnancies of, 57, 59, 67, 68, 74
and Super Bowl III loss, 121
at Super Bowl VII, 193, 195
at Super Bowl VIII, 203
in trip to Hungary, 217
wedding of Don and, 55
Shula, James, 7
Shula, Jane, 7
Shula, Jeanette, 7, 8–9
Shula, Joe, 5, 8, 10
Shula, Mary Anne, xix, 312–14, 325, 327, 329, 332, 334, 340, 341, 344, 346, 349
Shula, Mary Miller, 3–5, 6–7, 9, 14, 23, 203, 256, 217, 293, 340
Shula, Mike, xvi, xix–xx, 277–78, 295, 336,342
coaching career of, xix–xx, 305, 309, 314, 347
Shula, Sharon, 68
Siemon, Jeff, 201
Sievers, Eric, 282
Simmons, Chet, 265
Simms, Phil, 282, 295
Simpson, O. J., 177, 212, 220, 237
Sims, Keith, 302, 315, 321
Skorich, Nick, 182
Small, Gerald, 243
Smith, Billy Ray, 66, 81, 83, 85, 116
Smith, Bruce, 311
Smith, Bubba, 91, 103, 143, 149, 165
Smith, Charlie, 214
Smith, Jerry, 191
Smith, Sammie, 298, 303, 307
Snead, Norm, 180
Snell, Matt, 106, 113, 115
Snow, Jack, 93, 94
Snyder, Cameron, 84, 99, 102, 125–26, 151–52
Sochia, Brian, 297
Solomon, Freddie, 218, 219, 237, 285
Southall, Terry, 91
Sports Illustrated, xix, 61, 88, 89, 104, 138–39, 166, 174, 194, 196, 214, 218, 230, 232, 242, 253, 254, 255, 258, 275, 279, 281, 284, 285–86, 299, 302, 318, 324, 327, 334
Spurrier, Steve, 91
Stabler, Ken "Snake," 200, 208, 210, 213, 214–15, 218, 345
Stallworth, John, 211, 243, 284
Stanfill, Bill, 141, 150, 177, 178, 181, 192, 346
Starr, Bart, 61, 76, 81, 82, 84–85, 89, 100
Staubach, Roger, 166–67, 169
Steadman, John, 43, 46, 65, 86
Stenerud, Jan, 161
Stephens, Mary Anne, see Shula, Mary Anne
Stephenson, Dwight, 283, 290, 297, 340
Stevens, Gary, 298, 335
Stewart, Mike, 327

Stofa, John, 150, 159
Stonebreaker, Steve, 81
Stowe, Otto, 157
Stoyanovich, Pete, 315, 316, 317, 323
Stradford, Troy, 296–97
Stram, Hank, 106, 160, 161, 201, 217
Strock, Don, 197, 205, 220, 231, 238, 239, 246, 248, 252, 253–54, 256, 262, 269, 274, 278–79, 289, 297, 341
Stuckey, Henry, 214
Studley, Chuck, 279
Stukes, Charlie, 124
Sule, Denes, see Shula, Dan (father)
Sule, Frank, 2–3, 5, 6
Sule, Paul, 2
Sule, Rosa, 2, 5, 6
Sullivan, Dan, 72, 109
Super Bowl, 222, 228, 233, 240, 244, 254, 288–89, 304, 311, 324, 343
Super Bowl III, x, xx, 105–20, 258
Super Bowl IV, 201
Super Bowl VI, x, xiii, 165–70
Super Bowl VII, 185–86, 187–95
Super Bowl VIII, 200–203
Super Bowl XVII, 260–63
Super Bowl XIX, 286–87
Svare, Harland, 177
Swann, Lynn, 211, 213, 243
Swift, Doug, 150, 156, 182, 191, 213, 224
Szymanski, Dick, 66, 123

Tagliabue, Paul, 335
Tampa Bay Buccaneers, 256, 294, 298
Tarkenton, Fran, 98, 176, 200, 201–2
Taseff, Carl, 18, 19, 20–21, 22–23, 31, 35–36, 147, 335, 340
as Browns player, 28–31, 32–33, 34, 36
as Colts player, 37, 42, 47, 49, 52
death of, 345
as Dolphins assistant coach, 140, 227
Tatum, Jack, 183, 213
Taylor, Charley, 185, 191
Taylor, Jim, 81, 82, 85
Taylor, Otis, 160
Theismann, Joe, 157, 226, 260, 261, 279
Thomas, Duane, 166, 167, 168, 169, 171, 172
Thomas, Emmitt, 160
Thomas, Jimmy, 125
Thomas, Joe, 43, 139, 158, 171, 197, 198, 218, 228, 237, 250–52, 255, 264
Thomas, Norris, 231, 243
Thomas, Thurman, 303, 307, 310, 311, 329, 330
Thomas Harvey High School, 7, 10–11
Tillman, Andre, 210, 218
Time, 187–88
Tippett, Andre, 291
Tittle, Y. A., 71, 281
Todd, Richard, 258, 259
Towle, Steve, 218
Trump, Donald, ix, xi, 1–2, 271–73, 293
Tunney, Jim, 85, 87
Turner, T. J., 297
Twilley, Howard, 149, 150, 151, 156, 177, 190, 218, 221, 347
Tyler, Wendell, 285

Uhlenhake, Jeff, 302
Underwood, John, 167, 174, 209, 236, 248,
    250–51, 253
Unitas, Johnny, xiv, xv, xviii, 50–51, 53–54, 56,
    61, 65, 80, 98, 108, 121, 123, 136–37, 152, 153,
    156, 178, 180, 274, 281, 340, 345
  1963 season of, 70, 71–72, 73
  1964 season of, 75–76, 77–78
  1965 season of, 81, 82, 83–84, 85
  1966 season of, 88–89
  1967 season of, 91–94
  1968 season of, 98, 99–102
  1969 season of, 124, 125, 126
  in 1971 AFC title loss to Dolphins, 164, 165
  Shula and, 51, 68, 74, 75–76, 78, 100–101,
    120, 143
  in Super Bowl III, 114–16, 120
United States Football League (USFL), ix, 260,
    264–65, 268, 269, 271, 289, 293
Upshaw, Gene, 200

Van Brocklin, Norm, 32, 35, 45, 49, 298
Vincent, Troy, 323, 326, 330
Virgin, Charles, 179, 341
Virgin, Herbert, 179, 199, 213, 225, 341
Virginia, University of, Shula as assistant
    coach at, 54–56
Vogel, Bob, 67–68
Volk, Charlene, 117
Volk, Rick, 91, 92, 97, 105, 106, 109–10, 112, 113,
    114, 117–18, 123, 125, 126, 164, 232, 346
von Schamann, Uwe, 254, 256, 257, 271, 282
Voris, Dick, 54–55, 56

Walker, Doak, 37
Walker, Fulton, 262
Walker, Herschel, ix, 265
Walker, Wayne, 60
Wallace, George, xi
Walsh, Bill, xiii, 280, 285, 286, 287, 300
Ward, Arch, 26
Ward, Jim, 91, 98, 101
Warfield, Paul, xii, xviii, 77, 142, 144, 149, 158,
    168, 169–70, 212, 223, 224, 277
  in defection to WFL, 205–6, 210, 211–12, 216,
    219–20
  1970 season of, 151, 153–54
  1971 season of, 160–61, 164–65
  1972 season of, 177, 180, 182, 184
  1973 season of, 197, 198
  in Super Bowl VI, 169
  in Super Bowl VII, 190–91, 192
  in Super Bowl VIII, 202

Warren, Don, 260
Washington Redskins, 42, 53, 73, 95, 122, 125,
    157, 200, 212, 225–26, 235, 238, 279
  Shula as player on, 52, 53–54
  in Super Bowl VII, 185–86, 187–95
  in Super Bowl XVII, 260–63
Weaver, Earl, 122
Webb, Richmond, 302, 321
Webster, Larry, 315
Webster, Mike, 211, 285
Westhoff, Mike, 315, 335
White, Dwight, 183
White, Jeris, 210
White, Reggie, 271
Wicker, Tom, 117
Wilbur, John, 191
Wiley, Ralph, 284
Williams, Delvin, 237, 238, 239, 242, 248–49, 252
Williams, Edward Bennett, 185, 236
Williams, Jarvis, 302
Williams, Kevin, 316
Williams, Ronnie, 321
Willis, Bill, 26, 27
Wilson, Butch, 98
Wilson, George, 58, 59, 62, 64, 66, 130, 166, 195,
    240, 340
  as Dolphins head coach, 129–30, 132, 134,
    140–41, 144, 145–46, 147
Wine, Steven, 327
Winner, Charley, 251
Winslow, Kellen, 252, 253, 254, 258
Winston, Roy, 176
Woodley, David, 246, 248–50, 252–53, 256–57,
    259, 261–62, 268–69, 270, 274, 278–79,
    283, 345
Woodruff, Dwayne, 284
Woodson, Marv, 75
World Football League (WFL), xviii, 204, 205,
    210, 211, 216, 219
World Hockey Association, 205
Wright, Rayfield, 167
Wyche, Sam, 309

Yary, Ron, 200
Yepremian, Garo, 144, 152, 160, 161–62, 191–92,
    193–94, 196, 214, 218, 231, 345
Young, Dick, 208
Young, George, xv, 98, 217, 246
Young, Steve, 271, 294

Zimmerman, Paul, xii–xiii, xviii–xix, 44–45,
    46, 110, 114, 253, 257, 258, 259, 267, 273,
    274, 281, 286, 318